Political Disaffection in Cuba's Revolution and Exodus

The Cuban exodus is estimated to be from 12 to 15 percent of the country's population. It also harbors several distinct waves of migrants, alike only in their final rejection of Cuba. In this book, Silvia Pedraza links the revolution and exodus not only as cause and consequence but also as profoundly social and human processes that range from the political and economic to the cognitive and emotive. But, ironically for a community that defined itself as being in exile, virtually no studies of its political attitudes exist, and certainly none that encompass the changing political attitudes over the nearly 50 years of the exodus. Through the use of two major research strategies – participant observation and in-depth, semistructured interviews with 120 Cubans who were representative of those who left between 1959 and 2004 – Pedraza captures the processes of political disaffection of participants in this major historical drama. She emphasizes the contrasts among the four major waves of the exodus not only in their social characteristics but also in their attitudes as members of different political generations.

Silvia Pedraza is Professor of Sociology at the University of Michigan. She is the author of *Political and Economic Migrants in America: Cubans and Mexicans* (1985) and the coeditor of *Origins and Destinies: Immigration, Race, and Ethnicity in America* (1996, with Rubén G. Rumbaut). She has also published articles in such journals as *Social Science History* and the *Annual Review of Sociology*. A child of the Cuban refugee exodus, she lived through both a dictatorship and a revolution, which left an indelible mark on her research.

Cambridge Studies in Contentious Politics

Editors

Jack A. Goldstone *George Mason University*
Doug McAdam *Stanford University and Center for Advanced Study in the Behavioral Sciences*
Sidney Tarrow *Cornell University*
Charles Tilly *Columbia University*
Elisabeth J. Wood *Yale University*

Ronald Aminzade et al., *Silence and Voice in the Study of Contentious Politics*
Javier Auyero, *Routine Politics and Violence in Argentina: The Gray Zone of State Power*
Clifford Bob, *The Marketing of Rebellion: Insurgents, Media, and International Activism*
Charles Brockett, *Political Movements and Violence in Central America*
Gerald F. Davis, Doug McAdam, W. Richard Scott, and Mayer N. Zald, *Social Movements and Organization Theory*
Jack A. Goldstone, editor, *States, Parties, and Social Movements*
Doug McAdam, Sidney Tarrow, and Charles Tilly, *Dynamics of Contention*
Kevin J. O'Brien and Lianjiang Li, *Rightful Resistance in Rural China*
Sidney Tarrow, *The New Transnational Activism*
Charles Tilly, *Contention and Democracy in Europe, 1650–2000*
Charles Tilly, *The Politics of Collective Violence*
Deborah Yashar, *Contesting Citizenship in Latin America: The Rise of Indigenous Movements and the Postliberal Challenge*

Political Disaffection in Cuba's Revolution and Exodus

SILVIA PEDRAZA

University of Michigan

CAMBRIDGE UNIVERSITY PRESS
Cambridge, New York, Melbourne, Madrid, Cape Town, Singapore, São Paulo, Delhi

Cambridge University Press
32 Avenue of the Americas, New York, NY 10013-2473, USA

www.cambridge.org
Information on this title: www.cambridge.org/9780521867870

First published 2007

Printed in the United States of America

A catalog record for this publication is available from the British Library.

Library of Congress Cataloging in Publication Data

Pedraza, Silvia, 1946–
Political disaffection in Cuba's revolution and exodus / Silvia Pedraza.
    p.   cm. – (Cambridge studies in contentious politics)
Includes bibliographical references and index.
ISBN 978-0-521-86787-0 (hardback) – ISBN 978-0-521-68729-4 (pbk.)
1. Cuban Americans – Politics and government.   2. Cuban Americans – Social
conditions.   3. Cuban Americans – Interviews.   4. Immigrants – United States – Political
activity.   5. Cubans – Migrations.   6. Cuba – Emigration and immigration – Political
aspects.   7. United States – Emigration and immigration – Political aspects.   8. Cuba –
History – Revolution, 1959 – Influence.   9. Cuba – History – Revolution, 1959 – Public
opinion.   10. Public opinion – United States.   11. Public opinion – Cuba.   I. Title.
II. Series.
E184.C97P43   2007
304.8′730729109045–dc22   2006100710

ISBN   978-0-521-86787-0 hardback
ISBN   978-0-521-68729-4 paperback

$28.09

To my mother, Silvia Lubián Pedraza,
and my cousin, Alicia María Pedraza,
both of whom did everything they could to help me

Contents

List of Tables   *page* xii

Acknowledgments   xiii

List of Abbreviations   xvii

1   FALSE HOPES   1
    Cuba's Refugees: Manifold Migrations   1
    Political Disaffection   9
    Theoretical Framework   14
    Data and Methods   19
    Studying Refugees   26

**Part I   For and against the Republic, for and against the
Revolution: The Cuban Exodus of 1959–1962 and 1965–1974**

2   THE REVOLUTION DEFINES ITSELF   35
    Sociology of Revolution   35
    Democracy   37
    The Church for the Revolution   56
    Humanism   58
    The Revolution Betrayed   62
    The Church Dissents   64

3   THE REVOLUTION DEEPENS   66
    Nationalism   66
    The First Wave: Those Who Wait   78
    The Church versus the State   87
    The Revolution: Political and Social   89

ix

4	THE REVOLUTION REDEFINES ITSELF	92
	Socialism and the Bay of Pigs	92
	The Church Is Silenced	107
	Marxism-Leninism	109
	The First Wave: Those Who Escape	110
	The Cuban Missile Crisis	112
5	THE REVOLUTION CONSOLIDATED	115
	Consolidating the Revolution Within	115
	The Second Wave: The Petite Bourgeoisie	120
	Political Prisoners	128
	Tending Bridges	139

Part II The Children of Communism: The Cuban Exodus of 1980 and 1985–2004

6	*LOS MARIELITOS* OF 1980	151
	The Third Wave: Refugee "Vintages"	151
	Race, Class, Gender, and Sexuality	159
7	AFTER THE SOVIET COLLAPSE	177
	The Fourth Wave: The Special Period	177
	The *Balsero* Crisis	183
8	THE LAST WAVE	205
	Political or Economic Migrants?	205
	Familial or Economic Motives	210
	Both Political and Economic Motives	215
	Political Motives	228

Part III Civil Society Returns

9	THE CHURCH AND CIVIL SOCIETY	239
	The Church in Cuba	239
	The Church among the Immigrants	259
10	DEMOCRATIZATION AND MIGRATION	264
	Exit-Voice Relationships	264
	Four Theses	267
11	THE IMPOSSIBLE TRIANGLE	283
	Cuba, the United States, and the Exiles	283
	War by Another Name	291
	Neutralizing the Exiles	294

Contents

Transitions in Cuba 295

Transitions in Exile 299

Refugees as a Social Type 307

Appendix: List of Interviews 313

References 319

Index 341

List of Tables

1.1 Cuban Immigrants in the United States by Year of
   Immigration, 1990 and 2000 U.S. Censuses   *page* 5

1.2 Cuban Immigrants in the United States by Year of
   Immigration and Sex, 2000 U.S. Census   6

6.1 Racial Composition of Cuba, 1899–2002   156

6.2 Cuban Immigrants in the United States by Year of
   Immigration and Race, 2000 Census   156

7.1 Typology of Migration   202

11.1 Attitudes toward Cuba among Cuban Americans in the
   Miami Area, by Waves of Migration, in 2000   300

Acknowledgments

I am truly grateful to many colleagues and friends for the support they gave me during my research. Above all, I want to thank the 120 Cubans for the interviews they granted me, long and sincere, and the documents they shared with me. Without their help, this book would not have been possible. Their names are listed in the Appendix. Although my insights and conclusions issued from what I learned from them, I am solely responsible for any errors that remain.

In addition, many people went out of their way to help me procure an interview. For this, I am grateful to Concha, Olga, and Benito Besú; Alfredo and Liana Blanco and Maricusa Repilado Blanco; Joaquín Calvo and Emma García-Menocal; Max Castro; Jesús and Idalmis Cruz; Emilio Cueto; Himilce Esteve; Andrés Gómez-Mena; Eulogio González; José Manuel Hernández; Francisco León; Melchor Loret de Mola; Nicole Lucier; José Martín and Victoria López-Pedraza; Bernard Mulaire; Patricia and Daniel Pastor; Christine Reinhard; Natalia Revuelta; Oscar Luis Rodríguez and Barbara Grau; Carmen Rodríguez and María Rodríguez; Angelina, Luisa, and Norma Rodríguez; Pedro Romañach; Nicolás Sánchez; Gladys Santana; and Silvia Villalón.

Many people also lent me photos, poems, and works of art to use for illustration. For this, I am grateful to Robert Aponte; Ricardo Blanco, artist; Elvis Brathwaite, from Associated Press AP/Wide World Photos; Alberto de la Cerra; Elly Chovel from the Operation Pedro Pan Group; Arturo Cuenca, artist; Belkis Cuza-Malé, poet; Rafael Díeguez, artist; Isabel Ezquerra from the University of Miami's Otto Richter Library, Cuban Heritage Collection; Alina Salgado; Dawn Hugh and Melissa Mame from the Historical Museum of Southern Florida, Miami; Joanne Leonard, artist; Huber Matos and María Luisa Matos; Lissette Elquezabal, from the *Miami Herald*; Ben Osborne and Charity Schmidt; Angel Pardo; Felix Peña; Coiré Rodríguez; and Jesús Selgas, artist. Jessica Cepelak and Ciara McLaughlin from Cambridge University Press assisted me with the photos and illustrations.

Still others helped me find important sources: Father Juan Manuel Dorta-Duque, from the Antiguos Alumnos del Colegio Belén; Cynthia Harris, from the *Jersey Journal*; José M. Martínez, from *La Voz Libre*; Isabel Tejera, from *Desafíos*; Yuzuru Takeshita, Professor Emeritus of Public Health, the University of Michigan; Lesbia Varona, from the University of Miami Otto Richter Library, Cuban Heritage Collection; as well as Karen Mike, Leif Backman, and Anthony Davis from the University of Michigan Interlibrary Loan. The Sánchez family provided invaluable help in transcribing the interviews.

At the University of Michigan, many staff members were helpful. Some helped me learn new data analysis techniques, in particular Al Anderson, Ren Farley, Lisa J. Neidert, and Patrick Rady of PDQ, Inc., and JoAnn Dionne, data librarian from the Library. Still others helped me learn the new digital world, in particular Rick Smoke and Carrick Rogers from the Sociology Department, as well as Monica Trujillo, my research assistant, who was sponsored by the Summer Research Opportunity Program. Patricia Preston from the Sociology Department and Peggy A. Westrick from the College of Literature, Science, and Arts Office of Research processed my Faculty Research Assistance Awards.

A number of colleagues went out of their way to offer useful comments, some of which I heeded. For this, I am grateful to Nelson Amaro, Jesús Barquet, Heriberto Brito, Steven Gold, Pedro Ladislao Guerra, Bert Hoffman, Richard Sukjo Kim, Enrique Pumar, Joane Nagel, Doug McAdam, Vicky Unruh, my student Jordi Martínez-Cid, and two anonymous reviewers.

I am particularly grateful to Joane Nagel at the University of Kansas, Jorge I. Domínguez at Harvard University, and Sueann Caulfield at the University of Michigan for supporting my grant applications.

Ruth Homrighaus helped me copyedit the original manuscript, and Brian MacDonald served as my production editor for Cambridge University Press. I am grateful to both.

Lewis Bateman, senior editor at Cambridge University Press in New York, was both supportive and exacting, and I thank him for seeing value in this work.

Acknowledgments

This research project was initially supported by a seed grant from the American Sociological Association's Fund for the Advancement of the Discipline (1995–96). The necessary support came from the University of Michigan's Horace H. Rackham School of Graduate Studies' Faculty Grant and Fellowship (1997–99), for which I am particularly grateful to Provost Nancy Cantor and Dean Homer Rose. A grant from the Rockefeller Foundation's Scholar in Residence Program at the Rockefeller Foundation Study and Conference Center in Bellagio, Italy (Summer 2003), allowed me to spend a peaceful summer working through difficult intellectual issues. Travel to Italy was made possible by the University of Michigan's Horace H. Rackham School of Graduate Studies' Discretionary Funds, for which I am especially grateful to Dean Homer Rose, from the University of Michigan's Rackham School of Graduate Studies, and Dean Terrence J. McDonald, from the University of Michigan's College of Literature, Science, and Arts. Associate Dean Susan Gelman of the College of Literature, Science, and Arts helped me obtain a Faculty Research Grant. Joseph P. Marino, Associate Dean for Research of the College of Literature, Science, and Arts, and Lester P. Monts, Senior Vice-Provost for Academic Affairs, helped me obtain Faculty Travel Awards that made participant observation in Cuba and Puerto Rico possible. With sincerity, I express my gratitude to all of them. Without their support, this research would not have been possible.

Abbreviations

ACU	Agrupación Católica Universitaria (University Catholic Group)
Auténticos	Partido Revolucionario Cubano Auténtico (Auténtico Political Party)
CANF	Cuban American National Foundation (Fundación Nacional Cubano Americana)
CCL	Consejo Cuban por la Libertad (Cuban Liberty Council)
CDR	Comités para la Defensa de la Revolución (Committees for the Defense of the Revolution)
CIA	Central Intelligence Agency
CID	Cuba Independiente y Democrática
CONIC	Confederación Obrera Nacional Independiente de Cuba (Cuban Independent Federation of Trade Unions)
CSDC	Corriente Socialista Democrática Cubana (Cuban Democratic Socialists)
CTC	Central de Trabajadores Cubanos (Cuban Workers' Confederation)
CUJAE	Instituto Politécnico Juan Antonio Echeverría (Polytechnic Institute Juan Antonio Echeverría)
DRE	Directorio Estudiantial Revolucionario (Revolutionary Students' Directorate)
ENEC	Encuentro Nacional Eclesiástico Cubano (Cuban National Ecclesiastical Congress)
FEU	Federación Estudiantil Universitaria (University Students' Federation)
FMC	Federación de Mujeres Cubanas (National Association of Cuban Women)

FNTA	Federación Nacional de Trabajadores Azucareros (National Sugar Workers' Union)
FRD	Frente Revolucionario Democrático (Democratic Revolutionary Front); later renamed Consejo Revolucionario Cubano (Cuban Revolutionary Council)
INRA	Instituto Nacional para la Reforma Agraria
INS	Immigration and Naturalization Service
JUCEPLAN	Junta Central de Planificación Económica (Central Economic Planning Board)
MDC	Movimiento Demócrata Cristiano (Christian Democratic Movement)
MH	Ministerio de Hacienda (Treasury Department)
MININT	Ministerio del Interior (Ministry of the Interior)
MRP	Movimiento Revolucionario del Pueblo (Revolutionary Movement of the People)
MRR	Movimiento de Recuperación Revolucionaria (Movement for Revolutionary Recuperation)
Ortodoxos	Partido del Pueblo Cubano Ortodoxo (Orthodox Political Party)
UJC	Unión de Jóvenes Comunistas (Communist Youth League)
UMAP	Unidades Militares de Ayuda a la Producción (Military Units to Aid Production)
UNEAC	Unión Nacional de Escritores y Artistas de Cuba (Cuban Writers and Artists Union)

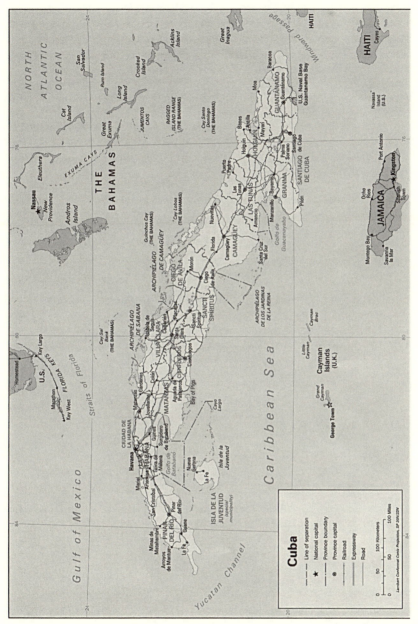

Map of Cuba

Political Disaffection in Cuba's Revolution and Exodus

1

False Hopes

¡El vino, de plátano; y si sale agrio, es nuestro vino!

Our wine is made from plantains; though it may be sour, it is our wine!

José Martí, "Nuestra América" (1891)

Cuba's Refugees: Manifold Migrations

The triumph of the Cuban revolution was one of the most popular political events of the 20th century. A social movement that the majority of the Cuban population initially applauded, and for which many risked their lives, the Cuban revolution had the capacity to capture the imagination of most of its citizens. Romantic in its execution, expressing a call for social justice, it had vast international support. Yet by the end of the century, 40 years later, a very sizable proportion of the Cuban population had left for other lands. Working both with U.S. and Cuban statistics, Antonio Aja-Díaz (2006) of the Center for Migration Studies at the University of Havana estimates that between 1959 and 2004 roughly 1,359,650 Cubans left Cuba for various countries and by different means. Because the Cuban population has grown from 5.8 million at the time of the 1953 census to 9.7 million at the 1981 census and 11.2 million in 2000 (Martínez-Fernández 2003a), that number probably represents from 12 to 15 percent of the Cuban population. Certainly, it is larger than the population of Cuba's second largest city – Santiago de Cuba – at present. This study captures the process of political disaffection – the disappointment and sense of betrayal – that led so many Cubans, many of them ardent supporters of the revolution initially, to leave their homeland for other lands.

To date, analyses of the Cuban revolution have focused on the changing stages of the Cuban revolution, with only a slight mention of the exodus of Cubans as a consequence of the vast upheaval of revolutionary transformation in Cuba (e.g., Horowitz 1995; Eckstein 1994; Domínguez 1978a). At the same time, analyses of the Cuban migration have focused on the incorporation of Cuban immigrants in comparison to other immigrant groups in the United States, with only a slight mention of the changing stages of the Cuban revolution as the backdrop to the immigration (e.g., Portes and Bach 1985). By contrast, this research links the two – revolution and exodus – not only as cause and consequence but also as profoundly social and human processes that were not only political and economic but also cognitive and emotive.

In my earlier work on "Cuba's Refugees: Manifold Migrations" (1996), I traced the development of the Cuban community in the United States as the result of four major waves of migration and described them with data from the U.S. census and other surveys on the social and demographic characteristics of each of the major waves. The research reported here goes beyond this work to capture the processes of political disaffection of participants in this major drama. Through the use of the two major research strategies of ethnography – participant observation and interviews – I emphasize the contrasts among the four major waves of the exodus not only in their social characteristics but also in their attitudes as members of different political communities and political generations. As such, this research project expresses the dual intellectual heritage of sociology as a discipline that can best be described as a melding of the principles that guide science and the principles that guide the humanities.

First, I will set the historical stage by briefly describing the nature of the Cuban exodus that is now nearly half a century old and has brought more than a million Cuban immigrants to American soil, an exodus that harbors distinct waves of immigrants, alike only in their final rejection of Cuba. In contrast to economic immigrants, as Peter Rose emphasized, refugees are more "pushed" by the social and political processes in the society they leave than "pulled" by the attractiveness of the new (Rose 1981; Kunz 1981, 1973; Lee 1966). Each of the major waves of migration has been characterized by a very different social composition with respect to its social class, race, education, gender and family composition, and values – differences that resulted from the changing phases of the Cuban revolution. They render the Cuban community in the United States today an extremely heterogeneous one, comprising different "vintages," depending on their social characteristics and their processes of political disaffection. E. F. Kunz (1973:137) called refugee groups that leave the country as "distinct in character, background, and avowed political faith" different "vintages" because they lived through different social processes of maturation. This research captures that dual variability – in social characteristics and political attitudes – across the four major waves of the Cuban exodus.

The First Wave: Cuba's Elite

Nelson Amaro and Alejandro Portes (1972) portrayed the different phases of the Cuban migration as changing over time with the exiles' principal motivation for their decision to leave. With the unfolding of the Cuban revolution, they argued, over the years "those who wait" gave way to "those who escape," who were then followed by "those who search." To update their analysis, I added "those who hope" and "those who despair" (Pedraza 1996a).

In the first wave (1959–62), those who left were Cuba's elite: executives and owners of firms, big merchants, sugar mill owners, cattlemen, representatives of foreign companies, and professionals (see Figure 1.1). They left Cuba when the revolution overturned the old social order through measures such as the nationalization of American industry and agrarian reform laws, as well as through the United States' severance of diplomatic and economic ties with Cuba. "Those who wait" characterized these first refugees that came imagining that exile would be temporary, waiting for American help to overthrow Cuba's new government. This first phase of the exodus began with the triumph of the revolution in 1959 and ended with the failure of the exiles' Bay of Pigs invasion in April 1961.

"Those who escape" constituted the second phase of the first wave, which was engulfed by the growing political turmoil. The Catholic Church, which denounced the revolution after supporting it, was silenced; the electoral system and civil society collapsed, particularly when the independent press and radio and television stations were closed. Removing any doubt, Castro announced that he had always been a Marxist-Leninist and would be so until the day he died. As a result, the exodus doubled. As Amaro and Portes noted, the inverse relationship between date of emigration and social class in Cuba began to show. Still largely a middle-class exodus, now it was more middle than upper: middle-class merchants and middle management, landlords, middle-level professionals, and a considerable number of skilled unionized workers who wanted to escape an intolerable new order.

3

Figure 1.1   Cubans from the first wave of the exodus (1959–62) were often middle and upper middle class. Here a family is being resettled by the Cuban Refugee Program in Cleveland, Ohio, in 1962. (Historical Museum of Southern Florida/ *Miami News*)

Table 1.1 gives both the 1990 and 2000 census estimates of the number of Cubans who came to the United States by their year of immigration. The 1990 census provides a better estimate for the early waves of migration, the 2000 census for the more recent waves. According to the 1990 census estimates, from 1960 to 1964 around 172,919 Cubans arrived. The first wave ended in October 1962, when, as a result of the Cuban Missile Crisis, all flights ceased.

The Second Wave: Cuba's Petite Bourgeoisie

In the fall of 1965 a chaotic flotilla exodus began, when hundreds of boats left from Miami for the Cuban port of Camarioca, where they picked up thousands of relatives to come to the United States. As a result, the U.S. and Cuban governments negotiated the orderly departure of Cubans through an air bridge, the Vuelos de la Libertad, which brought Cubans to the United States on daily freedom flights. They began in 1965 and lasted until

Table 1.1. *Cuban Immigrants in the United States by Year of Immigration, 1990 and 2000 U.S. Censuses*

Year of Immigration[a]	Number of Cubans[b]	Percentage
2000 census		
1959–64	144,732	17.5
1965–74	247,726	29.9
1975–79	29,508	3.6
1980	94,095	11.3
1981–89	77,835	9.4
1990–93	60,244	7.3
1994–2000	174,437	21.0
TOTAL	828,577	100.0
1990 census		
1960–64	172,919	25.5
1965–74	284,642	42.9
1975–79	27,713	4.1
1980–81	120,605	17.8
1982–90	71,633	10.6
TOTAL	677,512	100.0

[a] The 1990 census precoded the variable on year of immigration; hence, this recoding is the best possible approximation of the waves of migration. The 2000 census left the variable on year of immigration as single years; hence, this recoding is more accurate for the waves of migration. For this reason, results for the two censuses are reported separately.
[b] Tables do not include Cubans born in the United States.
Source: U.S. 1990 and 2000 Censuses (1993; 2003), Public Use Microdata Sample, 5 percent, unweighted.

1974, when the Cuban Refugee Program ended. Kunz (1973) distinguished between acute and anticipatory refugee movements. The joint policy of the U.S. and Cuban governments turned this initially acute refugee exodus into a coordinated and orderly anticipatory refugee movement. In the largest wave to date, according to the census estimates, around a quarter of a million Cubans immigrated to the United States (see Table 1.1).

According to Amaro and Portes (1972), "those who search" characterized this wave of migration, which was largely composed of the working class and *la petite bourgeoisie*: employees, craftsmen, small merchants, skilled and semiskilled workers. They left Cuba during some of the leanest and most idealistic years of the revolution. While the Cuban government

Table 1.2. *Cuban Immigrants in the United States by Year of Immigration and Sex, 2000 U.S. Census*

Year of Immigration	Number of Men (%)	Number of Women (%)	Total Number
1959–62	55,252 (46.1)	64,670 (53.9)	119,922
1963–64	12,009 (48.4)	12,801 (51.6)	24,810
1965–74	105,053 (42.4)	142,673 (57.6)	247,726
1975–79	15,047 (51.0)	14,461 (49.0)	29,508
1980	55,540 (59.0)	38,555 (41.0)	94,095
1981–89	38,689 (49.7)	39,146 (50.3)	77,835
1990–93	32,060 (53.2)	28,184 (46.8)	60,244
1994–2000	94,315 (54.1)	80,122 (45.9)	174,437

Source: U.S. 2000 Census (2003), Public Use Microdata Sample, 5 percent, unweighted.

made real efforts to spread access to a basic education and health care across all social classes and from city to countryside, the hemispheric trade embargo began to be felt, the exodus continued to be a "brain drain" of skilled professionals, and Cuba failed in its attempts to cease being a sugar monoculture. Thus, in Amaro and Portes's judgment, the migration increasingly ceased to be a political act and became an economic act. Yet their distinction ignored that, while life in Cuba grew harsh for all, it turned bitter for those who had declared their intention to leave. When the migration began in the early 1960s, 31 percent of the arriving Cubans were professionals or managers; by 1970, only 12 percent were, while more than half the arrivals were blue-collar, service, or agricultural workers (Aguirre 1976: table 2). Table 1.2, based on the 2000 U.S. census, shows the gendered nature of the Cuban exodus. The early waves of the exodus were female-dominated, in part because refugees resemble those caught in a sinking ship – women and children first. Moreover, the second wave was an anticipatory refugee movement, governed by family reunification criteria and prior approval by both countries.

When the air bridge ended in 1974, refugees who had first lived in Spain arrived. Alejandro Portes, Juan Clark, and Robert Bach (1977) found that these émigrés represented Cuba's "middling service sectors": cooks, gardeners, domestics, street vendors, barbers, hairdressers, taxi drivers, small retail merchants. They left Cuba when Castro launched a new "revolutionary offensive" in Cuba, confiscating more than 55,000 small businesses that were privately owned (Mesa-Lago 1978). This policy "pushed" out the little entrepreneurs and their employees.

With the economic transition to socialism accomplished, in the 1970s the Cuban government cast the shape of the political system – an institutionalization during which Cuba took on the features of Eastern European communism (cf. Roca 1981). The old idealism and romanticism of the 1960s gave way to what Carmelo Mesa-Lago (1978) called pragmatism. In 1978 a dialogue took place between the Cuban government and representatives of the Cuban exiles. As a result of the Dialogue, the Cuban government agreed to release 3,600 political prisoners and to promote the reunification of families by allowing Cubans in the United States to visit their families.

The Third Wave: Cuba's Marielitos

Those visits were partly responsible for the third wave – the chaotic flotilla exodus from the harbor of Mariel in 1980 that brought close to 125,000 more Cubans to America. From Miami, Cubans sailed to bring their families to the United States. At times they succeeded, but sometimes they brought whomever angry officials put on the boats. Toward the end, this included Cuba's social undesirables, whom Castro called *escoria* (scum): those who were in prisons (whether they had committed real crimes or had only challenged the state), those who were mental patients, and those who were gay (cf. Montgomery 1981).

Robert Bach's (1981–82; Bach et al. 1980) studies showed that the most salient characteristic of the *Marielitos* was their youth: most were young men, single or without their families, characteristic of an acute refugee movement that results from a crisis (see Table 1.2). Moreover, there was a visibly higher proportion of blacks than earlier. Their occupations showed that most were from the mainstream of the Cuban economy, hardly scum. This exodus was overwhelmingly working class – close to 71 percent were blue-collar workers. In addition, a significant number of young intellectuals were also part of this wave (the most famous being Reinaldo Arenas). These writers recognized themselves as belonging to a political generation, which they themselves called *la generación del Mariel*. "Those who hope," I said, might well characterize this wave (Pedraza 1996a).

Because of their youth, the *Marielitos* clearly constituted a different political generation, one comprising individuals of approximately the same

7

age who share, in their coming of age, certain politically relevant experiences that shape their outlook (Mannheim 1952). The *Marielitos'* coming of age occurred long after the early revolutionary struggle that demanded enormous sacrifices but affirmed the loyalty of many. Roughly half of the Mariel immigrants came of age during the late 1960s or the 1970s, at a time when problems of freedom of expression became acute, especially for artists and intellectuals, and deviance, particularly homosexuality, was dealt with by prison sentence. The *Marielitos*, therefore, were significantly different from the early exiles. At the two poles of twenty years of exodus stood two "vintages" that at best could hardly comprehend one another and at worst might be hostile. Over time, the dramatic changes the Cuban revolution underwent interacted with the social characteristics of those affected to produce markedly different processes of political disaffection.

The Fourth Wave: Cuba's Balseros

As the 1980s came to a close, a new Cuban exodus began that has yet to cease. Cuba's economic crisis reached new depths when communism collapsed in the Soviet Union, on which Cuba had been enormously dependent. The impact of these losses was devastating, so that Castro himself declared this "a special period in a time of peace." Such a *período especial* was supposedly temporary but, coupled with the United States' tightening of the embargo, went on for many years. Abject need and hunger defined Cubans' lives.

Initially, this new Cuban exodus was mostly illegal (cf. Rodríguez-Chavez 1996; 1993). Cubans became so desperate they left on *balsas* (rafts, tires, makeshift vessels), risking death due to starvation, dehydration, drowning, or sharks (see Figure 1.2). From 1985 to 1993, close to 6,000 *balseros* managed to reach the United States safely; more than 34,000 left just in the summer of 1994 when, in the midst of a crisis, Castro suddenly instructed the Cuban Coast Guard to let them go. Due to the high risk entailed in this acute refugee movement, it was mostly male-dominated (Table 1.2). In the United States, an abrupt change in policy took place, as the new attorney general, Janet Reno, saw the *balseros* as illegal aliens trying to enter the United States. This contrasted sharply with the long-standing U.S. view that Cubans were victims of communism. Hence, the Cubans were now criminals who had to be stopped, rather than refugees deserving a welcome. The U.S. Coast Guard blocked their progress at sea and directed them to Guantanamo. The United States and Cuba signed a new Migration

Figure 1.2 Cuba's refugees from the fourth major wave of the exodus (1989 to the present) often fled Cuba on makeshift *balsas*. Here *balseros* signal to a rescue plane in December 1993. Of their initial crew, five survived six days of cold December seas, but one died along the way. (*Miami Herald*/Hector Gabino)

Agreement, and Guantanamo's *balseros* were resettled throughout the United States "Those who despair," I stressed, constituted this last wave.

Political Disaffection

Using Luis Aguilar-León's (1972) 1958 analysis of the political generations in Cuban history, Maurice Zeitlin (1966) studied the support the various political generations in the working class gave the revolution. Zeitlin found the strongest support came from the generation of '53, their consciousness marked by the anti-Batista struggle, followed by the two generations that came of age during the anti-Machado struggle of the '30s, while the generation of '59 and the republican generation of the '40s gave the lowest support. Thus, the historical period in which individuals became adults was significant in the formation of their political identities. These studies emphasize the need to study refugees taking into account their different political generations, as my research has done.

To illustrate the contrasts to be developed in the following chapters, I will simply offer a few brief illustrations from the interviews I conducted that focus on the contrasting processes of political disaffection that Cubans from the various waves underwent. For this, I rely on interviews with Rafael Peláez (pseudonym), Serafín García-Menocal, Carlos Gómez, Rafael Saumell, and Olguita Gómez (pseudonym).

Among those who had reached adolescence and adulthood in the 1950s, when the Cuban revolution first succeeded in its uprising against the dictatorship of General Fulgencio Batista, one finds three very different types of exiles. The first group, the *Batistianos*, sided with Batista against the incipient revolution. The second group, on the contrary, believed in the revolution that was gathering force and lent it their support. Some fought for it, in the underground movement in the cities or in the armed struggle in the hills of Oriente and Las Villas. Among them, a distinct third group resulted from those who felt the social and democratic revolution they believed in and fought for had been betrayed by Fidel Castro. These exiles, like Rafael Peláez, bore arms twice – first against Batista and afterward against Castro in the mountains of the Escambray. They speak of "the revolution betrayed."

As an adolescent, Rafael Peláez had fought side by side with Fidel Castro when he attacked the army barracks of *el Moncada* on July 26, 1953, triggering the revolution as an armed struggle. Rafael was also among those who chose the colors of the flag for the new revolutionary movement that began calling itself the 26th of July Movement – red and black, to symbolize blood and mourning. The Manifesto of the 26th of July Movement spoke of a social and democratic revolution and expressed a social populism that was long a part of Cuban history. Soon after the revolution triumphed in 1959, however, Rafael was horrified by the massive killings Castro ordered in a stadium, brutality that was reminiscent of a Roman circus, and he also realized, due to his very proximity to the revolutionary center, that Castro was handing the revolution over to the communists. "The hatred," he said, "the killings. . . . That was not the revolution we fought for. The revolution we fought for was not red, but 'green as the palm trees,' as Fidel himself said in one of his speeches, and it was to take place through the democratic process." When the armed struggle against Fidel's treason ensued, Rafael joined the organization that was most to the left, the Movimiento Revolucionario del Pueblo (Revolutionary Movement of the People, MRP). He then took to the armed struggle in the hills of the Escambray Mountains. Caught speeding down Havana's seaside *malecón*, with a carload of arms, Rafael spent 10 years in prison and 8 more in Cuba bearing the stigma of "former political prisoner" before arriving in the United

States in 1980 – too old to complete his education as an engineer and start anew. Still a handsome man, talkative, tense, he became a city bus driver in New York.

Also in this first wave came most of Cuba's professional class, whose lives had possessed the grace and pace that often accompany the lives of the middle and upper classes in underdeveloped countries, together with all the trappings of modernity that came from their rich neighbor to the north. Those fortunate enough to live the lives of the professional middle class in Cuba in the 1950s lived a *belle époque*. Serafín García-Menocal, a tall, thin, blue-eyed, well-mannered, and quietly elegant man, was an engineer educated in the United States. He returned to Cuba and eventually became the director of the Compañía Cubana de Electricidad, which provided electrical power for the whole island. He left Cuba in 1960 when the company was nationalized. He argued that "in Cuba, there was no need for a social revolution at that time." He pointed to Cuba's leading social indicators in comparison to other Latin American countries. Like so many in his social class who left early, he could not credit the revolution with having done anything worthwhile. Giving vent to his nostalgia for the inordinately beautiful city he had left behind, he added, "Havana then was like a bright, shining star, whose light shone throughout the Americas." After he left Cuba, for the next eight years he went everywhere giving a talk on "The Lessons the U.S. Should Learn from Cuba." After working in Panama as president of the Panamanian Electrical Company for eight years, and thereafter in Brazil, the merchant marine, and Guayaquil, he retired to a modest home in West Palm Beach, next to other family.

Carlos Gómez, by contrast, belonged to a younger generation and felt a deep attraction toward the revolution. His early adolescence in the mid-1960s coincided with the development of the philosophical base of Marxism in Cuba. He had grown up in Trinidad, a most traditional and conservative city, perhaps due to its colonial beauty and its distance from the modernity of Havana. Carlos's adolescent rebellion led him to break away from tradition, from his Catholic religious education, from a petit bourgeois social milieu, from traditional family values, from the past. "As I became an adolescent I saw the social transformation taking place in Cuba," he remembered, "and there were aspects of it that I fell in love with: the profound change in social values and philosophy, all the romanticism that a revolution can hold." Yet, when he was invited to become a member of the Communist Youth League (Unión de Jóvenes Comunistas, UJC), he declined. He participated politically in the activities perceived as normal, such as joining the

11

militia and making the security rounds, but he wanted to avoid the burden of excessive political participation because, given his musical vocation, he preferred to devote his time to playing the guitar. As a musician, he was among those who initiated the movement called La Nueva Trova, some of the best music to come out of the revolution. Initially an artistic brigade, a grass-roots movement of young musicians who expressed their belief in the revolution in song, it eventually became an official institution, a symbol of the revolution that played a public role under the control of the Ministry of Culture.

By the 1970s, for Carlos the revolution had lost its romanticism. The political disappointment resulted from a number of experiences that had accumulated, as was the case for most I interviewed. The Soviet Union's invasion of Czechoslovakia in 1968 was the first major blow. Fidel sided with the Soviet Union, a stance that shocked many of his generation: "Until then, we thought we really were nonaligned," Carlos emphasized. "We thought we really supported the weak – we would never side with an empire. Fidel justified his behavior." In addition, in 1970 the failure of the sugar harvest proved a turning point for many. To cut the projected 10 million tons of sugar, Fidel mobilized the whole nation to the countryside. Cuba's honor depended on making that *zafra*, Castro stressed. Doctors, engineers, everyone went to the rural areas to cut cane. A grandiose effort, its failure profoundly impacted many. Cubans then became polarized between those who placed themselves unconditionally behind Castro and those who, like Carlos, saw him as a madman leading the country down the wrong path. Carlos realized that "Fidel had become the state, he had usurped and alienated the concept of *la patria*, the fatherland, because he had become the state, *patria*, everything." Though change was, thus, impossible, he tried to remain honest and to express his disagreements, even in collective assemblies and meetings, where he began to be seen as a troublemaker. When the Mariel exodus began in 1980, seeing that the government fanned the flames of the *actos de repudio* toward those who left, repudiating, insulting, and humiliating them, he resigned and told the other members of La Nueva Trova that he was leaving. Neither they nor the Committee for the Defense of the Revolution in his block engaged in any act of repudiation toward him, as they appreciated him. Still, because La Nueva Trova was a symbol of the revolution itself, he was not allowed to leave until 1985, when he finally left for Spain. Those five years he lived in a situation of utter marginality, in which only a few friends remained by his side: "People avoided me or would not shake my hand, or they pretended not to have seen me, or they simply refused to greet me." While in Spain, Carlos met his wife, Marta, born in the Canary Islands. Together they formed the duo "Carlos y Marta" that now plays in Miami.

In contrast to the early exiles, those who left Cuba recently nearly always point to Cuba's advances in health and education as real social advances and go on to highlight that the social ascent they experienced – coming from a humble family of origin and going on to the university to become well-trained professionals – was real. But immediately thereafter they point out that the government, the system, was unable to accept that such training requires the freedom to be, to think, to express oneself. Rafael Saumell, a mulatto in his early 40s, came face to face with such limits. Although he came from a poor family, he received a good education and graduated from the university with a degree in foreign languages. He rose to become a television producer of an extremely popular children's program; from 1979 to 1982, he also worked in the program called *Todo el Mundo Canta*, which made new singers known to the public, work in which he took great pride. For him, as for many in Cuba then, the impact of the Mariel exodus in 1980 was decisive. From Mariel harbor sailed many of his closest friends; until the day they left, everyone believed most of them were strong supporters of the government. Suddenly, Rafael felt as if Havana had become an empty shell. "Cuba was one before *el Mariel*," he said, "and another afterward."

In retrospect, those who left had worn many masks: they had often been members of the Young Communist League or the Committees for the Defense of the Revolution and were card-carrying members of the Communist Party. Rafael himself was a member of the Cuban Writers and Artists Union (Unión Nacional de Escritores y Artistas de Cuba, UNEAC), which was founded after the revolution. To narrate these events, he wrote a collection of fictional short stories and, as a result, was sentenced to five years in prison, convicted on a charge of disseminating enemy propaganda. Yet, he said, "in prison, I discovered another Cuba," a more profound Cuba than any he had known until then, composed of the resistance of many. As a result, he became a dissident and joined the human rights movement that was then emerging in Cuba, partly out of the dismal prison conditions many experienced. He arrived in the United States in 1986 and eventually became a faculty member at Sam Houston State University in Texas.

At 26, Olguita Gómez had recently come of age. A pretty and vivacious young woman, her adolescence was carefree, with much partying and dancing. As smart as she was pretty, always the best student in her class, Olguita won a trip in the early 1980s to the Soviet Union, where she spent a month touring the country together with her teachers. Though finding it somewhat colorless in comparison to Cuba, she firmly believed that communism was a good system until its collapse in the Soviet Union, which also ushered in Cuba's "special period" of hunger and hardship in the 1990s. "They told us that communism was a good system," she said, "but then we could see that it wasn't." She and her husband arrived in the United States in 1994.

Theoretical Framework

Political Communities

Living the revolution inside the island, joining the exodus that left the island, living *el exilio* (the exile) in Miami, and being active in the dissident movement within Cuba entailed becoming a part of or exiting political communities that defined themselves against one another. Those who chose to leave Cuba left behind family and friends they deeply loved, though at times they also rejected and denied them, as reflected in their labeling them "communists" or "opportunists." Those who chose to stay in Cuba lost their loved ones who left, though at times they also rejected and repudiated them, as reflected in their use of pejorative labels to describe them, such as *gusanos* (worms) for the first wave and *escoria* (scum) for the third. Those who chose to become deeply integrated into the revolution by becoming militant Communist Party members were prohibited by government decree from ever writing to their family and friends in exile. Those who chose to become actively integrated into the Miami exile community were prohibited by the reigning conservatism there from ever visiting or helping their struggling family and friends back in Cuba, despite the acute shortages of food, clothing, and medicine there. Those who left Cuba suffered enormous losses – not just the material loss of property and status but also the loss of their memories, childhoods, comfortable old ages, and their peers in schools, neighborhoods, and work with whom they shared the emotional space of their lives. Those who joined the dissident movement that eventually emerged in Cuba in the 1980s and 1990s found themselves repudiated and shunned by even the most intimate of family and friends. They experienced an isolation that was social, becoming pariahs within their own country, and often also physical and mental, if they suffered imprisonment. Those who chose the path of exile had been profoundly alienated while in Cuba; once in Miami, some again found themselves socially alienated, now from the oppressive conservatism of *el exilio* – victims of a double alienation, possibly, a double exile.

In short, the revolution and the exodus are deeply intertwined, a combination of both historical and political processes and cognitive and emotional processes. Fear, repudiation, loyalty, sympathy, distrust, isolation, humiliation, denunciation, rejection – these permeated the lives of all Cubans as they lived through a historical and political process that forced them, over and over again, to define and redefine themselves, to side with one political community against another. To date, this attitudinal and emotional dimension of the Cuban revolution and exodus has not been explored or seen in the historical context in which I place it. As Ron Aminzade and Doug McAdam (2001) emphasized, the time has now come to pay attention to the role of emotions in contemporary politics. Damián Fernández (2000) also argued that the Cuban revolution cannot be understood without understanding the politics of passion.

Using the distinction developed by Albert O. Hirschman (1970) in *Exit, Voice, and Loyalty*, I conducted 120 in-depth, semistructured interviews with people who were representative of the four major waves of the exodus and the four major political communities. As I see it, the four major political communities that developed are the supporters who never wavered and became highly integrated with the revolution (*loyalty*); those who remained in Cuba but were uninvolved in the political process (*neglect* – an option some say Hirschman forgot); the exiles who rejected the revolution and joined the Miami political community (*exit*); and the dissidents who, living their criticism within, both support the revolution and reject it (*voice*). All of these communities exist at any time; over time, people also left one to join another. My interviews mined the participants' political biographies to explore this dynamic dimension of change over time, in its historical setting. Hence, I sought to capture the difference that time makes in two senses: time as age and time as history. In this, my effort is quite similar to Glen Elder's (1979; Elder and Hareven 1993), whose work also focuses on the intersection between moment in the life cycle and moment in history as crucial in determining social outcomes that are markedly different from one generation to another.

To capture the effect of time as both age and history, several main concepts guided my interviews: "vintages," political disaffection, political communities, and political generations. They helped identify the changes in political attitudes across time, for the same person, and across social groups at the same historical moment. For example, in the early 1960s the dramatic social changes taking place in Cuba were those associated with the transition from capitalism to communism, while in the early 1980s the enormous changes taking place in Cuba reflected the debates then raging within the communist world – *glasnost* and *perestroika*. Young people who lived through such distinctly different stages of the history of Cuba and the revolution constitute different political generations. As such, their loyalty to the revolution, their dissent within it, and their exile vary in meaning. A central finding of this research is that the critical experiences that promoted their processes of political disaffection varied quite markedly across the major waves of migration because they represented the different political generations that lived through distinct stages of the revolution.

Political Alienation

While virtually all who joined the exodus out of Cuba were people who became profoundly alienated from the society there, that estrangement from the political institutions manifested itself differently than in other societies, such as the United States. The most consistent finding of political alienation research in the United States is that the alienated participate less. As James Wright in his study of *The Dissent of the Governed* put it, "the alienated participate less in politics because they believe that all political choices are vacuous" (1976:111). By contrast, alienation and participation often coexisted in Cuba because, quite simply, the meaning of participation contrasts markedly in the two societies.

In the United States and other Western capitalist democracies, to participate (as is often measured in surveys) means to turn out to vote; to attend political meetings or rallies; to work for a party or candidate; to belong to a political organization; to give money; to wear a campaign button or put a campaign sticker on one's car; or to follow a campaign with interest in newspapers, magazines, and television (Wright 1976:227). These are all activities from which an individual can derive much intrinsic satisfaction – but no extrinsic benefits. Hence, in societies like this, the politically alienated, to whom all political choices seem vacuous, participate less in these activities than the nonalienated. By contrast, in Cuba, as well as in other communist societies, the rewards to participation are not only intrinsic but also extrinsic. For example, when new cars were imported from the Soviet Union, they were distributed among party members. Likewise, membership in the Communist Youth League greatly facilitated admittance to the university, whereas church membership greatly impeded it. That changes the social psychology of participation. Political alienation manifests itself in our society by participating less, by withdrawal. In Cuba, too, political alienation manifests itself by withdrawal (what Alex Inkeles and Raymond Bauer in their 1959 study of daily life in the Soviet Union called "the inner emigration"), but it can also coexist with participation in the political institutions of the society that supposedly indicate strong political integration, such as the party or the Committees for the Defense of the Revolution. When political alienation coexists with this type of political participation, I called the resulting behavior "dissimulation" (Pedraza-Bailey 1983). These days, Cubans are very upfront about the extent to which they lived *la doble moral* (the dual morality). Writers often refer to it as "the masks we wore."

Furthermore, as Wright expressed it, all societies are characterized by "some mix of consent, assent, and dissent" (1976:268). The stability of any regime, therefore, depends partly on the makeup of the mix – although empirically we hardly know what levels of consent, assent, and dissent are tolerable. The distinction is important for the study of political disaffection because, as Wright argued, it can help us distinguish between the always alienated and the recently alienated, a distinction seldom made. The always alienated and apathetic are people for whom alienation may be an accurate reflection of their powerlessness. By contrast, the recently alienated are people who initially were strong supporters and believers in the regime and its norms (consenters) but who suffered what Wright called a "disconfirmation" experience, a "political disappointment," so that their political alienation is experienced as a loss. My interviews searched for these disconfirmation experiences. As Max Weber pointed out so long ago, whatever their origins, ideas, once established, take on a life of their own and guide action. Working from a Weberian perspective, I believe that both material and ideal interests govern conduct (see Bendix 1977:46).

In the study of political alienation, the distinction between assenters and dissenters is crucial. Assenters are people who just "go along" with things as they are, who are politically alienated but also politically inactive and uninvolved. In general, they doubt the utility of any political activity and therefore live outside the margin of politics. Dissenters, on the other hand, are politically alienated but also politically engaged, and their hostility toward the political system is translated into political action. Following Wright, in my research I expected to find that dissenters would not come from people who initially were assenters because assenters are for the most part "spectators to somebody else's game" (1976:276). Instead, I expected that dissenters would come from those who were consenters. My research findings confirmed this. My interviews showed that people who bore arms against the revolution had formerly borne them for the revolution, such as Rafael Peláez fighting for the 26th of July Movement and then for the MRP. Likewise, Rafael Saumell initially was a member of the UJC and the UNEAC, and then he founded the human rights movement in Cuba. Between their days as consenters and their days as dissenters lay the "disconfirmation experiences" that promoted their political disaffection and that my interviews searched for.

A Period of Transition

Exit, Voice, Loyalty, Neglect are one set of images; *Assent, Dissent, Consent,* another. These images, or analytical distinctions, represent the varying political choices people made at different historical moments. The historical moment in which I conducted my research was appropriate to capture the change in and out of political communities and the political options just described. For one brief moment, people who represented all waves of the exodus were still alive. Also, the political spectrum is now richer than ever (cf. García, 1996). Over the course of nearly half a century, generational change has taken place. Moreover, a transition out of communism is now imminent in Cuba. Hence, in both Miami and Cuba a new civil society began to emerge, with new organizations and associations. That made them excellent sites for fieldwork. A range of political opinion now exists in *el exilio* in Miami. At one end are organizations such as the original Cuban American National Foundation (CANF or la Fundación) and Unidad Cubana (Cubans United) that support the U.S. trade embargo of Cuba and oppose a dialogue with Cuba's government because they feel it legitimizes the Cuban government. At the other end are organizations that oppose the trade embargo and the Helms-Burton law tightening the embargo and seek a dialogue with the Cuban government regarding a peaceful transition, such as the Committee for Cuban Democracy, as well as activist organizations, such as the Movimiento Democracia (Democracy Movement), that pattern their actions after the nonviolent struggles of the American civil rights movement.

Also in Cuba there is now a civil society emerging with the proliferation of independent groups of professionals (i.e., non-government-affiliated journalists, teachers, lawyers, economists, trade unionists), all of whom put themselves at risk to provide news, classes, and legal defense free of government dictate. The risk is quite real because a charge of "enemy propaganda" – a charge that covers all ideas that do not have the approval of the government – is sufficient to land people in jail. Moreover, within all the major institutions there are now *reformistas* (reformers) who seek to promote change within limits, but change nonetheless. And the dissident movement is now composed of myriad different organizations. Some are for, some against the embargo, but all have issued a call for parliamentary elections that will issue a freely elected democratic government and a peaceful, nonviolent transition. Even more, the Catholic Church, which the revolutionary government silenced in the early years, has now become a political actor. Once it was the church of the upper classes, whose mission was to train Cuba's future leaders. Today the church is closer to the common people and is also a major institutional presence. For many Cubans – especially after the collapse of the Soviet Union and communism – religion provides an alternative vision of the world and a place within which to exist (existentially speaking) amid the hardships of life in Cuba. The "transition" out of communism in Cuba is underway and is being led by Cubans. Like any social movement, however, it houses contradictory tendencies and is fraught with danger regarding the future.

Data and Methods

The research for this book entailed a great deal of fieldwork and participant observation in the major communities of Cuban exiles. Of the 120 interviews conducted over the course of four years, close to two-thirds took place in Miami, capital of the Cuban exile, corresponding to the proportion of Cubans settled there. The Cubans interviewed were representative of those who left the island from 1959 to 2004. A list of all the names and the city where I interviewed them is in the Appendix. From them, I chose the interviews with which to illustrate the book.

The research for this book used five primary research strategies:

1. observing and participating in the life of the community, particularly in Miami and in Cuba, but also in the other major cities where the interviews were conducted;
2. conducting the 120 formal, in-depth, taped, semistructured interviews;
3. collecting documents (such as political manifestos, photos, and letters) and analyzing their content;

4. analyzing quantitative census and survey data on the various waves of Cuban immigrants; and

5. reviewing electoral data and opinion polls.

This triangulation – the combination of different methodologies and different types of data in the study of the same phenomena or program – strengthened the research design (cf. Patton 1990; Denzin 1978).

The Interviews

The interviews were conducted in many different cities where the Cuban diaspora settled: in Miami, Hialeah, Homestead, and Key West; New York (in its various social worlds of the Bronx, Brooklyn, and Manhattan); Union City, Paterson, and Elizabeth; Boston and Amherst; Chicago; Los Angeles; Houston and Huntsville; Phoenix; Ann Arbor, Detroit, Flint, Ypsilanti, and Lansing; St. Louis; and New Orleans; as well as in Montreal, Canada; San Juan, Puerto Rico; and Madrid, Spain. I easily logged more than 100,000 miles by air, bus, train, and car to complete the interviews. Many good people opened their homes to me and even fed me and found me a place to sleep.

The taped interviews were in-depth. In a more informal manner, I easily interviewed three times more people, and I grew to know well many more whose experiences also became part of my understanding. The 120 interviews, therefore, are those people whose stories I chose to tape because they represented many others. Many of the people whom I interviewed were chosen by members of the community themselves. As McAdam recalled regarding his own interviews with those who participated in the civil rights movement's Freedom Summer in 1964, "By turns, I felt confused, exhilarated, depressed, and enriched" (1988:9). John Lofland, David Snow, and Lyn H. Lofland (2006) also underscored that, when engaging in fieldwork, the interviewer faces a number of emotional challenges. A major challenge is that the fieldworker traverses a vast emotional range with respect to his or her informants: from distance at one end to surrender at the other, with feelings of loathing, marginalization, sympathy, and identification in between. Snow et al. encouraged fieldworkers not to rush to disaffiliate or embrace their subject, but rather to experience the pulls as a tension from which insight might be derived. My own effort was to regain the center, where there is both some measure of distance and some measure of empathy.

My sampling strategy consisted of choosing the respondents on two bases: by the social and demographic characteristics that typified the immigrants of that wave (social class, race, education, gender) according to surveys and census data analyses (cf. Pedraza 1996a); and by the nature of their political participation in the key events that defined the particular historical moment. This is a form of what Anselm Strauss called "theoretical sampling" – where the researcher, after previous analysis, is seeking samples of population, events, or activities guided by his or her evolving theory (1987:16). Theoretical sampling is harnessed to making comparisons between and among those samples of populations, events, or activities that the emerging theory points to, so as to shed light on them as it evolves. The sample selection was, thus, guided by two different principles: the search for *statistical representation* of social and demographic characteristics that guides quantitative research, as well as the search for the *best exemplar* of social types that guides qualitative research. The first resulted from the statistical descriptions of the various waves of migration that came from the census and sample surveys; the second from the knowledge of the community I gained from my fieldwork among them. In a small sample (N = 120), statistical representation alone would fail to include minorities such as Cuban Jews or Chinese Cubans. Hence, I sought to represent Cubans as social types, so as to better represent the full gamut of what it means to be Cuban. Moreover, within each wave I selected respondents who lived through the defining events of the unfolding historical process. For example, I interviewed those who participated in the Bay of Pigs invasion in 1961; those who were among the more than 14,000 children who came to the United States alone, as part of Operation Pedro Pan in 1960–61; those who were part of the generation of artists that left through *el Mariel* in 1980; and those who joined a dissident organization in the early 1990s. Choosing the particular individuals to interview, I exercised great care because, as Blumer pointed out, "One should sedulously seek participants in the sphere of life who are acute observers and who are well informed. One such person is worth a hundred others who are merely unobservant participants. A small number of such individuals ... is more valuable many times over than any representative sample" (1969:41).

In choosing my respondents, I entered the community in many different ways: through the rich and the poor, through hospitals, schools, organizations, and neighborhoods. I sought to give expression to the full range of political views. In the United States, this range is usually understood as right and left – terms that, above all, express the degree of state intervention in social and economic questions Americans think is desirable. In the Cuban exile community, the range of political expression does not depend on their attitudes toward state intervention. Prior to the revolution, the two major political parties in Cuba were the Auténticos and the Ortodoxos, which together represented about two-thirds of the electorate. Both were social democratic parties. Those social democratic attitudes still encase the political attitudes of most exiles today. Cubans who grew up during the revolution also espouse socialist values. However, their experiences with both the revolution and the exile, their opposition to Fidel Castro's communism, have cut deep. Today, among exiles, the range of political expression indicates the extent to which they are for or against the U.S. trade embargo, for or against a political dialogue with Cuba's government. Cubans in exile define themselves instead as ranging from *los intransigentes* to *los moderados*, with some radical supporters of the revolution.

While the research concentrates on only one country, Cuba, and as such it constitutes a case study, the research design makes it a *comparative study* across four major waves of the exodus over nearly half a century. In particular, I emphasize the enormous divide between the first two and the last two waves. As immigrants, the first were the children of a democratic, capitalist society, who remember *la Cuba de ayer* (the Cuba of yesteryear); the recent immigrants were the children of communism in *la Cuba de hoy* (today's Cuba), who knew no other Cuba. That divide is enormous in experience, attitudes, and memories.

To improve the reliability of the data, I tried to correct for subjective distortions of reality as well as for lapses of memory over time, by interviewing various family members (cf. Johnson 1990; Kirk and Miller 1987). I also wanted to show that the social and historical processes lived were lived as family, rather than as lone individuals. For example, only one son may have become a political prisoner due to his conspiratorial activities against the government, but the whole family became the family of a political prisoner – branded, ostracized. Moreover, a major issue I explored in this research was how siding with or against the revolution divided families. Americans have lived through this experience only during the days of the Civil War in the middle of the 19th century. It is, however, part of the experience of all peoples who lived through failed or successful revolutionary movements in the 20th century, in Europe, Latin America, Africa, and Asia. Perhaps only Americans have been spared the trauma of loving those who chose to be on the other side.

Cuba is a small island with a population around 6.5 million at the time of the revolution, around 11.2 million today. Thus, social networks are quite dense, and people who share a similar life circumstance – for example, going to private school prior to the revolution, sharing the experience of prison in the 1970s, or participating in the dissident movement in the early 1990s – all know one another. Hence, to a large extent, tapping into someone's network is unavoidable. I chose, however, to do so deliberately because I wanted to observe the events people were describing from several viewpoints, both to corroborate the details and to give them depth.

The interviews, conducted in Spanish, focused on the different processes of political disaffection the émigrés underwent and the reasons why they chose to leave Cuba. I developed the questionnaire during preliminary travels to Miami and Cuba, a period of exploration. It included questions in the following areas:

1. the respondents' social and demographic characteristics (social class, occupation, race, education, gender, age, marital status) and the role these played in their lives and their political engagement over time;
2. their level of integration into the political organizations of the revolution (e.g., participation in the early revolutionary struggle against Batista in the 1950s, in the revolutionary government, or in the dissident movement in the 1990s) as well as the exile (e.g., participation in the Bay of Pigs in 1961 or the Cuban Committee for Democracy in 1992);
3. their family's changing attitudes toward the revolution over time;
4. the "disconfirmation experiences" that were critical in promoting their political disaffection, particularly for those who were strong supporters of the revolution initially;
5. their experiences in prison, if applicable;
6. their judgment regarding what was positive and what was negative about what happened during the revolution (using the image of the revolution on a balance);
7. their changing attitudes toward U.S. policy concerning Cuba (from the trade embargo, to the recent Migration Agreement, to the Helms-Burton Act); and
8. whether they wanted to return, given their expectations for Cuba's future and the role they might play in it.

All of these dimensions of the Cuban refugee experience to date remain unexplored.

During the interviews, I also collected relevant documents. For example, I collected the political manifesto of the organization or movement they belonged to; letters written between relatives in Cuba and the United States at a moment in their lives when they made the effort to express their thoughts and sentiments regarding the meaning of the exile and the family separation (or their reunion, when the family returned); and photographs and paintings that visually portrayed, or symbolized, the conditions of people's lives.

Typically the interview took place in the people's homes, secondarily in their offices. This allowed me to build trust and to ask probing questions regarding the family by pointing to their family photos or to the trophies they took pride in. The typical interview took five hours to complete; some took fully two days. I also selected both respondents who were public intellectuals – whose names often appeared in the newspapers – and respondents who were private individuals. When I interviewed more than one family member, I counted the interview as one interview if they had made the decision to leave Cuba together (e.g., as husband and wife); I counted them as two interviews if they had each made that fateful decision individually and later met each other and married in the United States.

The research also constituted an analysis of the two major institutions in Latin culture: the church and the family. Not only are they central in Latin culture, but they are also the two institutions around which fascism and communism erected themselves as mass social movements. Both fascism and communism were political projects that aimed to re-create the self – to develop in their subjects new identities as citizens of fascist or communist nations.

In the case of fascism, Mabel Berezin (1997) argued that the fascist government sought to incorporate the Italian love and respect for the family and the church into the fascist movement by creating fascist selves that were partly defined by them. I argue further that *both* fascism and communism depended on public spectacles – ritual parades, rallies, celebrations in the public plaza – to create a new political community and identity, fusing the public and the private selves. The relationship between the leader and the led was one of Max Weber's central concerns, as he paid particular attention to the types of legitimate domination (1978). Both fascist and communist governments created a culture of mobilization in which the leader aroused the masses through powerful, rhetorical speeches, while the masses replied with applause, chants, and flag waving. In both cases, the intent was to create men and women whose identities were bound to the regime – in fascist Italy, by appropriating their deep cultural ties to the family and the Catholic Church; in communist Cuba, by destroying them.

I gathered the interviews over the course of four years, which involved a sabbatical semester, four summers, and all semester breaks. During that

24

time I also made four trips to Cuba, varying in length between a week and a month. After the interviews were gathered, I continued the relationships established with many; hence, I was able to share their reactions to events that happened beyond the interview date, giving many interviews a longitudinal quality, as well as more depth.

The Fieldwork

The interviews influenced the fieldwork, and the fieldwork influenced the interviews. For example, when I began interviewing the exiles who were representative of those who left Cuba in the first wave, 1959–62, many of whom supported the Bay of Pigs invasion, I began to hear about the Agrupación they belonged to. The Agrupación Católica Universitaria (University Catholic Group, ACU) was an organization of young Catholic men whose aim was to put their spiritual beliefs into practice as social concerns. Soon I realized that within the Agrupación three political movements were born: the Directorio Estudiantil Revolucionario (Revolutionary Students' Directorate, DRE), the Movimiento de Recuperación Revolucionaria (Movement for Revolutionary Recuperation, MRR), and the Movimiento Demócrata Cristiano (Christian Democratic Movement, MDC), all founded and led by members of the Agrupación. Thereafter, I visited the site of the Agrupación in Miami, where it successfully transplanted itself and continued to bear fruit. While there, I was able to speak with Father Llorente, an influential leader of that generation, and to confirm the importance the Agrupación had, first in Cuba and later in exile, for young, Catholic professional men. Its appeal rested on its simplicity and the values it held out for that generation (see Hernández 1999; 1981).

Likewise, my fieldwork in the Cuban community in the area of Miami known as Little Havana led me to Cuban Memorial Way, off of Calle Ocho (8th Street, the symbolic heart of the Cuban community) to see the long row of monuments where Cuban exiles symbolized important events. There I discovered La Casa del Preso, a cooperative of former political prisoners that not only houses office space for their meetings and work but also was a home to several of them. They came to the United States after so many years in prison that they lost a substantial part of their families, remained childless, and were often so crippled and maimed as to be unable to work. Nothing taught me more about what political imprisonment was like in Cuba than to see La Casa del Preso and to come to know the men who lived there. When I interviewed former political prisoners thereafter, I did so with full knowledge of the consequences of their political stance. Thus, the fieldwork and the interviews had a profound reciprocal influence.

The fieldwork took place not only among exile communities but also in Cuba. Though I was quite young at the time, I am old enough to remember the origins of the Cuban revolution, moments that remained stored in my consciousness for a lifetime. Moreover, since 1979 (the first year Cuban exiles were allowed by the government to return to Cuba), I returned to Cuba on 11 very different trips. My participation in Cuba ranged widely. For example, I traveled there to observe the impact of the pope's visit on the Cuban people. I also participated in several conferences at the University of Havana on the Cuban exodus – the first few times that Cuban and Cuban American academics whose research specialized on the exodus came together to share ideas and research findings. Despite the tense political situation in the island at the time, my efforts to come close to the lives of people there were quite successful. Thanks to my friends there, I was able to visit Cubans in their homes, staying in the very modest quarters where Cubans live today, and to attend their churches. I also grew to know the families my respondents had left behind or saw their former homes and schools. I traveled the full length of the island, cities and rural areas both, often far from the madding crowd of Havana and the government. I sat with the privileged and the poor, blacks and whites, men and women, supporters and opposition. I listened to all. Although my research focuses on the Cuban exodus, an eyewitness understanding of the social conditions in Cuba is essential to understanding those who chose the path of exile. However, I never interviewed anyone there formally because the necessary social and political conditions are not present.

Studying Refugees

Refugees are one of four major types of immigrants, identified by Portes and Rumbaut (1991) as labor migrants, entrepreneurial immigrants, professional immigrants, and refugees. While refugees are as old as human history, over the course of the 20th century, in what has become the age of genocide (Power 2002), their numbers have grown by leaps and bounds. Yet, as refugees, they have been little studied to date, and theoretical syntheses of migration (e.g., Massey 1999) focus on labor migration.

The defining feature of a refugee exodus is that people left their homes wrapped in fear – fear of persecution, imprisonment, at times even death; hence, they made the coerced decision to leave seeking refuge, safety

(Rose 1981). As E. F. Kunz explained, a refugee is "a distinct social type." The essential difference between refugees and voluntary migrants lies in their motivations: "It is the reluctance to uproot oneself, and the absence of positive original motivations to settle elsewhere, which characterizes all refugee decisions and distinguishes the refugee from the voluntary migrants" (1973:130).

Hence, the key idea necessary to understand the refugee in flight is that of the "push" rather than the "pull" that prompts people to migrate (cf. Lee 1966). While ordinary immigrants are more likely to be "pulled" by the attraction of the opportunity to fashion a better life, as Barry Stein (1981:322) succinctly expressed it, "the refugee is not pulled out; he is pushed out. Given the choice, he would stay." Political exile is the last step of a process of profound political disaffection that, as Kunz (1973) stressed, is often accompanied by the refugees' fear for their safety given their interpretation of events and self-perceived danger.

To explain the enormous variance among refugees' experiences, Kunz spoke of "vintages" – refugee groups that are distinct in "character, background, and avowed political faith" (1973:137). When dramatic changes in the society take place gradually, individuals react differently. Some oppose changes that others support, some call for compromises that to others smell of collaboration: "As the political situation ripens for each, they will leave the country as distinct 'vintages,' each usually convinced of the moral and political rightness of his actions and implicitly or openly blaming those who departed earlier or stayed on" (1973:137).

Basing themselves on their analysis of the Mexican labor migration, Massey et al. (1987) pointed out that when a migration flow has gone on for so long that the social networks that drive it become mature, the migration that was initially propelled by structural causes (e.g., poverty, landholding patterns) acquires an internal dynamic (family reunification). Thus, migration comes to fuel itself. Such has also happened in the Cuban case. However, refugees are distinct from other immigrants. Not only are their motivations different, but also they do not intend to return to their homeland as other immigrants do. The old world as they knew it, in which they were targets or victims of persecution, simply ceased to exist. Fear of persecution remains.

Whether immigrants are refugees or voluntary migrants is determined not only by the contrasting nature of their motivation – a social and psychological distinction – but also by the governments that regulate their exit and arrival – a legal distinction (see Table 7.1). The distinction is also between micro- and macrolevels of analysis. This research focuses both on the nature of the decisions the refugees made to leave Cuba and the larger social structures that shaped the exodus, a dialectical relationship between the micro and the macro. As C. Wright Mills (1961) said so long ago, the sociological imagination lies at the intersection of personal troubles and historical issues.

Methodological Implications

Studying refugees also holds implications for the research methodology used. The qualitative method of ethnography – particularly the research strategies of interviews and participant observation – was the appropriate methodology for this research for two reasons: because it is a study of *refugees*, immigrants that possess distinct characteristics; and because the study explored the *process* of attitudinal change.

Given the highly politicized nature of the Cuban community, and a political process that has not yet ended, most of the people who are politically involved in the community make themselves accessible only to those they know and trust. Fear defines the refugee experience. Oftentimes their fear is not for themselves but for those left behind. For both reasons, most of my sample had unlisted phone numbers. Thus, the standard sampling strategy in the social sciences, which consists of drawing a random sample of a community via the telephone directory, was inappropriate, because it would have never yielded a sample of those politically involved and daring or those uninvolved but afraid – the defining characteristics of the refugee experience. Second, the research sought to capture the *process* of political disaffection – exploring the experiences that brought attitudinal change about. Although one can capture the attitudes held at one moment versus another with survey research, qualitative research involving in-depth interviews is the appropriate methodology to understand the process of change. Moreover, ethnography is the appropriate method to place people's lives in their historical and social setting, as this research also sought to do.

Given the problem of fear and mistrust that exists in a refugee community, I asked those I interviewed whether they wanted the interview to be reported with their real name or with a pseudonym. In general, those who were public persons chose to be interviewed with their real names. To them, the interview was yet another form of political participation that would serve as a testament of their lives. By contrast, those who were private persons usually chose to have their interview reported under a pseudonym.

Because most interviews took place in the respondent's home or office, I was able to ask questions about family photos or even meet family members, which gave depth to the interviews. For respondents who were public intellectuals or activists, I read about them in newspaper accounts or watched them on television. Here the methodology was closer to that of historians who engage in reconstructing people's lives through archival research and the collection of materials handed down in the family. Historians engage in reconstructing the past because the past is dead. My respondents lived in the present, but many had left Cuba never to return again; hence, it was necessary to reconstruct their old lives.

Without doubt, part of the methodology used in this study is historical, not only because the time span covered by the period of the revolution spans nearly half a century now, involving distinct historical stages of the revolution and the exile, but also because social life is always historical – shaped by distinct political and economic stages, disrupted by historically contingent events. The present is historical, as is the past. Moreover, as Charles Tilly (1981) pointed out, social science history results when sociologists reach out for historically grounded theoretical explanations, and historians reach out for the social scientific tradition that involves explicit conceptualization of the phenomena under study, painstaking measurement, and the deliberate use of comparison. Then sociology meets history.

Moreover, a study of refugees involves a different type of data collection. Interviewing refugees entails handling sensitive matters that can be disclosed only under conditions of trust. A refugee community is a wounded community. Hence, rather than the impersonal relationship between the interviewer and the respondent that characterizes survey research and leads to quantitative analysis, in studying refugees it is crucial to first develop a trust relationship with the respondent or to have a third party who is trusted by the respondent broker the interview.

Self-Reflexivity

The social sciences used to be characterized by the quest for an impossible objectivity and detachment between the researcher and his object of study. As Gunnar Myrdal (1975) pointed out, such objectivity was, in fact, impossible because our values intruded at every stage of the research process – in the very choice of the problem to be studied, for example. Fortunately, over time, the social sciences have moved to a more self-conscious stance in which the relationship of the researcher to the object of his or her research is made evident. While such self-reflexivity can easily degenerate into a form of self-indulgence (see Pedraza 2002), the effort to become conscious of one's stance vis-à-vis one's object of study seems worthwhile. In my case, both sides of my family became deeply divided by the Cuban revolution between those who rejected it summarily and those who accepted it and rose within it. On my father's side, for example, my uncle Rafael Pedraza, was a doctor and was deeply identified with the goals of the revolution. A director of several hospitals, he was also a committed, idealistic communist since his early years when he was studying medicine at the Sorbonne in Paris, France, in the late 1920s and early 1930s. During the revolution, he became a member of the Central Committee of the Cuban Communist Party (Partido Comunista de Cuba, PCC). My father, however, was an American enthusiast who graduated from MIT as a chemical engineer in the early 1940s and went on to work in Cuba for an American company, B. F. Goodrich, for whom he also worked for most of his career after he left Cuba (cf. Morello 1998).

A similar split took place on my mother's side as many of her closest cousins, the Lubián and Gómez-Lubián of Santa Clara, sided with the revolution. Marta Anido (Gómez-Lubián), for example, was a woman who specialized in many facets of Cuban culture – ballet, history – and was a founding member of the Cuban Communist Party. Her ideals led her to believe in the egalitarian thrust of the revolution. For Marta and others on this side of the family, the death of my cousin Agustín (*el Chiqui*) Gómez-Lubián, a student at the university then, when he was fighting for the revolution against Batista, weighed greatly in their commitment. My mother, however, continues to mourn the loss of her house and her life in Cuba to the revolution, although she went on to have a rewarding life outside Cuba. Above all, she was always a committed teacher: in Cuba, at the Instituto de la Víbora for many years; for 10 years thereafter in Bogotá, Colombia, at the Colegio Nueva Granada; then in Akron, Ohio, at Thomas-town Elementary; and in Hialeah-Miami for the last 25 years of her career as a bilingual education teacher in Hialeah Junior High. I myself feel only the loss of my close family and friends: my cousins, the women who raised me, school classmates – all those with whom I would have liked to share my life from birth to death. Everything else I have more than found in this country. Surely the person I am today is the result not only of my upbringing but also of the harshness of the refugee experience, the sense of loss and disorientation I felt for many years. Throughout the book, I have chosen to bring myself in, though humbly and briefly, because I also am part of the historical drama.

Because my love for both those who stayed and those who left never wavered, and I understood them both to be motivated by principles and beliefs, never expediency, from a very early age I was able to see the revolution from both points of view. That made me sensitive to all political stances regarding the revolution in a way that many Cubans cannot achieve. It allowed me to develop what Max Weber called *verstehen* – an empathetic understanding (cf. Gerth and Mills 1981). I recall that, in an interview regarding his PBS documentary *The Civil War*, Ken Burns remarked that what had allowed him to work on the American Civil War was the fact that he had family on both sides of the line. So say I.

In addition, the social movements that were blowing in our time when I was an undergraduate at the University of Michigan and later a graduate student at the University of Chicago, during my own political generation, also made me sympathetic to the claims that the Cuban revolution had delivered enormous benefits to the Cuban people. Thus, I joined the Antonio Maceo Brigade, in the summer of 1979, and returned to Cuba for a month of travel throughout the island, to see for myself how I could weigh on a balance the achievements and the failures of the revolution. I, of course, also returned to capture my lost childhood, to find what was still left of my family and my past. Over the course of a couple of return trips, my own perspective developed. In my view, the social advances of the revolution in the areas of health and education were real, and the effort to overcome the systematic marginalization of blacks, peasants, and women laudable. Yet it was also clearly evident that the denial of civil liberties and civil rights to all of the population also constituted an enormous setback, as did the widespread poverty that robbed most Cubans of material goods and dignity. In my view, both had to be put on the balance (Pedraza-Bailey 1983). My encounters with Cuba in revolution allowed me to develop my own perspective: bread with liberty. It is a perspective that is, at once, social-democratic and profoundly (Judeo) Christian: the society needs to redress the excesses of the unregulated market, its tendency to lead to exploitation, without violating the dignity of the human person, the individual need for personal freedom.

I am a child not only of the Cuban revolution but also of Cuba's history. Both sides of my family, Pedraza and Lubián, distinguished themselves in the struggle for Cuba's independence. I feel most identified with my grandaunt Victoria Pedraza, who as a young woman sewed and embroidered the flag that Máximo Gómez defiantly raised. This book is like her flag, my contribution to Cuba's history.

I am also a child of the American social movements of the '60s. I also believe in nonviolent forms of social protest exemplified by the life and work of Martin Luther King Jr., Mahatma Gandhi, and Cesar Chavez. Their influence makes me sympathetic to the courageous men and women who struggle at present in the dissident movement in Cuba for universal human rights – for the right to free elections, the right to own and use personal property, the right to self-expression and free association, the right to dissent – the principles embodied in the proposals for a democratic future that came out of Cuba in recent years. The transition out of communism has already begun in Cuba; there will be *un nuevo amanecer* – a new dawn, a new democratic awakening. Cuba's struggle around the achievement of democracy has taken place over the full length of the 20th century, since the achievement of independence. To my mind, it will cease only when we come to value the democratic institutions that have proved so difficult to consolidate. Until then, we will continue to sweat our fevers, as José Martí said.

I believe this research will help us develop an understanding of how our lives, our biographies, are shaped by and, in turn, seek to influence the limits imposed by society and history. As such, my hope is that it will contribute to the development of the sociology of the refugee as well as the sociology of revolutions.

PART I

For and against the Republic, for and against the Revolution

THE CUBAN EXODUS OF 1959–1962 AND 1965–1974

2

The Revolution Defines Itself

...Ya que nacer es aquí una fiesta innombrable

...Since being born here is a remarkable feast
José Lezama-Lima, *Enemigo Rumor* (1941)

Sociology of Revolution

The changes – political, social, economic – that took place in Cuba at the end of the 1950s and beginning of the 1960s were so dramatic, profound, and irreversible that they truly deserve the name of "revolution" in the original sense of "taking a full turn." In an extremely brief time – less than four years, from January 1, 1959, until October 1962 – the Cuban revolution progressed through several distinct stages. Yet Fidel Castro, who became the maximum leader of that revolution, repeatedly promised that it was not a communist revolution but an authentically Cuban one – "green as the palm trees." His insistence lasted until the revolution was consolidated after the failure of the exiles' attempt to restore the republic by invasion. During this time, all Cubans were forced to choose their political stance.

Throughout Latin American history, *caudillos* – political leaders whose mandate to lead is based on their person – rather than political parties have most often spearheaded political change. Two *caudillos* shaped the history of the Cuban revolution: Fulgencio Batista, who relied on the support of the army; and Fidel Castro, who relied on the support of the common people. The Cuban people became completely polarized by these two men. Some fought for or against Batista's government; others fought for or against Fidel's government; still others fought twice – first, against Batista, then against Fidel. In the end, it was the republic that fell – vanquished both by Batista's and Castro's dictatorships.

The three chapters that cover this time period are based on 67 interviews I conducted with Cubans who lived through the origins of the Cuban revolution and remembered it well: those who left Cuba during the first two waves of the exodus plus 10 others who were imprisoned then for their political activities. Many of them were responsible for the course the Cuban revolution took in the island; many were responsible for the political organizations and the political culture that developed in *el exilio*. Others tried to remain at the margins.

To organize the data from the interviews, I chose to employ Nelson Amaro's (1977) periodization of the processes of social change in the Cuban revolution into five stages: democracy, humanism, nationalism, socialism, and Marxism-Leninism. Amaro's notion of stages echoes Crane Brinton's (1965) natural history of the great revolutions. I use the interviews to tell the story of the unfolding Cuban revolution; to identify its root causes; and to illuminate the changing stages of the revolutionary process. I also use the interviews as evidence of the different political tendencies that existed at the time, focusing on the process of political disaffection the émigrés underwent. The men and women I interviewed had a great deal to say about the unfolding of the Cuban revolution and the course it took, as well as the development of social revolutions more generally. To illustrate the onset of the revolution, I rely on interviews with Alfredo Blanco, José Antonio Costa, Fernando Roa, Antón Nuñez (pseudonym), Olga Mallo, Manuel Díaz, Julio Rodríguez, José Ignacio Rasco, Juan Sánchez ("Novillo"), Antonio Reyes and Cecilia Mestre (pseudonyms), Carlos Franqui, Rafael Peláez (pseudonym), Manolo Ray, Jorge Valls, Himilce Esteve, Fermín Mejía (pseudonym), Rosario Rexach, and Carlos Méndez.

In his reviews of the literature on the causes and consequences of revolution, Jack Goldstone (2001; 1982) identified four generations of theories of revolution. The first generation of theorists, the natural-history school, examined only the great revolutions (the English, American, French, and Russian), comparing them in terms of the stages they traversed (e.g., Brinton 1965). The second generation of theorists considered the great revolutions together with other forms of collective political violence, such as peasant revolts, riots, unsuccessful revolutions, and civil wars (e.g., Tilly 1978), an approach that has once again gained currency (e.g., McAdam et al. 2001), though now in a dynamic, relational way. The third generation of theorists, the structural-functional school, focused its attention at the level of the state, its strength or weakness and vulnerability to revolutionary challenges (e.g., Skocpol 1979). The fourth generation of theorists has critiqued the overly structural emphasis of earlier scholars and insisted on the need to bring leadership, ideology, and political identity back into the study of revolution (e.g., Aminzade et al. 2001). The challenge at present lies in connecting structure and agency, macro- and microsocial processes (McAdam et al. 2001), a challenge present also in the study of immigration (Pedraza-Bailey, 1990). McAdam et al. (2001) call for a study of "contentious politics," an umbrella term for all related social processes that are dynamic and relational, such as revolutions, social movements, and civil wars. This study forms part of the effort of fourth-generation scholars. As such, it seeks to identify not only the causes of the Cuban revolution (and of the exodus) and its outcomes, but also the processes through which it was lived. Simply put, my aim is not only to identify the *why* and the *what*, but also the *how*.

Goldstone (2001) emphasized that one can develop a typology of revolutions by their outcomes or by their main actors. Defined by their outcomes, one can distinguish between political revolutions, social revolutions, palace coups, abortive revolutions, and unsuccessful revolutions. The Cuban revolution was a response to Fulgencio Batista's military coup – a political revolution that aimed to restore the republic. It became a social revolution under Fidel Castro's leadership – a radical transformation of the total structure of Cuban society. Throughout this process, lurking in the background was the memory of the revolution of 1933, a successful political revolution against the dictatorship of Gerardo Machado (see Farber 2006).

Democracy

The first stage of the Cuban revolution was that of democracy: the restoration of the republic. Cubans who fought for the revolution at this time wanted to restore the constitutional elections that Batista's 1952 coup had brought to a halt. This stage began with the 26th of July Movement that Castro organized and spearheaded, which took its name from the day in 1953 when he and 165 others (2 of them women) participated in an attack on the Moncada army barracks in Santiago de Cuba. It lasted into the first few months of the revolutionary victory of 1959 with the first social reforms the government promulgated.

Social Conditions on the Eve of the Revolution

To understand who supported or rejected the revolution, it is necessary to understand Cuba's social and economic conditions on the eve of the revolution. As Carmelo Mesa-Lago (2000:171) stressed, comparing Cuba in the 1950s to other Latin American countries puts it "among the top two or three countries in socio-economic development." In the 1940s and 1950s, the state began transforming an overwhelmingly market economy by regulating labor conditions and intervening in economic affairs. The Constitution of 1940 introduced the notion of social rights and aimed to shape a social welfare state. Still, as Mesa-Lago emphasized, both state ownership and regulation were at low levels in comparison with other similarly developed Latin American countries, and they primarily affected education and health care. To Louis Pérez (1995:296), however, despite "this appearance of well-being, the Cuban middle class was in crisis," as the decade of the 1950s was a period of mounting instability and uncertainty. While Cuba enjoyed one of the highest standards of living in Latin America, the "apparent affluence" concealed tensions and frustrations, dependent as they were on the United States' economic system and its consumption patterns.

In Cuba's plantation society of the 1950s, 81 percent of all exports consisted of sugar, and about a quarter of the labor force was employed in work that revolved around the *ingenios*, the sugarcane mills and fields (Pérez-López 1991; Moreno-Fraginals 1978). Sugar production is particularly prone to "boom" and "bust" cycles, which characterized the Cuban economy throughout the century. The instability of world market prices for sugar and the shifting sugar quotas and prices fixed by the United States fostered instability in Cuba's gross national product. Moreover, the sugar sector was basically stagnant, and other sectors could neither absorb the excess labor from agriculture nor provide the dynamism necessary to make the economy grow (Mesa-Lago 2000:173). Two-thirds of Cuba's trade was with the United States. The Cuban economy was fully integrated into and dependent on the United States economy.

Social inequality was vast, particularly between city dwellers and those who lived in rural areas, but a social welfare state was well advanced. Labor legislation and social security were among the best in Latin America. The trade-union movement and collective bargaining were quite strong, though often controlled by the government, as they were under Batista (see Córdoba 1995). Alfredo Blanco came from a family of *colonos* (independent sugar producers who grew cane for the sugar mills) who later on became sugar mill owners, *hacendados*. He also remembered the poverty of the sugar workers during Machado's government. In 1933, he stressed, there was no minimum wage; the salary paid to the employees in *el ingenio* was 25 cents for a 10-hour working day; even less for those who worked in *el campo*. After Machado, "it was Grau-San Martín's government that gave labor its victories: he established the minimum wage of 80 cents, the eight-hour working day, and supported the development of the trade unions." The national labor union, the Central de Trabajadores Cubanos (Cuban Workers' Confederation, CTC), was organized in 1933. The sugar workers' *sindicatos* became quite strong. Every sugar mill had its own *sindicato*, all of which were part of the FNTA – the Federación Nacional de Trabajadores Azucareros (National Sugar Workers Union).

José Antonio Costa knew firsthand the poverty of the countryside and the struggles of the labor movement. As an adolescent, he saw the sugar workers become unionized on the heels of Machado's fall from power. Costa was typical of the poor *campesinos*, the peasants, descended from Spaniards – mostly Gallegos and Canarios – who immigrated to Cuba in the early part of the 20th century, looking for work. He grew up in Camagüey province in an American sugar mill called "Vertientes." There he was a *machetero*, cutting the sugarcane and doing a bit of everything else – planting, reaping. One of seven siblings, he had only a third-grade education, though he continued studying while employed at the sugar mill. He devoted his life to the labor struggle and rose to become recording secretary of the Confederación Nacional de Trabajadores Azucareros de Cuba (National Federation of Sugar Workers). There he served until in 1959, under the impact of the enormous popularity of the revolution, the communists took over the *sindicatos*, labor unions, in every sugar mill and threw him and others out. "Before you had the *patrón*, the worker, and the government. Now the government is the *patrón*," he emphasized.

Costa remembered the misery that reigned in the Cuban countryside prior to the development of the labor movement, misery that became "a disgrace" during the Great Depression. Workers were jobless, but, when they worked, they would earn only 12 cents for cutting and lifting 100 *arrobas* of sugarcane – about 2,500 pounds. During the "dead season" at the end of the harvest, there was no other employment. World War II changed the situation by inflating the price of sugar, and prosperity arrived "like a river flowing with money." By 1949 the sugar workers' union comprised 180 *sindicatos*. As a result of collective bargaining, workers obtained impressive labor legislation: delimiting the workday, establishing a minimum wage, and providing maternity benefits for their wives, as well as retirement benefits.

Mesa-Lago (1981) pointed out that gains such as those Costa described came at the expense of the unemployed and the peasants. In Efrén Córdoba's (1995) view, however, unemployment in Cuba was structural – the result of the sugar industry that provided employment for only a few months of the year. In 1956–57, 16 percent of the labor force was unemployed and 14 percent was underemployed; during the "dead season," unemployment more than doubled (Mesa-Lago 2000:172). In 1957–58, according to Mesa-Lago, Cuban education, sanitation, health care, and social security were among the best in Latin America. But, as Costa's recollections suggest, the national averages masked a great deal of internal inequality. Modern conveniences, health care, education, and social services were mainly concentrated in the cities. In 1953 the illiteracy rate in Cuba was 23.6 percent, just slightly higher than Costa Rica's (20.6) and Chile's (19.8), but that overall rate masked a rate of 41.7 percent illiteracy in rural areas versus 11.6 percent in urban areas (in Mesa-Lago 2000:172). The same was true with respect to infant mortality, access to safe drinking water, and sewerage and sanitation services. In 1953, 82 percent of the urban population had access to potable water, but only 15 percent of the rural population did (in Mesa-Lago 2000: table V.23). As a result, there was a substantial rural-to-urban migration, which resulted in peasants living in shanty towns. At best, they found work in the low-paid service occupations, as domestic servants or peddlers; at worst, they became beggars who made a scant living, depending on the mercy of others.

The middle class grew considerably and played an important part in the economic life of the country but seldom had a role in politics. Due to Cuba's history of government corruption (both electoral and administrative), average Cubans came to feel that politics was a dirty business. They called it *politiquería* and stayed away from it (Farber 2006). Jorge Mañach (1959:6) called such corruption "the great problem" of Cuba's "public sphere."

Batista's Dictatorship

In *The Old Regime and the French Revolution*, Alexis de Tocqueville (1955) argued that to understand how a new society is born, one needs to visit the grave of the old. With his coup of March 10, 1952, Batista put an end to the new era of democratic government and to the best aspirations expressed in the Constitution of 1940. Though Cuba had been a republic since 1902, when it won its independence from Spain, the republic was not yet deeply rooted. It was dependent on the political tutelage of the United States, as the Platt Amendment, which allowed the United States to intervene in Cuban affairs when it deemed such intervention necessary, made clear. The amendment remained in force until 1933, at which point a period of authoritarian rule ensued under Gerardo Machado's presidency, which provoked deep social rifts and a social movement of protest called "the revolution of 1933." Thus, the Constitution of 1940 was the "fruit of a long historical process full of sorrow," as Mañach, one of Cuba's leading social scientists, stressed (1959:7). It was a document in which Cubans took great pride. Fernando Roa, *magistrado* (superior judge) of the Havana court, remembered the writing of the Constitution itself as admirable, as the Constitutional Assembly represented all political tendencies – left and right, including the communists. It "fundamentally guaranteed both individual rights and social rights, which should remain for Cuba in the future," he stressed.

Batista's coup was popularly called *el madrugonazo* (literally, the enormous event that took place in the early dawn) because the surprise attack occurred only a few weeks before the scheduled presidential elections. At this time, Cuba had a multiparty system. The three largest parties consisted of the Partido de Acción Unitaria (United Action Party, PAU), the Partido del Pueblo Cubano Ortodoxo (Orthodox Political Party, popularly called the Ortodoxos), and the Partido Revolucionario Cubano Auténtico (Revolutionary Authentic Political Party, popularly called the Auténticos). The last two were both social democratic parties, as the Ortodoxos were an offshoot of the Auténticos. Batista, who had risen in the army from sergeant to colonel and then to chief of staff, was running as the PAU candidate. He had served as Cuba's elected president from 1940 to 1944. Running against Batista were Carlos Hevia, for the Auténticos (the party of former presidents Ramón Grau–San Martín and Carlos Prío Socarrás); and Roberto Agramonte, for the Ortodoxos, former vice-chancellor of the University of Havana. Senator Eduardo Chibás, who expressed the deep social populism in Cuba, was an Ortodoxo (see Farber 2006). Smaller parties, including the Partido Liberal, the Partido Nacional Cubano, and the Partido Conservador also had candidates in the race.

The coup was motivated by Batista's low probability of winning office. A national survey by the Instituto Nacional de Investigaciones published in *Carteles* magazine in 1952 asked the Cuban people for whom they intended to vote. Although Batista was the best known of the political candidates (see Figure 2.1), Agramonte was the top vote getter, with 34 percent, while

Figure 2.1 Fulgencio Batista was president of Cuba twice: from 1940 to 1944, after he was elected, and from 1952 to 1959, after his coup d'etat. Here General Batista is with his wife, Marta Fernández, and supporters at a political rally in 1951. (University of Miami, Otto G. Richter Library/Cuban Heritage Collection)

Batista gathered only 24 percent, and Hevia came in a distant third with 13 percent. *Carteles* published the third installment of the survey on February 10, and Batista's coup occurred exactly a month later, 80 days before the scheduled June elections. As Portell-Vilá emphasized, the events of

March 10 took Cuba's citizens by surprise, as they thought that military might and privilege had effectively been buried by the Constitution of 1940 (1975:438).

During his second stint in government, Batista's emphasis was on public works, such as the Central Highway that cut across the length of the island. He also gave organized labor his support. Alfredo Blanco recalled that Batista enacted a number of populist measures that benefited *el obrero*, the worker. He raised their salaries by 10 percent and reduced their work week from 48 to 44 hours. He also enacted legislation that helped their retirement benefits. "Batista wanted to win the support of *el pueblo*," said Blanco, "which he lacked, but it was Grau–San Martín they idolized."

In addition, Batista made efforts to promote tourism and gambling, which increased both corruption and prostitution. For many American visitors, Cuba became the playground of the Western Hemisphere. Despite the excellent public works he spearheaded, Batista failed to gain what he most wanted – the support of the Cuban people. A general prosperity reigned in Cuba at this time, as indicated by the equivalence between the United States dollar and the Cuban peso and by overall economic indexes, but, as Mesa-Lago emphasized, this largely benefited capital and employed labor (2000:173).

Some of the Cubans I interviewed were *Batistianos*, and they expressed their satisfaction with the accomplishments of his government. The artist Antón Nuñez, for example, remembered that those were "years during which money flowed." The survey of public opinion published in *Carteles* revealed that women were an important social base of support for Batista (Instituto Nacional de Investigaciones, February 10, 1952:32). Olga Mallo was one of these women. In her mid-40s when Batista took over the presidency, she came from a middle-class family of professionals. Her father frankly admired the Americans, so when the students revolted against Machado in the 1930s and the university closed, he sent Olga and her older brother to study in the United States. He went to Georgia Tech and then to work for Westinghouse briefly. She went first to high school and then to the women's college of the University of North Carolina at Greensboro. She returned to Cuba after *el Machadato* was over and studied at the University of Havana, specializing in physics and mathematics, while her brother went on to work as an engineer and manager in several sugar mills: "Jaronú" in Camagüey; "Boston" in Banes; and "Soledad" in Cienfuegos. Olga recognized the negative aspects of Batista's presidency – the broken democratic process – but she laid her stress on the positive, especially the progress Cuba experienced under Batista. She recalled that one could pay with pesos at a department store like El Encanto and receive change in dollars. She had once met Batista at a friend's house and found him likable – despite others' objections to his being mestizo and to his coup. But she was aware that "in truth, he was not popular."

Early Rebellions

Batista lost the meager backing he had due to his government's corruption and repression during his last few years in power. People began to refer to him as "the tyrant." In the issues of *Bohemia* magazine published immediately after the triumph of the revolution in 1959, one can see evidence of how Batista's police force imprisoned, beat, and tortured the opposition, particularly university students in the cities and peasants in the countryside.

Because he failed to gain a legitimate mandate in the eyes of the Cuban people, twice his authority was challenged from within the military. The first time was in April 1956, when a group of high-ranking career officers developed a powerful conspiracy. Led by Coronel Ramón Barquín and Major Enrique Borbonet, they were called *los puros* (those who were pure) because they opposed Batista's corruption and crimes. Young, middle-class, educated (many in the United States), *los puros* opposed the military's role in politics (Barquín 1978). At the same time, Rafael García-Bárcenas, a philosophy professor at the University of Havana, a Catholic and a leftist, who came from the social democratic tradition of the Auténticos, founded the Movimiento Nacional Revolucionario (National Revolutionary Movement, MNR). He sought to join the university students' social movement to that of *los puros*. The rebellion was premature, however, because Batista continued to control the army. The military recruited its men mostly among the poor peasants in the countryside, who tended to support Batista, despite his thirst for money and power (see Mañach 1959:168).

Manuel Díaz, for example, was a young, strong peasant who was the son of Spanish immigrants. He served in Batista's army, he told me, not because he was a *Batistiano* but because the army provided a decent living for a poor peasant. Moreover, Batista, who was mestizo, had risen from the rank of sergeant to lead the country and had created a class of mulatto civil servants around his government. The survey published in *Carteles* showed a differential pattern of support for the candidates by race. Only 18 percent of whites supported Batista, in contrast to 34 percent of mestizos and 44 percent of blacks (Instituto Nacional de Investigaciones, February 10, 1952: 32).

Julio Rodríguez, together with his brother Israel, was also driven to join the army not by sympathy for Batista but by his family's poverty. Only 19 years old when he enlisted, he hoped the army would be an avenue of social mobility. He had only a ninth-grade education and hoped to continue his schooling when the fighting was over. He worked in a *quincalla* (a small-goods store) earning only three pesos a week, wages so meager he could not help his mother support the family. When the revolution triumphed, he became unemployed and had to suffer the shame of being called *casquito* – a derogatory term for soldiers who joined the military in 1957 expressly to fight Castro's rebels.

The conspiracy of *los puros* failed, and the conspirators were arrested and sentenced by a military court to several years' imprisonment on the Isle of Pines. The second challenge to Batista's control was more broad-based and more successful. Many Cubans who fought to restore the republic did so after concluding Batista had made an electoral solution to Cuba's problems impossible. José Ignacio Rasco founded the Movimiento Demócrata Cristiano, Cuba's Christian Democratic Movement, in December 1959, as a Christian middle road between capitalism and communism (Rasco 1961). Many years later, Rasco also founded the Partido Demócrata Cristiano de Cuba, its expression as a political party, in Miami in 1990.

Rasco described himself as someone who had always been in the opposition – against Grau, Prío, Batista, Fidel. Rasco entered political life looking for an electoral, nonviolent solution to the problem of Batista's dictatorship. "But unfortunately," Rasco told me, "we saw that the government was just as intransigent as the opposition, that it was unwilling to find an agreement." To Rasco, yesterday as well as today, the formula that should be used is that of a dialogue and "the formula of the ballot box, which is preferable to arms." But only an armed solution remained: "The father of the 26th of July movement was the 10th of March," Rasco explained. The aim of this originally middle-class revolution was to restore the Constitution of 1940, elections, and "an honest, civil government."

The revolutionary armed struggle encompassed two major tendencies: first, the 26th of July Movement, centered in Oriente province, where the rebel *barbudos* (bearded men) fought in the Sierra Maestra and, later, in the Escambray Mountains in Las Villas; second, the Directorio Revolucionario Estudiantil, whose university student combatants fought mostly in the capital and other cities. However, the national and international spotlight fell only on Fidel Castro and the 26th of July Movement when in February 1957 *New York Times* correspondent Herbert L. Matthews (1961) interviewed

Fidel Castro in the Sierra Maestra, and Castro's story and photo appeared on the newspaper's cover page. That interview made Fidel Castro the undisputed leader of the Cuban revolution, concealing the equally important role the student movement played in the victory as well as its commitment to democratic values.

In this first phase, the vast majority of the Cuban people sided with the revolution against Batista's dictatorship. Had it been possible to measure the extent of the popular support through electoral returns or surveys, surely it would have been 90 percent. In its early days, the Cuban revolution was a very broad-based movement of popular opposition that progressively garnered the support of all social classes and groups. Juan Sánchez, nicknamed "Novillo" (Colt), Batista's soldier in Oriente, said the popularity of the revolutionary movement was such that very often Batista's soldiers would "pass from our side to the other." Antonio Reyes and Cecilia Mestre were typical of committed revolutionaries from the middle and upper classes. A young married couple in Oriente province, they came from a family of *colonos*, cattlemen, and professionals. Their farm neighbored on Castro's family farm. In the early stages of the revolution, they sewed uniforms and crossed enemy lines to take food and vital information to the rebels' second front of Mayarí Arriba, in the Sierra Cristal. The women in their family also hid important rebel figures in their homes, including Haydée Santamaría and Melba Hernández, who participated in the attack on the Moncada. They also visited rebel men who were imprisoned. The doctors in their family assisted the wounded rebels and even saved Gustavo Arcos-Bergnes, who nearly died from the bullet wounds received during the attack on the Moncada barracks.

In support of the revolution, Cecilia joined the march down the streets of Santiago staged by middle-class mothers dressed in black to signify their mourning. They marched under a placard that read: "Stop murdering our sons and daughters. Cuban Mothers" (*Bohemia*, January 11, 1959:179). In their family, the hatred for Batista was intense, and the 10th of March, the anniversary of Batista's coup, was a day of mourning.

Rural Poverty

The economy's performance in the late 1950s gave Cubans another good reason to remove Batista from power. While 1957 was the best year ever, in 1958 an economic deterioration took place, a decline that began in Oriente, the province that could be counted on to follow suit to calls for revolutionary activity. Organized labor also turned against Batista, even though he had cultivated its support (Domínguez 1978a:120–22).

Extreme social inequality also drove many Cubans from humble backgrounds to join the revolution in the late 1950s. Behind the prosperous Cuba of the urban middle classes lay another Cuba – that of blacks in the city slums, docks, ports, and sugar mills; that of whites of Spanish and Canarian ancestry who lived the rural poverty of *el campo*, the countryside. In 1957 the Agrupación Católica Universitaria issued a report resulting from the survey of 1,000 interviews its members conducted on foot in the nation's countryside. The report stressed the inequality between the city and the countryside and advocated agrarian reform: "The city of Havana is living in extraordinary prosperity while in the countryside people are living in incredible conditions of stagnation, misery, and despair" (1957:1). In a plantation society, 44 percent of the Cuban population lived in rural areas and 40 percent of the labor force worked in agriculture. The survey showed that the Cuban peasant (*el guajiro*) lived on a meager diet mostly consisting of rice and beans, supplemented only rarely with meat, fish, or vegetables; that he labored exceedingly hard for the five months of the harvest but was unemployed the rest of the year; that his family typically consisted of six members, but his average salary was only 45 pesos a month, which made it impossible for him to buy shoes; that his health was poor, and he often contracted typhus, parasites, or tuberculosis. Fully 43 percent of the peasants surveyed could not read or write due to the lack of teachers and schools in the countryside. Nearly all lived in the classic *bohío*, wooden houses with dirt floors and thatched roofs made with palm fronds. *Bohíos* lent their grace to the beauty of the Cuban countryside, but they had no indoor plumbing, electricity, or running water. Peasants used kerosene lamps for light and obtained water from rivers, springs, and wells. The Agrupación's report called these conditions a social sin that all Cubans were responsible for and, as Catholics and Cubans, had a responsibility to change.

Carlos Franqui is a prominent example of a peasant-born revolutionary. One of the *barbudos* in the Sierra Maestra with Fidel, Franqui became a linchpin of the revolution. He was director of Radio Rebelde, the radio station that became the voice of the revolution. He came from a family of *campesinos* that lost everything in the war of independence. Franqui's father cut sugarcane as a laborer. As Franqui put it, "he was condemned to fight for the revolution" because he saw his family's life as akin to slaves', and the world he knew needed change. As a young man, Franqui had been a communist, working as a journalist for the newspaper *Hoy* (Today), the organ of the Communist Party, the Partido Socialista Popular (People's Socialist Party). But soon he discovered that communism made the ample criticism and social challenge he sought impossible. When Batista's coup occurred, Franqui began editing an underground newspaper, *Revolución*, the organ of the 26th of July Movement. Batista's men detained him, imprisoned him, and tortured him. Thanks to the pressure exerted by many, he was able to leave prison after a few months, and he went into exile as an organizer for the 26th of July Movement until June 1958, when he was called to the Sierra Maestra to direct Radio Rebelde, to broadcast to the whole nation the progress of the rebel forces.

Castro's Charisma

The impact of Castro's leadership on the course the Cuban revolution took is undeniable. Yet, as Ron Aminzade, Jack Goldstone, and Elizabeth Perry (2001) pointed out, most research on leadership focuses on what kind of person becomes a leader, rather than on its effects. The three major theoretical approaches to the study of collective action and social change – structuralists, culturalists, and rationalists – all tend to relegate leadership to the status of a dependent variable, thereby robbing it of much of its agency. Yet leadership dynamics play a pivotal role in the outcomes of contentious politics, as they so clearly did in the Cuban case. As Aminzade et al. emphasized, the question of whether a revolution has a democratic outcome also depends on the character of the main revolutionary leaders, the catalytic role they play (2001:141). Hence, it is necessary to bring the study of leadership back in to the study of revolutions and social movements.

Rafael Peláez, who joined the 26th of July Movement as an adolescent, offered an analysis of Castro's emergence as a national leader. With the attack on the Moncada army barracks in 1953, Peláez explained, Fidel manifested himself as the leader of the Cuban revolution, and "armed struggle became the only solution to the problem of Batista." Of the 165 people who took part in the raid, about 80 died. Peláez emphasized that "militarily, that day's action was a failure, but politically it was a success. Although Fidel was imprisoned, Cuban politicians utilized it to condemn Batista's government, as a result of which Fidel came out alive." Many priests and bishops initially lent the revolution their support. The archbishop of Santiago de Cuba, Enrique Pérez-Serantes, interceded for Castro's life, saving him.

While in prison on the Isle of Pines in 1953, Castro, a lawyer, was allowed to conduct his own defense, resulting in his first great speech: "History

Will Absolve Me." In it, Castro denied that the attack on *el Moncada* was illegitimate and argued that it was really Batista's government that was illegitimate, the result of an unconstitutional power grab. Castro argued that to rebel against tyranny and despotism is legitimate (Castro 1973 [1953]:98–105). Hence, while the judge might condemn him, in the end, history would absolve him.

As a political and social program for the future of Cuba, "History Will Absolve Me" proposed social reforms, as did the second major statement, the Manifesto of the 26th of July Movement in 1956 (in Bonachea and Valdés 1972). Castro articulated several plans: restoration of the Constitution of 1940; safeguarding the property of small landholders; profit sharing for employees and workers of the large industries, mines, and sugar mills, as well as for *colonos*; and the nationalization of the electrical and telephone industries. He also pledged to seek solutions to the problems of industrialization, unemployment, education, and health, "together with the conquest of civil liberties and political democracy" (1973:43). One of Cuba's foremost economists, Felipe Pazos, also an author of the Manifesto of the 26th of July Movement, characterized the program as typical of all social democratic parties in Latin America, as recorded in the documentary "Castro's Challenge" (Domínguez 1985). As Domínguez (1978a:116–17) pointed out, the themes of political corruption and Batista's illegitimacy were far stronger than that of nationalism.

Castro's speech was widely disseminated, as a pamphlet, all over the island. He used this moment, Rafael Peláez emphasized, to "come out to the public palestra, to stake himself on something," because until then "he had been a rather mediocre university student leader." Peláez recalled: "From this moment forth, however, he was able to show himself before the Cuban people as a legendary figure, as a romantic figure." This, together with the armed struggle, attracted the young. The revolution increasingly gathered support among the Cuban people and much of the Catholic Church. Father Guillermo Sardiña climbed the Sierra to become chaplain to the rebels. Other priests became members of the urban resistance movement (Hernández 1999:96).

Rafael was among those that formed the 26th of July Movement as such – attracting others to it, carrying out sabotages, setting fire to the sugarcane fields. He placed the red and black flag of the movement on public display and wrote on public walls "M26-7" (the signature of the movement) or "Batista assassinates students" (referring to the DRE). He did so to create the perception that there was a state of discontent in Cuba and a social movement for change existed. Rafael defined himself as "a man of action," a man who "was capable of giving his life for a cause." As leader of the Action and Sabotage Brigade of the urban clandestine movement, he killed and he saw many die alongside him.

After Castro delivered his "History Will Absolve Me" speech, he and other political prisoners were granted amnesty and he went into a brief exile in Mexico. In September 1956, the leaders of the two groups of young Cubans engaging in armed struggle against Batista met in Mexico. Fidel Castro, representing the 26th of July Movement, and José Antonio Echeverría, representing the Federación Estudiantil Universitaria (University Students' Federation, FEU) as well as the DRE, signed the Mexico City Pact, agreeing to combine their efforts to overthrow Batista's tyranny. Franqui remembered: "We came back from our meetings in Mexico with renewed spirit and the firm conviction that we could not lose. With the pact, we had established the unity of Cuba's fighting youth under one ideology, although it had not been possible to come up with a common strategy.... So we agreed to follow separate plans that would culminate in Frank País's uprising in Santiago, Fidel's landing in Oriente, and the Revolutionary Directory's attack on the Presidential Palace" (1980:112).

Fidel and 82 others were to arrive on the coast of Cuba from Mexico in the yacht *Granma* on November 30, 1956. Rafael was among the group still in Cuba led by Frank País, a young university student in Santiago de Cuba, called El 30 de Noviembre. This group was supposed to assist the invasion force when it arrived. But due to inclement weather, Fidel and his men did not actually arrive until December 2, and they put in at a beach called Las Coloradas, rather than in Santiago de Cuba, where they were expected. Thus, they were able to escape the army unit sent to search for them by running to the nearby Sierra Maestra, where soon they established guerrilla operations. Henceforth, Peláez said, "Fidel Castro became a legend." Castro's charisma as leader exemplifies that "gift of grace" that Max Weber delineated is a type of legitimate authority that can break through as a revolutionary force (1978, vol. 1:241–45).

The 26th of July Movement

Rafael Peláez came from the upper middle class, and he could have left Cuba to study abroad, for many families sent their young sons overseas, to remove them from Cuba's troubled politics. He did not have to join the revolution, but he did so out of a quixotic sense – "a sense, perhaps romantic, of social injustice," a desire "to fight for the betterment of the country and to improve the situation of the poor," with whom he identified.

Manolo Ray was also a member of the 26th of July Movement and the urban clandestine movement. From his youth, he had been greatly preoccupied with social injustice – with poverty, unemployment, and, especially, racial discrimination. As a member of the Partido Ortodoxo, he was an enthusiastic follower of party leader Eduardo Chibás prior to his suicide. Chibás's political leadership expressed a profound social populism in Cuba. "That type of focus on social problems is what I saw in the 26th of July Movement," Ray explained. He saw the militants in the movement as people who fought for their ideals, without personal aspirations, and "without ever being at all communist." Ray said that no one had "a radical idea of a communist type; rather, it was a social democratic idea." When the revolution triumphed, Ray, a civil engineer, became minister of public works, as part of the first Provisional Government. This government, which lasted only about a year, was akin to what Brinton (1965) identified as "the rule of the moderates."

The 26th of July Movement clearly meant different things to different people. Carlos Franqui identified four major political currents: a Marxist, pro–Soviet Union current, that of Raúl Castro, Che Guevara, Carlos Rafael Rodríguez, and other old communists; a nationalist revolutionary current, that of Frank País, Faustino Pérez, David Salvador, Carlos Franqui himself, and organized labor; a liberal-reformist, democratic current, that of Raúl Chibás, Manolo Ray, and others, including a large part of the petite bourgeoisie and the better-off peasantry; and a conservative current, that of the upper middle classes connected to the civic resistance, such as Cecilia Mestre and Antonio Reyes, and leaders of civic institutions. "On top of all of this," Franqui explained, "was Fidel Castro, whose thoughts no one really knew."

Franqui believed that Fidel Castro's *caudillismo* and militarism impeded others' efforts to develop civic institutions within the movement or in the labor unions, to develop what today we call civil society. Franqui believed in the importance of these institutions, as his being an editor of several newspapers and a radio broadcaster indicate. Because of this belief, when Castro made him an offer to be a minister in the first Provisional Government, Franqui turned it down. Instead, he sought to create institutions that would render society more democratic. As editor of *Revolución*, Franqui attempted to both deliver the news of the day and promote criticism and debate. He hoped the newspaper would encourage the development of institutions that could provide a balance to Fidel's leadership, while at the same time strengthening the arts and culture, the labor movement, and a good-neighbor relationship with the United States. "If *Revolución* was neither official nor the mouthpiece of any ideology, it was, it turned out, the newspaper of the revolution," Franqui remembered, because "it posed a challenge" (1983:17). But, he argued, Fidel's popularity, the failures of U.S. policy toward Cuba, and the failed exile-led invasion attempt all made the development of countervailing forces impossible.

The Student Movement

While the 26th of July Movement led the struggle in Oriente, the Directorio did the same in Havana. Jorge Valls was part of the student movement. Only 19 when Batista staged his unexpected coup, Valls, like other student leaders at the university, refused to accept the illegitimate disruption of power. The student revolutionaries ratified the Constitution of 1940 and declared war on Batista. As Mañach (1959:8) expressed it at the time, "the students at the University of Havana situated themselves at the vanguard of a struggle they felt obliged to wage given their revolutionary tradition that harks back to the colonial period."

Together with many other students in the university, Valls engaged in several conspiratorial efforts against Batista, denouncing the blood the dictator spilled. He was persecuted by the police and went into hiding, but he was able to leave for Mexico in the spring of 1954. In the fall, conscious that the struggle had to be waged inside of Cuba, he returned. Continuing to make people aware of Batista's dictatorship, he landed in prison for 90 days, which served to mobilize the students throughout the island on his behalf. On September 30, 1955, an enormous act of protest was staged at the university, which the government tried to sabotage – without success – by cutting the electricity. The students held the protest on the *escalinata* (the long stairs) of the University of Havana. There, the founding of the DRE was announced. Drawing on the thought of José Martí, revered leader of the struggle for independence, the students called Cubans to the armed revolution: "When peace is unjust, war is necessary. My people, I ask you to join us in a just war" (Valls 1991:125, 144–45).

Valls was one of the students involved in drafting the DRE's, manifesto, which analyzed Cuba's problems in their political, economic, social, psychological, and moral dimensions. He and others in the Directorio distrusted Fidel's *caudillismo*, the emotional hysteria, and the exaltation of the

52

maximum leader that pervaded the 26th of July Movement. Thus, they felt it was important to state clearly the principles for which the Directorio stood. It was founded to promote political liberty (democracy), economic independence (nationalism), and social justice (socialism) (Valls 1991:126). In the midst of the tragedy that Batista's usurpation of constitutional power provoked, Valls felt it was necessary to lift those principles like a banner, especially because both the communist People's Socialist Party and the labor movement under Eusebio Mujal's leadership were collaborating with Batista. José Antonio Costa remembered labor's response to Batista's coup: "We stopped the sugar mill that was grinding the sugar in protest." The strike was quite large, and it went on for two or three days, joined by many other *sindicatos* in the mills and others throughout the island. Mujal guaranteed Batista that the labor unions would not continue to strike against him. In exchange for this discipline, he won more than a few privileges for labor (Mañach 1959:81).

Militarily, the Directorio was responsible for two major revolutionary accomplishments: the attack on the Presidential Palace on March 13, 1957, and the opening up of the second armed struggle front in the Escambray Mountains, in Las Villas province. Che Guevara afterward took over this second front, decisively influencing the last phase of the revolution. The Presidential Palace attack was a virtually suicidal, romantic action that was masterminded by Menelao Mora. The attackers intended to kill Batista while he worked in his study, effecting a coup d'etat that would result in a new provisional president of the republic. The result was to be announced on the radio by José Antonio Echeverría, leader of the Directorio and the FEU, whom many called Manzanita (literally, small apple). José Antonio went to Radio Reloj, the major radio station, to announce Batista's death to the people. A couple of minutes after he made his premature radio announcement and was on his way to the university, he was shot by a police car that sped by.

Armed with rifles and pistols, the students who participated in the Presidential Palace attack managed to reach as far as the second floor, but they did not find Batista there. Some were wounded but managed to leave the palace, only to be killed by the police waiting outside. Quite a number of students died in this way, Menelao Mora among them, and four more were killed in a surprise attack on their apartment at Humboldt # 7, a few weeks later (del Cueto 1959:56–59, 160–61).

The death of Manzanita left a vacuum in the leadership of the Directorio that was never filled. It meant the loss of a leader who was fiercely committed to constitutional principles and may have been able to channel the revolution in a democratic direction. After his death, and the failure of the attack on the palace, Valls stressed, the revolutionary student forces felt perplexed, lost. The death of Frank País on July 30, 1957, had a similar effect, for although the Frank País Museum in Santiago de Cuba today represents him as both a revolutionary and a communist, those who knew him well knew that he was a committed revolutionary but not a communist. Rather, his commitment was to the restoration of democracy to Cuba (Morán-Arce 1980).

With Fidel in *la Sierra*, the movement was now "totally in the hands of the 26th of July," said Valls. Most of the remaining Directorio students joined the armed struggle in the Escambray Mountains. Valls himself worked with the underground, helping the labor movement and the military conspiracy that was being planned by Rafael García-Bárcenas. He left for a short exile in Mexico in July 1958, a few months before the end of the struggle.

The Revolutionary Triumph

It was Franqui who first received and announced the news to all of Cuba that Batista had fled. When Batista departed Cuba on December 31, 1958, he left as he had arrived – "wrapped in the shadows of the night" (Portell-Vilá 1986:699). By the end, Batista's support base was minimal, consisting only of the politico-bureaucratic clientele he had developed and a small minority of capitalists and labor leaders beholden to him. His strength was "purely physical and rested on bayonets" (Mañach 1959:168). The victorious general strike of January 1, 1959, dealt the finishing blow to the regime. As Domínguez (1978a:133) summed it up, "Modernization without modernity, weak political institutions and an economic depression in a context of political illegitimacy" are the basic ingredients for a classic revolution, as they were in Cuba.

After seven years under dictatorship, which Cubans widely regarded as tyranny, Batista's departure provoked an enormous joy in Cuba. "An explosion of happiness shook the country," José Manuel Hernández recalled. Crowds "poured into the streets to celebrate the downfall of the tyrant, cheering, chanting, and singing into the night" (1999:115). I can remember the joy expressed in that New Year's Day celebration, in an outpouring of triumphant songs that could be heard everywhere. As Himilce Esteve, 40 years old when the revolution triumphed, remembered, "It was a moment

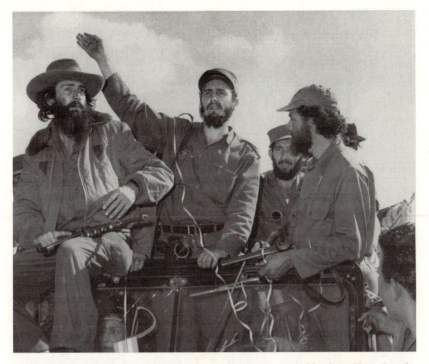

Figure 2.2   Initially, the Cuban revolution had various rebel leaders. Here Camilo Cienfuegos, Fidel Castro, and Huber Matos enter Havana victorious, on January 6, 1959, after a long caravan from Oriente province. (Huber Matos)

of hope." The vast majority of the Cuban people hoped for the return of democracy to Cuba.

For a week after Batista's departure, Fidel toured the island from one end to the other – in a caravan led by a jeep of the *comandantes* (the highest rank in the rebel army), arriving in Havana on January 6 (see Figure 2.2). Franqui remembered Fidel's entrance into Havana as really "an apotheosis" (1983:12–13). From the balcony of the Presidential Palace, Fidel asked the multitudes to open a path, and he crossed the sea of people like "a hero out of Greek mythology," with the crowd expressing an enormous collective, civic joy. Fermín Mejía, who was about to turn 15, witnessed that great enthusiasm as he saw Fidel pass by in front of his house in Vedado. As Franqui (1983) portrayed it, and I remember it, the crowds applauded and in delirium cheered "*Fidel, Fidel, Fidel, Fidel!*" Castro's speeches lasted six, seven,

even eight hours, and the crowds on the street hung onto every word; those who remained at home sat motionless for hours in front of the television.

Amid the joy over Batista's overthrow, Franqui felt sadness "because he could see the danger in what was occurring." He felt caught in a situation in which fighting against Batista made it impossible to break with Fidel. The power of Fidel as the revolutionary *caudillo* could be balanced only by the development of civic institutions, "but at the moment of the victory," Franqui argued, "Fidel emerged with such an enormous popularity that such an institutional balance was impossible." Even the 26th of July Movement, with which 90 percent of the people identified, disappeared soon after the revolution's victory. The problem, Franqui stressed, was *Fidelismo*: "The war had been over for months, yet we still never met. It was incredibly hard to see Fidel. You could call Celia Sánchez again and again. If you were lucky and Fidel felt like talking to you, you talked. If not, it was nothing. If you ran into him in public, he was always surrounded by people, and it was only he who did the talking. We had lots of problems and no place to discuss them. And Fidel, like God, was everywhere and nowhere" (1983:29).

What, then, was the revolution, to those who sacrificed everything for it? To Jorge Valls, the revolution had an economic dimension, a social dimension, but the best was its human dimension. "We learned to live," he said, "as one always lives when one is near death.... Your friend's house is your house; my friends are my mother's sons"; and "my best friend would have defended my sisters as if he were their father or me. The revolution meant that human beings found their original humanity – their capacity for will, intelligence, goodness, and beauty." To Carlos Franqui, "the revolution was a necessity, a dream, a myth. The problem was that afterward it became barbaric. But that is another story."

The Church for the Revolution

Because Cuba is a predominantly Catholic country, the role of the church in the revolution was key. Initially, many important figures in the church supported the revolution. On January 3, 1959, Archbishop Enrique Pérez-Serantes, who had been instrumental in saving Castro's life when he was imprisoned, sent a message to all regarding the "Vida Nueva," the new life that was to begin in Cuba (Poyo 2002). Full of admiration for Fidel Castro, he nonetheless made some recommendations for the revolutionary government to take into account.

Members of the Agrupación Católica Universitaria were at the forefront of the struggle against Batista and later of the opposition to Castro and the exile community. The goal of the ACU was "to breed a new and different type of Catholic" (Hernández 1999:6). From its founding in 1931, the members of the ACU were young men who were interested not only in searching for the relationship between their faith and the public good but also in participating in the political system and influencing the implementation of public policies consistent with the Catholic social doctrine of assisting those in need. The Agrupación held night classes at a church for workers and served in the poorest of neighborhoods, such as the slum of Las Yaguas in the outskirts of Havana, where nearly 5,000 men, women, and children lived in shacks.

Likewise, the Juventud Católica Cubana (Young Cuban Catholics) and the Juventud Obrera Católica (Young Catholic Workers), which became part of Catholic Action in the 1940s, were organizations through which Cuban youth worked in hospitals, asylums, prisons, and other sites for the poor. In December 1959 José Ignacio Rasco (1961) also founded the Movimiento Demócrata Cristiano. Led by Catholic intellectuals, such as José Ignacio Lasaga, Father Amando Llorente, and Father Manuel Foyaca, these organizations sought to address Cuba's problems through structural social reforms and not just charity. Many of them advocated the principles of social democracy and the notion of social rights expressed in Cuba's Constitution of 1940, which included agrarian reform, labor legislation, and employment rights. While influenced by European thinkers, Latin Americans and Cubans evolved their own form of Christian democracy and social democracy. Poyo noted that "part of the general process of the emergence of Christian Democracy in Latin America involved rupturing the long-standing unquestioned relationship between Catholicism and conservatism" (2002:18).

During Batista's dictatorship, the church hierarchy was divided regarding the revolution, but more and more Catholics chose to join the revolutionary movement despite its use of armed resistance because Batista left no other option. Parish priests often used their homilies and bulletins to condemn Batista's violence and sought to help the rebels when necessary. After Batista fled, Catholic intellectuals, such as Father Ignacio Biaín, editor of *La Quincena* (The Fortnight), the most influential Catholic magazine, voiced their strong support for the revolution, which they saw as both radical and Christian (Poyo 2002:48).

Still, it is important to acknowledge that in a predominantly Catholic country, the vast majority of Cuban Catholics did not necessarily heed the leadership of the church. Catholicism exerted a much greater weight on the culture than on its social behavior. The ACU conducted another survey in the early 1950s regarding religious attitudes among the Cuban people (1954). It showed that 72.5 percent of Cubans declared themselves to be Catholic, while 6 percent identified as Protestants and 0.5 percent as Jews. Those who did not identify with a particular religion were 19 percent. The remainder called themselves Santeros (0.5 percent), Espiritists (1.0 percent), or Masons (0.5 percent). When those identified as Catholic were asked how observant they were, however, only 24 percent said they regularly attended mass. Forty-two percent said that they occasionally attended; 31 percent, that years had passed without their attending; and 3 percent, that they had never been to Mass.

Humanism

In the second stage of the revolution, Fidel Castro defined it as humanistic in his visit to the United States in April 1959. "Humanism," he said in New York, "means that man's dearest desire, his liberty, need not be sacrificed in order to satisfy his material needs. Yet man's most essential freedom does not mean a thing without the satisfaction of his material needs. Neither bread without liberty, nor liberty without bread. No dictatorships of man, nor dictatorship of castes, or class oligarchy. Liberty without bread, without terror. That is humanism" (in Amaro 1981:237–38). Castro also assured his audience that elections would be held within the next four years.

Soon after Castro made these declarations, however, a political and social crisis began to unfold in Cuba. In the early moments of the revolution's victory, the media had pointed fingers at the police and the military for collaborating with Batista, focusing on what the *esbirros*, or criminals, had done as they humiliated, beat, tortured, maimed, and killed their opponents (e.g., Brunet 1959). With the Cuban people's anger incited by newspaper articles and documentaries shown in movie theaters, the *esbirros* began to be called before military tribunals. At the same time, the victorious revolutionary government began to implement social reforms, such as the rent control law, agrarian reform, and tax reform. These social reforms began to incorporate the groups that were socially marginal in Cuba, such as the peasants. Thousands of peasants came from the provinces all the way to Havana, to attend the massive demonstration on July 26, a moment in which they raised their *machetes* in unison ("Medio Millón de Campesinos Respaldan la Reforma Agraria" 1959).

In this period, many Cubans felt truly confused regarding the turn the revolution was taking. Quite possibly, the least confused were Jewish Cubans and Chinese Cubans – those whose families had already confronted communism before they immigrated to Cuba. Such was the case of José Bober, the son of a Russian immigrant who had opened up a *bodega*, a grocery, in Cotorro, on the outskirts of Havana. Later, he came to own an auto repair shop, and both father and son became distributors for B. F. Goodrich tires. A student leader at the Instituto de la Habana, Bober protested against Batista "for the shameless way in which he grabbed power."

The revolutionary government insisted that the revolution was not communist. In the first interview Fidel Castro gave after coming down from the Sierra Maestra, to Carlos Castañeda (1959) of *Bohemia* and to Jules Dubois of the *Chicago Tribune*, Fidel insisted that it was President Manuel Urrutia, not he, who was truly the head of state, and he promised to be a friend of the United States. Castañeda noted that from Castro's neck hung the medal of Cuba's patron saint – la Virgen de la Caridad del Cobre (Our Lady of Charity) – and that many of the rebels accompanying him had rosaries in their pockets. To him, as to most Cubans then, these outward signs of faith gave the lie to the allegation that the revolution was communist.

Throughout his visit to the United States in April 1959 and when he returned to Cuba in May, Fidel underscored that the revolution was not communist. While in the United States, Fidel repeatedly stated he was seeking only its friendship. In his appearance on the television program *Meet the Press* in Washington, D.C., he defined the revolution: "I am not a communist, nor do I agree with communism. . . . In Cuba, we have revolutionary power. . . . We could have repressed everyone, but we have instead allowed freedom of expression, religious freedom, and human rights. . . . To me, democracy and communism are not the same thing. Our ideals are called humanism" (Castro 1959a:2). His government was not a dictatorship because public opinion backed it. While calling himself the defender of elections, however, he also noted that "in many public events when elections were mentioned, thousands and thousands of persons told him they were not interested in elections at this time" (Castro 1959a:7).

In his analysis of the sources of legitimacy of the Cuban revolution, Domínguez maintained that it was clear that "two basic decisions were made before this trip: there would be no elections and no United States aid would be accepted." The purpose of the visit, rather, was to gain time free of U.S. interference in which far-reaching social transformations could be implemented (1978a:45). Domínguez noted that these "crucial decisions struck at the heart" of the two most important sources of legitimacy in Cuba throughout the 20th century: elections and closeness to the United States. As Castro stated, the source of governmental legitimacy in Cuba had changed, becoming popular support.

Upon his return to Cuba in May, Fidel appeared on television a number of times and publicly denied the accusations that the revolution was communist. In his television interview on *Before the Press* on May 21, a week after the Agrarian Reform Law was signed, he explained in great detail the need for the agrarian reform, as the pillar of revolutionary change, and discussed its implementation. In so doing, he gave the revolution its definition: "With its thesis of humanism and social justice," he said, this revolution "will solve Cuba's problems, because this revolution is not red, this revolution is olive green" (Castro 1959b:38). Later, in replying to an interviewer's request to define the revolution's democratic humanism more precisely, Castro stressed that the revolution was neither capitalist nor communist but sought to find its own way: "This revolution is 'olive green' because that is the color of our revolution that came out of the Sierra Maestra" (Castro 1959b:63).

Writing in the newspaper *Información* on August 6, José Ignacio Rasco noted that the popularity of the regime was indisputable: "The great mass of the people is jubilant, and full of hope toward the revolution." Yet he stressed that Cubans still needed to cure themselves, once and for all, of "the virus of dictatorship." The people and the revolution needed to be joined in a democratic, electoral wedding (Rasco 1962:26–31).

While most Cubans believed at this time that the revolution was not communist, some knew otherwise. Himilce Esteve, a professor at the Instituto de la Víbora, recognized the true course the revolution was taking long before other Cubans did. Himilce was unusually well educated for a woman of the time, having studied in the United States, where she earned a master's degree in history at the University of North Carolina. She returned to Cuba to work and, three years later, returned to earn a doctorate in Latin American history at Harvard. Her studies were interrupted when she fell in love with Miguel Angel Campos, a Cuban career diplomat, while on a trip to Paris with her aunt and uncle. They were married in 1956.

Her husband was the Cuban consul in Hong Kong when he received an offer in 1958 to be Cuba's ambassador in Taipei, an offer he refused, not wanting to represent Batista. When the revolution triumphed in 1959, Himilce returned to Cuba with their daughter, Carmen, to continue working at the Instituto. The daughter of a father who was the representative to Congress from Oriente province and a mother who founded the first Montessori school in Cuba, Himilce was quite a formidable woman of her generation. In the 1950s, she was immersed in Cuba's cultural life. She was friendly with bohemian artists, such as the painter Victor Manuel. "A cultural *renacimiento*, rebirth, took place then, in which women played an important role," she pointed out. The Lyceum – a cultural institution run by women and for women – took force, "becoming a place women could lean on."

In January 1960, a year after the revolutionary triumph, Himilce's husband went on to The Netherlands, to help open up Cuba's embassy there. Himilce joined him there six months later, with their two children. When they saw each other again, her husband immediately asked about the situation she had just left behind in Cuba. She replied that there was still "an ongoing struggle between the groups with a communist orientation and those who want the revolution that has been promised, 'green like the palm trees.'" But Miguel Angel replied that the democratic cause had already been compromised. In his work in the embassy, he had been asked to give visas to Eastern European experts. He soon realized their expertise lay not in agriculture or other needed fields but in intelligence services. A Czech expert had bluntly told him he was going to Cuba to organize and train others in intelligence and counterintelligence services.

Women were often imbued with revolutionary fervor, though not Rosario Rexach. She was 47 years old and president of the Lyceum when the revolution triumphed. The Lyceum offered Cuban women their first public library, classes in activities such as ballet and tennis, training in areas such as social work, vocational classes in the evening for the poor, and conferences and exhibits that drew national and international artists and intellectuals. It enabled many women to develop their leadership abilities and to channel their desire to be of service. The Lyceum women wanted to go beyond charity to reforming society (Guerrero 1991).

Rexach's class origins were extremely poor. She was the daughter of a lithographer who designed covers for cigar boxes. She grew up in Juanelo, a Havana neighborhood where there was not a single public school, so she attended a rural school in the outskirts of the city. In her youth, Rexach helped the anti-Machado struggle. That political experience turned her against the communists, because she knew them and did not trust them. Adamantly opposed to Batista, she nonetheless considered the guerrillas to be communists in hiding.

Though Rexach opposed the revolution, the other 30 women on the executive board of the Lyceum unanimously voted for the Lyceum to lend its public support to Fidel Castro. Among them was Elena Mederos, who fought for women to obtain suffrage in Cuba and was part of the Pro-visional Government. Only Rexach refused to support Fidel Castro in a public gesture; hence, she resigned from the presidency. She left Cuba in September 1960.

The Revolution Betrayed

This second stage of the revolution came to an end with Huber Matos's denunciation of it in October 1959. Matos was a *comandante* who had fought side by side with Fidel in the Sierra Maestra and had ridden with him, triumphant, in the *comandantes'* jeep during the revolutionaries' victory tour (see Figure 2.2) (Matos 2002). Matos had seen how the revolution was being handed over step by step to the communists, who had hardly participated in the actual struggle. He wrote a letter to Fidel on October 19, 1959, in which he denounced the communist turn the revolution had taken and asked Fidel to rethink what he was doing. At the same time, Matos resigned his high position in the Rebel Army and in Camagüey's provincial government (Matos 2002:325–52). For this, he was arrested.

It was events like Matos's denunciation that caused Rafael Peláez and many others who left Cuba during the first wave to change their political posture. Peláez realized, despite being outside of Cuba, that the first to rebel against Fidel were his own people – those like Matos who were the closest to him and, therefore, could best understand what was happening. His disaffection was also due to the impact the executions of the *Batistianos*, such as General Sosa Blanco, had on him (Domínguez 1985). *Bohemia* published a number of articles with photos of the moment in which *Batistianos'* brains were blown out by the firing squad at *el paredón* – the execution wall (e.g., Salazar 1959). The executions took place in an amphitheater, resembling a roman circus. "That was not what we had fought for," Peláez said.

Like Huber Matos, Rafael believed that the revolution was "betrayed" by Fidel Castro when he channeled it toward communism. The political groups that backed Fidel did so in the faith that "when the armed struggle ended we would return to a civil movement once again," and that elections and democracy would follow. To Peláez's mind, Fidel's first treason consisted of his "betrayal of all the political people of all the movements that gave him their backing, and thanks to whom both he and the revolution triumphed." His second treason consisted of his betraying all the ministers who became part of the first Provisional Government, who believed in the restoration of democracy to Cuba – people like Manolo Ray, Felipe Pazos, Justo Carillo, José Miró-Cardona, Manuel Urrutia, and Elena Mederos.

José Ignacio Rasco felt not only that the revolution was betrayed but also that Castro was a traitor. Although the revolution could visibly be seen to be taking a communist direction, Fidel Castro did not declare it to be such; thus, confusion reigned. To this day, the question is still asked: When did Fidel become a communist? Was Castro a communist from early on in his youth, who hid his affiliation until the revolution was consolidated, or did he become a communist only after the United States' punitive measures forced him to turn to the Soviets for aid? Rasco, who was Fidel's classmate in Belén, believes that Castro was a communist from a very young age. Fidel told him that he was a communist on one occasion while they were at the university. Fidel was a traitor, Rasco explained, because he utilized the good people in the Provisional Government to hide behind, to pretend that the revolution was not communist, before getting rid of all of them when they were no longer useful to him.

In June 1959 Rafael Peláez returned to Cuba to conspire against Fidel's government. To this end, he began working in the armed forces, in aircraft maintenance, which allowed him to travel throughout the island. Rafael was in the Camagüey air base when the government sent for Huber Matos, and Camilo Cienfuegos personally accompanied him by plane from Camagüey to Havana. A couple of weeks later, the Cessna plane in which the *comandante* Camilo Cienfuegos traveled became lost. Camilo was very much loved by the people. Even today, it is unclear whether Camilo's loss was due to a deliberate attempt against his life or an accident.

Following Huber Matos's arrest, Manolo Ray, Elena Mederos, and others in the Provisional Government resigned their cabinet posts. Mederos resigned with sorrow (Guerrero 1991). Ray emphasized that his doubts had been there from the start, when he and other members of the 26th of July Movement saw that Che Guevara preferred to give high-ranking government jobs to members of the Communist Party, even to those not qualified for the tasks. To those near the center of power, the communists' penetration of the government became more and more evident. Many of them still trusted Fidel to rectify those excesses, but Ray, though he admired

Fidel's capacity as a politician, could see his limits as an administrator. Ray believed that the agrarian reform was necessary, for example, but the form in which it was carried out was destructive. But more than anything else, he remembered, "the basic problem was that against civil liberties, the terror." Manolo Ray left for Puerto Rico, where he continued to work as a civil engineer whose designs were esteemed.

The Church Dissents

Leaders in the church also began to worry about the direction in which the revolution was headed. The *Agrupados* were deeply concerned with social justice and had firsthand knowledge of the deep rural poverty in Cuba. Thus, they initially were quite supportive of the Agrarian Reform of May 1959 and its profound changes to the *latifundio* system. José Ignacio Lasaga and others expressed concern, however, about the excessive amount of power given to the Instituto Nacional de Reforma Agraria (National Institute for Agrarian Reform) under *el Ché* Guevara. This power, Lasaga stressed, could help carry the reform through, but it could also undermine private property rights (Poyo 2002).

At first, most of the *Agrupados* sided with the revolution and wanted to contribute professional and technical expertise to implementing its social programs. As Hernández wrote, they "volunteered in a number of specific projects, in which they joined hands with the guerrillas to correct social ills and meet the expectations of the populace" (1999:121). Initially, their assistance was well received, but after a while they began to notice their services were disregarded or rejected. Such was Fermín Mejía's experience. Since his father died, his mother and sister had lived at the margin of politics and with fewer means than would otherwise have been the case. Thus, though middle class, Fermín went on scholarship to Belén, possibly the best private school for boys in Cuba. While a student, Fermín felt the attraction of the Campaña contra el Alfabetismo (Literacy Campaign), and in February 1959 he volunteered to *alfabetizar* the rebel soldiers in the military camp of Managua, south of Havana. Every night, he and other students from Belén, joined by friends from the ACU, would give classes, using the *Manual de la Alfabetización* (Literacy Manual) which said: "F for Fidel," "Fi – Fidel," "Fu – *Fusíl* (Rifle)." In April 1960 Fermín Mejía and the others were told the government did not want them to go to Managua again to *alfabetizar* because it did not want any more Catholic influence in the army. This was a great blow to Fermín, who felt he was giving, not

64

asking. This was the first manifestation of the change in the relationship between the church and state.

When the church became truly concerned about the course the revolution was taking, Acción Católica called a National Catholic Congress on November 28–29. On the evening of the 28th, a procession took place in the Plaza Cívica that was conducted in the traditional Hispanic manner. The Virgen de la Caridad del Cobre, Cuba's patron saint, was brought all the way from her sanctuary in Oriente and carried on the shoulders of the faithful. Castro and President Osvaldo Dorticós were also present. From all parts of the island the faithful arrived, about a million persons (Alfonso 1985:60–69). They shouted "Caridad! Caridad!" The phrase had two senses: the Congress defended the principle of charity as a Christian way of giving to those in need, rather than as a consequence of the Marxist-Leninist class struggle; it also defended their *virgencita* by that name – that is, their culture and popular religiosity (see Martín-Villaverde 1959; Pérez-Serantes 1959). Of all the speakers that day, none delivered the message of the Catholic Church better than José Ignacio Lasaga when he shouted "Social justice, yes; communism, no!" (Hernández 1999:129). Carlos Méndez, a young seminarian who walked in the incessant, heavy rain for the entire six hours the procession lasted, remembered: "Our candles were lit, and we carried them in the rain, but they were not extinguished." This was the last public religious procession the government allowed for 39 years.

Despite making its enormous presence felt at that Congress and clarifying its anticommunist pro–social reform position, the church, in Pablo Alfonso's (1985) judgment, failed to provide the experienced leadership to help people sail through the turbulent political waters. Soon the church and Acción Católica became divided between those who followed the pastoral line and those who advocated armed struggle against the revolution. By the end of the year, the latter began to join the underground opposition.

Accused of treason and sedition, Huber Matos was tried on December 11, 1959. As a result, he suffered 20 years' imprisonment in Cuba, before he left for Costa Rica (Matos 2002). In October 1980, commemorating the date when his troubles began, together with Himilce Esteve and others, he founded el CID – Cuba Independiente y Democrática (Cuba Independent and Democratic). With his imprisonment, the stage of humanism and the rule of the moderates came to an end.

3

The Revolution Deepens

¡Ay, que este paraíso terrestre haya de estar siempre envenenado por la vieja serpiente!

Oh, that this earthly paradise should always be poisoned by the old serpent!
Fredrika Bremer, *Cartas desde Cuba* (1995 [1851])

Nationalism

The third stage of the revolution was that of nationalism, which emphasized "Yankee" imperialism. During this stage, "Patria o Muerte" (Fatherland or Death) became the slogan that spread throughout the society. The receptionists used it as a greeting to answer the telephone. The old five-peso Cuban coin that had read "Patria y Libertad" (Fatherland and Liberty) since the achievement of independence from Spain was now minted to carry the new slogan. This stage began with the trial of Huber Matos in December 1959 and lasted until the government completed the nationalization of the big industries – Cuban and American both – that took place from July to October 1960.[1] To illustrate how the revolution deepened, I rely on interviews with Alfredo Blanco, Jorge Valls, Ramón Espino, Gastón Vázquez (pseudonym), Augusto Vidaurreta, Nicolás Morejón, Aimée Vazquez-Simpson, Eloísa García and Rita Fuentes (pseudonyms),

---

[1] There is an inconsistency regarding dates in Amaro's (1981) article. In one part of the text, he notes that the nationalism stage lasted until September 2, 1960, with the Declaration of Havana, while in another part of the text he defines the subsequent period of socialism as beginning on October 13, 1960. I think it is more accurate to say that the socialism period began on October 13, 1960, because on that date the process of nationalization of the American industries, such as B. F. Goodrich, was completed. Thus, I have adjusted the beginning and ending of the periods to reflect this.

Bonnie and Gary Anderson, José Bober, Juan Manual Salvat, Estela Rasco, Elly Chovel, Fermín Mejía (pseudonym), and Rafael Peláez and Juanita Peláez (pseudonyms).

Domínguez pointed out that, while nationalism had been an important ideology in the 1930s due to blatant U.S. interference in Cuban affairs, by the 1940s and 1950s it had paled in significance, largely as a consequence of the nationalization during these decades that brought the majority of the country's sugar mills under Cuban ownership (1978a:114–15, 119, table 3.2). Nationalism was a minor theme in the two major statements of the 26th of July Movement, while political corruption and legitimacy were major themes. Domínguez used the survey of 1,000 urban Cubans conducted by Lloyd Free (1960) in the spring of 1960 to show that as late as that point in the revolutionary process, when substantial conflict had already taken place between the United States and Cuba, the frequency of nationalist responses was extremely low. Thus, Domínguez (1978a:118–19) concluded that "nationalism was a useful theme in the Cuba of the 1930s and of the 1960s, but not in that of the two decades in between" (cf. Montaner 2002).

Alfredo Blanco assented. A *hacendado* who came from a family of independent *colonos*, he lived in a number of sugar mill settlements throughout the island, both as a child and as a young man. He went to Boston to study in the preparatory school Chauncy Hall and thereafter went on to the Massachusetts Institute of Technology, from which he graduated as an electrical engineer in 1941. He returned to Cuba to live and work, initially in the sugar mills called "Xavier" and "Central America." Eventually, the family bought "Ramona," where he became the general manager and worked for 15 years. He left Cuba for the United States in 1960, after they called him *latifundista* and came looking for him. The "Ramona" finished its harvest on May 5, he recalled, and he left Cuba on May 6. Knowing both Cuban and American culture well, he did not agree that in 1959 there was a strong anti-American nationalism in Cuba. Rather, he reflected on how Cubans and Americans resembled each other in their idea of progress and "in their character: enterprising, open, humorous, informal." While Cubans were friends with the Americans, they still harbored resentment against the Spanish, the wounds inflicted by the war of independence still fresh in his generation's memory.

In 1960 the Cuban revolution took its definitive course, the diplomatic and economic war between the United States and Cuba ensued, and the Soviet Union became Cuba's protector. Che Guevara established contact with the Soviet Union. In February 1960 Soviet deputy prime minister

Anastas Mikoyan arrived in Cuba to sign the first important Soviet-Cuban agreement. Throughout the relationship, the Soviet Union's impact would be deeply felt in three areas: defense, trade, and aid. From the spring to the fall of 1960, relations with the United States worsened. Under President Eisenhower, the United States cut Cuba's sugar quota in July. Cuba retaliated by nationalizing all large U.S.-owned enterprises, agrarian and industrial operations in August, banks in September. In October the United States replied by prohibiting exports to Cuba, and Cuba enlarged its wave of nationalizations by socializing all U.S.-owned wholesale and retail trade enterprises. The government then went further, and on October 13 Cuban-owned enterprises were also socialized, including all sugar mills, banks, large industries, and large wholesale and retail enterprises, while the Urban Reform Act socialized all commercially owned real estate (Domínguez 1978a:146–47). Domínguez emphasized that the socialization of the means of production was the result of decisions taken earlier, in 1959, and not just the result of the conflict at this time, although Castro did not declare the socialist character of the revolution publicly until April 1961.

The diplomatic and economic war that ensued did inflame nationalist sentiments among Cubans. Clara Estrella Gómez-Lubián, my cousin who became integrated to the revolution, was in her late 40s then. When I first saw her again in 1979, she recalled the change in her sentiments: "Up until then we had seen the Soviet Union as 'the Iron Curtain.' But then we saw the United States was trying to choke us – and the Soviet Union lent us a hand." During this third stage of the revolution, Cuba's economic and political dependence on the United States shifted to the Soviet Union, where it rested for nearly 30 years, until the Soviet Union itself fell apart in 1989. Nationalism, the fight against U.S. imperialism, and the nation under siege became major themes in the Cuban revolution (Castro 1960). These themes were cemented by the Bay of Pigs invasion and the U.S. trade embargo. Fidel Castro regularly fanned the flames of these themes, as he has continued to do for nearly half a century. Today, they are a major – perhaps the only – source of legitimacy.

Civil Society Collapses

In 1960, the revolution effected its definitive turn. After Matos's trial, the First Provisional Government was immediately reorganized. In the beginning of the year, the government took over the newspapers and magazines, and the independent press collapsed. Labor unions retained their names, but their leaders were replaced with communists (see Montaner 2001). At the same time, the Catholic Church lost its ability to lead the society and was silenced. After the collapse of the press, the priests had only one means of communicating with the people – through pastoral letters, which increased in frequency, as the bishops laid aside a neutral stance and began to criticize the government openly. But these warnings were not widely heeded: Cubans allowed civil society to collapse because of the enormous popularity of the revolution and its leaders at this time. Fidel Castro ably articulated a vision in which a large part of the Cuban people, especially those at the margins of society, placed their hope.

On May 1, 1960, in a massive May Day demonstration celebrating the International Workers' Day, Fidel Castro (1960) gave a major speech in the Plaza of the Revolution in Havana, in which he attacked the democracy of the past, concluding that elections were unnecessary because the people had already chosen: "*This* is democracy. The Cuban revolution is democracy.... This democracy has been expressed directly in the close union and identification of the government and the people, in this direct relationship, in this working and fighting in favor of the majority of the country and in the interests of the great majority of the country.... Our enemies, our detractors, ask about elections.... The presence of such a large crowd is the best proof that the revolution has fought for the people."

To Jorge Valls, the legal order – the notion of political rights as the normative underpinning of society – collapsed with this speech. That crisis had begun with Batista's coup in 1952; it reached its climax with Castro in 1960.

Class Inequality

Ramón Espino's landed wealth exemplified the wealth that existed in the countryside in a society that was predominantly agrarian, yet also extremely close to the United States. As many young men of the upper and professional classes, Espino was educated in the United States, at Georgia Military Academy. After he returned to Cuba, he married Conchita (Concepción) Navarrete, whose father was very wealthy. Espino managed his father-in-law's businesses, including the *finca* called Baitiquirí, which consisted of both the salt mines that supplied all of Cuba's salt and 32,000 head of cattle of all types. Thousands of cattle were milked daily to provide all the milk for Guantanamo and Baracoa, the towns in the middle of which the farm lay, as well as for the naval base of Guantanamo. "The Navarrete family received that land from the king of Spain, during colonial times. It was a consider-able amount of land – 1,042 *caballerías*, and the *caballería* is 33 acres," noted Espino. The original title, he recalled, read "from here to where one can hear a 20-pound cannon."

Yet, for all their wealth, his wife's family was typical of the upper classes of Oriente in supporting the revolution. While Espino was never a *Fidelista*, he sympathized with them due to the way Batista's police arbitrarily misused power. "In Oriente, you could not go out on the street," he said, "because the *Batistianos* might kill you without reason." Fidel himself visited Baitiquirí just a few weeks after the revolution triumphed. He ate there and slept overnight – "He fell in love with it, without a doubt." A few days later, he gave a speech at the university for several hours, in which he announced that Baitiquirí should belong to the state. A couple of weeks later, the property was confiscated by the government.

The Agrarian Reform Law that went into effect in May 1959 allowed a maximum of 150 *caballerías* to remain in private hands. Baitiquirí was reduced to 150 from its 1,042 *caballerías*. Espino recalled the envy class disparities had given rise to. The poor peasant who worked in the *fincas* was very badly treated, he recalled. The middle class envied the rich; the poor envied the middle class. What made the government takeover of private property possible was the envy that existed. Espino left Cuba in 1960, with the help of the American consul. After working in Costa Rica for a few years, in a sugar mill with another Cuban partner, he returned to the United States, where he became executive vice-president of a shipping company. Apolitical, he greatly helped the Catholic Church provide assistance to people in Central America after the earthquakes. The church rewarded him by making him a Knight of Malta.

Also wealthy, Gastón Vázquez was content to live "the life of a 'play-boy,'" as he put it, prior to the revolution. He was the son of a Spanish merchant, a typical "Gallego" from Galicia. Gastón particularly enjoyed the yacht and country clubs his family belonged to. His father imported and exported goods between Cuba and Spain and owned a number of busi-nesses. Their shoe store in Centro Habana carried fine men's designer shoes made in Cuba. Excellent in quality, the shoes were sought after by Maurice Chevalier, the French star, whenever he visited Cuba.

Initially, Gastón sympathized with the revolution and bought 26th of July bonds to support it, because of "the malaise" that existed then in the nation under Batista. But immediately after its triumph, he "saw the looting, the envy, the common people set loose." A crowd of people broke the window of his father's shoe store and stole all the shoes. Other stores on that street were also vandalized – the social revenge of the masses. His father told him, "This is a disaster, this is chaos, this is anarchy." "In truth" he stressed, his own change in political attitudes had to do with "their taking everything that was mine." After the nationalizations were completed and the Rent Law went into effect, his parents were left with nothing but the apartment where they lived.

Together with other friends, relatives, and in-laws, Gastón began to conspire against the government. They sought help from the outside, from the Americans, without whose help, they believed, nothing could be accomplished. From 1961 to 1967, Gastón worked for the Central Intelligence Agency (CIA), which he and his friends referred to as *los amigos*, the friends. He left Cuba in February 1961, just when leaders of the opposition with whom he worked were caught and executed. Afterward, *los amigos* trained him in intelligence work, turning him "into a James Bond." In the next few years, he entered Cuba seven times to gather vital information and to promote unity among several factions of the opposition inside the island.

Augusto Vidaurreta was a lawyer for the municipality of Santa Clara, and his father was a respected Provincial Court judge and then Supreme Court judge. His respect for the courts, the parliamentary process, and civil rights was deeply ingrained. He also participated in the civic life through institutions like the Lions International Club, whose district governor he became. In 1957 he became a leader of the Conjunto de Instituciones Cívicas Cubanas (Association of Cuban Civic Institutions), an institution that asked Batista to resign because he imposed a dictatorship. Hence, they constituted the civic front of the struggle. As a lawyer, he aided revolutionaries in the courts, which earned him and others in the Conjunto death threats. Santa Clara was the only city taken by military force, by the forces led by Che Guevara, from the Segundo Frente del Escambray, and Rolando Cubelas, from the students' Directorio. Santa Clara gave the revolution its decisive victory, for there Batista's army was overtaken.

Although he was proud to help bring the dictatorship to an end, his disaffection with the revolution was immediate. When Fidel marched toward Havana, after the January 1 victory, he stopped in Santa Clara and spoke at the Marta Abreu park. Right then, Augusto perceived him as a demagogue: "In that moment, it seemed to me he wanted to manipulate the envy and class hatred, and from that moment I decided I did not want to be on their side." He tried to resign from his position, but his resignation was not accepted, so he remained a lawyer for the city. Having decided that leaving the country lacked dignity, he began to conspire against the communist revolution. He continued such activities until he was imprisoned in 1964. He helped the *alzados*, the insurgents in the Escambray Mountains, by raising funds. "It was shameful," he said. "The potentates would give so little. Sometimes I think they deserved what happened to them because they were unable to lend support to those poor souls."

Not only the upper classes and the professional class turned against the revolution early on, however. Nicolás Morejón came from *el pueblo*, the common people, as he put it. A *guajiro* from the countryside, he lived in the swampy area of the Ciénaga de Zapata and barely knew how to read and write. He mostly worked cutting down lumber, making charcoal for the train line. But he was proud of the progress he made, working day and night, as he owned a pig, a couple of cattle, three trucks, and a jeep. When Fidel was in the mountains, he sympathized with him, but by the end of the first year he had turned against him. The *milicianos* took one of his trucks for themselves, as well as the pig and the cattle. But more than the actual loss, his disaffection resulted from seeing how the *milicianos* treated *el pueblo* – without respect. They stopped people on the road to search them and "abused their power," he recalled. "The army should treat *el pueblo* with courtesy, not berate them and humiliate them." Moreover, they began to lie, he emphasized. He saw them making a documentary that focused on the poverty and the hunger Cubans faced in the Ciénaga, but it was made up for the film. The film makers told the people to go and put on clothes that were dirty and tattered. Soon he was *conspirando*, helping the rebels in the Escambray Mountains, transporting arms for the *alzados*, giving them coffee. Like him, most of them were working class in origin. He joined the Movimiento Revolucionario del Pueblo in Jagüey Grande and did all he could to help them. Many wound up in prison; others were executed. He was imprisoned in February 1963. A friend saved his life by warning him they planned to kill him in an ambush. He lost a brother and a leg in the struggle. In prison for 17 years, he was released as a result of the Dialogue in 1978 between the exiles and the Cuban government.

Racial Discrimination

By and large, black Cubans were enthusiastic about the revolution. Their support can be gleaned from the differential migration of the races during the first two waves of the exodus. In the 1950s the racial composition of Cuba given by the 1953 census reflected the different social definition of the races in the Caribbean than in the United States (see Wagley 1968). While in the South of the United States the dual racial classification used – black versus white – was based on ancestry ("one drop of black blood"), throughout the Caribbean the definition of race was based on phenotype buttressed by social status – "money bleaches," the Brazilian proverb says. Moreover, three major racial categories were recognized – black, white, and an intermediate category for those who were mixed, variously referred to as *mulatos* (Cuba and Puerto Rico), *pardos* (Brazil), *Indios* (Dominican Republic). Using this tripartite definition, the 1953 Cuban census put the proportion black at 12.4 percent, the proportion mixed race (*mulattos* or *mestizos*) at 14.5 percent, and the proportion Asian (no doubt Chinese Cubans) at 0.3 percent – 27.2 percent nonwhite. The proportion that identified as white was 72.8 percent (Cuba, Oficina Nacional del Censo 1984: table 39).

Data from the 1990 U.S. census show that about 91 percent of the immigrants who came over during the first wave were white, as were around 83 percent of those who came over during the second wave (Pedraza 1996a: table 2). Two different social processes, Benigno Aguirre (1976) concluded, were at work. At the outset, the revolution pulled out the power from under the upper classes that had deliberately excluded blacks from their midst. The immigration proceeded through the chain of extended family and friends, further selecting whites. In addition, the migration policy of the United States and Cuba contributed to blacks being excluded, as they gave priority to close relatives of Cubans already in the United States.

Moreover, blacks in Cuba did benefit from the revolution. Cuba never had a "Jim Crow" "separate but equal" legal system of segregation. Nor were there two entirely separate cultures, as Cuban culture was a creolization of white Spanish and black African cultural traditions – a cultural *mestizaje* in which both black and white Cubans participated. This can best be seen in the music Cubans identify with – and love. Yet prerevolutionary Cuba excluded blacks from the pinnacles of society: yacht and country clubs, the best vacation resorts and beaches, hotels, the social clubs, the private schools reserved for the elite. As Aimée Vázquez-Simpson, a professional black Cuban who came over in the second wave, expressed it, "discrimination in Cuba was in *lo social*, the social." Even Batista, who was seen as *mestizo*, had been denied admission to the Havana Country Club when he was president. In her stay in Cuba in the middle of the 19th century, Fredrika Bremer (1995 [1851]) perceived the race problem was the serpent that poisoned Cuba's remarkable beauty.

One of the first acts of the revolution was to make these exclusive facilities public, available to all, regardless of color or wealth. In addition, the Cuban government promoted new opportunities for blacks in employment and education. Richard Fagen et al. (1968:120) noted that the race problem in Cuba was "a boon to Castro." The revolutionaries found it extremely useful for discrediting the old social order. With the "instant liberation" of blacks "tens of thousands of disadvantaged Cubans were recruited into the ranks of revolutionary enthusiasts."

Still, some black Cubans left Cuba at this time. Among them was Celia Cruz, Cuba's *guarachera* who left in 1960 to sing with the orchestra La Sonora Matancera in Mexico and never returned. As she took her music everywhere, with her humor and rhythm, Celia became a symbol of *Cubanidad*, of Cuban identity. She was also involved in the development of *salsa* – the blend of Cuban and Caribbean rhythms with strains of American jazz. When she died in New York, 43 years later, in July 2003, the Cuban community said its last good-bye to "the Queen of Salsa" with a splendid funeral in which thousands participated.

Other black Cubans, however, like Nicolas Guillén, one of Cuba's foremost poets, threw their support decisively behind the revolution at this time. Guillén, the son of the senator for Camagüey, had been a member of the old Communist Party since the 1930s. He spoke of his mixed ancestry in the poem "Balada de los Dos Abuelos" (Ballad of Two Grandfathers) (Guillén 1986). In 1961 he became the head of the newly organized Unión de Escritores y Artistas de Cuba. In one of his poems, "Cualquier Tiempo Pasado Fue Peor" (Any Time in the Past Was Worse), he remembered the cabaret closed to people of color, the major hotel accessible only to the wealthy, the many institutions, such as banks, that employed only whites, except for the janitors (Guillén 2002).

Eloísa García was part of the mulatto middle class. Her mother, Ana, was a seamstress; her father owned a barbershop. Eloísa was educated well in the school for girls of lesser means that was situated right next to the major private school El Sagrado Corazón (The Sacred Heart) for girls. Her tuition was paid for by her godmother, the rich society lady for whom her grandfather worked as a chauffeur. She left Cuba in 1960, at the age of 12, with her widowed mother who was a nanny to the children of a white family. Even before the revolution, her mother longed to go to New York, thinking she could become a seamstress to some black American artist and join the black Cuban and Puerto Rican enclave that existed in New York in the 1950s, where Santería flourished. Santería, the syncretic blend of

West African and Spanish Catholic beliefs and rituals that developed in Cuba, was important to Eloísa's family. Her great-great-grandmother was the daughter of slaves and a Santera, a priestess. From her down to Eloísa descended the line of possible Santeras – women who could be initiated. Her mother became a famous Santera in New Orleans and part of the African American Yoruba Movement.

Although Eloísa's mother left Cuba, her aunt Rita (her mother's sister) was enthusiastically integrated to the revolution. Rita Fuentes was a teacher in her 20s during the years of the revolutionary struggle. She was an active member of the 26th of July Movement in Oriente, where she worked with the most dangerous underground unit that set the sugarcane fields on fire, placed bombs, and the like. When the revolution triumphed, she went back up into the Sierra Maestra as one of the *maestros de la Sierra* to teach the illiterate peasants. She remembered the changes the revolution made that benefited blacks: "Suddenly there was more freedom; we could move freely; there was less prejudice." But when others highlighted what the revolution did for blacks, she invariably insisted that it was blacks who gave much to the revolution. Once, while cutting sugarcane in the fields with a *machete*, she lost two fingers. Hence, she often stressed that she gave everything for the revolution, including a hand. For many years she worked for the Ministry of Tourism, helping foreign delegations to the island. Rita left Cuba in 1988, having only partially lost her affection for the revolution. Above all, she left so that her niece would not be alone. Never a Santera, Eloísa went on to become a nurse – another form of healing. Many of Eloísa's family never left the island. When Eloísa returned many years later, they let her know their feelings. "The revolution did remove the obstacles that prevented blacks' progress in the island," they said, but they not only received but gave – "We *are* Cuba," Eloísa's family emphasized, which it conveyed through the tradition of the *orishas* (deities) and Santería.

To many leading black intellectuals in Cuba at this time, the road Cuba was taking toward communism was not objectionable. As early as the 1930s, influenced by the old Communist Party, they understood the Marxist-Leninist argument that society was fundamentally divided into social classes to mean that, with the disappearance of capitalism and its class divisions, racial inequality and discrimination would thereby disappear (see Fernández-Robaina 1994). Still others believed that racial discrimination could be fought best through the self-help efforts black Cubans made, an argument that Guillén repeatedly claimed could result only in their ghettoization – "the road to Harlem" (1929).

Gender Inequality

Though women held levels of education comparable to those of men in Cuba, their labor force participation was quite meager, especially in comparison to women in other fairly well-developed countries of Latin America. In 1956 only 12.6 percent of Cuban women were in the labor force, in contrast to 16.3 percent of Costa Rican women in 1963 and 22.0 percent of Chilean women in 1960 (Mesa-Lago 2000: table V.17). In addition, women were overrepresented in low-income, low-status jobs and underrepresented in high-status occupations.

Even more, *machismo*, with is stress on male dominance, characterized the social relations between men and women, as throughout the Mediterranean world. A sexual double standard reigned that allowed and encouraged men to pursue numerous sexual adventures, while women were expected to remain virginal, always pure, their honor safeguarded by their fathers and brothers (see Péristiany 1966). As Lourdes Casal (1987) pointed out, *machismo*'s cluster of values entailed a strong rejection of male homosexuality and anything effeminate, and virtually denied women's homosexuality. *Macho* men also "wanted to keep 'their' women in the house, away from '*la calle*' (the street), where they could meet other men" (Casal 1987:42). Virginia Domínguez and Yolanda Prieto noted the change: the Cuban revolution "challenged the traditional place of women in Cuban society by bringing them out of their homes to take jobs" (1987:4).

In my view, women's participation in the revolutionary process itself first challenged the traditional role of women. Analyzing the role women played in the political process in El Salvador, Chile, and Cuba, Julie Shayne (2004:115) stressed that while in the 1950s in the United States women donned skirts, tended to homes, and served as wives, in Cuba "the skirts were sometimes used to transport weapons, the houses to hide guerrillas, and the matrimonial status to camouflage male militants." Women became what she called "gendered revolutionary bridges" that aided the revolutionary struggle and lent it moral authority (see García-Pérez 1998). Actively participating in the revolution raised women's self-esteem and challenged traditional notions of women's subservience. Many women became quite attached to the revolutionary ideal, as a result. Lloyd Free's survey of the urban population of Cuba in the spring of 1960 gave evidence of women's support for the revolution. Although there was no difference in overall support for the revolution between men and women (about 86 percent of the urban population of Cuba), women were more likely than men to be fervent supporters (46 percent of the women, as opposed to 41 percent of the men) (1960:7). Free also noted that many of the women's comments in the interviews "bordered on the fanatic in their expressions of fervor" for Fidel and the revolution (1960:6).

As Smith and Padula argued, "the significance of women's participation in the Cuban insurrection was not lost on its male leaders" (1996:32). In 1960 Castro created the Federation of Cuban Women, though most of the women who participated in the revolutionary struggle "disappeared from public view after 1959." A few went on to play important roles, however. Vilma Espín married Fidel's brother, Raúl, and was appointed director of the Federation of Women, a position she held for 35 years. Celia Sánchez remained Castro's right arm and intimate friend, until her death from lung cancer in 1980. Haydée Santamaría married Armando Hart, who became minister of education and culture. She founded Casa de las Américas, a major literary and public relations organization. She committed suicide in the summer of 1980, when the Mariel exodus was in full force.

An Anti-American, Pro-Soviet Revolution

As Irving Louis Horowitz pointed out, from the war of independence on, U.S.-Cuba relations were marked by a profound ambiguity: "Into such a situation Fidel Castro came to power – not as living vindication of Marxism-Leninism, but as part of an effort to move Cuba beyond ambiguity and to nationalist closure, and, in consequence, beyond the suffocating sphere of American influence" (2002:60).

The political battle waged with the United States entailed numerous agreements with the Soviet Union and other communist countries, intensifying an anti-American climate. The climax of this period came in 1960, when the Russian ships bearing oil arrived at Cuban ports. Years later, the Mexican writer Carlos Fuentes described the moment, as he was in Havana that day and saw the first Soviet tanker sail into the harbor: "I said to myself then that the history of our continent, for better or for worse, had changed forever" (1981:32). The Cuban government asked the oil refineries to accept the gasoline; the refineries refused, so the government confiscated them. In the diplomatic war that ensued between Cuba and the United States, the United States cut the sugar quota. The diplomatic and economic war reached its apex on October 13 when President Eisenhower announced the end of all exports to Cuba, with the exception of medicines and some food products. Cuba's reaction was swift, as it ratified the Nationalization Law, through which all American industries were nationalized.

"Cuba Sí! Yanquis No!" was the slogan often heard that expressed Cubans' anti-Americanism, sentiment that Castro fanned the flames of in his speeches. That anti-Americanism may have been responsible for the death of Howard Anderson. "Andy," as they called him, was an American who lived in Cuba with his wife and four children. The Andersons were friends of my family, first in Cuba, and later in exile in Colombia. In Cuba, Howard Anderson owned several gas stations and sold automobiles. All of his family enjoyed a life that included boating, sailing, and the beauty of Cuba's ocean and beaches. He sent his family to the United States in March 1961, at the insistence of the U.S. Embassy. He returned to Cuba to take care of his business, started by his father-in-law. His daughter, Bonnie, five years old at the time, grew up to become a journalist who described the events: "Communist officials were to say later that my father returned because he was a chief contact between the CIA and the Cuban counterrevolutionary forces. The charges also connected my father to an arms-smuggling operation that had been discovered on another side of the island" (1979:3). Her father denied all the charges. He was executed during the Bay of Pigs invasion, which he had nothing to do with, in Pinar del Río, along with eight other men.

The First Wave: Those Who Wait

Cuban society became completely polarized – between those who were in favor and those who were against the revolution, who were called *contra-revolucionarios* (counterrevolutionaries) and *gusanos* (worms). Those who did not side with the government were eliminated from universities, professional associations, labor unions, and the government. Activists were condemned to prison; many were executed. The exodus became massive.

In the first wave, those who left were Cuba's elite. These upper and upper middle classes were not tied to Batista's government but were bound to a political and economic structure that, as Amaro and Portes underlined, was completely interpenetrated by the demands and initiative of American capital: "These executives and owners of firms, big merchants, sugar mill owners, manufacturers, cattlemen, representatives of foreign companies and established professionals, were those most acquainted with the United

States' political and economic guardianship of Cuba, under which they had created or maintained their position, and were the least given to believe that the American government would permit the consolidation of a socialist regime in the island" (1972:10).

Hence, amid the economic and political war that ensued between Cuba and the United States, they decided to leave. These refugees came to the United States driven by Cuba's overturning of the old order through revolutionary measures, such as the nationalization of American industry and the Agrarian Reform Law, as well as by the United States' severance of diplomatic and economic ties with Cuba, all of which entailed serious personal losses. José Bober was working as a salesman with B. F. Goodrich when it was nationalized in October. In the large plant in Havana, he tried to organize a strike in protest but, given the enormous backing of the Cuban people for the government at that time, was unable to do so: "With a regime that has the entire people with them, what could one do?" Together with his family, he left Cuba a few months later.

"Those who wait" characterized those first refugees who came imagining that exile would be temporary, waiting for the inevitable American reaction and aid to overcome Cuba's new government. In this first stage, the exile's political activity was intensely militant, supporting military counterrevolution against Cuba. The exiles' invasion of the Bay of Pigs in April 1961 was the largest and most tragic action they undertook.

The Opposition Develops

While to many observers the incorporation of the socially marginal groups taking place was social justice, to others the manner in which it was carried out – by confiscating the private homes of the middle classes who left and giving them to the poor or using them to house the students who came from the countryside – was a miscarriage of justice. Jorge Valls remembered that for many years we "lived in profound agony. The first few years after 1959 were marked by the acme of the public plaza, the concentrations, the declarations, the screams, the collective hysteria." As Richard Fagen (1969) pointed out, a transformation in Cuba's political culture indeed took place. It was Hannah Arendt's (1979 [1948]) insight that communism and fascism, as systems, had a great deal in common, despite their left and right orientations, as both were forms of totalitarianism rooted in mass phenomena. They both created a new political culture in which public ceremonies were mass events held in plazas, attempting to create a new self in their citizens – a self where the private individual fused with the public citizen (see Berezin 1997).

To those who were not socially marginal, however, the revolution was not tearing down the barriers in their way but was tearing down the civic fabric of society Cubans had painstakingly achieved with the enactment of the Constitution of 1940 and elections. Such was the case for many of the middle- and upper-middle-class students in the university. Juan Manuel Salvat – today the owner of Ediciones Universal, a Miami publishing company that preserves Cuban history and culture – was 18 years old when the revolution triumphed. After graduating from the Instituto de Sagua la Grande, he went to Havana to attend the Universidad La Salle, where he was elected vice-secretary of the Social Science Association of the FEU. Salvat also became a member of the Directorio Estudiantil that took shape after the death of José Antonio Echeverría and, in his honor, was renamed Directorio Revolucionario 13 de Marzo. As before, it expressed a Christian social-democratic ideological current.

Salvat emphasized the struggle taking place in the university was between students who had democratic ideas and students who were communists. The final rupture between the two came when Anastas Mikoyan, first deputy chairman of the Soviet Union's Council of Ministers, came to Cuba to restore formal Cuban-Soviet relations and to provide economic assistance. Salvat participated in the protest against Cuba becoming part of the Soviet sphere of influence. On February 5, 1960, Mikoyan took a wreath of flowers and placed it before the statue of José Martí, Cuba's revered patriot, in the city's Central Park. The wreath represented the hammer and sickle lying on the Western Hemisphere. As soon as Mikoyan left, Salvat, along with other students, among them Alberto Müller and Juan Clark, staged a peaceful protest. The students destroyed Mikoyan's wreath, stepping on it, and laid down a wreath in the form of the Cuban flag, along with banners that read: "Long live the revolution! Down with communism!" The police crushed the protest by beating them with cudgels and iron rods and then jailed many of them, among them Salvat. The students were also expelled from their elected offices in the student government.

From this incident, Salvat and others learned that a peaceful opposition was not possible. Shortly thereafter, the students were expelled from the university; hence, they joined the underground movement. They formed the student wing of the MRR. Through an embassy, Salvat left for Miami, where he hoped to contact the U.S. government and to gather arms for the underground struggle in Cuba.

Operation Pedro Pan

In the early 1960s the massive exodus of more than 14,000 unaccompanied children took place that became known as Operation Pedro Pan. Victor Andrés Triay (1998), María de los Angeles Torres (2003), and Ivonne Conde (1999) detailed the history of the development of the program that brought them to the United States. At the age of six, Torres (Nenita, to her friends) was one of the children who arrived then, with her name pinned to her dress, together with the address of family friends in Miami. "It broke one's heart," Estela Rasco remembered, "when you saw them arriving at the airport, so small, alone, with signs that said their name. Sometimes, the sign said they did not speak English."

The program began in December 1960 and lasted until mid-1966. Some of the children were the children of the underground opposition, the *contrarrevolución*, who needed to leave Cuba safely – a CIA strategy. However, because issuing visas to these children served to identify their parents, the U.S. government granted Father Bryan Walsh permission to waive visas for children under age 16. About 200 children came, unaccompanied, to the United States then.

The second period began with the failure of the Bay of Pigs invasion in April 1961 and lasted until the October Missile Crisis in 1962 put an end to the flights between Cuba and the United States. Frightened parents wanted to take their children out of Cuba. A rumor had spread throughout Havana that the government had plans to pass a law that would abolish the parents' *patria potestad*, their parental rights. In Cuba, the government nationalized the private schools, closed the public schools temporarily, and began sending adolescents to the countryside to participate in the literacy campaign. Elly Chovel, herself a Pedro Pan and today the director of the Operation Pedro Pan Group in Miami, remembered her parents' fear that the children would be sent to the countryside to *alfabetizar*. Thousands of children came then. The third period began at this time and lasted until the beginning of the second major wave of the Cuban exodus in 1965 that both the U.S. and Cuban governments administered, providing for the orderly departure of family members.

The program was the result of the humanitarian efforts of two men, James Baker, who called himself "an American Cuban," and Father Bryan Walsh, an Irish immigrant priest working in Miami. Baker was headmaster of the Ruston Academy in Havana, where many of the children of the American colony studied, and Walsh was director of the Catholic Welfare Bureau and had earlier worked resettling Hungarian refugee children. Together, they joined forces to begin the program in December 1960, at the same time that the Cuban Refugee Emergency Center opened its doors. It was the press that dubbed their project to fly the children out of Cuba Operation Pedro Pan. For children without families in the United States, the program provided foster care funded by the U.S. government. Ideological considerations defined the children's exodus on both sides. Cuba saw it as a form of psychological warfare to undermine the revolution (Torreira and Buajasán 2000). The United States saw it as an effort to save the children from communist indoctrination.

After the United States broke relations with Cuba on January 3, 1961, and Jim Baker left Cuba, the effort continued through the assistance of Great Britain, whose embassy in Cuba arranged for the children to arrive in Miami through Jamaica. Visa waivers facilitated the exit. For many Pedro Pans, the experience at the airport itself was traumatic. Pury López-Santiago was a very young child, petite, who carried a little Chinese doll that she had just gotten at Christmas. She had been told by her parents to do whatever she was told. When they called her name, she gave the *miliciano* the pouch with her documents. After looking at her papers, he asked her for the doll. "So I gave him the doll," she said, "and I remember he just looked at it. And it was very methodical. He yanked off the arms, then yanked off the legs, and then gave me the doll back. I went back to my seat." After that, she did not remember much (see Cardona and de Varona 1999).

Most of these children did not have relatives in the United States who could claim them. They were met at the airport by "George" (George Guarch) – "Mister Rescue to the lone, often scared youngsters," as Triay put it (1998:59) (see Figure 3.1). As more and more children arrived, larger camps and receiving centers opened up – Kendall's Children's Home; Camp Matecumbe – then the boys were moved to Opalocka Air Base in Florida City. The staff was reluctant to force assimilation and, instead, made efforts to keep the atmosphere Cuban. Thus, Cuban holidays were celebrated, talent shows included tributes to Cuban culture, and for a time a statue of la Virgen de la Caridad brought from Cuba made the rounds of the camps (Triay 1998:57). Still, many of the children experienced fright and loneliness. They were eventually placed in foster homes or orphanages.

As the first in their families to arrive in the United States, thereafter the children could apply for a visa waiver for their parents. Children thus became the first link in the family chain migration networks through which all migrations take place. Many were reunited with their families only after

Figure 3.1 Operation Pedro Pan brought more than 14,000 unaccompanied children from Cuba to the United States in the early 1960s. Here George Guarch, working with Catholic Relief Services, met some very young children at the airport. To the frightened children, he was "Mister Rescue." (Operation Pedro Pan Group)

long separations. Some never saw many of their relatives again. At the time of the reunion, Pury López-Santiago no longer was the child her parents left behind: "The child they left was a child they themselves protected, a child that needed them, that they hovered over and kept from harm. The child they found was a child that had already learned to protect itself" (Cardona and de Varona 1999).

After the Bay of Pigs failure, the CIA reportedly lost interest in the children's exodus and disengaged itself. The visa waiver program continued with the assistance of Pancho and Berta Finlay, as well as Pola ("Polita") and Ramón ("Mongo") Grau, who were siblings. Thanks to them, about 4,000 children left Cuba. Polita was one of the island's leaders of Rescate Revolucionario, an anti-Castro organization led by Miami-based Antonio de Varona, with the support of the CIA, that engaged in antirevolutionary activities in Cuba. It spread the visa waivers throughout the island, giving first priority to adolescents who had been active in the opposition. The *patria potestad* rumor returned – this time a deliberate misinformation spread by Rescate, so as to instill fear in Cuba (Torres 2003:136–37).

At the time of Monsignor Bryan Walsh's funeral in Miami, exactly 40 years after Operation Pedro Pan began, I witnessed the gratitude so many of his Pedro Pans bore him. Juan and Aidée Pujol, a married couple both of whom were Pedro Pans, remained by his side every moment until his burial. Also accompanying him were some of the Pedro Pans who became well-known public figures, such as Mel Martínez, then secretary of Housing and Urban Development (HUD), afterward elected senator for the state of Florida.

Fermín Mejía became one of the Pedro Pans. He began to study law in Villanueva – a university that was both Catholic and American, the two great enemies of the revolution. In 1961, of the 18 classmates in his entering class, counting him, there were only 2 left. He wanted to leave via Spain, but because the visa he was able to obtain was through Operation Pedro Pan, he went to the United States instead. By chance, Fermín was supposed to leave Cuba on the very day that the Bay of Pigs invasion began, as a result of which the airport was closed. Because the invasion failed, he left a week later. Operation Pedro Pan also helped him to continue his studies in a small Catholic school in New England. However, 17 more years passed before Fermín was able to travel to Cuba to see his mother and sister.

Eventually, Fermín left the church because it "was unable to assimilate him," given his sexual orientation. Yet he remembered his years in Belén with gratitude, as "the institution that gave me the greatest happiness in my life." Never in favor of the revolution, Fermín preferred a dialogue and an aperture, emphasizing the cultural aspects that unite Cubans on both sides.

Much younger Pedro Pans were Carlos Eire and his brother Tony, who left in 1962 when Eire was only 11. Today a professor of history and religious

studies at Yale University, Eire (2003) told his story in *Waiting for Snow in Havana*. A child of privilege, he remembered his childhood as the son of a judge whose judgments and sentences were swift, in a neighborhood of Havana that was dotted with pools: "those pools spoke to me of the privileged life that I knew was mine" (p. 353). From that life, he was hurled into one at the bottom of the heap, where upon arrival at the refugee camp he was called "spic!" "Not easy, the transformation into a spic," stressed Eire. "Not at all like a chameleon changing his color" (p. 121). A child who until then did not have any responsibilities and did not know how to do any chores, he spent three years tumbling from one orphanage to another, one foster home to another.

His mother was supposed to come in a few months but was unable to arrive until 1965. When she finally joined her sons, they went on to Chicago, where she worked in a factory while the brothers went to school. Her sons appreciated her sacrifice. A woman who was handicapped, knew no English, had never worked, and knew only how to sew, still she came to take care of them. By contrast, Eire never saw his father again; he remained in Cuba ostensibly "to guard the precious art collection" he had accumulated from the state. Feeling abandoned by his father, Eire turned his surname (Nieto) into his middle initial (N.) so that his children would someday inherit his mother's name: Eire.

In its finality, my own story resembles many of the Pedro Pans'. It was the abrupt end of our childhood and the beginning of adulthood; the loss of adolescence was the loss of the chance to create one's identity based on one's culture, family, tradition. Shortly after I left Cuba, my father began working for B. F. Goodrich (for whom he worked in Cuba for 20 years) in Bogota, Colombia, where my parents lived for the next 10 years. I spent my high school years in a Quaker boarding school in Vassalboro, Maine, Oak Grove School, where the principals, teachers, librarians, and staff consciously sought to watch over this refugee child, to make up for the family I lacked. I was also fortunate to be close to my aunt and uncle's family, Fidelia Pedraza, Joaquín Fermoselle, and Rosa Suárez, in Washington, D.C., who also looked after me.

Still, my departure from Cuba was wrenching. Despite my parents' insistence that I would be back in six months, in time for Christmas, I had a child's certainty that my world had come to an end. I can see my own departure in a book of autographs, a popular item then among Cuban children. I brought my book with me among the few possessions allowed. Before I left, I asked those dearest to me to write something. The *cocinera*, the cook who raised me, Eloína Díaz ("Bibi"), and the nanny, Guillermina Torres ("Tata"), raised me as their own, though they were black. So I felt about them, too, as most nights I climbed the long stairs to their tiny room, to sleep on the same bed with them. Able to read and write partly because of the lessons I gave them after school, they both wrote in my autograph book. Unable to express the depth of her feelings, Bibi wrote: "Silvita, I hope that when you return, you will be able to pack your own suitcases." My uncle Rafael, an idealistic communist from his youth, wrote: "Silvita, may you learn a great deal, see a great deal, and return with all of that so it can be useful to you and others. Only in giving and in creating can we find full happiness.... Your uncle, Rafaelito."

When the plane actually lifted up in the air, despite the curtain of heavy tears, I framed the beauty of the Cuban countryside in my memory: the ochre red earth beneath, the green royal palms everywhere, the turquoise sea hugging the coastline, the clear blue skies above. So I have seen it every time I returned. So I kept it always inside.

No one who left Cuba in those early years was able to return until the Dialogue that took place in 1978, between the Cuban government and representatives of the Cuban exile community, made the return trips for family reunification possible beginning in 1979. Eire chose never to return and prefers to live solely with his memories. I did return and engaged Cuba over time, seeking to understand what had happened there, trying to accompany el pueblo in its process of social change. When I returned in 1979, expecting Cuba in revolution to be the brave new world I was told it would be at the university, Bibi had died, as had my grandmother, Abuela. The child's intuition regarding the end of its world had proved partly right. It took many years, trips, and efforts to find the family the exodus severed me from.

Families were deeply divided by the political sides they chose. More often than not, both sides insisted that politics should be placed above family. I recall my father telling me that if anyone asked me whether I still had family in Cuba, I should say no. But I never did. In Cuba, members of the Communist Party, such as my uncle, were forbidden to write to their relatives in exile. But my uncle wrote to me from the many countries he traveled to, representing Cuba and its public health advances. So we lived for 19 years, until the family reunification trips began. When I first saw him again, at the airport in Havana, he was now an old man, his hair fully gray (rather than the handsome middle-aged man I remembered). I realized he had grown abstract in my memory.

The Church versus the State

The open ideological confrontation between the church and the state began in the spring of 1960. The church provided an orientation for its faithful regarding how to behave amid these confusing times. The first pastoral letter pointing the finger at communism was written by Archbishop Pérez-Serantes in "Por Díos y por Cuba" (For God and for Cuba): "The fields of battle have now been traced between the church and its enemies. . . . We can no longer say that the enemy is at the door because, in truth, he is within" (1960a:107).

In an effort to bolster the church hierarchy at this time, Monsignor Eduardo Boza-Masvidal, who was chancellor of the University of Villanueva, was named auxiliary bishop. By now, crowds of people interrupted the religious services frequently, insulting the priests for being *esbirros* (criminals) wearing cassocks, *curas falangistas* (pro-Franco, fascist priests).

The church and the government entered into a profound ideological combat between two philosophies that saw themselves as not only different but also contradictory. The archbishop of Santiago de Cuba, Enrique Pérez-Serantes, who had saved Fidel's life in 1953, framed it as such in his pastoral letter titled "Rome or Moscow" (1960b) regarding the great ideological battle that was then being waged in the world, as well as in the heart and mind of every Cuban.

As 1960 was coming to an end, the armed struggle against Fidel developed, particularly in the Escambray Mountains (in Las Villas) and in the Sierra de los Organos (in Pinar del Río). Rafael Peláez became a member of the MRP. Many at the time characterized it as "*Fidelismo* without Fidel" or "the 26th of July without communism." Their manifesto exhorted the Cuban people to rise up against "the new tyranny." Rafael went to fight in the mountains of el Escambray, once more as chief of Action and Sabotage, but now for the MRP. The government called them "counterrevolutionaries"; they called themselves "revolutionaries" (see Figure 3.2).

In October 1960, when the diplomatic and economic war between Cuba and the United States peaked in the final expropriation of all American industries, a group of fighters in el Escambray was captured. It included Captain Porfirio Ramírez, president of the FEU in Las Villas, and Plinio Prieto and Sinesio Walhs, who were *comandantes* of the rebel army. On the 12th, they were executed. In Alfonso's words, "The revolution, like Saturn, was beginning to devour its own children" (1985:91). The period of terror

Within the image (holy card text):

eMadre de Dios y de los hombres, pósate ahora aquí sobre el corazón de tu pueblo.

Reina de los cielos y de la tierra, te rendimos homenaje de veneración.

Patrona del Universo, agradecémoste vuestro amparo y protección.

Nov 1959

Figure 3.2   As the revolution deepened, a strong identity developed between the Catholic Church and the opposition movement. Here a Holy Card of Cuba's patron saint, la Virgen de la Caridad, demonstrates it. Each stanza of the prayer began with the three letters – M, R, P – that identified the bearer as a member of the opposition's Movimiento Revolucionario del Pueblo (MRP) to another member. This one belonged to member number 197, Coiré Rodríguez. (Silvia Pedraza)

was among the stages that Brinton (1965) identified in the course taken by the first great revolutions.

The Cuban bishops continued to issue pastoral letters clarifying the position of the church. It was Monsignor Boza-Masvidal who went to greater lengths, candidly explaining why Castro's revolution could not be considered Christian, despite its clearly Christian aims of helping the poor, ending racial discrimination, and alleviating extreme social inequality (Hernández 1999:139–40). In an article published in *La Quincena* on October 30, Boza-Masvidal (1960) underscored that Castro's revolution was not Christian because the means to achieve this were not just, as they harmed the rights of others. For the revolution to be truly Christian, he said, it needed to base itself on a spiritual conception of life and of man, rather than the materialist conception that led to erasing the name of God from the Constitution. Moreover, the revolution needed to base itself on love, not on hate and on the class struggle. The revolution also needed to respect liberty of expression and association, as well as the right to private property, and to respect the good name of others, rather than to insult them and vilify them, even when they were enemies. Last, Boza-Masvidal objected to the exclusive relationship Cuba developed with the Soviet Union, while attacks on the United States were constant. "We Catholics are not against the revolution," he stressed, "which we helped enormously, and we do want the large-scale social transformations that Cuba needs, but we cannot give our support to communism, materialist and totalitarian, that would entail the total denial of the ideals for which so many Cubans fought and gave their lives." Rolando Cubelas, the president of the FEU at the University of Havana, replied with insults and disparaging remarks, calling him a "counterrevolutionary."

Amaro pointed out that in this phase the educational system was reorganized. The masses were now organized in new groups that were linked to the government, such as the Unión de Jóvenes Comunistas, the Pioneros (Pioneers, for children under age 12), the militia, and the Federación de Mujeres Cubanas.

Still, the revolution at this time had both extremely positive and extremely negative aspects. Positively, the revolution gave expression to the idealism of youth with the literacy brigades that would go to the countryside to *alfabetizar*, teaching reading and writing to the peasants. Negatively, surveillance intensified with the creation of the Comités para la Defensa de la Revolución. When the CDRs were initiated at the end of 1960 for surveillance, Raúl Castro reminded them: "You are supposed to keep an eye on everybody and a hand grasping onto their neck." These contradictions created serious conflicts in many. In the years following, with the revolution consolidated, the CDRs took on more positive functions; for example, their block-by-block organization helped to spread vaccines against infectious diseases.

The Revolution: Political and Social

The revolution started as a middle-class revolution, whose aim had been to restore the republic; by now, it had broadened to incorporate the groups that historically were at the margins of society, excluded from participation, particularly the peasants, blacks, often women. Their incorporation to the mainstream was accomplished through the social reforms the government enacted, such as the Agrarian Reform; through an end to racial discrimination in public social life; and through lifting high, for all to see, the revolution's accomplishments (e.g., Galaor 1959:16–18).

At this time, two contrasting social processes were taking place. The upper and upper-middle classes and the professional class were leaving the country, after seeing the antidemocratic, communist turn the revolution had taken, and suffering the loss of their enterprises and personal property, such as their homes. But a large part of *el pueblo*, especially the humblest of them, centered their aspirations and hopes in the figure of Fidel Castro. As Louis Pérez (1995:319) pointed out, in his leadership style Fidel became both cause and effect of a style of *personalismo* that fostered direct dialogue between the leader and his followers, as he increasingly became the repository of the people's belief in his ability to solve their problems. It is worth citing Huber Matos's recollection and the way he frames what Castro came to represent in Cuba, with which I concur. Matos saw Castro's capacity to express the hopes and aspirations of the Cuban people, not only as a function of his personal charisma, but also as a function of Cuba's past history, beginning with the war of independence, which was frustrated by U.S. intervention, and in which the best leaders, Martí and Maceo, died. "The people have tried to fill the void they left, generation after generation," Matos explained, "once again seeing their hopes frustrated by the mediocrity of the political leadership and by other tragic deaths, such as those of Antonio Guiteras, Eduardo Chibás, and José Antonio Echeverría." Finally, the country achieved democracy in the 1940s, but Batista's coup d'etat "miscarried the political process," he emphasized. The Cuban economy, when he reached power, had the third highest level of per capita production in Latin America, but this "was not able to attenuate it." "The people desire the Cuba José Martí depicted," Matos continued, "a genuinely independent nation, 'with all and for the good of all.' Fidel Castro, wrapped in the mysticism of the revolutionary struggle, came to represent more than sixty years of truncated aspirations and hopes" (2002:337).

The literature on the sociology of revolution has been overly dominated by structural approaches that ignore human agency as well as the importance of leadership. To my mind, understanding a revolution requires an understanding of both structure and agency – of the people who made it in circumstances not of their own making, to paraphrase Karl Marx. The Cuban revolution had multiple causes: Batista's illegitimate dictatorship; the vast inequalities of class, rural poverty, race, and gender; Castro's enormous charisma; and an anti-American nationalism. Under their multiple impact, the political revolution became a social revolution.

4

The Revolution Redefines Itself

¿Y si llegaras tarde,
cuando mi boca tenga
sabor seco a cenizas,
a tierras amargas?

And if you were to arrive late,
When my mouth
Tastes dry, like ashes,
Like bitter earth?
    Emilio Ballagas, "Poema
    Impaciente" (1953)

Socialism and the Bay of Pigs

The fourth stage of the revolution was that of socialism, which began when the large Cuban and American enterprises, *latifundios*, and private property were nationalized in 1960 and lasted until December 1, 1961, when Castro for the first time announced that he was and had always been Marxist-Leninist. The announcement was made more than seven months after the failure of the Bay of Pigs invasion.

The Brigade 2506 that invaded Cuba at the Bay of Pigs organized the opposition to the revolution's communist turn. To illustrate the plans for the invasion, its execution, and consequences, I rely on interviews with Raúl Martínez, Mariano Pérez, Marcelino Miyares, José Ignacio Rasco and Estela Rasco, José Basulto, Gastón Vázquez (pseudonym), Ramón Espino, Juan Manuel Salvat, Rafael Peláez (pseudonym), Father Eduardo Lorenzo, Carlos Franqui, Manolo Ray, and Augusto Vidaurreta and Esther María Vidaurreta.

92

The execution of Porfirio Ramírez and the other students in Las Villas was the event that turned Raúl Martínez into a fierce opponent of the revolution, as previously he was of Batista. He was in Miami at the time because his parents insisted he leave Cuba, at the age of 19, for his safety. But when he realized that Cubans were being executed not because of war crimes committed under Batista but simply for their opposition to the regime, he became radically anti-Castro. The next day he dropped the courses he was taking at the university and signed up to be part of *los campamentos*, the camps where young Cubans were being trained by the CIA in Guatemala. Two days later his father came from Cuba to try to dissuade him.

Raúl and his father, Urbano, were close; both were strong Auténticos. For two days they talked incessantly, as his father tried to convince him of the futility of his effort: "Not our social class, the professional class, but the vast majority of the people sides with the government," he stressed. "The armed forces are more powerful and consolidated than before, as they received armaments from the Soviet Union; their force is superior." Raúl, however, insisted that with the support of the United States, they could not lose. Raúl recalled that, with great foresight, his father admonished him that the great powers – the United States and the Soviets – would not fight over Cuba; rather, they would reach an agreement that would abandon both the exiles and the island.

Raúl, however, won the day when he asked his father whether he would enlist if he were a young man with a cause and found support for that cause. His father, seeing himself in his son, admitted that he would. With his father's acquiescence, Raúl enlisted in the brigade that was training to fight in the Bay of Pigs. The brigade was renamed Brigade 2506, after the young man with that number (Carlos Rodríguez Santana) who died during training. On January 6, 1961, Raúl left for Guatemala. There he was trained by the CIA as a parachutist for the invasion. Thirty years later, he was to fly with Hermanos al Rescate (Brothers to the Rescue) over the sea's 90-mile stretch between Cuba and Key West.

Mariano Pérez grew up in a *bohío* and as a boy milked cows for the owners of the farm where his family lived. His grandfather immigrated to Cuba from the Canary Islands, and his family knew the poverty of the peasant. His father admired Eduardo Chibás, whose social populism was well received among the working-class Cubans. He felt a visceral hatred for Batista, whom he saw as a thief who violated the Constitution. All the time Batista was in power, he kept Chibas's portrait hanging in the living room. His father worked hard in an *henequén* (sisal) plantation, and he was a

93

carbonero (charcoal maker) who transported the charcoal from the country to the city of Matanzas. He had never gone to school, but he could read and write thanks to his mother's instruction.

Mariano had just begun the fourth grade when a flood destroyed his school, which was not rebuilt until his adolescence. He joined Batista's army not because he liked Batista but because it was the only way he could escape the poverty of the countryside, and he liked being a soldier. Despite his lower-class background, he never felt any sympathy for the revolution, in part because the family who owned the farm his family worked for were revolutionaries. They were quite rich, and, as a farmhand, he felt exploited by them, working 18 hours a day for only two pesos. Early in 1960 Mariano joined those who were fighting in the *manigua*, the isolated wilderness of Las Villas, together with a friend who was in the rebel army under Che Guevara. For about three months, they spent most of the time running away from the *milicianos* who persecuted them "like ants running after us," he said. Eventually, in July 1960, they decided to leave Cuba in a small boat, together with another friend who was black. They asked him to pray, because as *guajiros* they did not know how to pray. Caught in the midst of tall, raging waves, they were rescued by a ship on the way from New Orleans to Puerto Rico. In Puerto Rico, he joined Rescate Revolucionario, an organization that intended to rescue the revolution by helping the opposition, and in December 1960 he joined those who were in training in Guatemala.

In this stage, the leaders of the major political organizations in prerevolutionary Cuba left. Together with the young men who joined the *campamentos*, their goal was to help the underground struggle with arms, strategy, and money. The Frente Revolucionario Democrático (Democratic Revolutionary Front) was founded in 1960 by combining all the principal organizations that opposed Batista: Tony Varona's Auténticos, Aureliano Arango's Triple A, José Ignacio Rasco's Democracia Cristiana, Justo Carrillo's Montecristi group, and Manuel Artíme's Movimiento de Recuperación Revolucionaria (MRR), all of them collaborating with the Americans through the CIA. Through this Frente, the Bay of Pigs invasion was organized, with the goal of restoring democracy in Cuba. Again the impact of the Agrupación can be seen in that two of the leaders, Rasco and Artíme, were *Agrupados*. Salvat, who founded the students' Directorio Estudiantil, was also an *Agrupado*. Later on, the Frente expanded when other political factions joined, such as those led by José Miró-Cardona and Manolo Ray. It was then renamed the Consejo Revolucionario Cubano (Cuban Revolutionary

Council). Miró-Cardona was president of the exile government that the CIA intended to establish provisionally in Cuba after the brigade's success.

The year 1961 opened with the U.S. government ending all diplomatic relations with Cuba and Kennedy becoming the new president of the United States. Publicly, he announced his Alliance for Progress to promote economic and social development of Latin America, which could help avoid other Cubas. Privately, he inherited the Bay of Pigs operation. In addition to the Frente, the students in the Directorio also prepared for Bay of Pigs. Salvat returned to Cuba in November 1960 on a boat that carried a full shipment of arms, entering the Cuban coast near the Naútico Country Club. Although they were independent, they coordinated their efforts with the United States and had U.S. backing in money and arms. Within Cuba, they sought to organize the student movement, to have their message reach the population, and to prepare the uprisings that were to take place throughout the island, coordinated by the underground. They sought to ready Cuba for the impending arrival of the invasion force at Playa Girón, so that it would arrive when the armed struggle was taking place in cities and mountains throughout the island, rather than be the lone and isolated event it turned out to be.

The invasion force consisted of 1,400 exiles, most of them young men. The *invasores* (invaders) were accompanied by three Catholic priests. Their uniforms bore shoulder patches in the shape of a shield bearing a Latin cross in the center. Their class composition reflected that of the first wave of the exodus – mostly middle- and upper-middle-class white Cubans. But a sizable number of working-class and peasants also joined, as had black and mulatto Cubans, including Erneido Oliva, the brigade's deputy commander, second only to José Pérez San Román, the commander of the brigade (Thomas 1971:1360–1361). They were assisted by a couple of American CIA officers who went by the names of "Gray" and "Rip" and identified deeply with the Cubans but were unable to do more than watch the unfolding tragedy (Lynch 1998).

Militarily, the Bay of Pigs invasion was a total failure. Denied the air cover that was vital for its success and abandoned on the beach with no ammunition and few supplies, the Brigade 2506 fought for three days with little food or water. Of the 1,400 exiles, 114 were killed, a few were executed immediately thereafter, and 1,189 were captured. About 150 were unable to land, were never shipped out, or made their way back (Wyden 1979:303).

Today, a monument with an eternal flame honors those who died, located on Calle Ocho (8th Street), the symbolic heart of Cuban Miami.

Unlike Mariano Pérez, Marcelino Miyares came from wealth. His father and uncles owned three sugar mills. He was among the few who managed to escape Castro's *milicianos* by hiding in the swampy area of the Ciénaga de Zapata as long as possible. His life was saved miraculously on the third day of the fighting. A few minutes after he left the house from which he transmitted on the radio, a bomb fell on the house and exploded. Also an *Agrupado*, thinking he had little time left to live, he began to pray. The leader of the brigade ordered the 50 or so men who were there to try to escape by going inland, into the mountains. On the way there, upon encountering a group of Castro's *milicianos*, they dispersed. Marcelino ended up alone, for which he was initially thankful. He began to search for fresh water, which he direly needed. Dehydrated under the hot sun, after three days, he was beginning to feel almost mad, but he continued searching. He knew he was near fresh water because he was in a charcoal plantation area, and making charcoal involves using water. Finally, he came upon a well. Entirely alone for a total of 16 days, he survived thanks to the well of water he found, but he grew weaker and weaker without food. During the day he walked, but he had to hide because the area was full of *milicianos*. He was so close to them that sometimes he could overhear them. Once he was able to hear Castro give his May 1st speech on television! At night, strong winds penetrated his uniform and made him feel overwhelmingly cold.

Luckily for Marcelino, the *milicianos* left their camp, and he found half a can of condensed milk they left behind – the first meal in 16 days. Continuing to walk, he managed to leave the arid zone and came upon a *bohío* where he could see a family gathered for lunch. He asked them for their help, especially for food. Though frightened, they helped him, as one of their sons, a *guajirito*, had joined the invasion and was in prison. But soon thereafter they asked him to leave, as the CDR had come to see them. They gave him clothes that made him look like a *guajiro*. He boarded a bus to the nearest town in Jagüey Grande, but two of the *milicianos* on the bus noted the incongruity between his physical appearance and his clothes, and they turned him into the military post nearby. When they interrogated him, he declared who he was. He had thus managed to survive until they caught him, without surrendering. He then realized that, unconsciously, that was his aim. He was taken to Havana, where he joined the rest of the brigade that had already been taken to the Palacio de los Deportes. Nine men did not survive an eight-hour trip in a *rastra*, a sealed truck, ordered by Osmany Cienfuegos. They died of asphyxiation.

For 20 days the survivors were questioned in Havana's Sports Palace. Judged as war criminals, they were taken to prison, first at the Castillo del Príncipe, later to the Isle of Pines. They remained in prison for 20 months. In the Isle of Pines prison, despite the inhuman conditions in which they lived, 105 men in one room, Miyares managed to turn the experience into a very spiritual one by studying the Old Testament in a small study group and helping others find solace. While in prison, he also made the decision to continue studying, though he had already become a lawyer in Spain and had initially returned to Cuba to work in the Ministerio de Relaciones Exteriores (in effect, the State Department). Years later, he obtained a Ph.D. in political science from Northwestern University. He also became a founder of both the Committee for Cuban Democracy and the Partido Demócrata Cristiano in Miami.

The Cuban government does not call it the battle of the Bay of Pigs, which they feel is undignified; rather, they call it the battle of Playa Girón – the site of "the first defeat of imperialism in America" (Wyden 1979:311). Because they had accepted the help of the United States, after the Bay of Pigs invasion failed Fidel called them *mercenarios* (mercenaries), as they were represented in the documentary on *Playa Girón* made in Cuba years later. But to José Ignacio Rasco, one of the leaders, the world was then divided into two camps – Russia and the United States – and if there was an alliance between Russia and Castro, the exiles had to forge an alliance with the enemy. "It was a struggle between major world powers, and we formed part of that struggle," Rasco emphasized. His opinion was that, had it not been for President Kennedy's treason – the Americans' lack of endorsement – the invasion would have been successful. That opinion was widely shared by others who participated. Enrique Ros (father of Ileana Ros-Lehtinen, who was elected to the U.S. Congress many years later) was coordinator of the Frente outside Cuba. In his history of the events that unfolded around Playa Girón, Ros (1994) detailed his efforts to have Cubans be part of the plans being made and in command of the operation. Neither was the case. According to Ros, the Americans traced the plans for the operation that was to decide the future of Cuba, with their backs turned to the Cubans. The failure of the invasion consolidated the revolution and sealed the identity between Fidel, *la patria*, and the revolution that, as Marifeli Pérez-Stable emphasized, came to characterize the revolution. Within the logic of Fidel-*patria*-revolution, dissent was not tolerated (1999:177).

Centrally involved in the Bay of Pigs operation was José Basulto, who 30 years later was to found and head the organization of pilots called Hermanos al Rescate to assist the *balseros* they sighted at sea. He was 19 years old when the revolution triumphed and was also a member of the Agrupación that exerted such a strong influence on his generation. Always an admirer of personal courage, he sympathized with the revolution against Batista because "it confronted the dictatorship and entailed an act of courage – the wish to confront the tyranny with arms." Because his father was vice-president of an American company, his family always wanted him to study in the United States. He left Cuba only a few days after the triumph of the revolution to study at Chauncy Hall, a preparatory school in Boston, and then at Boston College. However, he soon became convinced that Castro's revolution was full of duplicity; for example, he noted, Castro gave a speech where he repeated "¿Armas para qué?" (What do we need arms for?), while at the same time the government kept buying more and more arms. Castro's nationalist anti-Americanism also grated on him. Moreover, Basulto highlighted that his personality was such that he liked adventure – personal courage put to the test. Thus, he left for the United States again early in 1960 to be trained by the Americans. He was part of a small group in the underground resistance movement that was developing inside of Cuba to support the impending exile invasion.

When he returned to Cuba, early in 1961, ostensibly he was to continue his studies at the university, but this was a cover for his underground activities as a member of the MRR to rectify the wrong turn toward communism they felt the revolution had taken. His training by the CIA developed his expertise in communications as a radio operator and a telegrapher; more generally, he learned about explosives, foreign weapons, intelligence, psychological warfare, propaganda, cryptography, and parachuting – to enable the resistance fighters in Cuba to receive arms to support the Bay of Pigs invasion. Two types of teams existed, he explained: the "gray" teams that enabled military operations to take place, which he belonged to, and the "black" teams that carried them out. His mission as radio operator and infiltrator was both important and dangerous. As Wyden pointed out, the radio operators were special – the lifeline between the internal resistance and the Americans (1979:36).

In Santiago de Cuba he helped both the Directorio Estudiantil, under Alberto Müller's leadership, and the MRR. He successfully carried out his mission to help the Bay of Pigs invasion. Moving from one place to another, so he could not be found, he used telegraphy to send back to the United

States an enormous amount of information to support the invasion. He even told them the invasion would be a disaster, poorly planned and executed as it was. Due to the disaster that, indeed, took place, of the five radio operators in Oriente province, he was the only one to come out of it "in one piece." He drove to Guantanamo and climbed over a 10-foot fence to safety in the U.S. naval base.

Why was the Bay of Pigs invasion such a total failure? My answer is based on two excellent analyses as well as my own interviews with those who participated in the operation. Wyden's (1979) analysis of the reasons for the failure was based on interviews with the major political actors involved and the president's conversations with Theodore Sorensen soon after the events, which became the only full presidential postmortem, as well as content analysis of the available documents (Sorensen 1965). Enrique Ros (1994) also analyzed the reasons for the failure at Playa Girón, basing his work on the declassified secret CIA reports on the invasion (Kornbluh 1998), as well as his firsthand experience as the coordinator of the FRD outside Cuba.

As a military operation, the exile invasion was developed under President Eisenhower, who in March 1960 authorized the CIA plan for an exile-led invasion. When John F. Kennedy assumed the presidency in January 1961, he inherited a full-blown operation that was to be carried out only three months later. Although he assumed responsibility for it, his actions betrayed an enormous ambivalence. In March 1961, only weeks before the operation was to take place, he introduced key changes in the military plans the CIA had developed, changes that diminished the chances for success of the operation. The original plans for the Bay of Pigs project were drawn by the CIA. Richard M. Bissell Jr., the CIA's deputy director for plans (in effect, chief of all covert operations), second only to the director, Allen W. Dulles, had escalated the Bay of Pigs project from a guerrilla operation to a full-scale invasion, what was called the "Trinidad Plan." As Wyden (1979:70) noted, "with this escalation the importance of air power increased enormously." The Trinidad Plan involved concurrent air support and the landing of a provisional government once the brigade achieved a foothold. Wanting above all to conceal the U.S. hand, President Kennedy made key changes in the plan that, in effect, crippled the chances for success. He changed landing sites from the city of Trinidad to the isolated and difficult, swamp terrain of the Bay of Pigs and the Ciénaga de Zapata. He changed the arrival time of the brigade from night to day, so they lost the advantage of darkness. He also reduced the number of air strikes, effectively denying the young men entering the bay the necessary air cover – the "umbrella" of protection they were promised (Wyden 1979:56–57, 191–92).

Kennedy's changes were not the only cause of the failure, however. Kornbluh (1998) and Wyden (1979) both stressed that, despite the CIA's efforts to keep the operation a secret, it was foretold in American newspapers. Three months before the invasion, on January 10, 1961, at the top of the front page of the *New York Times* the headline read: "U.S. Helps Train an Anti-Castro Force at Secret Guatemalan Air-Ground Base." Paul Kennedy's (1961) article underscored that "the U.S. was assisting the effort not only in personnel but in material and the construction of ground and air facilities," as was, indeed, the case (Wyden 1979:46). Likewise, 10 days before the actual invasion, Tad Szulc's (1961) article in the *New York Times* announced the imminent invasion.

Moreover, the U.S. role in the preliminary air strike of April 15 – two days before the full invasion was due – was exposed to the world at the United Nations, making it impossible to deny U.S. responsibility for the attack, as both Eisenhower and Kennedy had intended. Adlai Stevenson, the U.S. ambassador to the United Nations, later on was to say that the Bay of Pigs invasion gave him the most "humiliating experience" of his years in public service (Wyden 1979:152). All this prompted Kennedy to cancel the second air strike that was planned for the very day of the invasion, which the CIA considered critical for the operation's success. Just a few days before the actual invasion, President Kennedy had stated at a press conference that under no conditions would the United States intervene by using any U.S. forces (Wyden 1979:168).

According to Wyden (1979:309), Kennedy's approval of the plan was based on two possible outcomes: national revolt or flight to the hills. Neither was possible. After three days of fighting without food, water, ammunition, or supplies, Oliva, San Román, and Artíme pushed into the swamps with their men, but the hills were too far away to provide them with cover. Despite Kennedy's efforts to conceal the U.S. hand, nationally and internationally the exile invasion was portrayed as an act of U.S. aggression, assisted by the CIA's secret army, the Cuban exiles. From then on, the Cuban revolution elicited the admiration of many for what may well prove to be its most enduring quality: that of David confronting Goliath.

Moreover, a few weeks before the invasion, Castro's forces broke the backbone of the resistance by capturing several of its leaders, the first of whom was "Francisco," or Rogelio González-Corso. He was caught shortly before the invasion. "Francisco" was director of the Ministry of Agriculture under Castro's government. Profoundly Catholic and anticommunist, he was also in the underground movement, where he became national coordinator of the MRR, as well as military coordinator of the FRD (Villegas 2003). Due to chance, he was found at a meeting with other underground resistance members, who included Humberto Sorí-Marín, a former *comandante* of the rebel army, as well as Rafael Díaz-Hanscom. All of them were worried that by itself, without the support of the urban guerrilla, the brigade could not succeed. Gastón Vázquez found the 200,000 pesos the captain of the G2 Police asked for, to ransom "Francisco" and Domingo ("Mingo") Trueba, but the contact who was supposed to meet them to receive the money failed to show up. Gastón then left Cuba and made contact with *los amigos* in the United States, returning to Cuba a week before the invasion, fully believing it would succeed. At the airport in Havana, however, the police interrogated him. They asked him whether he knew "Francisco," "Tomás," "Julio," and others – all of whom he knew intimately. As he left the airport, he could see "Julio," the right-hand assistant to Che Guevara, next to *el Che*, holding a copy of the newspaper *Revolución*. He then knew that Castro's police knew the leaders of the underground by their *noms de guerre*, but they did not yet know who they really were.

Captured in mid-March, the young men who led the underground were soon executed. In reply to the invasion force on April 17, Castro ordered that all political prisoners be executed. At La Cabaña prison, a total of seven young men were executed two days later, among them "Francisco" (Villegas 2002). They died shouting *¡Viva Cuba Libre! ¡Viva Cristo Rey!* (Long live Cuba! Long live Christ the King!). Ramón Espino's brother, Jorge, was also executed a few months later, in November, when they finally learned who he really was and captured him. Jorge was the head of the underground for the provinces of Matanzas, Havana, and Pinar del Río. They found him at 11 p.m., and executed him at 1 a.m. He died shouting the same words.

After the execution of "Francisco" and Mingo, Gastón's family claimed their bodies to bury them in the family's plot in the cemetery. Reading in the newspaper that he was condemned to death, Gastón sought a place to hide. He went to a church where a priest who was a friend had repeatedly offered him assistance, should he ever need it. Yet the priest betrayed him, telling him they could not help him. After the expulsion of the priests and nuns, the few remaining in Cuba were duly afraid. Finally, Gastón hid in a couple of embassies until he was able to leave Cuba. In the meantime, Castro's police imprisoned his father, condemning him to 30 years in prison, to force Gastón to turn himself in, but his father forbade him to do so.

When Gastón reached the United States, "Jimmy," one of *los amigos*, contacted him, expressed his sorrow at the loss of his friends and his father's imprisonment, congratulated him on his work, and handed him an envelope with $25,000 "to help him," promising that they would soon be in touch again. Between 1961 and 1967, he returned to Cuba and entered the island seven times. Twice he tried to bring his wife out, but she refused to leave, which led to their divorce. Altogether, he worked for *los amigos* for 25 years.

The capture and execution of the leaders of the underground had many consequences, as the link between the internal and external struggle was severed. Arms for the internal resistance ceased arriving in Cuba. Juan Manuel Salvat, who was inside Cuba then, remembered that all the resistance movements were coordinated and ready – the MRR, the MRP, the 30 de Noviembre, the Directorio. They wanted to fight, but they had nothing to fight with. When the invasion actually began on April 17, Salvat did not know it was coming but read about it in the newspapers and heard about it on the radio, just like everyone else. "It would have been very different," he said, "if first there had been an armed uprising in a number of cities throughout the island and then, in the midst of this, the invasion arrived." Too much emphasis was placed on the external invasion, not enough on the internal resistance, on the *alzamientos* (uprisings), Salvat emphasized. The massive exodus of refugees also hurt the internal resistance. They had fewer safe houses in which to hide, less support, Salvat remembered.

How much support there was among the common people inside of Cuba for this challenge to the revolution was not tested because the government rounded up thousands of Cubans who, they suspected, sympathized with the invaders. The prisons and the stadiums were full to the brim. At that time, Castro's real strength was his popularity. Basulto, however, felt the brigade also had their support. "Poor people helped us by giving us a place to hide," he pointed out. He was helped by two *guajiros* who kept him in hiding and gave him the little they had to eat, telling him they understood the risk he was taking on their behalf. The internal resistance on the island was quite widespread, he emphasized. Had the effort not taken the form of an invasion of exiles from the outside, but instead had taken the form of assistance to the internal resistance on the island, it could have been won, he felt.

While plans were being made for the Bay of Pigs invasion outside Cuba, inside Cuba the underground resistance was ready to back the invasion.

Rafael Peláez was among those who set fire to the department store El Encanto (The Charm) three days before the Bay of Pigs invasion. Without doubt, it was Cuba's largest and most beautiful department store; but more than a store, it was a symbol of the hopes and aspirations middle-class Cubans had, wanting to be part of the world that they saw as modern and civilized and that they knew existed in the United States, Spain, and the rest of Europe. The burning of El Encanto constituted the loss of that symbol, of that aspiration, but Rafael Peláez said that "it was a call...a code to let everyone know of the impending landing at Playa Girón," to prepare the groups inside of Cuba for their role in the resistance (Instituto de la Memoria Histórica 2000:1).

Basulto firmly believed the real problem with the Bay of Pigs invasion was that Cubans relied on the Americans to solve the problem for them, while they should have relied on themselves. Despite the enormous failure, Basulto continued working for the CIA in the United States until November, returning to Cuba once more. He thought there would be an effort to rectify what had gone wrong – not because he believed in the Americans, because he did not, but because he expected there would be others like him, willing to continue the struggle. He was wrong: "The demoralization that followed immediately after, the frustration after the failure of Bay of Pigs was immense." Cubans in the opposition lost hope, felt abandoned. Even more, the failure consolidated Fidel Castro in power. "And the warranty came with the October Missile Crisis," Basulto added.

He ended his association with the CIA's key officers and continued working on his own. A year later he organized the attack on the hotel Rosita de Ornedo, an attack that Salvat joined. They heard that a party was being given there for Russians, so they sailed along the coast in a little boat with a cannon, which they fired repeatedly at the hotel. Castro accused the United States of this aggression. The headlines read: "Cuba Accuses President Kennedy." In fact, the Americans were in the dark, Salvat noted.

Those who fought in the brigade were captured and imprisoned for 20 months. The jails were full, including the internal resistance fighters and anyone under suspicion. As prisoners, the brigade members were treated better than other prisoners because the eyes of the world were upon them (Johnson 1964). Many others served long prison sentences, as did Alberto Müller of the Directorio, who served a 15-year sentence after being caught in the struggle in the Sierra Maestra. At his trial, he spoke of the hammer that strikes and the sickle that blinds.

Raúl Martínez was among those who were imprisoned after the Bay of Pigs failure. On his mother's side, the Urioste, the family was deeply divided politically. The three sisters were Ondina, who strongly supported Batista; Dulce, his mother, who was anti-Batista and anti-Castro both; and Josefina, who strongly supported Castro. My mother's family, the Lubián of Santa Clara, were related to Josefina's husband, Agustín Gómez-Lubián. Hence, I also felt her son's death (my cousin) in the struggle against Batista. A handsome young man who studied medicine at the University of Havana, everyone called him *el Chiqui*, with great affection. His death was a searing event for his family; it left a deep mark on all who lived in Santa Clara, Las Villas.

El Chiqui, a member of the Action and Sabotage unit fighting against Batista in Santa Clara, was also a poet. Many of *el Chiqui*'s poems contradicted his youth and presaged his death. One, for example, was titled "Viejo" (Old), and pointed out that inside his soul was quite old, bearing too much sorrow for his few years (Gómez-Lubián 1978). In May 1957, about to turn 20 years old, he and another young man, Julio Pino, drove a car to place a bomb on a street corner. *El Chiqui* was driving the car, while Julio prepared the bomb. Due to a defective fuse, the bomb exploded ahead of time inside their car. Julio Pino died instantly. *El Chiqui* arrived at his father's medical clinic still alive, but he died soon thereafter. His family's pain ran deep; his loss prompted them to commit themselves deeply to the revolution, which honored him as one of its martyrs.

When Raúl was in prison in el Castillo del Príncipe, his aunt Josefina went to visit him, insisting that he was her nephew and, because she had lost a son, she knew how much his mother must be suffering. She admonished him that because he was still young, he would be able to adapt to the revolution and the revolution would reeducate him. When the visit ended and she tried to leave, however, a guard from the Ministry of the Interior obstructed her passage with a rifle and called her a *gusana*, meaning "counterrevolutionary." Raúl seized the chance to tell her, "This is why we came here to fight, so that you can have the freedom to walk wherever you want, such as you cannot have with these people." The rift between them never healed. Many years later, in the 1990s, she came to visit the family in Miami, but he remained distant, as he thought it was only her need for dollars and goods in the midst of "the special period" that drove her there.

Mariano Pérez, a parachutist, did not actually land in the Bay of Pigs, but in San Blás, with 80 others and a tank. They fought against Castro's army for three full days, though vastly outnumbered and outgunned. Some died, others took to the *manigua*, the isolated wilderness, and Mariano went to Playa Girón; but when he got there, he found that the troop was dispersing and the commanders gave the order for each man to save himself, as best he could. Mariano and a couple of other soldiers went to *el monte*, the hills where they hid until the 25th, but they were captured by some *milicianos* when Mariano set out to find some food, ravenous as they were. The *milicianos* rounded up all the young men. Arms crossed over their heads, they were lined up and taken to the Palacio de los Deportes (see Domínguez 1985). Fidel went to meet them at the Sports Stadium and spoke for hours with the young men, especially the parachutists, which suddenly began to be televised. Mariano stood up and declared, "We are not all rich, because I am a *guajiro* whose father worked in a charcoal plantation." To this Fidel replied: "You are here and you do not know that the revolution built a house for your father and your father now lives well, has electricity, a house." Not knowing whether it was true, because he had been out of Cuba for 10 months, Mariano sat down. Mariano remembered that Fidel then said to Tomás Cruz, a black Cuban, "And you? What are you doing here now that you can bathe on all the beaches of Cuba?" To this Tomás replied: "Comandante, I did not come here to bathe on the beach, but to liberate Cuba." To Mariano, the most difficult moment was at night when the young men could hear the crowd outside the stadium, chanting "mercenaries," asking for *paredón*, for their execution.

After a few days, they were taken to El Príncipe, where a trial took place and a price was set on each one of them, to be exchanged for food and medicine. For the leaders of the brigade, the price was set at $500,000 or $100,000 each; a poor *guajirito*, Mariano's price was set at only $25,000. Altogether, the United States paid $53 million in ransom. Of the soldiers captured at the Bay of Pigs, five were executed in the beginning, a few received long prison sentences, but most of them were released and arrived in the United States on December 23 and 24, 1962. Many of their parents arrived a day later, all on a boat. At a ceremony in the Orange Bowl in Miami, with the First Lady by his side, President Kennedy received the young men (see Figure 4.1). Jackie Kennedy spoke in Spanish and welcomed them. The President promised the brigade flag would someday fly over a free Cuba. He shook hands with each *brigadista* as he arrived. Mariano explained that he shook his hand out of duty, remembering how the Americans abandoned them. Hence, when he was invited to join the U.S. Army, he refused to do so because he felt betrayed by the Americans.

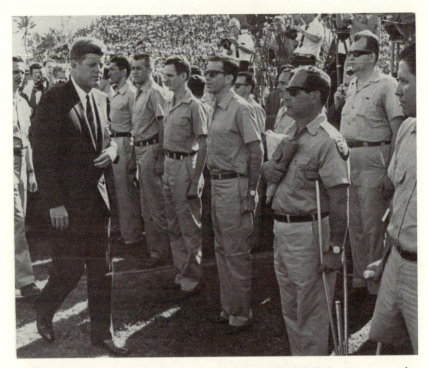

Figure 4.1 When the Bay of Pigs exile invasion of Cuba failed, the young men who participated in it were imprisoned until the U.S. government traded them for money, food, and medicine. Here President John F. Kennedy reviews the veterans after their return from the abortive attempt to overthrow Fidel Castro, at the ceremony in the Orange Bowl stadium in Miami, December 29, 1962. (Historical Museum of Southern Florida/*Miami News*)

After a couple of years, Mariano arrived in Detroit, where he got a job in an auto factory; he worked on the assembly line for almost 30 years. The pay and benefits were good and allowed him to save. He continued to involve himself in exile politics, becoming secretary of the military wing for Alpha 66 in the Midwest, possibly the most belligerent exile organization. Alpha 66 regularly organized and carried out commando raids of the island, as well as sabotage actions inside Cuba, intended to harm the Cuban economy (Telleda 1995). Like Mariano himself, most members of Alpha 66 were *humildes* (of humble origin, as poverty is signified in Latin America), from the rural areas, without much schooling, but valiant. Mariano was also very active in Abdala, an organization composed of young radically anti-Castro Cubans. In 1969 his father, whose enthusiasm for the revolution had waned, asked Mariano to help him leave Cuba. Mariano managed to bring both his parents to the United States through Mexico, and his parents spent the next 30 years in Michigan with him, working as custodians in a factory, until they retired and left the cold winters for Miami.

The U.S. government offered the *brigadistas* the chance to become a part of the armed forces. José Basulto himself became second lieutenant, upon receiving adequate training. Erneido Oliva, the military chief of the brigade and a black Cuban, became a general. Eventually, Basulto realized the intent was not to address the Cuban problem but for them to become integrated to the U.S. armed forces, and he resigned. His experiences led him to feel repeatedly betrayed, but from them he also learned that "Cubans have to take responsibility for their own problem." In his view, the exodus was a mistake; so was the reliance on the United States.

The Church Is Silenced

On May 1, 1961, after the attempt to restore the republic died on the shores of Playa Girón, Fidel Castro proclaimed Cuba a socialist nation. "The independent life of a society," as Vaclav Havel (1978) expressed it, a civil society that consisted of independent institutions – the press, media, labor unions, schools, universities, churches, and synagogues – was abolished. In June the government took over the private schools, most of them Catholic, and the seminaries where young men studied to become priests. The church was dealt a major blow, as large numbers of priests and nuns were teachers and professors. Most of them left Cuba.

On September 8, Cubans celebrate the festivity of la Virgen de la Caridad del Cobre. In 1961 Monsignor Boza-Masvidal prepared to celebrate the annual festival in the parish that bore her name, which included a procession. But the day before, the permission the government had granted was rescinded; the procession was canceled and the image taken away, so the people would not try to use it by force. Nonetheless, more than 4,000 persons showed up and, using a private image, marched toward the Presidential Palace, shouting *¡Cuba sí, Rusia no!* and *¡Viva Cristo Rey!* The police arrived, and shooting ensued; the melee ended with some wounded and one dead. The upshot was the expulsion of the priests (Alfonso 1985).

On September 17, 1961, Bishop Boza-Masvidal was expelled from Cuba. After a week in prison and then accompanied by the *milicianos*, he joined the other 132 priests already aboard the Spanish ship *Covadonga*. Among them was Agustín Román, who became auxiliary bishop of Miami years later. Boza-Masvidal went up the plank; as he stepped inside the ship, he turned and, looking back, blessed the crowd.

The expulsion and the related departure of many other priests and nuns was a mortal blow to the church in Cuba. According to the church's statistics, in 1960 the church had 723 priests for a population of more than 6 million people. By 1965 only 220 were left in Cuba (in Alfonso 1985:106). The silencing of the church lasted until the late 1980s or early 1990s (Menocal 2003).

Due to this crisis, Father Eduardo Lorenzo left Cuba. A young student at the Seminario del Buen Pastor (Seminary of the Good Shepherd) in Havana, Father Lorenzo's vocation took unexpected turns. He was ordained in the United States and ministered to the Mexican American community in Michigan, initially to the farm workers, afterward to the working-class community in Flint that had grown around the auto industry. Together with his parishioners, he built the church of Guadalupe, Mexico's patron saint, where a small altar was dedicated to Cuba's patron saint.

While still in Cuba, Father Lorenzo witnessed a great deal of the conflict. On one occasion, he was taken to jail and searched, accused of being a counterrevolutionary. On another occasion, at a major church celebration when he was in the company of many priests and the church's leaders, he saw rocks thrown down from the rooftops at them. He was also present on Sunday, August 7, 1960, when crowds screamed and threw rocks at Monsignor Boza-Masvidal, preventing him from reading the bishops' letter during the homily. As they left through the back door of the cathedral, Father Lorenzo saw people carrying sticks, ready to beat Boza-Masvidal. That pastoral letter expressed well the nature of the confrontation between church and state. The bishops stated their support for the social reforms the revolution initiated to improve the lot of the poorest Cubans (such as the agrarian reform), the expansion of health and educational services, the improved access to the beaches and public facilities, the construction of housing for the poor, and the elimination of racial discrimination. However, the bishops also emphasized they could not countenance the advance of communism in Cuba "because Catholicism and communism correspond to two opposite conceptions of humanity and of life, which it will never be possible to reconcile" (Arteaga 1960:117). As an atheistic and materialistic doctrine, communism was historically an enemy of the Catholic Church. Moreover, communism denied the religiosity of the Cuban people and their culture, which was Catholic. As a system, communism denied the most basic human rights. For all these reasons, the church explicitly condemned communism. The bishops concluded that the church would always favor the poor, but it would never side with communism.

Such was also Boza-Masvidal's message, which he repeatedly expressed in his Sunday homilies at the parish of Nuestra Señora de la Caridad, named after Cuba's patron saint, and in articles published in Catholic magazines. In his article in *La Quincena* (1997:67), he stated very clearly that the church wanted the Cuba Martí had dreamt of – "without *latifundios* and without exploiters" and with social justice for all, but also "without hatred or vengeance toward anyone" and with liberty. That was the last article he wrote in Cuba.

As 1961 ended, three years after the initial triumph of the revolution, the opposition it generated had largely been crushed. Like all social conflicts, it was lived in people's daily lives, as Cuban families became divided between those who supported the revolution, becoming integrated to it, and those who rejected it, taking the road to exile. For many Cubans, their allegiance to the church was at the center of that decision.

For Carlos Franqui, 1960 was "a year of great dogmatism, of great passion. That fever, in my case, lasted a year" because in 1961 he could no longer deny the communist course the revolution had taken. In his youth he was a communist, so he "already knew what communism was" and its capacity for total control of power. "The process of breaking with a revolutionary faith," he emphasized, "like any other faith, does not take only a day; rather, it is a long and difficult process, fraught with difficulties." The revolution he knew and fought for was lost; "and no one – neither the United States, nor the CIA, nor the internal struggle – could any longer save it." Instead, he realized the revolution such as it then was – communist, backed by the Soviets, immensely popular – would go on to last a very long time.

Marxism-Leninism

The failure of the Bay of Pigs invasion in April 1961 consolidated the revolution. The 26th of July Movement, the Directorio Revolucionario Estudiantil, and the Partido Socialista Popular were all merged into one group, the Organización de Instituciones Revolucionarias Integradas (Integrated Revolutionary Organizations). According to Pérez-Stable (1999:100), this was necessary for the revolution to defend itself against the internal opposition and the United States and to form a vanguard party.

Even after the Bay of Pigs failure and despite the lack of hope, Manolo Ray remained active and, in Puerto Rico, founded the Junta Revolucionaria Cubana (Cuban Revolutionary Junta), where the old ideals of social justice and democracy of the MRP were once again expressed. In September 1962 the Declaration of Río Cañas expressed the humanism of the second phase of the revolution, denouncing Fidel as an impostor: "The great impostor of the much needed social justice, with his false humanistic politics, has dehumanized the spirit substituting the beautiful slogans of 'Bread without Liberty' and 'Bread without Terror' for the sad realities of '*Neither Bread nor Liberty*' and '*Terror without Bread*' " (Junta Revolucionaria Cubana 1964:7).

Also part of the Provisional Government, Elena Mederos left Cuba in September 1961. She went on to work for UNICEF. Always on the side of the powerless, the last battle before she died was creating Of Human Rights in Washington, D.C., in 1976, to let the world know the abysmal conditions Cuba's political prisoners lived in (Guerrero 1991; Clavijo 1985).

The fifth and last period in the consolidation of the revolution was the Marxist-Leninist phase, when Fidel Castro declared for the first time publicly, on December 1, 1961 – more than seven months after the Bay of Pigs – his true political and ideological posture: "Some have asked me whether I thought at the time of the Moncada as I think today. I have told them: 'I thought very similarly to how I think today.' That is the truth." He continued: "That was the road the revolution had to take: the road of the anti-imperialist struggle, the road of socialism, that is to say, of the nationalization of all the large industries, of the large commercial enterprises; the nationalization of property and the socialization of the basic means of production, and the planned development of our economy.... Thus I began by telling you, in all frankness, that we believed in Marxism, that we believed that it was the most correct theory, the most scientific, the only true theory, the only true revolutionary theory. I am telling it here today with full satisfaction, with full openness: I am Marxist-Leninist, and will be Marxist-Leninist until the last day of my life" (in Alfonso 1985:110).

The First Wave: Those Who Escape

"Those who escape" constituted the second phase of the first wave of the exodus. As Amaro and Portes (1972) noted, the inverse relationship between date of emigration and social class in Cuba began to show. Still largely a middle-class exodus, now it was more middle than upper: middle merchants, middle management, landlords, middle-level professionals, and a considerable number of skilled, unionized workers – all who wanted to escape an intolerable new order. The exodus doubled.

The immigrants of the first two phases were not so much "pulled" by the attractiveness of the new society as "pushed" by the internal political process of the old. "What began as a trickle," wrote Richard Fagen et al. "was, by the middle of 1962, a small flood" (1968:62). Data from the 1990 census, which represents best the early waves of the exodus, show that of the 677,512 Cubans who immigrated to the United States from 1960 to 1990, 25.5 percent arrived during the first wave, 1960–64 (see Table 1.1). The Cuban Refugee Program that assisted most of the refugees in Miami began at this time (see Pedraza-Bailey 1985). The higher-class origin of these refugees has been well documented. This initial exodus overrepresented the professional, managerial, and middle classes, 31 percent, as well as the clerical and sales workers, 33 percent. Likewise, the educational level of the refugees was remarkably high (Fagen et al. 1968: table 7.1).

Casal (1979) observed that although the "highly belligerent" counter-revolutionary movements of the first two phases never actively engaged all exiles, they did draw on the financial or moral support of most exiles who hoped for Castro's overthrow with U.S. help and for their own return to Cuba. Unable to reach their goal, the Cuban communities became disenchanted with such activities and withdrew their support. As Kunz (1973:133) specified, when refugees realize "that the doors are closed behind" them, they begin to take the steps that change them from temporary refugees into exiles.

In Cuba, this period also entailed the creation of the Partido Unido de la Revolución Socialista (United Party of the Socialist Revolution) in March 1962.[1] From there on, as Amaro pointed out, the Cuban revolution underwent an essential change in its nature: "Emphasis was placed upon the enemy within, either due to the difficulties brought about by the shift from a capitalist to a socialist system, by excessive bureaucratization or by inefficiency in the area of production. All criticism had to be made within the revolution and never outside of it; otherwise, criticism was considered a 'counterrevolutionary' activity" (1981:59).

---

[1] In his article, Amaro (1981) dates the end of this stage as December 1, 1961, with Castro's speech or early in 1962, with the creation of the new revolutionary institutions for the masses. In my view, it is more accurate to date it as October 1962. The Missile Crisis closed the door to the massive exodus and to the exiles' bellicose struggle against the Cuban government. I have adjusted this last stage to end with the Cuban Missile Crisis in October 1962.

The Cuban Missile Crisis

Few who lived through them can forget the 13 days of the Cuban Missile Crisis in October 1962. A U-2 plane routinely photographing Cuba on October 14 had discovered that there were nuclear missiles standing, pointed at the United States. Previously, the U.S. perception held that the Soviets were supplying Cuba with defensive weapons. After this discovery, the United States realized Cuba had become an offensive military base, a situation it could not accept (Heath 1975:126–29). Thus, Kennedy presented it to the American public, on a television broadcast on Monday, October 22. This led to an eye-to-eye confrontation in which, as Secretary General Dean Rusk expressed it, "they blinked first" (Heath 1975:130). Over the next 13 days, the crisis peaked and then slowly subsided, as the first Soviet vessels to reach the U.S. blockade turned back and the Soviet Union responded to the United Nation's Secretary-General U Thant's letter calling for peace. On Sunday, October 28, Khrushchev broadcast his conciliatory reply to Kennedy's message publicly, declaring he gave a new order for the missiles to be dismantled and returned to the Soviet Union.

To most Americans, Kennedy emerged as a hero who managed to contain the threat via the imposition of a naval blockade of Cuba, which impeded further supplies from entering the island. Kennedy's policy choice of a blockade fell short of the military invasion the Joint Chiefs of Staff were proposing and proved effective (Robert Kennedy 1971). To Kennedy himself, the missile crisis was Khrushchev's test of America's will, as the missiles had changed the balance of power (Heath 1975:132). Still, to others Kennedy also brought the United States and the world dangerously close to a nuclear war. With both short- and medium-range missiles pointed at the United States, Miami was certain to disappear. Estela Rasco taught school in Miami, in St. Peter and Paul Elementary School, in the section for Cuban children who arrived without knowing English. She remembered how all the children who came to school bore two items: dog tags with their name and address, and a sheet for others to wrap their dead bodies in, should it prove necessary. She felt heartbroken when the children asked her, "Why do I have to wear this when I know my name and address?"

The missiles were dismantled under United Nations supervision, and the Soviet bombs were crated and returned to the Soviet Union. In exchange, the United States agreed to remove its missiles from Turkey and Italy. Khrushchev and Kennedy reached "a *quid pro quo* over Cuba," as Jim Heath explained it. "Kennedy promised not to invade the island, in return for the Russians' removing their missiles. Washington thus accepted the Castro regime, at least for the immediate future, as part of the prevailing balance of power" (1975:296). For many Cubans in exile, the Missile Crisis was the second defeat (Ros 1995).

The October Missile Crisis was a turning point for many. In the beginning of 1962, Augusto Vidaurreta joined a spy ring the opposition had created in Cuba. Although Augusto did not know it, it was part of the CIA. "After the fall of Girón," he said, "it was no longer just a struggle among Cubans but Castro's struggle against the United States," so he allied himself with the United States. He began to gather information – for example, regarding the military reinforcements along the coast, the state of the airport, and the introduction of missiles to Cuba. His daughter, Esther María, a young girl, remembered seeing him wearing gloves to read the messages he received, letters written in invisible ink that became visible when ironed. However, after the October Missile Crisis and the agreement reached between Kennedy and Khrushchev, Augusto felt nothing more could be done, as a long period of coexistence would ensue. He burned all the information he still had and ceased conspiring.

A couple of years later, he learned for the first time he had worked for the CIA. A good friend from the Lions Club, who was similarly involved, introduced him to a tall man who was a CIA agent. The tall agent asked Augusto to work for them again. Augusto declined, feeling that making a useless sacrifice was stupid. The agent threatened to kill him, but Augusto still refused and left. Immediately, agents of the Seguridad del Estado intercepted him on the road. Their interrogation led him to realize they knew everything that had just happened and the tall CIA agent was, in fact, a double agent, working for the Cuban government. Seguridad del Estado also tried to persuade Augusto to join them, to become a double agent. "Leonardo," they confronted him, "Fin, fin, fin" – his name and the phrase he ended all his reports with. He still refused, stressing his activities had ceased; and that their cause could never be his. His refusal saved his life, for his friend was executed. A few months later, he was imprisoned.

Nearly four years after the triumph of the revolution, the old civil society, independent of government, was destroyed. New organizations were created that linked the people with the government, representing them, but the people in them lacked independence from the government and the ability to check the power of the state. Politics was shaped into a single vanguard party. The masses of the people were mobilized behind the charisma of the maximum leader, Fidel Castro. No independent institutions existed that could limit his absolute power. The Marxist-Leninist ideology became the future basis of Cuban society. The influence of the United States was effectively counterbalanced. As a result, the republic so many fought to restore was completely vanquished.

5

The Revolution Consolidated

Si un niño quiere que tú le cuentes
lo que es la vida de un prisionero:
¡Canta una copla,
inventa un juego...!
Pero no digas a un pequeñuelo
lo que es la vida
de un prisionero.

If a young child should ask you
to tell him
what the life of a prisoner is like:
Sing him a song,
make up a game...!
But do not tell
a youngster
what the life of a prisoner
is like.

> Ernesto Díaz,
> *La Campana del Alba* (1984)

Consolidating the Revolution Within

The revolution effected radical social and economic changes that benefited *el pueblo*, but these went hand in hand with increasing social control over people's lives. The Bay of Pigs failure consolidated the revolution against its external enemies – the United States and the exiles. Wrestling power away from the old communists, as well as Che Guevara, discrediting the counterrevolution, and imprisoning those who challenged it consolidated the revolution against its internal enemies. Once consolidated, some exiles accepted the revolution, pragmatically; others grew to believe in it, with fervor. As some exiles began building bridges to Cuba, a wave of exile violence swept through its communities. To illustrate these events, I rely on interviews with Hilda Felipe, Víctor Mozo, Julio and Myriam Rodríguez, José Tenreiro, Luis Zúñiga, Andrés Vargas-Gómez, Jorge Valls, Seferina ("Fefé") Fernández-Yarzábal and Marcelino Heres, "Richard" (José) Heredia, Martha Oliva, Luis González-Infante, Augusto Vidaurreta, Lorenzo Dueñas, Yolanda Prieto, Eloísa García (pseudonym), Alberto de la Cerra, Jorge Duany, Flavio Risech, Bernardo Benes, and Miguel González-Pando.

Old versus New Communists

After civil society collapsed, the Communist Party became the sole source of power. However, a struggle developed between the old communists (e.g., Joaquín Ordoqui, Lázaro Peña, Aníbal Escalante) and the new communists (e.g., Fidel Castro, Raúl Castro, Alfredo Guevara). The Soviet Union backed the old guard, especially Aníbal Escalante, against Castro. As Domínguez (1978a:210) pointed out, of the organizations that made the revolution, only the old communists were well organized; thus, most of the power of the Integrated Revolutionary Organizations fell to them. As secretary, Aníbal Escalante was in charge of recruitment, promotion, and firing. A Communist Party member almost from its founding in 1925, he believed in the communist principle that the party politicized and educated through its cells, and Escalante gave preference to his old communist comrades, challenging Castro's authority; thus, he was ousted. On March 27, 1962, Fidel Castro appeared on television and radio, denouncing those who were plotting against him, who wanted to impose "a yoke, a straightjacket, so as to have an army of domesticated revolutionaries." The fall of Aníbal Escalante was the beginning of a complete restructuring of the Cuban party, as massive numbers of party members were also expelled. By 1965 the old communists' share of the Central Committee of the party had fallen from 40 to 23 percent. The road to power in Cuba then ran through close association with the Castro brothers and participation in the military (Domínguez 1978a:211, 310–15).

The Cuban Communist Party was again shaken by internal division in 1968. Led by Escalante, a "microfaction," as it was called, held discussions regarding Cuba's serious political and economic problems and the deterioration of Soviet-Cuban relations (Enzensberger 1974). As a result, 43 persons were arrested, 9 were expelled from the party and imprisoned, 26 others were imprisoned, and 2 were forced to resign from the Central Committee of the party (Domínguez 1978a:162; "Microfaction Unmasked" 1968).

Of the 43 persons arrested, one was a woman, Hilda Felipe. Hilda was sent to prison along with her husband, Arnaldo Escalona, an old-guard communist who was among the nine expelled from the party. She was imprisoned for 13 months and suffered domiciliary arrest for four years; her husband was imprisoned for six years, charged with "ideological diversionism" and with being a CIA agent. "Our crime was to think," Hilda stressed. Much older than Hilda, Escalona had been with the party since its beginning. A lawyer and journalist, he was editor of *Hoy*, the Communist Party's newspaper, and also a professor at the University of Havana, where he taught philosophy, Marxism, and economics.

A small woman who was very fair, Hilda came from a family that became poor through divorce. Thus, from an early age she worked in a textile mill and was involved in the labor struggles of the *sindicatos*. Although her father had come from the Canary Islands in the 1920s, her mother's family had been *mambíses* during the Cuban war of independence and struggled against Machado. She was also influenced by the Spanish Civil War because her father came from a Republican family that defended the democratic tradition. A member of the Communist Party Youth, she and her husband shared ideals and struggles.

A lawyer, Escalona defended many who helped the revolutionary struggle against Batista and was also the legal counsel for the Cuban Workers' Confederation. Along with other women (Marta Frayde, Natalia Bolívar, and Aurelina Restano), Hilda founded the Comité de Mujeres Oposicionistas Unidas, which united around 40 women in the opposition to Batista, and then the Comité de Ayuda al Preso Político, which helped those who suffered political imprisonment under Batista.

Hilda remembered Escalona as an idealistic man who never abandoned his principles. Escalona frequently disagreed with Fidel. He was opposed to Cuba's exporting revolution, because the country needed to follow its own revolutionary path; he was against Fidel's massive mobilization of Cubans to cut sugarcane, because he predicted it could not be achieved; he was against the constant sacrifices "the new man" was asked to make, because only a small vanguard could make them; and he was against the power of the Ministry of the Interior because it meant the police ran the country. At a meeting of the Central Committee of the party in January 1968, Escalona expressed his lack of confidence in the leadership: "Look. Tell them – the Soviets – that the main leaders of the revolution and this party do not have a communist background . . . their orientation is simply nationalist, reflects a chauvinist class tendency . . . " ("Microfaction Unmasked" 1968). Although he was a committed communist, such thinking made him a dissident. Even the experience of prison did not take away his idealistic belief in communism, however. "He died a Marxist," his widow stressed. "He thought communism was a more just society than capitalism; however, it needed to go hand in hand with democracy, which is what it lacks."

After prison, both Hilda and Escalona founded the Comité Cubano Pro Derechos Humanos (the Cuban Committee for Human Rights), which included Ricardo Bofill and Eddie López-Castillo (who were purged during the microfaction), Elizardo Sánchez-Santa Cruz, and Gustavo Arcos-Bergnes, its sole representative in Cuba until his recent death. After their children left Cuba in 1980, through the Mariel exodus, Escalona and Hilda felt forced to leave, to join them. "We would never have left the island otherwise." In Miami, no one ever offered Escalona a job, nor was he able to teach, despite his vast knowledge and experience. "It should put all Cubans to shame," Hilda stated. She became a seamstress. In Miami, no one could forget she had been a communist. When City Commissioner Tomás Regalado called her to be his assistant in 1996, the newspaper's headlines read: "Tomás Regalado has chosen the communist Hilda Felipe." Still, she continued her work for human rights in Cuba.

Che Guevara

Che Guevara exerted a major influence on the revolution, seeking to channel it in particular directions. The major ideology became the creation of "the new man," along with an emphasis on rapid industrialization, at the expense of agriculture, and a commitment to proletarian internationalism. An Argentine doctor (hence, the affectionate nickname of *el Che*), he was given charge of agrarian reform at the INRA, the Instituto Nacional de Reforma Agraria (National Institute for Agrarian Reform) after the triumph of the revolution. The large landowners were expropriated, and their land was distributed in small plots to thousands of families. As president of the National Bank also, he signed the bills that read "Patria o Muerte" (Fatherland or Freedom) with a rapid *Che*. Together, Fidel and Che nationalized all the American companies and the large Cuban-owned enterprises, toppling down the industrial, capitalist, and landed infrastructure of the economy.

When Castro appointed Che as minister of industry, Guevara's plan was to change the attitudes of the Cuban people, creating *el hombre nuevo* – the new man (Guevara 1970). Under communism, work would mean the fulfillment of a social duty. Work was often voluntary labor, rewarded not materially but by moral incentives (e.g., inclusion in the vanguard workers). Always a romantic theoretician, Guevara famously said: "Let me say, at the risk of seeming ridiculous, that the true revolutionary is guided by great feelings of love."

As a result of the new policies, the economy plummeted, particularly the sugar industry. Thus, the sugar sector was withdrawn from Che's ministry and Fidel Castro resumed Cuba's emphasis on sugar and agriculture (Domínguez 1978a:383–91). But it was his criticism of the Soviet Union, which was keeping Cuba afloat through a generous subsidy and thousands of specialized technicians, that most likely caused him to be sent outside of Cuba, to foment revolution elsewhere (Dugowson and Kaflon 1997). With his influence over Cuba's internal affairs declining, Che became a roving ambassador, railing against Western imperialism and against the socialist countries as accomplices of imperialist exploitation.

Cubans were perplexed by the disappearance of *el Che* from Cuba. In October 1965, while Che was in the Congo, Fidel publicly read Che's farewell letter, which he wanted read only after his death. In the letter, Che made explicit that he resigned from all his posts, so that nothing tied him to Cuba any longer. As a soldier, he noted, other lands claimed his modest efforts. When Fidel read the letter, Che responded: "I have nothing more to seek in Cuba – it is no longer my Cuba!" (Dugowson and Kaflon 1997).

Che turned his revolutionary fervor first to the Congo and then to Bolivia, from where he hoped to spread the revolutionary fire to all of Latin America. By the fall of 1967, he was in the rough terrain of the Bolivian *altiplano*, wounded, asthmatic, and isolated. He suffered both from the loss of his men in combat and the Bolivian peasants' lack of interest (see Guevara 1968). There, Che Guevara met his end at the hands of the Bolivian army (Alarcón-Ramírez 2003; Dugowson and Kaflon 1997). Before he died, Che met Felix Rodríguez face to face – a Cuban exile sent by the CIA to help capture him (Rodríguez 1989). Today, Felix Rodríguez is the president of the Association of Bay of Pigs Veterans.

Although it is quite possible that Castro sent Che to a certain death, in Cuba *el Che* today remains a symbol of revolutionary fervor, as posters and murals quote him and declare that "Tus ideas perduran" – his ideas remain. As an icon, more than a man, he continues to inspire revolutionaries everywhere (cf. Kunzle 1997).

Although Cuba's foreign policy failed in Latin America, it was a success in Africa. From the mid-1970s on, Africa became the main theater of operations, particularly Angola and Ethiopia, to which Cuba supplied a military aid program involving not only troops but also educational services. After the Angolan war, Cuba began to stress that it was an Afro-Spanish country. However, to Carlos Moore, a black Cuban in exile, this "Afrocastroism" was politically motivated. Victory in Africa – the weakest link in the chain of world imperialism, Fidel Castro called it – would decide who would rule the world: capitalism or communism (1988: 323). Nonetheless, Cuba's assistance with the decisive victory in Angola strengthened its position with African countries (Del Pino 1991; LeoGrande 1980; Domínguez 1978b).

The Second Wave: The Petite Bourgeoisie

The second major exodus from Cuba began in the fall of 1965. A chaotic period ensued when hundreds of boats left from Miami for the Cuban port of Camarioca, where they picked up thousands of relatives to come to the United States (see Figure 5.1). "Those who search" characterized this next major wave of the Cuban migration. It was organized in response to President Lyndon Johnson's "open door" policy that welcomed refugees from communism. In October 1965, at the Statue of Liberty in New York, President Johnson (1965) announced he would open the nation's gates to all Cubans, so that "those who seek refuge here will find it. The dedication of America to our traditions as an asylum for the oppressed will be upheld." On that very day, he signed the bill that constituted a major overhaul of the nation's immigration policy (Semple 1965). Following this change in policy, for eight years, the United States and Cuban governments administered an orderly air bridge as the Vuelos de la Libertad, or Freedom Flights, brought Cubans from Varadero to Miami. Around 3,000 to 4,000 refugees arrived every month. The Cuban Refugee Program swiftly processed them, dispersing them throughout the United States.

Kunz (1973) distinguished anticipatory refugee movements from acute ones. The joint policy of the United States and Cuban governments turned this acute exodus into an orderly anticipatory refugee movement. The U.S. and Cuban governments have often "cooperated with the enemy," as Domínguez (1991) stressed. Pablo Alfonso (2005a) emphasized that the

Figure 5.1 The second wave of the exodus (1965–74) was sent out by the flotilla exodus from the port of Camarioca. Here are two women who just arrived in Florida from Cuba on a boat, looking distraught. The one in front holds both a child and a doll. (*Miami Herald*)

Camarioca exodus 40 years ago was the first time Fidel Castro used the massive exodus of Cubans as a weapon in his conflict with the United States, turning his internal problems into an American domestic crisis. When the refugee airlift closed in 1974, more than 3,000 flights had brought 260,000 persons. The 1990 census showed that 43 percent of Cuban immigrants after the revolution came during the years of the air bridge (see Table 1.1).

Throughout this period, a Memorandum of Understanding regulated the immigrants' departure, giving priority to the immediate family of exiles already living in the United States (Thomas 1967). Both countries compiled their master lists; jointly, both governments decided who would emigrate, and the migration proceeded through family networks. Cuba barred from exit young men of military service age (15 to 26), as well as professionals and technical and skilled workers whose exit would cause a serious disturbance in production or delivering social services, such as doctors (Clark 1992). Women thus predominated in this wave, making up 58 percent (see Table 1.2), as did young students, and the elderly.

With this phase, the exodus of the upper and upper-middle classes came to an end. This wave of immigration was largely working class and petite bourgeoisie: employees, independent craftsmen, small merchants, skilled and semiskilled workers. Amaro and Portes judged (1972:13) that over time the political exile increasingly became an economic exile as "those who search" sought greater economic opportunities than were provided in a socialist society that instituted a new ethic of sacrificing individual consumption to achieve collective goals.

The years of the second wave of emigration were some of the leanest and most idealistic of the Cuban revolution. To spread access to a basic education and health care, young, educated Cubans went to live in the countryside, working in the Literacy Campaign to educate the illiterate peasants and in public health campaigns to provide basic health care. The impact of the hemispheric trade embargo imposed by the Organization of American States in 1964 resulted in a spare-parts crisis and other economic dislocations (Schreiber 1973); the exodus drained technical and administrative skills; and Cuba failed in its attempts to industrialize and diversify.

The social transformations the Cuban revolution effected were so pervasive that they always "pushed" Cubans. America, in facilitating the migration, always "pulled" them. As both the United States and the Cuban governments facilitated the exodus, together they set in motion a system of political migration that for many years proved beneficial to both. The loss of the educated, professional middle classes indeed proved erosive to the revolution, but it also served the positive function of externalizing dissent. At the same time, in the United States the arrival of so many refugees who "voted with their feet" also served to provide the legitimacy necessary for foreign policy actions during the tense years of the Cold War. From the Cold War issued a period of real war in Vietnam. Détente followed for some years, until the 1980s opened with a resurgence of the Cold War. My content analysis of the statements of public officials revealed that, during the peak years of the Cold War, the multitude of political refugees from communist societies served as touching symbols around which to build the legitimacy necessary for foreign policy actions (Pedraza-Bailey 1985). The U.S. Congress, recognizing the need to give over a quarter of a million Cuban refugees already in the United States a legal status, in November 1966 approved the Cuban Adjustment Act, which allowed Cubans who entered the United States legally to adjust their status to permanent residents one year and one day after arrival.

The Cuban community in the United States became increasingly heterogeneous, varying widely in social class. When the migration began in the 1960s, 31 percent of those arriving were professionals or managers; by 1970, they constituted only 12 percent. More than half the arrivals were blue-collar, service, or agricultural workers (Aguirre 1976: table 2). After the air bridge ended came those who first lived in Spain, who represented Cuba's "middling service sectors": cooks, gardeners, domestics, barbers, taxi drivers, retail merchants (Portes et al. 1977). They left Cuba when Castro launched a new "revolutionary offensive," confiscating more than 55,000 small businesses that were still privately owned (Mesa-Lago 1978), "pushing" out the little entrepreneur. The Cuban government labeled them *parásitos* (parasites).

The Counterrevolution

While life in Cuba grew harsh for all, it turned particularly bitter for those who declared their intention to leave. They lost their jobs, became unemployable, and were ostracized as enemies. Their belongings were "inventoried" and were confiscated when they left, as houses, clothing, cars, housewares, clothes all became the property of the state, to the benefit of the local CDRs. Some men were even sent to the Unidades Militares de Ayuda a la Producción or UMAP (Military Units to Aid Production) (cf. Ros 2004). Norberto Fuentes (1999), a writer who for many years was quite close to Fidel and Raúl, noted that most of the 30,000 to 40,000 young men who were sent to these camps were Catholic seminarians and Protestant ministers, many of them Jehovah's Witnesses; young men who wanted to leave Cuba; persons who practiced self-employment; university students expelled from the university for ideological incompatibility; and peasants who refused to join the cooperatives. The government spread a rumor that these camps were for homosexuals, so as to exploit Cubans' homophobic attitudes. For months, the men were separated from their families, with only an occasional visit.

Among the young men who were sent to the UMAP was Víctor Mozo, only 16 years old, after two and a half years in the seminary San Basilio Magno in el Cobre, Oriente. Ironically, it happened just at the point when he began to ask himself whether his vocation to become a priest was true. His friendships with other young people in the Cathedral were some of the happiest moments in his adolescence. Moreover, affirming his belief in God was affirming his self, as it ran deep. But the vow of chastity was impossible for him, ever more attracted to the opposite sex. Hence, he left the seminary and went to work with his father in the cafeteria he still owned, with a partner. The draft citation arrived for him to leave for the military late in June 1966. Young as he was, he was glad it gave him a chance to first enjoy the carnival's revelry, thinking he was being drafted for the obligatory military service. But it was the UMAP instead, where there were hundreds of men, 16 to 50 years old, of every color and race, about to be rehabilitated through forced labor – an idea that came from the Soviet Union. Over the next two years, he spent time in several camps: "Mexico," "Jaronú," "Kilo 7," and the sugar mill "Stewart." The work in these camps varied: from forced labor in agriculture, to making the rounds of the camp with loaded guns, to gardening, to heavy construction work in the sugar mill. Water, soap, and food were scarce; the 12-hour workdays under the hot sun were extremely long; and more often than not, they were treated with contempt by the guards working for the MININT. Fortunately, occasionally a decent person made the load lighter, as was the case with the man who distributed the letters from their families at "Mexico." Even then, the arbitrary misuse of power was evident, as Jehovah's Witnesses never received any letters. By the time he got to "Jaronú," they could not even be found – they were all in prison. With the goal to rehabilitate them, political instructors arrived to read to the men from the classic political texts. One of them could barely read, having been recently taught during the Literacy Campaign. Rather than have him read haltingly, Mozo offered to do the reading for him.

With ingenuity, Mozo managed to get a medical leave for a couple of days from the camp on a few occasions. Once, during a religious holiday, he even sang with the choir at the Cathedral in Camagüey! He also managed to steal some brief romantic moments with a young *guajirita* who looked after him, bringing him some food. Because the work hours were long, they did their best not to work too hard – the only way they could combat the system. At the sugar mill, they were surrounded by "vanguard workers," who saw them as the scum of the society, to whom the revolution had done a favor, giving them the opportunity to become rehabilitated. His parents could visit him, but only for a couple of hours. When they finally let him go free, they handed him a document with the four letters UMAP printed extremely large, so that no one could ever miss he had been there – a permanent stain in his work file.

Finally able to leave Cuba in 1983 – 17 years after his induction – he set-tled in Montreal, Canada, together with his French Canadian wife, Danièle Cardin. He now translates French-language films to Spanish, which are then distributed to Spain and all of Latin America. He still has occasional nightmares about his time in the UMAP. Although he is quite satisfied with the life he has built in Canada, he feels the years in the UMAP robbed him of his youth, his adolescence. He cannot forget his parents' suffering.

The counterrevolution continued to exist within, as young men went up into the Escambray Mountains to fight the government's forces with their *machetes* (cf. Encinosa 2004). The government discredited them by telling the people in the surrounding areas they were *bandidos* (bandits). Among them was Israel Rodríguez, Julio Rodríguez's brother, who had been in Batista's army. Occasionally, Israel came down from the mountains to see his family. He was captured by the police in his grandmother's home. Taken to La Cabaña prison and tried along with three others, he was accused of being a CIA spy who brought arms and documents from the United States for the counterrevolution. The defense lawyer pointed out that the evidence for these charges was never presented. Israel denied being a CIA agent but stressed he was not afraid to die. The four men rose and, as they were taken away, Israel turned to his brother Julio, his family, and friends and waved good-bye to them. "We were not allowed to touch one another, to give a last embrace," said Julio. Israel was executed that very evening.

After this, Julio only wanted to leave Cuba, as he did in 1969, together with his wife, Myriam, and their daughters, through one of the Vuelos de la Libertad. First, however, he had to work in a *granja*, a farm called El Encanto, for two years, seven days a week for seven pesos. The men cut sugarcane, gathered potatoes, and dug out yams; at night they slept on the floor or in hammocks. Sometimes, he ate beans that had *gorgojos*, weevils, growing in them. When the time to leave finally came, Myriam could gather only three changes of clothing.

Exile Violence

With the economic transition to socialism effected, in the 1970s the Cuban government cast the shape of the political system: the new Cuban

Communist Party held its first congress; a new constitution was declared; and Fidel Castro became president. The old idealism and romanticism of the 1960s gave way to pragmatism (Mesa-Lago 1978). The failure of the 1970 mobilization of all Cubans to make the national goal of cutting 10 million tons of sugar led to this new phase. Cuba reintroduced material incentives and wage differentials; mass organizations, such as the Poder Popular (Organs of People's Power), took form. With this institutionalization, Cuba took on the features of Eastern European communism (cf. Roca 1981). With the revolution consolidated, externally and internally, for the vast majority of Cubans in the United States the issue throughout these years continued to be life in America. Yet the cultural impact on the young who lived face to face with the social movements of the 1960s in America gave birth to a denser ideological pluralism than ever before (Casal 1979). At a time when the sympathy toward Cuba peaked among Americans, some exiles tended bridges to Cuba because they felt Cuba was there to stay; others went further and developed an identity with the revolution they openly supported. Both gave rise to substantial exile violence. One source of the violence was paramilitary groups, such as the Omega 7 commandos, who sought to put an end to the bridges to Cuba by intimidating those who promoted them with bomb scares and death threats. Sometimes, the violence went further, putting an end to their lives. Omega 7 advocated: "Violence against violence; violence against hypocrisy; violence for dignity and liberty." They also made it clear they would not answer for the lives of traitors and *vendepatrias*, an insult designating those who, literally, "sell their nation."

Tragedy resulted. In Miami, Emilio Milián was a radio newscaster who in April 1976 had both his legs blown off by dynamite when he turned on his car. He was broadcasting editorials condemning exile terrorism and advocating tolerance, even after receiving death threats. Another victim of the violence was Orlando Letelier, former Chilean ambassador to the United States under Salvador Allende's government, assassinated in Washington, D.C., in September 1976. Chilean secret police, agents from DINA (Dirección Nacional de Inteligencia), were convicted for the murder. As they confessed they had hired several anti-Castro Cuban exiles to booby-trap Letelier's car, some exiles were sentenced to prison. Two weeks after Letelier's murder, the Cubana airlines bombing took place, as the plane was in midair, killing 73 people. Though no one ever claimed responsibility for it, the Cuban government repeatedly blamed Orlando Bosch and Luis Posada-Carriles, CIA operatives. Posada-Carriles tried to kill Fidel Castro on several occasions. Once, his jaw was broken by a bullet.

José Tenreiro served three years in prison, for his supposed participation in terrorist acts. In Cuba, in his early 30s, he had worked with the *sindicatos*, especially the one representing cafeteria and soda fountain workers. He rose quite far in the Cuban Workers' Confederation. Like organized labor under Mujal, he supported Batista initially, believing he would be a good president, but the Batista who arrived the second time around, with the coup, was "a poor bargain for the working class." Tenreiro also participated in the Unión Nacional Obrera, the national labor association that sought to depose Batista.

In exile, Tenreiro joined groups that were involved in subversive actions, trying to infiltrate Cuba to support the resistance against Castro. In 1963 a failed action landed him in jail in Tampa. "After the Missile Crisis the Americans were totally against the Cuban exiles," he stressed, "whose efforts they impeded, rather than helped" (cf. Cuesta 1988). In the mid-1960s, he joined the Movimiento Nacionalista, a paramilitary group that fought for Cuba's liberation, and a few years later he moved to Elizabeth, New Jersey, where he continued working with the group. The movement had strength, organization, enthusiasm. It was guided by the conviction that "against a reign of terror, such as exists in Cuba, where they execute people, only armed struggle can succeed." The movement ended when the brothers Guillermo and Ignacio Novo were sentenced as responsible for the death of Orlando Letelier. The Movimiento Nacionalista fought for them to be free; when the Novos were freed, they put an end to the movement. In 1980, Tenreiro was sentenced to prison, accused of terrorist acts in New Jersey and Miami. He was suspected of involvement in the death of Eulalio José Negrín, director of the Cuban Refugee Program in Weehawken, New Jersey, who had been his friend for many years but "had changed his destiny" after he went to Cuba and "began to openly support the regime." Omega 7 claimed responsibility for the execution-type murder (Torres 1980). Tenreiro insisted on his innocence.

Who really was responsible for the wave of terrorism that coursed through the Cuban communities in Miami, New Jersey, and Puerto Rico in the 1970s may never be known, but it is certain that the many arrests involved led to the demise of groups such as Omega 7 and the Movimiento Nacionalista. Moreover, the rise of the Cuban American National Foundation at the start of the 1980s also shifted the political strategy. Most exiles, Tenreiro among them, supported it and placed their hope in it. One of the directors of the original Fundación, Luis Zúñiga, noted the goal became to build an institution financed by the economic success of the exiles to lobby the U.S. Congress regarding policies toward Cuba. Though many saw the CANF as frankly proannexation in intent, la Fundación also worked for human rights in Cuba and helped bring Cubans spread all over the globe to the United States through the Program Exodus.

Political Prisoners

In authoritarian and totalitarian societies, both right and left, only two alternatives exist for effectively dealing with the dissent they inevitably generate: emigration and imprisonment. Over the course of nearly half a century, Cuba exercised both. Altogether, I interviewed 20 Cubans who were political prisoners. I soon learned that a significant proportion of the exile leadership, both hard-liners and moderates, came from those who were former political prisoners. Of the 20 interviews, 11 were with Cubans who were part of *el presidio politico histórico* – the historical prisoners jailed in the revolution's early years. They had participated in actions the government deemed to be "against the powers of the state," such as conspiracy, insurrection, sabotage, assaults. These were part of *la lucha*, the struggle against Castro's communism, for the restoration of democracy to Cuba. Because a human rights–monitoring group was not allowed in Cuba, America's Watch could not write its country report. Instead, it sponsored the publication of Jorge Valls's (1986) prison memoirs, *Twenty Years and Forty Days: Life in a Cuban Prison*, which I also use to describe the prison conditions. The other nine interviews were with younger Cubans who struggled for the same democratic principles but in nonviolent ways, when the dissident movement began to emerge in Cuba in the late 1980s.

Imprisonment

Andrés Vargas-Gómez spent 21 years in prison. The grandson of Máximo Gómez, a major leader of the 19th-century movement for independence, he was middle-aged when the revolution triumphed. Politically active in his youth, he was part of *la generación del '30*, the revolution of the 1930s against Machado's dictatorship. As a student, he joined the original Directorio Estudiantil, which earned him his first prison sentence at 16. He was part of the *ala izquierda*, the leftist wing of the students (cf. Ros 2005). Though they were not communists, he explained, they were anti-imperialists, and they struggled side by side with the workers for the development of social reforms, such as minimum wage and the eight-hour working day.

It was only natural for him to struggle against Batista, as part of the Montecristi Movement led by Justo Carrillo, a group of professionals who wanted to restore democracy. Proud to be Máximo Gómez's grandson, he explained his nationalism was due to the *tradición mambisa*, the tradition of independence, behind him – a tradition both our families shared.

Vargas-Gómez was imprisoned when he returned to Cuba as a member of the Frente Revolucionario Democrático to support the Bay of Pigs invasion. For the FRD, he initiated a radio news program, urging Cubans to rebel. He arrived in Cuba before the invasion, on a special mission to deliver a cargo of arms. Like everyone who was part of the underground resistance, he waited for the order to join the combat, but it never came. He went into an embassy and spent a year there. He thought some of the people who were supposedly helping him had informed against him, resulting in his imprisonment. After serving a 21-year sentence, he came to the United States as part of Operation Jesse Jackson, along with some 20 other political prisoners. Upon arrival, Jackson asked him to be the one to speak. In his speech, Vargas-Gómez expressed their gratitude to Jesse Jackson, but underscored that Fidel Castro wanted the world to see this as a humanitarian gesture, when "in truth, he was a terrible tyrant." In exile, he continued the struggle for a democratic Cuba in several ways: with Tony Varona's Junta Patriótica Cubana, and then with Unidad Cubana, the large umbrella organization that united thousands of exiles who identified with the hard-line position and that elected him president.

Jorge Valls was imprisoned for his participation in the trial of his best friend, Marcos Rodríguez, with whom he shared revolutionary activities. In 1964 Marcos was accused of betraying to Batista's police the four students who were conspiring against Batista's government in the apartment at Humboldt # 7. Batista's police stormed the apartment, killing all four members of the Directorio who were inside (del Cueto 1959). The new revolutionary government tried Marcos as the informant responsible for their deaths. Valls remembered Marcos when he appeared in public: "he was like a piece of rawhide, unable to stand by himself or hold up his head." Valls believed he was innocent, though many of their friends did not, and he assembled evidence to prove it. Marcos's trial "was a mockery of justice" (Valls 1986:5). Valls was forcibly taken to Fidel Castro's apartment, where he was interrogated. The following day, Valls testified for the defense. As a last resort, he went to see then President Osvaldo Dorticós, who made it clear that they were interested only in the political implications of the trial. Marcos was shot on April 25, 1964; on May 8, Valls was arrested.

Felo Fernández-Yarzábal lived in Sagua La Grande, part of a well-to-do family that owned the largest department store in the city, La Villa de París. Friend and collaborator of Justo Carrillo and Rufo López-Fresquet, who were part of the Provisional Government, Felo joined Rufo in the administration of the Ministerio de Hacienda, the Treasury. When he realized the revolution was communist, he resigned and joined the struggle against Castro's communism. His sister Fefé remembered he was imprisoned several times. He often told his friends: "Castro's populism will lead us toward tyranny; this needs to be avoided in time" (Otazo 1976). Felo left Cuba in 1961, together with his brother-in-law Marcelino Heres, the owner of a store in the "Santa Ludgarda" sugar mill. Soon he returned to Cuba and was imprisoned again.

José Heredia was known to all his friends as "Richard" because that was the name he used in the underground struggle against Batista, of which he was a major leader. At the university, he was secretary-general of the FEU in the School of Engineering. His friends looked up to him and described him as a mulatto who was *sesudo*, meaning brainy, and *culto*, with a broad culture. The goal of the student movement was to restore the Constitution and the electoral process Batista had broken, Heredia stressed. In 1952, in a symbolic protest, the students stressed the illegitimacy of Batista's government by holding a wake, marching around the Constitution with lighted torches. They intended to restore it when the revolution triumphed.

"Richard" was the national leader of the 26th of July Movement's student wing and was in the rebel army. He also organized the workers for the general strike on January 1. When the revolution triumphed, Heredia was made the commissioner for the province of Oriente, a position that issued from the new juridical structure put in place then. "That showed there was no intention to restore the Constitution," according to Heredia, so he left the rebel army. Raúl Castro, leader of the Segundo Frente Oriental Frank País, in which "Richard" fought, offered him an important position in the army, but he declined. He returned to the city to create new "revolutionary cells" of those who cared about the restoration of the Constitution because, under Fidel's dominion, the 26th of July Movement had become "nothing but a shell."

Heredia also went back to the University of Havana to try to keep the student movement from being controlled by the communists. However, his efforts for election to the leadership of the FEU in the University failed. Rolando Cubelas – backed by the Castro brothers – was supposed to run against Pedro Luis Boitel – the choice of the students who were not

130

communists. But on October 20, 1959, Fidel wrote to the major newspapers requesting that no elections be held; rather, he insisted that the president of the FEU be chosen by popular acclaim, designating Cubelas as the new university leader.

Heredia organized the prodemocracy forces into a new 30 de Noviembre Movement, composed of workers, students, peasants, and military who wanted to impede the consolidation of communism. "Richard" recalled how, in effect, 28 labor leaders gave up their positions, protesting the communist direction in which the labor movement was headed, but those positions were then filled with communists. He was imprisoned in December 1960, due to a friend's treason. To discredit him, they dressed him in Batista's military uniform and accused him of "terrorism." He was certain that, during his prison years, the government had kept his case in "low profile" because he had been "in the rebel army, in the 26th of July movement, and he was also black."

Martha Oliva was falsely accused of working for the CIA. As a student in the University of Havana, she was a strong supporter of Pedro Luis Boitel, so her opposition was known. Moreover, she refused to join any of the newly formed government organizations, such as the Federación de Mujeres Cubanas (National Association of Cuban Women). Though she was expelled from the university due to the political problems in the FEU, she remained in Cuba for many years because she worked as a certified public accountant and an auditor.

Martha went to work for the Ministerio de Salud as a key administrator for the hospitals and polyclinics, nationwide. She also helped many doctors and nurses with their permission to leave Cuba, because first they had to be replaced in the hospital. After this, she went to work at the Calixto García Hospital, as director of the Department of Information, Statistics, and Clinical Archives. Her marriage collapsed due to her husband's belief in the revolution – "He saw through Fidel's eyes," she said. She decided to leave Cuba. She prepared boxes to mail, which contained books she wanted to keep; the survey and record-keeping instruments she helped to design; the annual reports she prepared. She was accused of sending information to the CIA and was tried for espionage. Everyone at the trial was part of the government: "the prosecutor, the judge, the defense lawyer, they were all *verde* [olivo green]." They sentenced her to 15 years.

Luis González-Infante was a mulatto from a humble family. His father worked as a mason, and his mother worked in a tobacco factory. They also came from a *tradición mambisa*, as his grandfather fought against Spain in the struggle for independence. His father was a soldier in the old Cuban army but resigned in protest when Batista usurped power. Their life improved, economically speaking, when he became head of construction for the "Santa Teresa" sugar mill.

When the revolution triumphed, "Infante," as his friends call him, was 15 years old. He had begun to study *bachillerato* in the Instituto de Santa Clara and had gone on to study at the vocational school. While his family was largely apolitical, he deeply admired Porfirio Ramírez, whom he called "el negro Ramírez," with affection, though he was not black, but dark-skinned, *trigueño*. Admired by many, Porfirio Ramírez fought against Batista in the mountains of the Escambray and became a captain of the rebel army. Afterward, he became president of the FEU. When Porfirio Ramírez, an important role model for Infante, turned against Castro, so did Infante. The government executed Porfirio Ramírez in October 1960, and Infante joined the opposition, as a member of the MRP, despite his parents' admonitions. He became head of Acción y Sabotaje, the underground resistance, for the province. Infante was imprisoned in April 1964, betrayed by a young man in their movement. He served 21 years in prison. When I visited Santa Clara on my return trips to Cuba, thanks to our common friend, Coiré Rodríguez, I visited his family. To this day, one can feel the ostracism under which the families of former political prisoners live in Cuba; few dare to visit them or be seen as their friends.

Prison Conditions

Vargas-Gómez was the first person to tell me about the conditions in Castro's prisons in detail. Learning about the extreme degradation human beings can endure hit me hard. Afterward, I went to a church and quietly prayed. Eventually, after so many interviews, I was able to build a callous surface.

In the first few years, the prisoners were housed in La Cabaña, the fortress prison that dominates the Bay of Havana. As supreme prosecutor, Che Guevara had declared that revolutionary justice was true justice (Dugowson and Kaflon 1997). Vargas-Gómez remembered how every night they could hear the executions, the *fusilamientos*. In the six months he stayed there, Vargas-Gómez heard 170 executions. Valls described how they could hear the squad arriving and the car that brought the convict pulling up: "Then there would be the sound of a door opening and footsteps in the night. We could hear the prisoner being tied to the pole, his last cries, the command to fire, the volley, and finally the shots ringing out; then the squad retiring and the corpse being taken away" (1986:26).

Vargas-Gómez remembered how almost every night they could hear the victims crying: *¡Viva Cristo Rey! ¡Abajo el comunismo!* (Long live Christ the King! Down with communism!). Afterward, the head of the squadron would give the fallen bodies a coup de grace, to make certain they were really dead. Then the bodies were taken to the Colón Cemetery to be disposed of in an unmarked, mass grave. Vargas-Gómez was among the prisoners transferred to the Isle of Pines prison. When Vargas-Gómez returned to La Cabaña a year and a half later, the executions were still going on.

At La Cabaña, the jails that housed the men were meant for at most 70 men, with only two small bathrooms, but they crowded more than 300 men in them. The beds were filthy, crawling with bugs; mice ran down the passage ways and gnawed at people. Valls recalled: "Each prisoner had his belonging in a bag that hung from the bed or from a nail on the wall. Three hundred and four men would not all fit," he continued, "so some had to stand while others tucked themselves inside the niches of the beds. At night, those who had no bed would fit themselves on the floor like pieces of a puzzle, under the beds and in the passage ways" (1986:21–22). America's Watch summed it up: "all available evidence indicated that the lowest point for Cuba's political prisoners, both in terms of severity of sentences and living conditions, occurred in the mid-1960s" (Valls 1986:v). They went on to note that many prisoners' testimonies corroborated these accounts of frequent beatings and bayoneting, subhuman nourishment and medical care, and agonizing isolation – all of which I also heard during my interviews.

Food and water were always extremely scarce. The isolation also cut deep. The constant harassment was the worst: the soldiers arriving in the middle of the night with their arms, beating the prisoners with their bayonets, the wounded. Some prisoners found release from these conditions in madness; others, in suicide. Still others accepted the government's "reeducation plan"; later on, the "progressive plan." It is difficult to estimate how many prisoners were kept in these conditions under Castro's regime. Valls estimated there were easily 8,000 prisoners at Isle of Pines and between 30,000 and 35,000 total prisoners. The Cuban government's own estimate was 70,000 (Alfonso 2005a).

Many became *plantados*. For the many years they were in prison, Vargas-Gómez, Valls, González-Infante, Vidaurreta, Zúñiga, Pardo, all were *plantados*. The term came from the peasants, meaning they were people who

Figure 5.2   During the revolution, many Cubans who were in the opposition languished in prison. *Plantados* were those who demanded recognition as political prisoners, refusing to wear the common prisoner's uniform. Instead, they wore boxer shorts. Plácido Díaz, Roberto Montenegro, Juan Soto, Eusebio Peñalver, and Angel Pardo in 1988 were at Combinado del Este prison, in Havana. (Angel Pardo)

dug in their heels, who refused to participate in the various "reeducation" plans and also refused the discipline of the common prisoners. The *plantados* refused to wear the blue uniform of the common prisoners. Instead, they made a bid for respect, by using different uniforms or simply boxer shorts – *calzoncillos* (see Figure 5.2). The common prisoners treated them with awe; even the guards treated them with "a certain respect," as Infante put it. But Infante also stressed that prisoners who belonged to the social categories favored by the revolution – such as blacks, peasants, former communists – were singled out for special abuse. Such was his case, as a mulatto, as well as the case of Guillermo Rivas-Porta, a former communist.

Those who accepted the "reeducation plan" derived benefits. If the prisoners were ready to state publicly that they were mistaken to fight against the government, they could get out of prison after serving only a quarter of their sentences. They could also have a bit more food, more visits, less harassment. "The real purpose," argued Martha Oliva, "was to put the communist dogma inside people's heads." Those I interviewed refused to allow such indoctrination to make a dent. In a community where being a *plantado* signified courage, accepting the reeducation plan was deemed dishonorable.

Some prisons were worse than others. In Boniato prison in the 1970s, prisoners were held in solitary confinement in cells that were *tapiadas*, completely enclosed without exterior views, conditions that were designed to lead the prisoners to despair. Angel Pardo was held inside such a cell for over a year before he was able to see the sun again (1992:163). The conditions there were so extreme that a revolt ensued that armed guards put down by firing on the prisoners. It came to be known as *la masacre de Boniato*. On September 1, 1975, a prisoner was killed – Gerardo González-Alvarez, a Protestant minister. Many others were seriously wounded with gunshots or were beaten.

The women in prison may well have suffered more than the men. As prisoners, women were cut off from their children, their families, and their causes. But, as Martha Oliva pointed out, often the younger women grew closer to the older women, who treated them in a maternal way. In the "América Libre" prison, Martha worked in agriculture – fruit, coffee, tending every crop – 12 hours a day; and in the kitchen – cooking and cleaning for the 600 women there. The women were beaten and insulted, not only by their women guards but also by men at the prison who took advantage of them.

The dominant experience of "the island," as the prisoners called the Isle of Pines, was defined by forced labor and irrational brutality, Valls (1986:42–43) stressed. The guards were trained to hate them; they were told the men were murderers, traitors, capitalist exploiters, torturers, or CIA agents. The harassment and ill treatment were intended to humiliate them. Such is exemplified by Felo Fernández-Yarzábal's testimony. He was sentenced to 15 years, which he served. When he was released from prison, late in June 1976, he came to the United States and Puerto Rico, where his family eagerly awaited him. He was suffering from cancer of the stomach, in an advanced stage. In prison, they had diagnosed him as suffering from parasites and treated him inappropriately. When he arrived in the United States, his friend Julio Otazo (1976), former journalist in Cuba, recalled the conversation they had soon after Felo arrived in Miami. Felo underlined that if he were to tell others what life in Castro's prisons was like, they would not believe him. Once, Felo told him, they took a group of prisoners out to clean a *potrero*, an animal stall. "How should we do it?" asked some, seeing there were no tools. "With your mouth," was the reply. So they had to cut the grass, while crouching down, biting it off. Over the course of eight hours, more than 200 prisoners fell unconscious, exhausted.

The harsh prison experiences led a group of prisoners in the Combinado del Este prison to prepare a document on the "Human Rights Violations in Cuba, Based on the Universal Declaration of Human Rights" (Pardo 1988). A 13-page document, it was prepared by Angel Pardo, Luis Zúñiga, and Luis Rodríguez and signed by all the political prisoners. They handed it to the United Nations' Human Rights Commission, which finally visited Cuba for the first time on September 21, 1988. Until then, the United Nations had kept silence – "a silence of complicity," as Valladares (1986:304) put it. The change in their attitude came about because of Armando Valladares' work. Adopted as a prisoner of conscience by both Amnesty International and the PEN Clubs in both Sweden and France, he was released. His publications began to crack down the wall of silence and indifference that existed regarding Cuba's human rights violations.

Faced with extreme conditions, a strong sense of duty and honor existed among the prisoners, Augusto Vidaurreta explained. Accepting the reeducation plan reduced their sentences, yet most prisoners did not accept it; rather, they accepted the harsh prison conditions. However, many of the prisoners simply did what they had to do to get out and accepted the reeducation plan, as did "Richard" Heredia and Martha Oliva. Heredia served 10 years in prison; Martha Oliva served more than 4 years.

In addition to the reeducation plan, in the 1970s another plan was created, the *plan progresivo*, with the support of the Catholic Church, through the initiative of Monsignor César Zacchi, the Vatican's apostolic nuncio in Cuba, together with the Cuban government. Accepting the progressive plan reduced one's sentence by half; work was no longer forced labor but paid labor and useful labor. Yet some of the *plantados* felt betrayed by those who accepted the plan. "That was quite hard for us," explained Infante. Others felt the church also betrayed them: "Never, in the 21 years I was in prison, did we receive any help from the church," said Vargas-Gómez, a committed Catholic who gave communion to the others. To Valladares, "it was not only a silent church, but something much worse, a church of complicity" (1986:283).

The political prisoners had only one means to force the guards and the prison administration to make changes: the hunger strike. They became quite adept at it. At La Cabaña, for example, in 1969, 600 prisoners out of nearly 1,000 went on a hunger strike to demand minimal living conditions, including food, medical attention, visits, and mail. "We went for 35 days without food, breathing the stink of our own rotting flesh," recalled Valls (1986:61). Angel Pardo (1992:115), a black Cuban who was in prison for 24 years and was also a *plantado*, described his physical condition after so many days: "My muscles had wasted away. I then realized I had become only skin and bones." Prison conditions improved as a result.

How was it possible for the prisoners to bear the inhuman conditions? While in Ariza prison, Felo Fernández-Yarzábal wrote to his brother, on June 10, 1969, a letter that his sister "Fefé" shared with me. He said: "At times, when in the darkness that envelops us, we feel the strength to continue this living death that is our daily lot, and we ask ourselves from where does the strength to resist come, I find three reasons: optimism, strength, and faith. My father's optimism; my mother's strength; and the faith God gave us."

Every sector of society was present, every form of political and religious belief. Some were architects of the revolution. Mario Chanes de Armas, for example, was Fidel Castro's companion in arms both in the yacht *Granma* and in the attack on the Moncada army barracks. He served the longest sentence of any prisoner: 30 years. While in prison, he received the news of his son's birth and, many years later, of his son's death (Cancio-Isla 2007).

To Valls, the bravest were the peasants, who expressed themselves in popular folksongs, *corridos* and *décimas*. Union leaders were common. With so many years spent in prison, eventually a different generation of political prisoners arrived. They were against the state, but "they did not believe in us old fellows, nor did they have any reverence for the past" (Valls 1986:86).

Lorenzo Dueñas, however, did heed the advice and teaching of the older prisoners. Born in 1958, he truly was a child of the revolution. His family was a black working-class family that became involved in the revolution. His father had been a *miliciano*, always ready to defend the revolution, while he was also a chef in Casalta, an excellent restaurant. He wanted to impose his belief in Palo Monte, a form of Santería, on his children, but none of them accepted it. Even more, Lorenzo grew close to the Catholic Church: "They talked to me about God, about Jesus Christ, things that I had never been told when I was a child. And I began to change. When I realized it, I had already changed." As an adult, he worked in the nursing home at the church of San Rafael, in Marianao, where he helped the elderly.

The failure of the 1970 mobilization also had an impact on him. Nearly 14, while studying in the military school called Playa Girón, he began to see Fidel Castro as one who was always promising but never delivering, wanting to give the world false impressions. Thus, he wanted to leave Cuba. When in 1985 a rumor made the rounds that the French Embassy was giving visas to leave Cuba, he entered the embassy. When the police started to catch those who entered the embassy, he ran and ran, but they shot him in the leg and captured him. For expressing his intention to leave Cuba, an illegal act at that time, and being found in dubious company, they sentenced him to five years in prison, as a traitor.

At Combinado del Este prison, they put him in with the political prisoners, so he was able to talk with them, take classes, learn English, and pray in the evenings. It was in prison, he said, that he truly became a political prisoner because there he learned the Universal Declaration of Human Rights.

Beyond Prison

By chance, I learned how political prisoners feel when they regain their freedom. When I traveled to Cuba and gave the inaugural Lourdes Casal Lecture at the University of Havana in January 1996, the only flight available for me to return to the United States was full of young men who were political prisoners. At the takeoff, I heard their shouts of joy as the plane lifted us away.

The prisoners I came to know led quite purposeful and diverse lives. After leaving Cuba, some were reunited with their spouses and families, while others began new families; many became involved with exile politics in various ways. For example, Andrés Vargas-Gómez was reunited with his wife, who waited for him for 20 years, and went on to head Unidad Cubana, while Augusto Vidaurreta established a new family and stayed outside of exile politics altogether. Felo Fernández-Yarzábal was reunited with his family when he had only a few months left to live. On September 8, the feast day of Cuba's patron saint, Felo spoke to those present at the Church of the Immaculate Conception in Brownsville, Texas, and asked them not to forget the thousands of men and women who still remained in prison in Cuba due to their patriotism (Fernández-Yarzábal 1976). Lorenzo Dueñas went on to work at the Doctor's Hospital, helping patients in wheelchairs around the hospital, and studied physiotherapy at Miami-Dade Community College. Martha Oliva began working at the Jackson Memorial Hospital as a Certified Tumor Registrar; after retirement, she worked for the League against Cancer, coordinating the cancer program. Jorge Valls continued working with the Partido Social Revolucionario Democrático de Cuba, a socialist-democratic party. Luis González-Infante served twice as the president of

La Casa del Preso (the Home for Former Political Prisoners), to help them in the arduous tasks of being free and adjusting to life in the United States, while also expressing their patriotism. The former prisoners, in fact, built it on Cuban Memorial Boulevard in Miami. There, those without family or in need could live.

Tending Bridges

In her analysis of exile literature as shaped both by the prescribed and the prohibited, Olga Connor (2005) notes that at a time when the name of the game was to close the door, the Antonio Maceo Brigade broke through and opened it. The brigade, whose first trip to Cuba was at the end of 1977, also made the Dialogue between the Cuban government and representatives of the exile community in November 1978 possible. The Dialogue fractured the Cuban community into two opposing camps, creating a division that has never healed. But it also bore multiple fruits.

The Antonio Maceo Brigade

Among other splits, such as social class and waves of migration, the Cuban community is certainly cleft by age, by generations. Typically, immigrants experience a pronounced generation gap when parents raised in the Old World confront their children raised in the New. But this gap reflects more than that; it is the difference between the political generations that came of age in Cuba and that came of age in the United States under the impact of the civil rights and anti–Vietnam War movements.

The 55 progressive young people who formed the Antonio Maceo Brigade in December 1977 first broke through 19 years of hostility, abuse, and isolation. Their visit throughout the island left behind a profound mark. In Cuba, Jesús Díaz (1978) filmed the event – 55 Hermanos (55 Brothers and Sisters) – and turned it into a book (1979). Both captured their search for cultural identity; for some, for political identity. Widely shown in Cuba, it proved heartrending: evidence of the suffering the exodus had caused the family.

Like the journal Areíto, where young Cubans who supported the revolution expressed themselves, the brigade was Lourdes Casal's idea, the result of her own process of change that led her to support the revolution. The very name of the Antonio Maceo Brigade expressed her sentiments. Lourdes was a black Cuban in a largely white exile. Casal explained to me in Chicago, soon after I joined the brigade, that she named it after Antonio Maceo, general of the war of independence, because he was black and thus often ignored in Cuban history. Those who worked editing *Areíto* were strong supporters of the revolution, while those who joined the brigade varied in their commitment. To Yolanda Prieto, Lourdes Casal was both an intellectual and moral force. Casal taught at Rutgers University at a time when Abdala, the radical anti-Castro youth group, was quite strong in New Jersey. "Lourdes was many Lourdeses," Prieto recalled. "She changed her convictions a number of times, but always remained committed." Part of Acción Católica and the Directorio Estudiantil, Lourdes actively opposed the revolution when she first left Cuba. But a trip to Africa changed her attitude. A black Cuban, there she was confronted both with extreme under-development and the problem of race and colonialism. She then began to believe in the Cuban revolution and returned to Cuba in 1973. One of her poems defined the condition of exile she never stopped feeling: *Exilio es vivir donde no existe casa alguna en la que hayamos sido niños* (Exile means living where there is no house where we were children) (Casal 1981:31).

Under Lourdes's influence, Yolanda became more radical and involved herself with *Areíto*, which she worked hard editing for its 10 years. Lourdes returned to Cuba when she learned her kidneys were failing and spent the last year of her life there, undergoing dialysis. She died on February 1, 1981, after witnessing the Mariel exodus from inside Cuba. I recall the photo that appeared in *Granma*: Lourdes's coffin was surrounded by many who loved her, among them Marifeli Pérez-Stable, Yolanda Prieto, and Albor Ruíz.

Despite Lourdes's intent, the brigade remained mostly white and upper middle class. Eloísa García was one of the few black Cubans in the brigade, so she felt isolated and confused. Nonetheless, regaining touch with her family in Cuba was important. They strove to show her both sides of the revolution: they emphasized both the spread of public health services and the enormous problems they had finding an ambulance for her grandmother.

Alberto de la Cerra felt similarly out of place. Though white, he came from a working-class family. When he arrived in Cuba, they looked at him and said: "What are you doing here? Don't you see what this is really like?" As a student at the University of Wisconsin at Madison, he had grown to sympathize with the revolution and was against the trade embargo, but he fell short of unconditionally supporting it. Such was also my case.

What caused these young people to return to Cuba? The opportunity to participate in the brigade was open to all young Cubans who had left due to their family's decision; were against the trade embargo; and supported the normalization of relations between Cuba and the United States (Díaz 1979:18–19). For some, the return expressed a political identity, best expressed by Marifeli Pérez-Stable, a member of its executive committee: "Look, the Antonio Maceo Brigade is the end of a road that began in the sixties, especially in the Universities, when they became polarized by the Vietnam War, and earlier by the black American Civil Rights Movement.... In those movements there were people who sympathized with Cuba, including the Venceremos Brigade. And they would say to us, 'And you? ... What do you think of Cuba?' 'No. Not Cuba, because they are communists,' we would reply" (Díaz 1979:92–93).

That attitude lasted until the 1970s, when the radical, young Cubans began to develop several "fronts," as they called them, such as the journals *Areíto* and *Joven Cuba*. The idea of the brigade was to return to Cuba, not only for emotional reasons, but to work and live with the people there, to *reencontrarse*. Working hard to put out *Areíto* for many years when she lived "intensely," Yolanda differed from others who were deeply involved in that she was very religious. Hence, she was interested in the relationship between Marxism and Christianity. *Areíto* and *la Brigada* virtually ceased in the mid-1980s, due to the impact of the Mariel exodus. When it became clear that those leaving Cuba were the poor, the working class, and black Cubans, the radical young could no longer accept the revolution unquestioningly. Reflecting on her own journey, Yolanda noted that while her working-class background in Cuba inclined her to accept the revolution's goals enthusiastically, her deep religiosity was a stumbling block. She continued to define her own attitude as one of "support, but with criticism." In recent years, though, she felt she was in a state "of flux," no longer able to be fully supportive of the revolution, but unable to join the opposition.

While the 55 who composed that first trip were quite homogeneous in their level of political commitment to Cuba and their participation in activities like *Areíto*, subsequent trips were much larger and politically heterogeneous. I participated in the second *contingente*, with around 178 young Cubans. Although I shared many of their views, my schooling in Michigan and Chicago had isolated me from participating in these ventures, centered as they were in Gainesville, Florida; Puerto Rico; and New York. Hence, my own attitude, like that of many others, can best be described as feeling caught between a rock and a hard place – between the political division in my immediate family and the romantic attitude toward Cuba in American universities. Hence, I simply needed to see Cuba with my own eyes.

Figure 5.3   In the late 1970s and 1980s, young Cubans whose parents had rejected the revolution and left often returned to Cuba as part of the Antonio Maceo Brigade. Some were in open sympathy with the revolution, others needed to see it for themselves. Here is a group who worked in the construction of apartment dwellings for factory workers in the outskirts of Havana in July 1979. Silvia Pedraza is on the right. (Alberto de la Cerra)

Brigade members stayed at the Campamento Julio Antonio Mella, where we slept in bunk beds with mosquito netting, bathed in cold water, shared the bathroom with frogs and lizards, and ate on tin trays. We worked plastering the walls of the apartments being built for the workers of the Textilera Ariguanabo in the outskirts of Havana (see Figure 5.3). We also toured the whole country for weeks, as we met with leaders of the revolution, who lectured on their areas of expertise, such as the economy, the political system, history, and culture. Everywhere we went, we were treated warmly and respectfully, often with amazement. We were the *Maceítos* who had returned. Yet despite the lectures, visits, and museums, this first trip was more psychological than social or political. Above all, it involved the reencounter with our childhood, with what was left of the world we knew. In three letters I wrote to my husband then, Lee Bailey, I described my own encounter with my island, my family: "The countryside looks to me like I last saw it yesterday. It's really beautiful! Hilly, undulated, very, very green, and studded with palm trees." My senses and my memories were one, as I felt the hot sun, the evening breezes, the sound of the crickets, the fragrance of mangoes and flowers. My encounter resembled that described by Marcel Proust in *A la Recherche du Temps Perdu*, where sensory experiences constantly triggered memories, making me aware of the past. Most profound was the encounter with my uncle, *tío Rafaelito*, whom I loved deeply as a child.

The weekend I was able to spend with my family in their home, only one house away from the one where I grew up, when all the children ran back and forth between the three family houses, a seamless extended family. To me, "it was one of the most beautiful days of my life... to be confronted by all my memories and all the people I loved for so long." On that day, while we were at dinner, my uncle stole away and began to play the piano, as always – with precision and feeling. Suddenly, many emotions swelled up inside, and I began to cry. The family rushed to give me coffee. Recuperated, after some time, I decided I would show them how I could also play the piano. As I played the sentimental "Corazón" (Heart), suddenly there was a big silence and I realized, behind me, *they* were all crying! Afterward, we talked for hours about Cuba, the revolution, the trade embargo, why some family had accepted and others denied the revolution.

Jorge Duany, raised in Puerto Rico, expressed the different psychological attitudes involved in every return trip: "In the first trip, I felt as if I was at home.... 'At last I know who I am: I am Cuban.' I felt as if I were one piece. In the second trip, I began to have doubts.... In the third trip, I realized I could not live in Cuba – not only for political reasons, but because I felt more Puerto Rican than Cuban.... On the fourth trip, I realized how difficult it would be to live the daily life in Cuba, given the social conditions there: from the lack of hot water to owning a car, which is a privilege in Cuba."

Flavio Risech became very involved with the brigade. His parents had left Cuba at the end of 1959, when he was only five years old. He grew up in Miami's *"Sagüesera"* the southwest of the city. In his 20s, he settled in Massachusetts, where he still resides. Having lived in several distinct communities, Flavio used the image of cross-dressing to express his views. Going from exile Miami to Cuba to other U.S. cities, each time he crossed and recrossed these boundaries he wore different identity garments, making decisions as to how to present himself.

Growing up in Miami, he felt constrained in high school and at times insulted by teachers who supported the Vietnam War due to their anti-communism. But the principal rescued him by placing him in an honors class, taught by an American who was against the war, which pleased him. His father and he would often lock horns, not so much over politics as over sexuality. When Flavio let his hair grow, hippie-style, and attended the anti–Vietnam War protests, his father worried about his masculinity, his ability to be *macho*. "It was bad to be a communist, worse to be gay, a *maricón, el colmo* [the ultimate sin] to be both" (Risech 1994:531). But in the end it was politics that made the gap between the cultures of Cuban Miami and the Anglocentric school world unbridgeable. He could date the political break with his family and Cuban Miami to May 1970, when they were watching television coverage on the four Kent State students killed by the National Guard during the antiwar protests. His grandfather said, "four less communists" (Risech 1994:530).

For Flavio, his work as a lawyer in legal aid services, seeing poverty up close, meant the allure of Cuba was abstract: a socialist society where there was greater equality, social justice. But in his return trips to Cuba, he also realized his sexuality, as a gay man, marginalized him there, too. As he put it, both the identities of *revolucionario* in Havana and anticommunist *gusano* in Miami "require unambiguous and unquestioned masculinity for their constitution" (Risech 1994:531). With time, Risech came to realize that the government also lacked respect for the people, for the individual. "The only explanation is that they treat people without respect to remain in power." Clearly, the brigade allowed the *Maceítos* to make a peace with the family division exile and politics wrought.

To others, like Jesús Díaz, the *Maceítos* temporarily brought relief, a reason to believe, once more, in a revolution that had grown tarnished. While in Cuba, for many years Jesús Díaz had tried to express his commitment to socialism while also trying to create a liberal intellectuality within, with the journal *Pensamiento Crítico* (Critical Thinking) and its supplement *El Caimán Barbudo* (Cayman is an image for the island itself; bearded is an image for the revolution). Initially euphoric for the revolution, the failure of the 10-million-ton sugar harvest in 1970 prompted his disaffection (Díaz 2000; Guerrero 2002). The failure, he thought, was due to Fidel Castro's limitless ego, at the expense of the Cuban people's blood, sweat, and tears.

Jesús Díaz left Cuba in 1992 to teach at Berlin's Film Academy. His own experiences as a man of the left led him to realize that Castro's totalitarianism could not be reformed from within (Díaz 2000:118). He criticized Fidel openly, for running Cuba "as if it were a private *hacienda*." Cuban officials expelled him from the party and UNEAC (Rojas 2002). In 1996, in Spain, he founded the journal *Encuentro*, literally a place where Cuban intellectuals on the island and in the diaspora could find one another. His untimely death in May 2002 made it the last project of an intellectual whose organizational capacity was as vast as his commitment to Cuba, who lived the revolution passionately and tried to do so lucidly.

The Dialogue

In November 1978 a dialogue took place in Havana between representatives of the Cuban community in exile and the Cuban government that resulted in deep rifts and further violence among the exiles. They became divided between those who supported it (*los dialogueros*, a term of contempt) and those who see any contact with the Castro regime as a way of legitimizing that regime politically (*los intransigentes*). No one else's story exemplifies that better than Bernardo Benes's, its architect, and Miguel González-Pando, part of the 75-member delegation who represented the exiles.

A Cuban Jew, Benes was a pillar of the Miami business community, a man who many called "the Cuban Henry Kissinger" (Laughlin 1994). Communism found Bernardo Benes's family twice: once in Russia, which his father left, as a young man, in the 1920s; and again in Cuba, which his family left in 1960, when Bernardo was young. Bernardo grew up in Havana, where his family was active in the substantial Jewish community there. His father had arrived in Cuba penniless, but eventually he grew to own a textile factory where they made *camisetas Perro*, cheap undershirts, and the family prospered. As a student at the University of Havana, Bernardo was involved in the anti-Batista struggle, both as a member of the FEU and the Directorio Estudiantil. As a lawyer, at 25, he worked for a major law firm and served as a legal consultant to Castro's Ministerio de Hacienda, the Treasury. However, he was horrified by the direction the revolution was taking, particularly the executions, and he left in November 1960.

In Miami, with time, Benes established himself as both a businessman and a humanitarian. During Jimmy Carter's presidency, with his tacit approval,

Bernardo met with two representatives of the Cuban government a dozen times, all over Central America, the Caribbean, and the United States, until early in 1978 he met with Fidel Castro in Havana. In the next few months, he met with him numerous times. Benes tried to convince Castro that "making certain human rights gestures could favorably influence the U.S. position on the embargo against Cuba" (Laughlin 1994).

Benes found himself reviled by the community for entering into a dialogue with Castro: "I went from being a business and community leader to a social leper" (Laughlin 1994:2). On the radio and on television, the signs read: "Bernardo Benes is a traitor," "Bernardo Benes is a Castro agent." The object of death threats, he and his wife, Raquel, had to live with constant fear. He wore a bulletproof vest, had police escort, and had security devices installed in his home. In May 1983, on a Friday evening after everyone had gone home, his bank office was blown up. Deeply depressed, Benes found his courage again only when he found the family his father had left behind in Russia (Laughlin 1994).

After participating in the Dialogue, Miguel González-Pando also found himself ostracized upon his return to Miami. His fellow veterans expelled him, a Bay of Pigs *invasor*, from the brigade. Twelve years later, on a television program remembering the Bay of Pigs, he was slapped on the face when he expressed a message of reconciliation – "I said that we should remember the dead on both sides," González-Pando remembered (Novo 1994:24). But he never gave up, becoming a chronicler of the exile community in various documentaries, such as *"Calle Ocho": Cuban Exiles Look at Themselves* (González-Pando 1994) and *Ni Patria Ni Amo: Voces del Exilio Cubano* (González-Pando 1996), both of which gave a voice to a broad gamut of the exile community. González-Pando died in his late 50s from leukemia, which he fought to the end. When he died in April 1998, many mourned his absence from Miami's cultural and artistic life (Montaner 1998). At his funeral, friends from the Veterans of the Brigade 2506 arrived to place the Cuban flag over his casket.

As a result of the Dialogue, all at once, the counterrevolutionaries (*gusanos*) of yesterday respectfully became "members of the Cuban community abroad"; the release of the political prisoners began; and the return visits of Cuban exiles commenced, promoting the reunification of families rent apart by the exodus. Most important was the release of the political prisoners who were languishing, forgotten in Cuba's prisons. Between 1978 and 1979, fully 3,600 political prisoners were released. As of April 1986, there were still 126 *plantados* in Cuba's prisons (Valls 1986). Eventually, they were also released.

As the 1970s drew to a close, the revolution seemed consolidated against both its external and internal enemies. Imagining that all who wanted to do so had already left Cuba, the Cuban Refugee Program ended. Few expected the chaotic flotilla exodus that burst next.

PART II

The Children of Communism

THE CUBAN EXODUS OF 1980 AND 1985–2004

6

![ornamental divider]

Los Marielitos *of 1980*

La memoria es un presente que no termina nunca de pasar.

Memory is a present that never ceases to pass by.
                    Octavio Paz (cited in Reinaldo Arenas, *Otra Vez el Mar* [1982])

The Third Wave: Refugee "Vintages"

Few expected the chaotic flotilla exodus that became the third major wave of the Cuban exodus. From April to September 1980, through the port of Mariel, a total of 124,789 Cubans arrived in Florida. They became known as *los Marielitos*. Of the 120 Cubans I interviewed, 13 were typical *Marielitos*. This chapter focuses on why they left Cuba and seeks to illuminate their distinct characteristics of race, class, gender, and sexuality. Considering why they became a distinct political generation, it also underscores issues of artistic freedom in this wave of emigrants. To show these contrasts, I rely on interviews with Teresita Sánchez, Rogelio Santos (pseudonym), José Macías (pseudonym), René Cifuentes, Jesús Selgas, Armando Alvarez-Bravo, and Fidelia Suárez (pseudonym).

As a result of the 1978 Dialogue, the Cuban government agreed to the release of political prisoners; to promote the reunification of families rent by the exodus; and to allow Cubans in the United States to return, to visit their families and their homeland. Since that day, approximately 100,000 Cubans have returned to Cuba every year – seeking the family they loved and the vestiges of the life they once led. Those return visits were partly responsible for the Mariel exodus. First, after many years of separation, families renewed ties of affection. Second, for many in Cuba the exiles' return constituted a discomfirming experience. The government had told them those who left for the United States led miserable lives, living in crime-ridden cities where unemployment was rampant and racism cut deep. But when the exiles returned, those in Cuba could see this was false; rather, it was clear they led decent, prosperous lives. Teresita Sánchez, who was in Cuba then, said: "The government made a mistake allowing them to return. We could see they were well!" With typical humor, Cubans in the island noted that the *gusanos* (worms) became *mariposas* (butterflies).

The chaotic flotilla exodus of 1980 began when six desperate young men drove a bus past the guards, straight into the Peruvian Embassy compound, asking for political asylum. A few days later, on April 4, Castro announced his decision to leave the embassy unguarded and to allow those who wanted to to leave Cuba. Within days, more than 10,000 persons had crowded into the compound. When this acute refugee exodus ceased the follow-ing September, it had brought close to 125,000 more Cubans to America, approximately 18 percent of all Cuban immigrants who had arrived until 1990 (see Table 1.1). This wave lacked order and process. From Miami, thousands of boats manned by relatives sped across the 90 miles of sea to Cuba's Mariel harbor. At times they succeeded in bringing their fami-lies; other times they brought whomever angry officials put on the boats. Toward the end, this included Cuba's social undesirables: those who had been in prisons (whether they were political prisoners, had committed real crimes, or had only challenged the state), mental patients, and homosexuals. The government called them *la escoria* (scum).

In Cuba, these "antisocial elements" represented a large public slap in the face: no longer were they the immigrants of the transition from capitalism to communism but the children of communism itself. In America they arrived in the throes of an ambivalent government policy that initially welcomed them "with an open heart and open arms," as President Jimmy Carter expressed it ("U.S. Opens Arms..." 1980), and subsequently sought to delimit the flow.

In the United States, after 20 years of celebrating the achievements of Cuban exiles, the press contributed to what it viewed as a damaging por-trayal, focusing on the criminals, the gays, and the many blacks, categories of people often accorded little respect. Who were the *Marielitos*? Were they "scum"?

Indeed, this wave had a distinct social composition. Among the most salient characteristics was their youth (most were young men, single or without their families); unskilled or semiskilled workers dominated

occupationally; Cuban blacks and mulattoes participated in larger numbers than ever before; there was a significant presence of gay Cubans; many
had spent time in prison; and a sizable number of artists and intellectuals
came in their midst. To dispel the more damaging and inaccurate portray-
als, Robert Bach (1980; Bach et al. 1981–82) and Gastón Fernández (1982)
studied their characteristics, sampling the *Marielitos* soon after their arrival,
while they were still in the processing centers and the refugee camps. From
their work, together with the census data, we can glean a fair portrait. Their
former occupations showed that most were from the mainstream of the
Cuban economy, hardly scum. Among Cuban immigrants, educational and
occupational attainment varies by waves. Data from the 1990 U.S. census
show that fully 25 percent of Cubans who immigrated during the first wave
had a college education, whereas only 7 percent of the *Marielitos* had the
same level of education. Also salient was their overwhelmingly working-
class origins – close to 70 percent were blue-collar workers. Mechanics,
heavy equipment and factory machine operators, carpenters, masons, and
bus, taxi, and truck drivers led the list of occupations (Bach et al. 1981–
82:34). These characteristics, stressed Fernández (1982), suggested new
generational strains might have developed from the more limited economic
and political opportunities available to the young when the older generation of Cubans who made the revolution held the key posts, as well as the
burden of military service in Cuba and overseas shouldered by the young
(cf. Díaz-Briquets 1983). Moreover, in the years prior to *el Mariel*, Cubans
lived through some of the leanest years of the revolution: housing shortages were severe; food was insufficient and controlled by *la libreta*, the strict
ration book; unemployment and underemployment were chronic; and a vast
black market developed in which most participated (Roca 1981). "We are
traversing through a sea of difficulties," said Raúl Castro, seven months after
the Mariel exodus. And he underscored that too often the U.S. embargo
had been used to hide "our own errors and inefficiencies." I characterized
the *Marielitos* as "those who hope" (Pedraza 1996a).

In the United Sates, the press focused inordinately on the criminal element. Indeed, there were many who had been in prison. According to the
Immigration and Naturalization Service, of the 124,789 Mariel refugees
around 19 percent of the *Marielitos*, or 23,970, admitted they had been in
jail in Cuba. But of those who had been in prison, 5,486 were political
prisoners and fully 70 percent of those who had been in prison had been
jailed for minor crimes or for acts not considered criminal in the United
States (Montgomery 1981). The Cuban *Ley de la Peligrosidad*, a law that

regarded certain behavior as potentially dangerous, made some forms of dissent "antisocial" behavior, controlled by prison terms, such as participating in the black market (buying or selling clothes and food); dodging military service or desertion; refusing to work for the state, particularly in the cane fields; and trying to escape from Cuba illegally (Bach et al. 1981–82:46). Of those who had been in jail, the Immigration Service considered only 7 percent to be serious criminals – less than 2 percent of all the *Marielitos* (Montgomery 1981). Nonetheless, their presence was felt in the United States. As Mercedes Cros Sandoval (1986:24) highlighted, "many of them were instrumental in unleashing a homicide wave in Miami" soon after their arrival. This damaged the Cuban community in the United States by tarnishing its reputation. The public stigma generated by the presence of this criminal element may also have been partly responsible for the riots in the camps (Fernández 1982).

Given their youth, the *Marielitos* clearly constituted a different political generation (cf. Mannheim 1952), one whose coming of age was long after the early revolutionary struggle and sharp social cleavages that demanded enormous sacrifices but also affirmed the loyalty of many. Roughly half of the Mariel immigrants came of age during the late 1960s or the 1970s. Clearly for this wave of young people, comparisons with the years of Batista could no longer serve to promote the consent of a generation that scarcely could remember them.

During these years, problems of freedom of expression became particularly acute for artists and intellectuals. A key incident was that sparked by Heberto Padilla's prize-winning poetry book expressing the marginality of those who lived *Fuera del Juego – Outside of the Game* (1998 [1968]). Moreover, deviance, particularly homosexuality, was scorned and dealt with by imprisonment. Zolberg et al. (1989) distinguished among different types of refugees: supporters of the *ancien régime*, targets of the government, and mere victims. Many of the Cubans who came through *el Mariel* were targeted for their political opinions, their religious beliefs, or their sexual orientation. These constituted stigmas that, as Erving Goffman's (1963) classic analysis of stigma noted, placed them at the margins of society – people who were seen as morally tainted, disgraced, to be avoided lest their social identity pollute others.

Whereas the first two waves of the Cuban exodus consisted of the émigrés who left when the transition from a democratic, capitalist society to a communist society was taking place, the *Marielitos* and the recent émigrés knew no other society than Cuba in communism. The *Marielitos*, therefore, were a significantly different "vintage" – one whose lived experience contrasted sharply with that of the early exiles. At best, they can hardly comprehend one another; at worst, they may be, as Kunz noted (1973), hostile. Despite the willing help of many in the Cuban community, many others exhibited a defensive prejudice against the newcomers, who might tarnish their reputation. The first and latest waves of Cuban refugees in the United States live side by side but remain aloof from one another. For them, as Kunz (1973:137) pointed out, the date of departure from Cuba signifies "the bona fide" of their "political credo." Thus, they tend to blame each other for having left too soon or stayed too late.

Moreover, every person who was uprooted suffers from a profound alienation, marked by sadness, despair, and nostalgia (Handlin 1973 [1951]). But different refugee vintages long for a different Cuba; the Cuba of memory and desire is not quite the same Cuba. One night when I was in Key West in the mid-1980s, facing the sea, with Cuba only 90 miles away, the difference struck me. Near me, four *Marielitos* were engaged in a conversation while fishing and listening on the radio to a baseball game being played right then in their hometown in Cuba. The early refugees' nostalgia attached them to the Cuba they knew – *la Cuba de ayer*, before the revolution. The Mariel refugees' longing was for *la Cuba de hoy*, of the revolution.

Prior to the Mariel exodus, both major waves of Cuban immigrants were predominantly white. Yet, while throughout the decade of the 1960s the occupational distribution of Cuban refugees became more representative of Cuban society, "paradoxically," said Benigno Aguirre (1976: 105), Cuban blacks "participated less in it."

A small island that throughout all of its history has both welcomed and seen depart huge currents of migrants, Cuba's racial composition has changed dramatically over time. Table 6.1, based on the Cuban censuses from 1899 to 1981 and 2002, shows the changing racial composition of Cuba. The enormous migration of Spaniards to Cuba in the early part of the 20th century, after independence, contributed to the predominance of white Cubans. As Table 6.1 shows, the 1953 Cuban census, taken just a few years before the revolution, gave the proportion of Cubans who were white as 73 percent, black as 12 percent, and mulattoes as 15 percent – by American standards, 27 percent nonwhites. In Cuba, like much of the Caribbean, social class and race overlapped in the extreme. But during the years of the revolution, while the social class level of the Cuban migration dropped, the immigrants to the United States remained overwhelmingly white. Table 6.2, based on the U.S. census of 2000 shows that, overall,

Table 6.1. *Racial Composition of Cuba, 1899–2002 (%)*

Race	1899	1907	1919	1931	1943	1953	1981	2002 (CIA)	2002 (Cuban Census)
White	66.9	69.7	72.2	72.1	74.3	72.8	66.0	37.0	65.1
Black	14.9	13.4	11.2	11.0	9.7	12.4	12.0	11.0	10.1
Mulatto	17.2	16.3	16.0	16.2	15.6	14.5	21.9	51.0	24.9
Asian	1.0	0.6	0.6	0.7	0.4	0.3	0.1	1.0	–

Sources: For all years except 2002, see Cuba, Oficina Nacional del Censo 1984: table 39. For 2002, the CIA estimates are in Central Intelligence Agency 2003. For the 2002 Cuban census, see http://www.ccsr.ac.uk/cuba/cepde2004/censomultimedia/c_iii.htm; Bustamante (2003); and D. Pérez-López (2006).

Table 6.2. *Cuban Immigrants in the United States by Year of Immigration and Race, 2000 Census(%)*

Year of Immigration	White	Black	Other[a]	Asian	Number
1959–64	93.3	1.2	5.3	0.2	144,732
1965–74	88.7	2.0	9.1	0.2	247,726
1975–79	82.6	4.0	13.3	0.1	29,508
1980	80.9	5.3	13.7	0.1	94,095
1981–89	85.7	3.1	10.9	0.3	77,835
1990–93	84.7	3.2	11.9	0.2	60,244
1994–2000	85.8	3.7	10.4	0.1	174,437
TOTAL	87.2	2.9	9.7	0.2	828,577

[a] Includes both those who designated themselves as being "some other race"; those who indicated they were mixed race, belonging to two or more race groups; and the minimal fraction who said Indian.

Source: U.S. 2000 Census (2003), Public Use Microdata Sample, 5 percent, unweighted.

87 percent of the immigrants were white Cubans, 3 percent were black Cubans, 0.2 percent were Asians (no doubt *Chinos Cubanos*), and 10 percent were "other race" or mixed race. Still, there are substantial differences in the racial composition of the various waves.

In the years since the revolution, dramatic changes took place in the racial composition of the island. These resulted from the disproportionate participation of whites in the exodus since 1959, the higher fertility rate of black Cubans, increasing racial intermarriage on the island, and changes in racial self-definition. As Table 6.1 shows, according to the 1981 Cuban census, 22 years after the triumph of the revolution, 66 percent of the population described itself as white, 22 percent as mulattoes, and 12 percent as black. For the present, I offer two estimates that vary widely. The data given by the Central Intelligence Agency (2003) place the proportion of Cubans of African descent on the island at more than 60 percent: white 37 percent; mulattoes 51 percent; black 11 percent; Chinese 1 percent (see also Martínez-Fernández 2003b). However, the Cuban census of 2002 placed the proportion white at 65.1 percent, black at 10.1 percent, and mulatto or mestizo at 24.9 percent (Pérez-López, Daniel 2006; see also Bustamante 2003 for the survey conducted by the Center for Demographic Studies at the University of Havana, which gives similar results). Thus, the CIA estimates describe Cuba as a predominantly nonwhite nation (63 percent), whereas the Cuban census estimates describe Cuba as a predominantly white nation (65 percent). In large part, this may reflect the two different social definitions of race that operate in the United States (the CIA estimates) and the Caribbean (the Cuban estimates).

Charles Wagley (1968) described the social definition of the races in the Americas. In the South of the United States, a dual racial classification was used – black versus white – that was based on ancestry (the "one drop of blood" rule). By contrast, throughout the Caribbean the social definition of race was based on phenotype buttressed by social status – "money bleaches," the Brazilians say (see Degler 1971). Moreover, three different racial categories were recognized – black, white, and the mixed group, variously referred to as *mulatos* (Cuba and Puerto Rico), *pardos* (Brazil), and *Indios* (Dominican Republic). Gastón Baquero (2003), a Cuban writer and poet who was a very light-skinned mulatto, reflected on the problem of race in Cuba. He stressed that in Cuba, as well as in other Hispanic American nations, it was not a problem of races but, rather, a problem of colors. He who appeared white was white, and he who appeared black was black. The mestizo and the mulatto would often go on to *adelantar la raza*, or "advance the race," as it was popularly expressed, by marrying someone white, gradually going on to classify themselves as white. Thus, it is quite possible for the same person to be seen as black in the United States and white in the Caribbean.

The differential migration of the Cuban races in the first two waves of migration was quite explainable. Two different social processes, Aguirre concluded, were at work. At the outset, the revolution pulled out the power from under the upper classes, which had deliberately excluded blacks from their midst. The immigration proceeded through the chain of extended family and friends, further selecting whites. In addition, the migration policy of the United States and Cuba has always contributed to blacks being excluded, as they gave priority to close relatives of Cubans already in the United States. As the initial exodus drew from the white middle classes, white Cubans had family networks in place outside of Cuba that pulled more whites to leave; black Cubans lacked these same family networks.

Moreover, blacks in Cuba did benefit from the revolution. Unlike the United States, Cuba never had a "separate but equal" system of legal segregation; and Cuban culture was a "creolization" of white Spanish and black African cultural traditions. Yet prerevolutionary Cuba excluded blacks from the pinnacles of society: yacht and country clubs, the best vacation resorts and beaches, hotels, private schools reserved for the elite. One of the first acts of the revolution was to make these exclusive facilities public, available to all, regardless of color or wealth. In addition, the Cuban government promoted new opportunities for blacks in employment and education. Richard Fagen et al. (1968:120) noted that the race problem in Cuba was "a boon to Castro." The revolutionaries found it extremely useful for discrediting the old social order. With the "instant liberation" of blacks, "tens of thousands of disadvantaged Cubans were recruited into the ranks of revolutionary enthusiasts."

While the nonwhite proportion was visibly higher in the Mariel exodus than ever before, the actual estimates vary. According to Juan Clark (1992), nonwhites constituted from 20 to 40 percent of the *Marielitos*. Table 6.2, based on the 2000 U.S. census, can serve to illustrate the changing racial composition of the Cuban exodus, though one should be aware of the limitations of the census. First, race or ethnicity in the census is the result of self-identification; second, the census has a serious problem with respect to the underenumeration of the poor, immigrants, blacks, and Hispanics. Table 6.2 shows that around 93 percent of the refugees who came over in the first wave, Cuba's elite, were white. But the proportion that was white declined markedly during the second wave. From 9 to 13 percent of those who immigrated from 1965 to 1979 designated themselves as "other race" or mixed. The *Marielitos* had the lowest proportion identified as white of any wave, close to 81 percent, while 14 percent were categorized as "other race" or mixed race (mulattoes or mestizos in Cuba), and 5 percent considered themselves black. By American standards, close to 20 percent were nonwhite.

Given the Cuban revolution's appeal to race, why such a large presence in recent years? As early as the 1970s, Geoffrey Fox (1971:21) remarked that "almost all those emigrating today are among the poorer classes in Cuba, the very people in whose name the revolution was made," blacks included. To study "the defections of the sans-culottes," Fox interviewed a few working-class émigrés in Chicago and concluded that for both white and black workers the salience of race in the revolution created strain – whites complained of favoritism, blacks of tokenism. Moreover, although discrimination was eliminated, racial prejudice persisted in Cuba, attitudes that Cuban blacks might have sensed as real, despite the changes that had taken place.

Whatever role their race may have played in the decision to emigrate, black Cubans find their steps uncertain in America. As blacks, they are not fully accepted by whites, while among blacks they are Cubans (cf. Dixon 1988).

Race, Class, Gender, and Sexuality

The following interviews illustrate these characteristics of the *Marielitos*: race, class, gender, and sexuality. Moreover, at this time, freedom-of-expression issues also loomed paramount. While interrelated, I group the interviews under the subheading that denotes the main thrust.

Class and Gender

Rogelio Santos was a man of humble origins, a semiskilled worker, like many of the *Marielitos*. He worked in construction and was also a *guaguero* who drove a bus. Politically engaged, he paid the high price of repeated prison terms for his anticommunism. Yet his wife was very integrated to the revolution, a gender difference I often noticed in Cuba. "As a woman," he explained, "she did not feel the pressures the revolution placed on men, for example, its militarism; instead, the revolution allowed her to rise, as a woman, to the level of her talents." His wife was grateful for the educational opportunities she was able to gain from the revolution. As a member of the Unión de Jóvenes Comunistas, she often spent weekends doing volunteer work. The government valued her worth; in return, she felt affirmed by the government. So after *el Mariel* set on, during the three months before he actually got on the boat, they each silently realized he would leave, while she would stay. He left without telling her that he was leaving, both because he wanted to protect her, but also because he was afraid she might be the one to betray him. This silence among intimate family members regarding their true thoughts and feelings is one that I have often encountered in Cuba. It is a silence that is difficult to understand for those of us who do not live in an authoritarian society, for whom intimacy means, precisely, the ability to share one's deepest thoughts and feelings with another. But Rogelio was aware that he lived "in a country that was full of all kinds of dangers," and the reality that your closest ones might betray you was a danger. He knew that innocent family members paid the consequences for their relatives' politics. On one occasion, Rogelio was sought after by the police, so they grabbed a brother as hostage, until he turned himself in.

Only nine years old when the revolution triumphed, Rogelio initially defended the idea of the revolution with sympathy and affection. He aspired to be a member of the Young Communists when he got older and participated with gusto, doing volunteer work, such as cutting sugarcane during *la zafra* and waving flags at mass rallies. However, when he reached adolescence, he began to experience a process of political disaffection. He began to act "less like part of a mass, and more as an individual," as he put it. Moreover, after so many years he began to feel tired of so much sacrifice, of so many revolutionary *lemas*, cheers like *¡Viva la revolución!*, and the practice of socialist emulation. A mulatto who considered himself very *macho*, he was quite attractive to women. As a young man, he wanted to look good and have a good time, which he found impossible given that clothes were rationed to two pairs of pants and one pair of shoes a year. Working in construction, he was earning only 67 cents an hour, less than 100 pesos a month, while a pair of pants was 200 pesos on the black market, as was a pair of shoes. So he joined the extensive black market that existed in Cuba at that time. To him, the black market was a way not only to procure the goods he needed but also to earn money. He became a bus driver, a much better paid occupation (1.05 pesos an hour), as well as comptroller for transport of goods via trucks, a rather good occupation because the trucks moved bulk food, such as coffee, rice, and black beans, from which he benefited. In those years, the black market in Cuba was illegal, but it became a way of life, a culture in which many people participated as they sought to make do or improve their lives; petty theft carried no moral stigma because everyone understood it as necessary. Cubans express this with the verb *resolver*, which means that one solves problems in any which way. Yet participating in this way of life also prompted his political disaffection because it exposed him to the corruption not only of the average Cuban *resolviendo* on the streets but also of government officials who took not just a little bit here and there but would disappear with a whole truck, for example, of rice (that afterward was sold on the black market at 5 pesos a pound); or a whole truck of bricks and mortar (that afterward was used to build their own houses). Rogelio participated in the black market making shoes, which meant he bought the leather from Communist Party officials, because they were the only ones who could take the leather, in bulk, out of the factory and then sell it to others, such as him. Rogelio learned the trade of making shoes from an older man who had been a shoemaker before the small shoe factory he worked in was nationalized. The shoes Rogelio made were bartered for other things he needed – a sack of rice, a shirt. In Cuba the 1970s were called *la danza de los millones* (the dance of the millions – a phrase used in Cuba to describe the affluence of the 1920s), he said, because there really was a lot of money on the streets but very little to buy at exorbitant prices. A shirt, for example, might cost 200–300 pesos. Participating in the black market made an enormous difference, he stressed: "While his regular monthly salary – above board – might bring in 140 pesos a month, in the black market he could easily make 600 pesos a week!"

His involvement with the black market was not the reason he was sent to prison, however. Rather, it was his antigovernment political activities and his plans to leave the country illegally. During his three years there, three times he escaped – a *fuga de rebeldía* (a rebellious escape), as it was called, because he had no place to go but home, where they easily found him again. He landed in one of the worst prisons, El Castillo del Príncipe, in Havana, where they placed him in "zone five," where the political prisoners were housed. There he could see Huber Matos from a distance. His antigovernment activities consisted of painting signs saying things like "Down with Fidel!" on city walls, the *malecón* wall by the sea, and store windows. In 1978, after leaving prison, he redoubled his efforts. He and his friends – a group without a formal name because dissident organizations had not yet emerged in Cuba – painted a bed sheet with huge, red letters that read *Fuera el comunismo de Cuba!* expressing his desire for communism to end. They tied two corners of the sheet with huge rocks while securing it on top with more rocks, and dropped the sheet down the side of a huge building for all to see. So he fell in prison for "revolutionary antipathy" and the attempt – illegal at this time – to leave the country. To punish him for his escapes, the prison guards put him in *la Leonera*, truly the lion's den, and beat him with a bayonet. "Here is the proof of my *bayonetazos*," he said, while pointing to the bayonet marks in his body. After he left prison, he continued making the signs but was careful not to speak against the government in public places, as he had freely done before, while driving a bus.

I first visited the family in the spring of 1981 in their home in Luyanó, only a few months after *el Mariel* had ended, and the trauma and desperation of families the exodus rent apart were still palpable. Rogelio came from a family whose ancestors were not only black Cubans and white Spaniards but also Chinese and Indians, so the six brothers and one sister ranged widely in color. But race (or color) did not have a direct bearing on their relationship to the revolution. Using the terminology used in Cuba, Rogelio described himself as *piel canela*, cinnamon-colored, as were his brothers Guillermo and Lázaro. Raúl was what Cubans jokingly call *Negro teléfono* (black as a telephone), while Juan was called *el jabao* for his nearly white appearance. The family was deeply divided politically; nonetheless, it kept strong bonds of affection intact.

Rogelio's father fought for the revolution, supplying the rebels with arms stolen from Batista's army while he lived and worked in the army barracks. He then joined the rebels in the Sierra Maestra, Oriente, and when the revolution triumphed in 1959, he returned as a *barbudo*, wearing a beard and the olive-green rebel uniform. By contrast, his mother's family had lost some of its independence and standing as the petite bourgeoisie. Like Rogelio, his brother Guillermo had challenged government authority and been in prison several times. He was an example of the dissimulation with which people live in Cuba – living one life in public and another hidden behind. Guillermo, a construction worker, came for me at the hotel, and phoned me from the lobby, greeting me as a comrade with *compañera*, what everyone called everyone else in Cuba then. It signified: we are with the revolution. Then we sat on a bench, just outside the hotel, alone, with no one near. He told me details about Cuba I had never heard before. At one point, he pulled out his identity card, which had his name, photograph, a number, addresses at home and work. "Everyone has one of these," he said. "You see this number. That number is a file. And in that file they have your life. They know where you are, where you work, where you live, when and where you were imprisoned. Each of us has a complete file." Over and over again, I became aware of the dissimulation, the double life, that people lived daily (Pedraza-Bailey 1982). Such was also the life their brother Raúl led. Publicly, he was a party member; privately, he was quite critical of the system. During my trip 15 years later, in 1996, we drove together in his Russian-made *motoneta* down the streets of old Havana at night. In the sidecar, I could enjoy the sound of the sea waves hitting *el malecón*, the stars out in the pitch black of the night above buildings in centuries-old Spanish architecture, the few people out late at night. Later, after a couple of rum drinks that enabled him to speak out, he pulled out his red Communist Party member identification, slapped it on the table, and, pointed to it: "We live better. My family has decent clothes to wear; twice a month we go out for dinner."

Guillermo and Raúl engaged in dissimulation, what Cubans call *la doble moral* – the dual morality that becomes a mask Cubans commonly wear; however, their brother Juan, *el jabao*, was quite honestly proud of his participation in the revolution. He rose to become a professor and administrator at one of Cuba's universities. Ranging as they did in political expression and opinion, all the brothers were glad Rogelio had left Cuba via *el Mariel* because, at the young age of 30, he had clearly reached a dead end. After Rogelio left Cuba, he received a letter from his brother Raúl, who accused him of not being able to survive in that system – as he himself had done, adjusting to it. Wearing a mask, as Raúl had done, was a common way to cope with the system, as Mercedes Cros Sandoval (1986) found. She was the director of a Community Mental Health Program in Miami at the time the Mariel exodus took place. For the next two years, she informally interviewed 439 *Marielitos* to assess their needs for program development and, particularly, to identify the most prevalent coping patterns, such as this.

Rogelio and his brothers also participated, to varying extents, in Santería – the Afro-Cuban syncretism – the blend of Catholic saints with West African religious deities (cf. Barnet 2001; Franco 1978). Rogelio himself had been a Palero. This is a similar though distinct religious expression whose origins lie in the people of the Congo, rather than the Yoruba people, the origin of Santería (Fernández-Robaina 1997; Sandoval 1975). These African-based forms of worship and ritual also came to the United States with the Mariel exodus. Here they have flourished with more abandon and openness than in the past. In Miami, for example, now there is a church where this form of worship is openly conducted – la Iglesia Lucumí Babalú Ayé. Rogelio had been to see a *babalao*, a Santería priest, in Cuba who had engaged in divination of the future by throwing the *caracoles* for him. With the aid of the cowrie shells, he told Rogelio that he could see him crossing the ocean – as he did.

Sexuality and Race

To José Macías, both his race and sexuality were decisive in the decision to leave Cuba. José was 12 years old when the revolution triumphed, and initially he shared in its great enthusiasm. He joined the Conrado Benítez Brigade for the literacy campaign. José taught a peasant who did not even know the vowels. He himself was so young that at night, rocking himself in a chair inside the family's thatched-roof hut, which in Cuba are called by their Indian-origin name of *bohío*, he would ask: "Which way is Havana? And I would begin to cry, like a child." That turned out to be his sole participation in the political institutions that denoted commitment, integration to the revolution. To thank the young men for their service, the government awarded them a fellowship to study further, and he spent four years studying accounting. But he was unable to enter the university to continue studying economics because "I was not part of the communist youth, and to study the career of economics you had to be a Young Communist." So his studies ended in 1968.

For Macías, the problems started early in the revolution. After his initial revolutionary enthusiasm, the constant obligation placed on Cubans became a problem for him. His mother made efforts for him to join other groups, such as the Jóvenes Rebeldes, but he did not last long in the Rebel Youth as he would not do even the expected *guardias del comité* – the security rounds to guard the CDRs on every block. You were always obliged to serve, and "I did not like the imposition." His homosexuality was also a problem: "Fidel *nos acorraló*. He hounded us, making gays out to be the worst part of the society, rather than a group where there are both good and bad people, like any other." Asked whether he participated in any dissident group, he replied that he never did because, given his homosexuality, if he landed in prison, they might even kill him. A friend he lived with for a year "had a scar here, from a bayonet."

José came from a decent, working-class, black family. His father was a contractor and handyman; his grandparents worked in the tobacco factories of Pinar del Río, where they chose the finest leaves to roll the best tobacco. His mother initially had been a *manejadora*, caring for the children of the upper middle class, and also sold popcorn and nuts in the schools, with José's help as a child. Later on, she had been a textile worker in a factory.

José's family was also divided deeply over the political question. But that family division cut even deeper than most due to, on the one hand, his being gay and, on the other hand, his brother's fame. Miguel was a famous baseball star, his name a household word in Cuba. He traveled the whole world pitching, representing Cuba. Because his brother had risen to stardom, no matter how deteriorated life became in Cuba, his brother continued to see *el lado bueno*, the good side of the revolution. All José could see was that he would have been a millionaire in the United States. "Fidel only harmed him by keeping him there," he said. He also thought his brother worked for the State Security police. When their parents divorced, José remained with his mother and another sibling, while Miguel and another sibling went on to live apart, though nearby. But the distance that separated them lay elsewhere, in José's homosexuality, because Miguel could not accept it. "Once he asked me when I was going to get married. I replied: 'You know my real preferences.'... And he began to cry."

His being gay left him totally isolated in Cuba. "I represented the worst things that can happen to anyone in Cuba: I was not a communist, I did not like the government, and I was a homosexual." When I asked him to compare what being black and being gay was like in Cuba and in the United States, he was quite precise: "In Cuba, being black was a bit..." and he shrugged his shoulders. "But oh – being gay!" and his arms gesticulated to say: it was enormous. "Here, being gay is a bit of a problem, but not a very big problem. But oh – being black!" and again his arms said: it is enormous. Despite this fine sociological contrast, he did not want to credit the revolution with doing much for blacks in Cuba. He recognized that Castro's government had opened up the private beaches to all, making them public; had ended the racial segregation in the private school system; and opened up other opportunities to blacks in Cuba. But, he explained, these were just like giving blacks some candy, while whites still retained the best opportunities. "Look at the Central Committee of the Communist Party," he stressed. "How many blacks are there? Only three.... Look at the sports teams – 80 percent black." Castro, he claimed, used blacks for his own ends. "And then you go to the prisons in Cuba, and they are full of blacks."

Macías confirmed that the initial return visits of the exiles had also affected Cubans' views of the revolution. Until then, Cubans were *conforme* – they had adjusted to the style of life they had, to everything they lacked. But when the exiles returned in 1979, Cubans could see they lived rather well – they had the latest model car, a house; they could travel. Those in Cuba could not see how dearly the exiles had to pay for these things, "how hard life is, in other ways, in this country."

The group he left with managed to avoid the *actos de repudio* that developed side by side with the exodus. Those who left were beaten, spat at,

165

insulted, thrown eggs at, humiliated – acts that went on for months. Carlos Victoria, a *Marielito* who is a writer, described it thus: "Seeing Cuba wrapped in that fever, where the basest of instincts (to humiliate and hit another because he has decided to leave his country) broke loose, seeing for the first time the real possibility of an escape, of a life that resembled what I vaguely understood as a life, awoke an instinct in me that I had thought dead. The instinct to change." He continued: "I recall as if in a fog the repudiation acts, with beatings, spittings (one landed on my mother's cheek), eggs and stones thrown with furor" (1998:134).

Macías's group avoided this because it left on a bus before dawn. He was 32 years old when he escaped, alone. After *el Mariel*, he was resettled out of Fort Chaffee to Los Angeles, where he became the food manager and diet clerk for a hospital.

Sexuality and Artistic Freedom

René Cifuentes was white, but because he was gay, all doors were closed to him. He could date with precision the moment in which everything in Cuba turned against him: Fidel Castro's speech at the Congreso de Educación y Cultura (National Conference on Education and Culture) in 1971 when René was 17. At the closing, he was able to hear Castro when he defined the "parameters" of the revolution, what Cifuentes was to title, many years later, "the parameters of paradise" (1984). Castro said that, with respect to homosexual deviations, the government defined them as "social pathology," and he went on to stress the government rejected its overt expression and would in no way allow its diffusion. At that moment, Cifuentes "realized that the 'equality' he had learned so well in school in the Marxist texts did not exist for homosexuals, that outright 'rejection' was to be the attitude in place toward them, given their 'pathological' condition and that, of course, he would immediately be expelled from his study center" (Cifuentes 1984:12). It was the first time that a Cuban president had publicly turned against homosexuals. A series of laws was subsequently passed that made homosexuality a crime, subject to fines and imprisonment, along with alcoholism, prostitution, and drug addiction, because it "clearly contradicted the norms of socialist morality" ("Leyes Cubanas contra el Homosexualismo" 1984). The consequences were felt as gay actors, singers, dancers, and artists were removed from their jobs.

For Cubans such as René Cifuentes, Reinaldo Arenas, Jesús Selgas, all of whom were the closest of friends, issues of artistic freedom and sexuality were closely linked – perhaps inseparable. Hence, soon after their arrival in the United States, they founded the literary and artistic magazine *Mariel*. They went on to live and work in New York, partly due to the lack of acceptance they also felt from the exiles in Miami. Probably few Cubans suffered as much as Reinaldo Arenas from both the lack of artistic freedom and the lack of tolerance for his sexuality. Unquestionably, he was one of Cuba's most gifted writers. Lezama-Lima, one of Cuba's most respected writers, juxtaposed the poverty of Arenas's origins in the Cuban countryside and the enormity of his talent: "Genius, when it blows, has no limits; it can reach even a shepherd from Holguín" (Estevez 1998:130). Arenas, whom I met briefly when he was weakened by AIDS, left his life behind for the world to see in his autobiography *Antes que Anochezca* (1992) that mixes autobiography and fiction, as was characteristic of all his work (Soto 1990; Estevez 1998). Recently turned into a movie, *Before Night Falls*, Arenas's life reached an even broader audience. Both portray the despair and ostracism that one of Cuba's most talented native sons endured; the censoring of his work, most of which he managed to smuggle out of the country; the necessity to publish in other countries – France, Spain – where he could not see his work, long before he left Cuba; the ill treatment regularly meted out in a Cuban prison like El Morro to those like him. As Juan Abreu, another writer who shared the label of *escoria*, explained, Arenas was persecuted because he was homosexual, because he was free (1998:137). Cifuentes was present in his final days, which ended in suicide. Arenas was an icon who brought together, around him, a generation of Cuban artists and intellectuals who felt they were silenced twice – once in Cuba and then again in exile (Ballagas 1983). Even more, he emphasized the hostility of the American academy to Cuban writers in exile. In return, Arenas used to call them "the festive left."

Arenas told the story of his political disaffection in his work. His first short story, "Comienza el Desfile" (The Parade Begins), written in 1965, recounted the euphoric triumph of the Cuban revolution seen through the eyes of a young man in the countryside who does not fully understand what he fought for but is happy to join the parade passing by. That story reappeared later in the anthology published in Spain after Arenas left Cuba, *Termina el Desfile* (The Parade Ends) (1981). In this work, he relived the onset of *el Mariel* in the Peruvian Embassy, the few days in April when more than 10,000 Cubans crowded, desperately, trying to leave Cuba (Soto 1990). For them, as for Arenas, the parade, indeed, had come to an end.

Roberto Valero (1983) and Jesús Barquet (1998) analyzed the various publications in which the work of *Marielitos* appeared (*Linden Lane*,

Término, Unveiling Cuba, Mariel) and delineated their common attitudes and values. Despite their lacking a common artistic vision and style that could make them a literary generation, what truly made them *la generación del Mariel* was their opposition to all dictatorships – of the left and of the right; their opposition to sexual intolerance, both in Cuba and in exile; their virulent anti-Castroism and anti-Sovietism, resulting from their lived experience; their admiration for José Lezama-Lima and Virgilio Piñera above all other writers; their shared goal of creating an art, in all its forms (including music, film, writing, painting) to which politics is subsumed; their private, though deeply held, religiosity.

Even more, social marginality and imprisonment were often part of this generation's experience. What René Cifuentes endured serves as an example. Because most of his family resided in the United States, including his mother, he was entitled to an exit visa, but the government denied it due to his homosexuality. So he attempted to leave Cuba illegally, for which he served in prison for three years. When he left prison, he found all doors closed. Unable to publish in Cuba, he published his first short stories in Venezuela. Soon that door also closed, as the government put in practice the Ley de Patrimonio Nacional (National Patrimony Law), by virtue of which all works of art belonged to the state. Thereafter, publishing overseas without the official state sanction meant prison (for him, the return to prison). For Cifuentes, Cuba became "a nightmare" from which he could not awake. Living in such a state of social exclusion, he discovered that, when the Mariel exodus began, being gay suddenly conferred upon him the right to leave Cuba. Thus, he, Reinaldo Arenas, and Jesús Selgas thankfully did.

The crossing itself was quite dangerous. Surrounded by hundreds of boats, overflowing with people, Victoria (1998:134) in his journey remembered being accompanied by common prisoners – *matones de verdad* (real thugs) – who displayed their tattoos in the sun, men who only the previous night had slept in prison, resigned to a long sentence, and now, perplexed, found themselves at sea. Jesús Selgas, for example, came in a shrimper designed to hold 80 persons but carrying more than 300 on board. The night he crossed, a tempest broke, boats overturned, some drowned, while others were rescued by helicopter. Pitch dark in the middle of the night, he could see neither the sea nor the sky. He only felt the waves passing over him, which made him think that he was already at the bottom of the ocean – strangely at peace.

Eventually coming to New York City, Selgas was able to actualize himself as an artist whose theme commonly is painting the saints and *orishas* (deities) whom Santería blends as one, as well as virgins such as la Virgen de la Caridad (Cuba's patron saint) or la Virgen de Fátima (revered in Portugal), that are expressions of popular religiosity. He painted la Caridad for the first time when his mother died and he was not allowed to return to Cuba to be with her. Shortly thereafter, he painted an unusual version of the image: the painted canvas is folded into the shape of a boat, and the boat is painted to become the virgin herself. Looking at it closely, one can see a number of symbols of Santería.

Cuban folklore became Selgas's theme when he no longer lived there. Such was the case with Lydia Cabrera, one of Cuba's foremost social scientists, who discovered *lo Cubano* when she was in Paris, at a distance, standing by the river Seine. She went on to write *El Monte* (1968), which explained the African backdrop of Cuban culture. Selgas's work also portrays an indelible characteristic of Cuban culture: the extent to which white Cubans' culture is penetrated by black Cubans' culture (see Figure 6.1). His work also contributed to the renewal of Cuban culture in exile. Prior to *el Mariel*, Cuban culture in Miami was often dedicated to preserving the past, *la Cuba de ayer* prior to the revolution; but through *el Mariel* also came an extremely talented group of artists, writers, and musicians who revitalized Cuban culture with their contemporary art, *la Cuba de hoy*, on this side of the ocean.

While Latin American culture can be said to be homophobic, given its Spanish and Catholic roots, its Mediterranean notions of *machismo*, and strongly held notions of sexuality expressing honor and shame, a cultural explanation seemed to me insufficient to account for what happened in Cuba in these decades – the outright persecution of homosexuals. Jesús Selgas, who was expelled from the Art School in the late 1960s for being gay, though he was so young then that he had no sexual knowledge, explained it best: because the revolution wanted to create "the new man," as Che Guevara (1970) had specified. And that *hombre nuevo*, Selgas stressed, was to live under the direction of the state, as a family man, a *macho*, lacking individualism and desire, wanting only to give selflessly to others. "The homosexual does not fit the mold. He goes against the grain." In her analysis of the intersections between race, ethnicity, and sexuality, Joane Nagel (2003:147) pointed out that nationalism, as an ideology through which to construct the modern state, erects moral boundaries regarding who is an insider (to be venerated) and who is an outsider (to be vilified) in that society: "The margins of nations – ethnic frontiers, gender frontiers, sexual frontiers, ethnosexual frontiers – are all locations where rules about citizenship and proper national demeanor are tested and contested." Nagel (2003:159)

Figure 6.1 Cubans who left in the third wave of the exodus (1980) were called *los Marielitos*. Among them were a sizable group of artists and intellectuals, such as Jesús Selgas, who painted this "Black Moon – Virgen de Regla." This is the black virgin Cubans pray to, whose shrine is in the town of Regla. In Santería – the blend of Catholic and West African beliefs – the Virgin is also the embodiment of Yemayá, a West African deity whose home is the sea. Here the black Virgin gives birth to a white child – a symbolic expression that white Cuban culture is penetrated by black Cuban culture.

also noted that the culture of hegemonic masculinity goes hand in hand with the culture of hegemonic nationalism, both because the nationalist state is an institution run by men and because the culture of nationalism is totally tied to the culture of manhood, thus becoming intolerant of sexual diversity, particularly homosexuality. Artists, too, were seen as people who could not be trusted. The government explicitly stated that the function of art was to educate – a socialist realism (see *Política Cultural* 1977). But to Selgas, artists came to the world *a confundir* (to confuse others), expressing themselves symbolically, which entails being free.

Asked what aspects of the revolution he would put on both sides of a balance that weighed the good on one side and the bad on the other, Selgas emphasized that the revolution had given him an education that had pulled him out of the very poor social milieu into which his family had fallen, partly due to his father's mental illness and partly due to the loss of the family business, the bakeries. Without the educational opportunity the government gave him, he might not have been able to realize himself, to join other artists. Yet, Selgas emphasized, what they had given, they had also taken away, condemning him to a life of social ostracism, insisting he should not be an individual. The revolutionary government claimed it was creating *una maravilla*, a marvel, in the future, while simultaneously it was creating "a terror," in the present. It gave gifts, he said: land to the peasants, houses to the homeless, decent health coverage, a free education; but it also took away the free press, forcibly reeducated the subversive, destroyed the opposition, and spread fear.

Artistic Freedom and Class

The parameters that the revolution defined at this time had to do not only with sexuality but also with artistic freedom. The case of Heberto Padilla (1990), a young man who had come out of the revolutionary process, in 1968 was key. His poetry book *Fuera del Juego* (Outside of the Game) (1998 [1968]) criticized the conformity demanded from those who were part of the game the revolution forced them to play. The poem that gave the collection its name said:

Al poeta, despídanlo!	The poet! Get rid of him!
Ese no tiene aquí nada que hacer.	He does not belong here.
No entra en el juego.	Takes no part in the game.
No se entusiasma.	Is not enthusiastic.

No pone en claro su mensaje.	His message is not clear.
No repara siquiera en los milagros.	Even miracles fail to impress him
Se pasa el día entero cavilando.	All day long he finds faults.
Encuentra siempre algo que objetar.	Always finds something wrong.
¡A ese tipo, despídanlo!	That guy, get rid of him!

The collection won the Julián del Casal Poetry Prize given by the Cuban Writers and Artists Union in 1968, thanks to a fair-minded panel of judges that included members of the union, such as Manuel Díaz-Martínez and José Lezama-Lima, and outsiders, such as J. M. Cohen, who came to Cuba to judge the contest. The government accused Padilla of engaging not in legitimate criticism but in counterrevolutionary activity (Ripoll 1981). In 1970 he was briefly imprisoned; then he was made to confess. He finally left Cuba in 1980. For many intellectuals, this incident was a turning point. Renowned intellectuals, such as Jean-Paul Sartre, Simone de Beauvoir, Italo Calvino, Julio Cortázar, Hans Magnus Enzensberger, Carlos Franqui, Carlos Fuentes, Gabriel García-Márquez, Octavio Paz, Juan Rulfo, and Mario Vargas Llosa, joined in letters to Fidel Castro, protesting Padilla's treatment, asking him to safeguard an intellectual space for criticism (for all the documents pertaining to this case, see Padilla (1998 [1968]), which includes the original documents published in *Casa de las Américas* (1971).

Armando Alvarez-Bravo witnessed the moment in which Padilla confessed publicly, an event that many colleagues attended, in the back of the garden of the UNEAC. Padilla's mea culpa – what he himself called "a ceremony of self-degradation" (1990:181) – was a turning point in the lives of many. Along with others who had fallen in disgrace (such as Reinaldo Arenas and Belkis Cuza-Malé, Padilla's wife), Alvarez-Bravo had a job that rendered him marginal – proofreading the texts to be printed in the official literary publication *La Gaceta de Cuba.* After that, he no longer had even that marginal form of employment. He then held out doing odds and ends for a living: giving private classes in his own home (an illegal activity), cleaning the church of San Antonio de Miramar. As Alvarez-Bravo noted, he lived a contradictory situation. On the one hand, given the critical situation that people like him were living through, a real solidarity developed among those who shared values and experiences. "Even more," he added, "a greater solidarity developed than there could be in an open society, such as this." On the other hand, he also began living an inner exile: "I did not serve in the military service, I was not a *miliciano*, I did not participate in anything," but never did he or his family cease to practice their religion. At that time, that was quite unusual; it also "made you into an enemy of the revolution." He described himself as a "Católico terco" (a hard-headed Catholic) at a time when attending church was seen as a counterrevolutionary activity. Until *el Mariel* came.

Initially, he and his wife sought to protect their daughters, who were humiliated and hurt by the *actos de repudio*. He painfully saw the crowds strip his daughters, 12 and 14, naked and beat them, calling them *burguesitas* – young bourgeois girls. They protected 10 young adolescents in their home in el Vedado, an exclusive section of the city known for its beautiful, old architecture.

As with so many other *Marielitos*, their family in both the United States and Spain made arrangements for a boat to go to Cuba and pick them up. But they could see that the exodus was coming to an end, and they were still there. Under those circumstances, many people who were not such declared themselves to be homosexuals, or drug addicts, or prostitutes – because if you were considered to be a *lacra social* (social scum) you were allowed to leave. As Victoria (1998:134), who was also present, noted, "violence was mixed with farce." But Alvarez-Bravo refused to incriminate himself falsely, to call himself what he was not. He experienced the contempt for the upper classes that typified the early years of the revolution. "They called me '*aristocratizante*,'" he stressed – a contemptuous rendition of "aristocratic." "So I decided to leave Cuba wearing a coat and tie." But soon he realized they would not let him go, so he gave his wife the legal power of attorney to leave with their daughters and her father, while he stayed behind. After a month in the camp "El Mosquito," his family finally left in September, just as *el Mariel* was closing, among the last to leave. Alvarez-Bravo himself was forced to do work in construction, filling carts with cement or bricks, under the sun, a brutal work regime, in a unit where others were common prisoners, many of them violent, even murderers. Yet they treated him very decently. Early every morning he was ready to begin again, with his metal spoon and cup dangling from his neck.

Thanks to the international pressure that his family and friends overseas exerted, in 1981 he was allowed to leave for Spain. There he lived and worked, primarily in literary magazines, for a couple of years, during which he was awarded a prize – the International Poetry Prize José Luis Gallego. Eventually he arrived in Miami, where he soon became a founding member of *El Nuevo Herald*, the Spanish-language version of the *Miami Herald*, and began to strive to bring the work of Cuban artists and writers to broader attention.

Alvarez-Bravo stressed that in Cuba, with all its censorship and lack of support, a lively intellectual and cultural life flourished. Even when they knew they would not be published, writers traded with each other. But in Miami he found a very poor intellectual life, despite the exiles' capacity to support it economically, with the exception of the work of Ediciones Universal – "the reservoir of an uprooted culture," he said.

Gender

Last, why did so few women participate in *el Mariel?* Fidelia Suárez wanted to leave through *el Mariel*. However, given the family responsibilities she shouldered as a woman, she was unable to do so, and arrived years later, in 1985. The youngest of six siblings, when the revolution first triumphed she was an architecture student at the university. Three of her siblings left Cuba in the early years of the revolution – for Miami, Spain, and Venezuela. Twenty years later, the only ones left were her father, who was 91, and she. She bore the responsibility of caring for him at home, while also being the breadwinner. An architect who specialized in public works, she earned the respect of her colleagues, though she did not participate politically. She lived surrounded by her paintings, her memories, a niece and nephew, a few close friends. In the small patio in the back of her house, she often rested after work, surrounded by verdant tropical foliage and bright flowers. Because there was no drawing paper in those years, she often painted miniature flowers on tiny pieces of paper. I first met her in Cuba in 1981, a few months after the closing of *el Mariel*. She gave me a watercolor she drew with just a few well-delineated strokes, depicting one of Cuba's loveliest beaches – Santa María del Mar. She painted it on an envelope left over from a letter she never mailed.

To her, what had left a mark on her life was to have remained alone in Cuba, with the weight of family responsibilities on her shoulders. At that time, simply to survive, day to day, was an achievement. Managing to put food on the table every day required ingenuity and connections with others. Friends and *socios* (partners who help one to solve problems) bartered this item in exchange for that piece of food, participating in the black market. Like many Cubans, she jokingly talked about *sociolismo* (rather than *socialismo*) as the system they utilized to solve problems, above and below board (see also Sandoval 1986:34). "*Sobrevivir a toda costa,*" she stressed, whatever survival may cost – that was the aim of her life then, as it was for most Cubans. This entailed living by the rules of the revolution, by its relentless, military-like discipline, while trying to protect one's individuality in a society organized into masses. To protect herself psychologically, she painted. Like many Cubans then on the island, she engaged in what Inkeles and Bauer (1959) in their study of the Soviet Union called "the inner emigration." For more than 20 years, leaving Cuba had been impossible for her, given the family responsibility she bore. Even if her family overseas had claimed her, she could not have given up her job, as required, waiting for months until the day came. But when her father died, at the age of 93 in 1982, at the funeral home itself she made the decision to leave. Thereafter, it took three years before she was able to leave, when she took an early retirement. She left for Spain, "as the last *escoria* – the very last scum."

In Spain, the Red Cross helped her as a refugee, not only economically but also psychologically, as she participated in the show they organized: "Artists in Exile." Fidelia showed her paintings at 30 of these exhibits, thus making a contribution to the cultural life of Spain, she felt. Painting again became the medium through which she found psychological comfort in her solitude. Apolitical in Cuba, she remained apolitical in exile. Never a churchgoer, she nonetheless lived "the mystery of life," as she called it, deeply and privately, often examining it in painting. Despite her need, sometimes she found it impossible to sell her work. A small collage she made particularly caught my eye. She placed a few torn pieces of letters and envelopes that had been mailed to and fro under a Cuban stamp that commemorated Amelia Peláez. Peláez was a revered artist and a close friend of hers. She explained: "These letters come and go, as you can see. They are the communication among those who love one another but are apart. A trip takes place. It is a trip with no return."

The *Marielitos* were a distinct wave because their social characteristics are the result of the particular conjuncture of the Cuban revolution. At this time, to survive economically entailed participating in the black market; women faced extreme familial burdens; gay Cubans were persecuted; and problems of freedom of expression loomed paramount. This exodus also raises the issue of Cuba's lack of tolerance for dissent. A society where the only choice possible is to "love it or leave it" provides too few choices. A truly democratic society is defined not only by its party structure, constitution, delegation of authority, or electoral representation, but principally by its capacity to tolerate and incorporate dissent. The Cuban exodus, now close to half a century old, was driven not only by the trauma of revolutionary change in

Cuba and by the economic hardships caused both by the inefficiencies of the new economic system and by the isolation imposed by the trade embargo, but also by Cuba's incapacity to tolerate dissent. The Cuban revolution's only solution to dissent has been to externalize it. Cuba has yet to provide political channels to express and incorporate the dissenting voices.

7

After the Soviet Collapse

Decidí romper mi amistad. . . . Pero ahora el abrigo [que él me había dado], una prenda grácil y tentadora, tendía un puente entre mi dignidad y mi miseria. Y allí, frente al espejo, pensé que si la verdadera historia de Cuba revolucionaria llegara a escribirse, en la portada del libro debía aparecer Esaú con su plato de lentejas.

I decided to break off my friendship. . . . But now the coat [he had given me], graceful and tempting, tended a bridge between my dignity and my misery. And there, in front of the mirror, I thought that if the true story of revolutionary Cuba were to be written, the book's cover should depict Esau holding his plate of lentils.

Carlos Victoria, "El Abrigo" (in Las Sombras en la Playa [1992])

The Fourth Wave: The Special Period

The new Cuban exodus – the fourth wave – began in the late 1980s and took force in the 1990s, during what Fidel Castro himself called "el período especial" – the special period that resulted when communism collapsed in the Soviet Union and Eastern Europe. The collapse meant the end of the generous Soviet subsidy that Cuba had received for nearly 30 years and the end of Cuba's economic and political dependence on the Soviet Union.

Over the many years the Cuban revolution now spans, its economic policy has swung from one economic and ideological cycle to another, cycles that are captured well by Carmelo Mesa-Lago (2004). He identified six cycles that oscillate between idealism and pragmatism, the one checking the other. When the Mariel exodus took place in 1980, Cuba was in the midst of a pragmatic cycle in which some economic reforms toward the market had been introduced, such as the introduction of free peasant markets and some forms of self-employment, as well as the construction of private homes and swapping (*permutar*). Moreover, as Mesa-Lago (2004:33) pointed out, "Soviet trade and aid peaked in this stage, particularly nonrepayable price subsidies to the island exports and imports, and Cuba entered the Council for Mutual Economic Assistance (CMEA), all of them positive external factors that contributed to implement and expand policies during this cycle." Even more, with President Gerald Ford's help, the Organization of American States lifted its sanctions in 1975, followed by President Jimmy Carter's further relaxation of tensions.

The pragmatic reforms of the 1970s and early 1980s constituted a swing of the pendulum away from the earlier idealism accentuated by Che Guevara's leadership. According to Mesa-Lago (2004:33), the "previous emphasis on egalitarianism, moral incentives, and labor mobilization were criticized as ineffective 'idealistic errors.'" Material incentives were reintroduced and expanded; wage differentials were defended; voluntary labor was deemed inefficient and drastically curtailed; and a parallel market arose in which demand and supply determined the price of goods. This cycle of pragmatism lasted 15 years. Many of the recent immigrants I interviewed remembered them as "the good years," when a period of stability ensued during which social inequality was not too great and the support of the Soviet Union was assured. Mesa-Lago noted that the highest economic growth was reached, particularly in 1971–75, aided by record sugar prices and sugar harvests that averaged more than 7 million tons a year.

This period was checked by the U.S. presidencies of Ronald Reagan and George Bush in the 1980s, both of whom continued the embargo of Cuba and spearheaded a crusade against communism, and by the premiership of Michael Gorbachev in the Soviet Union, who ushered in the reforms of *perestroika* in the spirit of the transparency of *glasnost*. Cuba felt the changes both politically and economically, as the Soviet Union could ill afford the weight of Cuba's burden. Thus, the Soviet Union's trade and aid to Cuba remained stagnant, while price subsidies were reduced. Mesa-Lago (2004:34) pointed out that the USSR began to pressure Cuba to reduce the trade deficit and better use the Soviet Union's economic aid. What Cuba really cost the USSR – not just economically but also politically – is a story yet to be told.

An idealistic cycle, the Rectification process of 1986–90 ensued, during which Humberto Pérez, the head of the Central Economic Planning Board (Junta Central de Planificación Económica, JUCEPLAN), was fired and tried for mechanically introducing an economic model not suitable for Cuba (Eckstein 1994). The new cycle was called the Rectification of Errors and Negative Tendencies, during which the government returned to the anti-market orientation of the Guevarist period, though in less extreme ways: private farms were eliminated; free peasant markets and self-employment were abolished; private housing construction and house swapping were reduced; voluntary labor was reintroduced; material incentives were sharply reduced and moral incentives reinstated; an emphasis on some of Guevara's ideals returned; the parallel market was eliminated and rationing was expanded; and decentralization measures were halted. As a development strategy, tourism began to be promoted, as was biotechnology, with the aim of making Cuba a world power in that area. Lasting only four and a half years, until the onset of "the special period" ushered by the collapse of communism, an economic recession was the outcome (Mesa-Lago 2004:35). During the years of Rectification, the rate of economic growth was negative, a fiscal deficit resulted, open unemployment continued to increase, and the trade deficit reached a historical record. This made Cuba even more vulnerable to the transition that perforce was to take place in the 1990s.

The *período especial* from 1991 to 1996 was Castro's euphemism for the abyss reached during the economic crisis that followed, when Cuba's trading partners, the Eastern European countries, disappeared, taking the regional trade market and heavy subsidies upon which Cuba depended along with them. As Mesa-Lago (2004:36) described it, Cuban-Russian trade was reduced to only bartering oil for sugar; all price subsidies ended; Russia ceased buying key Cuban products, such as nickel and citrus; Soviet loans and credits were drastically reduced; all trade with and aid from the Eastern European nations came to an end.

In addition, in the United States, President Bill Clinton, under pressure from the Cuban American National Foundation, represented by Jorge Mas-Canosa, tightened the trade embargo with the Torricelli Act of 1992. In the first three years of this cycle, when the crisis reached its full depth, the Cuban economy declined by about 35 percent of GDP – a precipitous decline. Now Cuba had to rely on itself, and the result was economic devastation. The real impact of the U.S. trade embargo was finally felt when these subsidies evaporated. Hunger, malnutrition, disease, and poverty became the daily lot of people. I traveled to Cuba several times during these years: in 1991, to attend the meeting of the Caribbean Studies Association; thereafter in January 1995, to participate in the Centro de Estudios de Alternativas

Políticas's workshop on "The Cuban Emigration" held at the University of Havana; and again in January 1996, when I gave the inaugural Lourdes Casal Lecture at the University of Havana, in which I presented my work on immigration to the United States, particularly the Cuban exodus. Thus, I was able to see the dire consequences of the early stages of the *período especial.*

The Mariel exodus had proved so traumatic, both for the United States and Cuba, that immediately thereafter the doors to further migration closed. However, in the mid-1980s both governments signed a new Migration Agreement that provided for the immigration to the United States of up to 20,000 Cubans and up to 3,000 political prisoners a year, as well as for the deportation of excludable *Marielitos* back to Cuba. In actual practice, however, only around 2,000 visas were given a year. When the economic and political crisis that took place in Cuba reached a new depth between 1989 and 1993, Cubans who wanted to leave Cuba were pushing against an almost insurmountable wall.

The "special period" was not only an economic crisis but also a crisis of legitimacy, of disbelief. Cubans on the island began to feel that their leaders were less than capable, and the hope they held of a future communist society with a decent life for all faded. Indeed, Cubans became so desperate that, in the summer of 1994, a massive riot ensued on the streets of Centro Habana on August 5, and the people began leaving en masse on *balsas* (rafts, tires, makeshift vessels) that drifted on the ocean, risking death due to starvation, dehydration, drowning, or sharks. More than 34,000 left in the summer of 1994. "Those who despair," I said, constituted this last wave of migration (Pedraza 1996a).

In the 1990s, the *balseros* risked the arduous crossing so regularly that from 1991 on Los Hermanos al Rescate (Brothers to the Rescue) began to constantly patrol the sea in small planes, searching for them. According to the U.S. Coast Guard, 5,791 *balseros* managed to reach safety in the United States from 1985 to 1992. As economic conditions worsened in Cuba, the numbers rose dramatically and illegal emigration became the major form of the exodus (Rodríguez-Chavez 1996; 1993). While the émigrés of the first two waves were those who became politically disaffected in the process of the transition from a democratic, capitalist society to a communist society, the young *Marielitos* as well as the recent émigrés are those who became politically disaffected from the only society they ever knew: Cuba in communism. As such, they are the children of communism, very different political generations than those of the early exiles.

The Sample

Of the 120 interviews I collected, 39 were with Cubans who emigrated during the new period, 1989 to 2004. On these interviews, I base this chapter and the next. In this chapter I portray the *balseros* and *balseras* who risked their lives to leave Cuba during the summer of 1994, as well as the conditions in Guantanamo when they lived there. To do that, I rely on interviews with Alberto Masa (pseudonym), Frank Fuentes, Juan López (pseudonym), Amelia Sosa and Arturo Llana (pseudonyms), Ricardo Blanco, and Raúl Martínez. In the next chapter, I present the range of political expression found among the contemporary émigrés. Because this wave of the exodus is still ongoing, we cannot yet characterize its definitive social and demographic characteristics – for example, the *balseros* (rafters) have recently given way to the *lancheros* (speedboaters), and the latter clearly have a great deal more money than the former – but it is possible that this latest wave may yet be the most heterogeneous to date.

Daniel Pérez-López (2006) compared the data for Cubans who were 25 to 44 years old in 2002 (i.e., born at the time the revolution triumphed or later) for Cubans on the island, Cuban immigrants in the United States, and the second generation of Cubans born in the United States. Data from the 2002 Cuban census put the proportion of Cubans on the island with the equivalent of a bachelor's degree or higher at 11.5 percent. Data from the 2000 census of the United States put the proportion of Cubans who immigrated from 1990 to 2000 with that same high level of education at 21.2 percent, and for Cubans who were born in the United States at 37.5 percent. To these estimates I add the most recent data available from the American Community Survey (ACS) microdata files for the years 2000–5. The ACS put the proportion of Cubans who immigrated in those years with that same high level of education at close to 27 percent of the men and 23 percent of the women (U.S. Bureau of the Census, 2000–5). Clearly the new exodus has brought Cubans with the highest levels of education on the island.

The social and demographic characteristics of my sample of 39 Cubans are congruent with those of other larger samples drawn on the same population of recent immigrants, such as those of Andy Gómez and Eugenio Rothe (2004) and those of the Measuring Public Opinion Project (MPOP) (Roberts 1999). Gómez and Rothe (2004) drew their sample in the fall of 2003, consisting of 171 Cubans who had been in the United States less than 72 hours and who were being resettled throughout the United States by Church World Service, a Protestant agency. Roberts (1999) drew the sample in the winter of 1999, consisting of 1,023 Cubans who had been in the United States three months or less. The survey was used by Ernesto Betancourt and Guillermo Grenier (1999), as well as Benigno Aguirre and Eduardo Bonilla-Silva (2001). All of these samples agree on the immigrants being preponderantly men (about 60 percent); on its being a relatively young population (mean age about 35); and on its being an urban population (about 80 percent).

Less agreement exists with respect to educational attainment and race. Although all samples agree that the population is very well educated, their descriptions vary. Roberts (1999) and Betancourt and Grenier (1999) described their levels of education as varying considerably: 19 percent of the immigrants had a secondary education; 40 percent had a preuniversity education; 22 percent had a technical school education; and 19 percent had a university or postgraduate education. Gómez and Rothe (2004), instead, drew a sample where only 9 percent had a university education; less than half, 46 percent, had a technical or vocational training education; 36 percent had a high school education; and 9 percent had only an elementary school education.

Their samples also disagree with respect to the racial description. The Measuring Public Opinion Project (Roberts 1999) drew a sample that was described as 87 percent white and 13 percent nonwhite (Betancourt and Grenier 1999). Gómez and Rothe (2004) drew a sample that was described as 76 percent white and 24 percent nonwhite, nearly twice the former rate. Even so, Gómez and Rothe felt that their sample underestimated the black, mulatto, and mestizo population of Cuba. That could be the result of their drawing the sample from the population served by Church World Service, a Protestant agency. Given the syncretism of Catholic and West African religious beliefs and practices evident in Santería, had they drawn their sample from the population served by Catholic Charities, it might have resulted in a sample with a larger nonwhite presence. The U.S. census of 2000 gives the proportion white among Cubans who immigrated in the 1990s at 85 percent (see Table 6.2), closer to the Measuring Public Opinion Project. My own sample of 39 respondents was closer to the percentage nonwhite found by Gómez and Rothe, with mulattoes in much larger numbers than blacks. The discrepancies demonstrate that the definition of race in Cuba continues to be fluid, subjective, and difficult to grasp by North American standards, particularly when researchers use different methodologies.

My own sample of 39 respondents who represented the recent immigrants included many professionals, university students, artists and intellectuals, and working-class Cubans who lived in the city and country-side. I spoke with Cubans who left in myriad ways: those who crossed the Rio Grande as *mojados* (wetbacks) or who left Cuba as *balseros* (rafters) and *balseros aéreos* (who came by plane because they had more money), those who lived in the tent city of Guantanamo Bay for about a year and a half, and those who left Cuba to study abroad (in The Netherlands, Italy, France, and Russia) and never returned to Cuba or returned to then leave again. The interviews included Cubans who formerly were active members of the dissident movement, as well as those who did their best to stay out of politics altogether, and those rebels who landed in prison for their political activism. My interviews also included Cubans of all races and ethnicities and religious persuasions, including those who grew up without any religious instruction and, as Amelia Sosa put it to me, wish they knew how to pray, but did not.

The Balsero *Crisis*

The *balsero* crisis reached its peak in the summer of 1994, but being a *balsero* has been a major mode of exit from Cuba throughout the years of the revolution. Holly Ackerman and Juan Clark (1995) compiled all the available data that tell us that the *balseros* have arrived in two major cycles: the first between 1959 and 1974, when more than 16,500 *balseros* arrived in the United States; the second, between 1989 and 1994, when more than 46,500 reached the United States alive. At the peak moment in the summer of 1994, the U.S. Coast Guard rescued 1,010 in July; 21,300 in August; and 11,085 in September – a total of 33,395. As mentioned earlier, August 1994 marked a historic turn in Cuba. On August 5, massive riots took place in the center of Havana, in which thousands of Cubans participated all day long, expressing the enormous material want that shaped their lives, their disdain for the privilege reserved for party members and foreigners, and the enormous wish for civil liberties that now also permeates Cuban society (Rivas-Porta 1994).

Shortly thereafter, Fidel Castro gave orders to the Cuban Coast Guard not to discourage the illegal emigration from Cuba's shores. Immediately, thousands of *balseros* put out to sea, in the hopes of reaching Miami. But an abrupt policy change made the Cubans unwelcome. President Clinton recalled the Mariel exodus, when Castro pushed people out from jails and mental hospitals, "all in an attempt to export all the problems of Cuba to the United States" (Clinton 1994). Both the president and Attorney General Janet Reno (1994) emphasized that such a crisis would not happen again.

On August 19, under orders from the attorney general and the president, the U.S. Coast Guard blocked their progress and directed them to a "safe haven" in Guantanamo (the U.S. base in Cuba). There about 30,000 people lived in tents for many months, some up to a year and a half, until they were allowed entry to the United States. Early in September the United States signed the first part of a new migration agreement. Moreover, Cuba agreed to discourage further emigration through persuasion.

The *balseros'* gratitude to their rescuers knew no limits. Early one morning in August, Lizbet Martínez, a 12-year-old girl with a long, blonde pony tail, climbed aboard a raft with her parents. She took aboard her most prized possession – her violin. When the U.S. Coast Guard rescued them, she played "The Star-Spangled Banner" on her violin for them – a plaintive melody of gratitude for those who saved her life (Balmaseda 1994a).

Many who set out for the United States died tragically at sea. Claudia Pérez was 15 months old when she died in her mother's arms – one hour before she was rescued. Raísa Santana died because she drank seawater, reserving the only drinking water left in their vessel for her son (*El Nuevo Herald*, December 26, 1993). The 33,395 rescued by the U.S. Coast Guard do not include these deaths, nor do they include those who arrived without their assistance or those who first reached land in other places, such as the Bahamas, Mexico, or Cayman Islands (U.S. Coast Guard 1995).

Ackerman and Clark (1995) developed a typology of the *balseros*: the "water taxi" mode – those who had money and connections, so that their travel was fast and safe; the "betting" mode – those who had access to boats, as well as knowledge of the sea, for whom it was a dangerous gamble; and the "do-or-die" mode – those who lacked resources and connections, risked imprisonment when leaving, and faced trauma or death at sea.

As a result of the crisis, a new Migration Agreement was signed in September 1994 that promised that the United States would henceforth actually give at least 20,000 visas a year for Cubans to immigrate to the United States. The visas were given to immediate relatives (and their families) of Cuban Americans who claimed them; to political prisoners; to temporary visitors; to those who qualified as refugees; and to those who did not have immediate relatives in the United States but won the lotteries held in Cuba in 1996, 1997, and 1998.

In May 1995, however, another abrupt policy change allowed the refugees in Guantanamo to come to the United States at the same time that the United States signed another Migration Agreement with Cuba that stipulated that *balseros* found at sea would actually be returned to

Cuba (Rodríguez-Chavez 1996). "Cuba bleeds," headlined Liz Balmaseda (1994b), "and the drops are called rafts." For the first time, the U.S. government denied Cubans' claim to be refugees and began to treat them as "illegal aliens," as Attorney General Janet Reno called them. This was quite a change from the days of President Johnson's policy, when all Cubans were seen as victims of communism and deserving of a warm welcome. The change, I think, was due to the end of the Cold War between the United States and the Soviet Union – yet another result of the Soviet collapse. With the Cold War no longer raging, refugees from communism no longer have the symbolic value they had. Then American policy makers encouraged their "flight to freedom" because they exemplified the rightness of our cause and served to legitimate U.S. foreign policy objectives (Pedraza-Bailey 1985).

From the many *balseros* and *balseras* I interviewed, I chose five to illustrate what impelled Cubans to risk their lives by leaving Cuba on a *balsa* and to depict the conditions in the camps at Guantanamo Bay. While the weight of the economic crisis of the "special period" can easily be seen, for most *balseros* (indeed, for most of all the recent immigrants, whatever their mode of exit), the political and the economic are deeply intertwined – in fact, are inseparable.

Alberto Masa felt deeply the weight of the economic problems during the "special period." A tall, attractive mulatto, he was born in 1957 and left Cuba on a *balsa* in the summer of 1994, at the age of 38. He had dreamed of leaving Cuba in 1980, during the Mariel exodus, but his mother had not wanted to leave, and he could not leave her behind. The seeds of the dream had been planted in his childhood, when his family had gotten the passports and the visas to leave Cuba, but the fact that his brother was of military age prevented his father from doing so. He refused to leave any of his sons behind. His father was part of the mulatto middle class that had surrounded Batista. He had worked for Batista's secret police. On the heels of the Bay of Pigs invasion, he was imprisoned under charges of conspiracy. While others could be said to have believed in the revolution and then lost their belief in it, Alberto never acquired it. He remembered growing up listening to his parents talking about what Cuba had been like before, how enjoyable social life had been, how life after the revolution had deteriorated. As an adult, Alberto tried to stay away from politics altogether, tried to work well but not to participate politically. Alberto thought that change from within was not possible; he expected the Cuban exile community to be the harbingers of change, from the outside.

As a sports teacher in a vocational school that housed around 6,000 students, Alberto had a good job. He invested his savings in buying a plot of land to build a house, together with his wife. The house was in the outskirts because he liked the peace of the countryside. Gradually, over the years, he bought the materials with which to build the house. After their first child, a girl, arrived and his mother died, they moved in with his wife's parents. Even though they had two incomes and his wife worked as an economist in the food industry, they could not make ends meet. So he began searching for another source of income. He learned to make shoes from a friend, aware that the leather and other materials were stolen from the government: "In Cuba, it is difficult to find something to do that is not illegal," he pointed out. So he made his shoes in hiding, afraid of being found. Alberto put all his efforts into finishing the house, hoping he and his wife could live alone, together, with their two children, without all her family. But then came the "special period" and, with the lack of transport in Cuba, his hopes were dashed. Aggravated by the lack of fuel then, the house was simply too far away for them to be able to live in it and also to take the children to the Círculo Infantil, a child care center.

Machista that he acknowledged he was, he felt that the responsibility for the family well-being rested mostly on his shoulders. He then began raising chickens, to eat and sell, to barter for other necessities. Then came the incident that "hit the nail on the head," as he put it, making him decide to leave Cuba. At the end of December, he bicycled to the countryside, about 40 kilometers distance, with some of the shoes he had made and some chickens, and he exchanged them for a small, succulent pig – a *puerquito* that would be big enough to eat in March, for a *fiestecita* in honor of his daughter's birthday. Moreover, he planned to sell part of the pig and buy his daughter some clothes with those dollars. Thus, the *puerquito* represented many efforts, many hopes. One night while they were sleeping, he heard the pig squealing loudly. He went to see what was happening and found four men trying to steal it. One hit Alberto with a wrench on the side of the head. The following day Alberto killed the pig and made the decision to leave Cuba: "There were no alternatives left; nothing more that I could do. I knew how dangerous the journey was, but I had faith in God and something inside of me said that nothing would happen to me." Alberto described how the conditions in Cuba made him into a *gusano*:

If you slept in a mattress with hardly any filling; and you got up in the morning, and had to brush your teeth with salt; and then you were told that breakfast as a meal did not exist; and you had to wait until lunch to eat, only *harina*, or even a good lunch of some rice and beans; accompanied by only tepid water, never a soda; and then the lights went off; and to fetch something you had to walk 20 blocks under the hot sun; and then you wanted to bathe but there was no soap, and no towels other than a rag; and if at night you suffocated in the heat, and could hardly sleep, without a fan, because even if you managed to have a fan, there was no electricity; you would think you were caught in a nightmare, a *pesadilla*, but it is not, because it continues, day after day – the day would come when you would become a *gusano* too!

Thus, he started making plans to leave. He and a friend had to come up with around 4,000 pesos to buy a boat and an additional $1,000 in U.S. currency for the motor. For this, he sold his bicycle, his gold chain, the few personal belongings he had. They managed to leave the day after President Clinton declared that the *balseros* departing from August 19 on would "not be allowed to enter the United States" but would be taken to the naval base at Guantanamo as a temporary "safe haven."

After 11 months in Guantanamo, Alberto was resettled to Lansing, Michigan. I interviewed him and others shortly after they arrived there. Alberto started to work immediately, at a restaurant, and lived an ascetic life-style in an apartment, saving all he could to telephone his family back in Cuba and to bring them to Michigan. In truth, his wish to leave Cuba, and his departure, created marital problems: "At first, my wife could not forgive me for having left them. But then she realized that I was right, like always, and it was the best I could do for the family."

Frank Fuentes was a *balsero* of the "do or die" type. At the age of 28, in September 1994, Fuentes joined a group of friends who were building a *balsa* with the help of a man who lived in Guanabo, on the beaches of Habana del Este. Frank sold his motorcycle for $300 so he could contribute to buying the supplies needed to make the *balsa* and the trip – the tires, tarps, oars, the sail, and the food. The *balsa* was built around seven tires – one in front and three on each side, on top of Styrofoam that someone had taken from the factories where it arrived with goods imported in containers. All of it rested on wood and was covered with a tarp. He left behind a daughter, less than two years old, with sorrow, but with the mother's consent. Seven of them sailed on the boat, with Frank managing the sail.

As they were finalizing the plans for their departure, with the boat ready to put out to sea, a man approached him to see if Frank would give up his place on the raft to the man's father for $150 – a hefty sum of money in Cuba. Frank refused, so eager was he to leave. "What pushes you into an adventure such as that," he stressed, "is the wish to be free – *ansias de libertad*.

I wanted to be free, not to be constantly watched, under surveillance, not to be asked to show my identification for no reason, not to be obliged to attend meetings." Despite the fear people live with in Cuba, when Frank and his friends left, people overcame some of it and dared to come up to them and say good-bye: "Good luck," they said. "May you have luck and arrive where you wish." Young boys swimming on tires accompanied them out to sea, encouraging them, and then returned.

When they were about 10 miles out, around 11 o'clock at night, the Cuban Coast Guard passed them by. They continued, knowing there was no return. Every two hours they would rotate duties, especially rowing, so as to be rested. Frank became seasick and repeatedly vomited. The first night they slept very deeply, tired from the rowing and the emotional stress of the day. They were able to sail about 40 miles out. When the new day dawned, they were able to see rather large boats in the distance, which made them hopeful they were either the U.S. Coast Guard or merchant boats. In the afternoon of the second day, a U.S. Coast Guard helicopter flew over them and the pilots waved. This gave them hope because the situation had become dire, as they had lost their drinking water. They had brought a huge 90-liter tank of potable water with them, which they placed on its side in front of the boat. But the weight of the tank made the boat sink gradually. When the level of the water inside the boat became quite high and the front tip of the boat leaned downward, there was no other choice left than to throw the tank of water overboard, after drinking as much as possible. Fortunately, they had some other water on reserve.

After they got rid of the water tank, the level of the water inside the boat improved, but the real problem became apparent: the wood underneath the *balsa* had cracked. The bread, the crackers, everything was wet. They had covered everything up carefully, but "the sea gets inside of everything." All in all, he said, luck was with them. They had fine weather all the way; the sharks did not follow them; and they were rescued just in time. As Frank was sitting down while manning the sail, the water reached his waist. Probably only a couple of hours more were left, he stressed.

Of the seven young men who left on the boat, all but one came from his neighborhood – Habana del Este. Four had attained a modest level of education, the *pre-Universitario*. One of them, from Pinar del Río, whom they called *el guajiro*, had less. Three were well educated. Frank had completed two years in the university, specializing in geography. Luis was older and had graduated from the University of Havana in international relations. He had been a member of the State Security working overseas in Cuban embassies, so he spoke English, French, and Portuguese. Carlos had completed the *pre-Universitario* and gone on to the Camilo Cienfuegos Military Academy, where future military were trained.

After the helicopter sighted them on the afternoon of the second day, they saw large ships fairly near, about five miles away. But they also realized they were not coming to rescue them right away because the sea around them was littered with *balseros*, whom they were busy picking up along the way. Finally, their turn came. The yacht stopped 500 meters or so away, and the crew lowered a speedboat with three persons to rescue them. As they pulled them onto the boat, they were checked for arms, and they took away their belts, which could be used to hang oneself or to hit someone else. The yacht was full of rescued *balseros*, from one end to another, ranging from the very young to the very old. They had to sleep literally on top of each other.

From their safe place inside the yacht, they saw how the Americans sank the *balsa*, so as to not leave it adrift, which could be dangerous to others. They remained in the yacht for more than a day, during which they picked up more than 500 persons, until the mother ship, the *barco madre*, as Frank called it, picked them up. Rescuing so many people in abject despair was an enormous task. In the yacht, the Americans had signs in Spanish asking questions like "Are you ill?" and "Does your head hurt?" so they would try to help them with the means available in the small clinic aboard.

Frank recalled that, as they entered the yacht, they took down their name and address on a piece of paper. These were transmitted to Florida. From there, Radio Martí sent the information back to Cuba. Usually, the information took 7 to 12 days to reach Cuba. It was the only way the family in Cuba could learn what had happened, as it took months before letters could be mailed from the camps.

That evening it poured rain, which made the waves break. The seawater poured inside the boat, and they were drenched. Now the sharks circled the boat, all night long, into the next morning. The next day came their transfer to the mother ship with the use of speedboats that could transfer around 70 persons at a time. The *barco madre* was a destroyer: "It was impressive – a monstrously big ship that must have held 3,000 persons, all dressed in white." As they entered the ship, they were given soap, white clothing, toothbrush and toothpaste, so they could bathe. In the *barco madre* the food was excellent. Coming from Cuba, where there was such scarcity of food, to be given fruit cocktail, scrambled eggs, toast, and milk for breakfast was *la gloria* – glorious. Lunch and dinner were equally good: chicken or beef, spaghetti or beans and rice, and milk. Considering how unprepared the Americans were for the massive exodus, Frank stressed, "they behaved very well with us. They took good care of us." After two days in the "mother ship," they were taken to Guantanamo Bay.

What impelled Frank, a "do or die" *balsero* to leave Cuba? Like many young people who left Cuba during this last wave, he came from a family that was very integrated to the revolution and knew no other world than Cuba in revolution, Cuba in communism. Frank's childhood had been "very sad." His father had risen to become an escort for Fidel and was a member of the Seguridad del Estado for 10 years, and then went on to become part of the Poder Popular (Popular Power). His mother was not a maternal woman, so he and his brothers and sisters were raised by their grandparents, who were also communists. His grandfather had been chief of personnel of the Granma Military Enterprise, in Casablanca, a huge industry with more than 30,000 employees. His father remarried a woman who also worked in intelligence.

As a child, Frank became very close to his two aunts, who were true believers in the revolution. For the revolution, they gave everything. Osília became a lieutenant in the MININT. Teresita also worked for the party for more than 20 years, in its provincial headquarters in Havana. But eventually they both realized they had made a mistake – "though late, because it *was* late." Osília left her job; Teresa resigned from the party. Frank could remember his aunt discussing the impact the Rectification of Errors Campaign had on her. His aunt Teresa often repeated Castro's speech in which he said that what they were doing until then to achieve socialism and to advance the revolution was wrong; hence, it was necessary to rectify the errors of the past. The situation confused his aunt because, until then, she thought the steps they had taken, *she* had taken in the name of the revolution, were correct. At that point, Frank remembered, she lost faith in the leadership and came to see the roads taken as only due to Fidel's ambition, his capricious decisions. A year later, she turned in *el carnet*, the party card, at a meeting of the assembly.

The symbolic repudiation resulted in the loss of her job, as well as constant surveillance wherever she went. Frank was 20 then, and his aunt's difficulties impacted him greatly. So did seeing how a neighbor who became a dissident and his dissident friends were treated. While the ill treatment of the dissidents was intended as an *escarmiento*, to keep others from joining the dissident movement, often it had the effect of making evident what the government was really like.

Other political events impacted Frank deeply. His brother was imprisoned because he had tried to leave Cuba as a *balsero* a couple of years earlier,
when exit was considered illegal. His ill treatment in the prison left a mark
on Frank. So did the nature of elections in Cuba. People in Cuba voted for
candidates up to a certain level, but not above it. There was a "pyramid" that
always peaked in the figure of Fidel, with Raúl below him. In an election for
the delegate of the city district, Frank had written in "no." A friend from
the UJC who was involved in the election let Frank know that thousands
of people had done the same. But the delegate was declared the winner,
nonetheless. Like so many young people who left Cuba in recent years, he
disliked the constant imposition to participate, the obligation to be part of
the system, the intrusion into one's life. "In Cuba there are no possibili-
ties to advance, unless you are a communist or an assiduous revolutionary;
nothing is possible for a young person who is not integrated to the nucleus
of the party. You cannot move forward, I can assure you."

Frank summed up his family's transformation and the toll it took on them:
"My family fought for the revolution; they were raised in the revolution;
they believed in the revolution; and they lost their faith in the revolution."
He felt that, in the end, his grandfather had died *de tristeza*, of sadness, in
addition to the normal illnesses of old age. I also believe that my uncle,
Rafaelito, died *de tristeza*, not just of an aneurism. The sadness belonged to
those who lost their hope in the cause they believed in and had sacrificed
themselves for.

Juan López's story is also instructive regarding how the political and economic were deeply intertwined for many people in Cuba in the 1990s. In
the summer of 1994, at the age of 29, he finally succeeded in his attempt –
for the third time – to leave Cuba as a *balsero*. By training an engineer, he
worked in a sugar mill in Camagüey. Later, he spent two years working in
the tourist industry, and he happened to be in Havana during the "5 de
Agosto" riots, a moment that caught him running away from the police
who were indiscriminately beating people to stop the protest. While his
parents and grandparents had never been in favor of the revolution, he
himself was born within it, been educated by it, and studied overseas as a
result. Hence, for him the experience of working in the tourist industry was
decisive, for there he had been able to see up close the double standard that
exists in Cuba today for foreigners versus Cubans, that everything was for
the tourists, while Cubans themselves had no access to that life-style and
were literally kept out of the hotels. He recalled Nicolás Guillén's (1986)
poem *"Tengo"* (I now have), written in 1963, that told how prior to the

revolution he was kept from entering a hotel, the "dancing," or a bar, because he was black. Now, Juan said, you cannot enter because you are Cuban, period. Asked whether he thought that people such as himself left Cuba predominantly because of the economic problems, he replied: "That really is the question for a *balsero*, isn't it?" And he went on to add: "It was the economic problems, yes. But they were the economic problems of *that* political system."

Amelia Sosa had studied physics and math at the State University of Minsk, Byelorussia, for close to six years, yet that experience did not promote a change in her values. "At that time, I still had a *venda* over my eyes, I was still blindfolded." After her parents became separated when she was 11, she had little contact with her father, so the major influence in her life had been her mother's family, all of whom were committed communists. Her father was sanctioned by the government and spent 45 days at Villa Marista, after which he spent two years in prison, working at a farm near Pinar del Río. A working-class man, mechanic and trucker, that humiliation deepened his hatred for communism. She remembered visiting him in jail, with her mother, but when he left jail, her parents divorced and her contact with him afterward was sparse, so her values and ideas were not challenged by his disaffection. His "political antecedents," as they are called in Cuba, did not hurt her career because she had established a solid political reputation for herself – first, as a young Pioneer student, then as member of the UJC. Ironically, in 1980, at the same time that she was leaving Cuba to study in the Soviet Union, her father was leaving Cuba through *el Mariel*. She was told he left because he did not love her, because she was the communist daughter, and he was willing "to exchange her for material things and for the consumer culture." She believed it then, yet at the same time she was profoundly "shocked by the violence *el Mariel* gave way to."

While she lived and studied in the Soviet Union, the winds of change – *glasnost* and *perestroika* – had not really started blowing yet. She returned to Cuba in 1985 to work at a research center in molecular biology. There she began to feel the winds of change, as other young people who had studied in the Soviet Union returned with fresh ideas, wanting to introduce *glasnost* and *perestroika*. At a meeting in their theater, for example, these students had the courage to stand up and freely say that they thought it was wrong to tie politics to work – to be obliged to do "volunteer work," which overloaded them, when their main work was to do research. Moreover, they asked for a greater *apertura*, an opening, so that people with different political opinions could participate at the workplace. Without doubt, these young researchers were surrounded by some informants. While she was still "blindfolded," as she put it, she met a young man, Arturo, who was in favor of change – so much so that they called him *el perestroiko*. Growing to love him opened up the possibility of her changing. He challenged her "blindness." He lent her George Orwell's *1984* and *Animal Farm* and other books that critiqued communism. Their circle of friends included other young people who took dissident positions, often at personal risk, wanting to change Cuba from within, rather than wanting to leave, as she increasingly did. Their friends participated in the "Declaración de Profesores Universitarios," a statement signed by 14 university professors. It asked for greater freedom of expression within the university; the return of its autonomy; the democratization of social and political life in the nation; as well as national reconciliation and unity among all Cubans, irrespective of their political beliefs and whether they resided in Cuba or in the diaspora (see González-Dalmau 1991).

Amelia Sosa left Cuba again in 1990, to study in Strasbourg, France, for two years on a fellowship. She had resumed a relationship with her father when one of his sisters came from the United States to visit the family in Cuba, bringing her a letter from him. In that letter, he explained his coldness at the time he left was due not to his lack of love for her but to his not wanting to cause her problems. When she went to France, their communication became quite regular. He expressed his hope that she would not return to Cuba but leave for the United States to be with him. Moreover, Arturo was able to join her in France the second year. Her brother had also left Cuba in 1988 and arrived in the United States, crossing the Mexican border illegally. His departure spurred a process of change in her mother. Eventually, her mother separated herself from the government and joined an evangelical church, although she had grown up without religious instruction.

Although reluctant to return to Cuba, Amelia did so due to Arturo's influence, because he had all his family there and he wanted to go to another country to do his thesis in another laboratory. They returned to "a total hell." Six months later, he left Cuba for Australia. After a two-year absence, she knew she would not be allowed to leave again, but she still tried by various means, including paying money for false documents, which did not work. "Then came the phase in which the person is totally destroyed," she recalled. She suffered through a meeting at work in which she was humiliated by her co-workers. She was expelled from the research institute and could no longer find work in Cuba. On September 5, five days before

193

the massive exodus was closed, she left on an unusually large *balsa* with 26 other persons, 8 of whom were extended family members. After 12 miles at sea, a day and a half, the Coast Guard picked them up.

The Guantanamo Camps

After the *balseros* were rescued by the Coast Guard, they were brought to the base in Guantanamo. Alberto Masa recalled that, as they descended from the plank of the boat, they were greeted by a woman in uniform who told them they would never enter the United States. Air-conditioned buses, such as they had not seen in Cuba, took them to the *campamentos*, the camps where they were given yellow uniforms to wear, a bag full of necessities, and some food. The camps were surrounded by a fence about six feet high. Every cabin held about 30 persons, with the cots placed tight next to one another because there were so many people. "At first it was very hard," Frank Fuentes remembered, "because they were not fully prepared for the situation." The base could hold 15,000 to 20,000 persons – not 30,000 persons. Food, milk for children, and vital necessities were missing. The situation was one of "despair, confusion, misinformation – a very hard start." His *campamento* was called "Uniforme." It held 300 persons with only six water pipes with which to bathe and to wash clothes. Later on, he moved to "Romeo" and from there to "Macara," the last one until he left Guantanamo. He recalled the confusion and anguish their arrival at the camps produced: "Cubans wondered how it was possible for the facilities to be so poor when they always thought the Americans were the most powerful people on earth." The Americans were simply unprepared for the massive exodus.

Little by little, over the next few months, life in the camps began to improve. Food, milk, vital necessities, and bathrooms were adequate. Dentists and doctors arrived. The *balseros* themselves re-created society. Newspapers sprouted; theater groups went from camp to camp to entertain; artistic expression began to flourish; schools were put in place; religious services became possible; a radio station called Radio Esperanza (Radio Hope) began to communicate news. In *periodiquitos*, small tabloids, they expressed themselves. *¿Qué Pasa?* (What's Happening?) had a series of informative articles that taught the *balseros* about American culture, gave them facts about the United States, gave news relevant to them, published the lists of names of those who gradually left for the United States, and included comic strips and cartoons where they expressed their frustrated aspirations (see Figure 7.1).

Frank Fuentes became part of a comedy group that went from camp to camp making others laugh. Alberto Masa carved a number of statues, inspired in the African wood-carving tradition. Amelia Sosa became one of the teachers in the schools that were improvised for the children, teaching them math. Ricardo Blanco, another *balsero* who was later resettled to Lansing, Michigan, started an art gallery. He used one of the white bed sheets and stiffened it with varnish to create a canvas. Painting in oil, using primary colors, he expressed himself. A small painting of his, depicting a white dove with an olive branch in her beak, now hangs in my living room (see Figure 7.2).

Frank felt that the experience of the journey and the refugee camps had "helped me mature; it turned me into a man." Because he had no family in the United States, after spending some months with friends in Miami, working at Wendy's restaurant, he was sent to Lansing, Michigan, by Catholic Charities. There, the charity provided an orientation program, teaching him aspects of life in the United States, such as what social security was and stressing the need to learn English. In my fieldwork in Miami, I spent time with both Catholic Charities and Church World Service, learning about the work they did with the refugees, how they operated, and the difficulties they faced. The Catholic Charities agency had, on the wall as one entered, a map with all the different cities it resettled the refugees to. The city was chosen randomly. Frank was assigned to Albuquerque, New Mexico, another of his friends to Lansing, Michigan. He did not want to go to Albuquerque, so instead he called a friend in Lansing who had offered him help. He was proud and did not want to accept the food stamps and the help; rather, he wanted to learn English, learn a trade, and stand on his own two feet.

He arrived in Michigan in the midst of winter, when the cold was at its worst – "violent," he said. Because he had been a cook in a number of good tourist hotels in Havana, he applied for the position of cook at the Kellogg Conference Center of Michigan State University. They called him to start working as a waiter, which he thought was harder, since it required some knowledge of English. Little by little, he began teaching himself English while on the job. He carried a notebook in which he wrote all the words he did not know. Soon, he became a U.S. resident. After a couple of years, he had the good fortune to meet Carmen, from Spain, who became his girlfriend, and he began learning a trade – dental technology, which she practiced. Eventually they left for Spain together, where he studied dental technology at the University of Valencia. They married and returned to work in the United States and now live in West Palm Beach.

195

Figure 7.2 Ricardo Blanco left Cuba during the *balsero* crisis of the summer of 1994. After jumping onto a *balsa* and then being rescued by the Coast Guard, he lived in the tents at Guantanamo Naval Base. There he painted this oil painting on a bed sheet. To him, the white dove symbolizes Cuba, which is choked by a strong hand wearing a metal glove. Blanco explained that both the Cuban and U.S. governments – their flags waving in the background – are hurting her. But she still hopes to be free. (Silvia Pedraza)

Immigration Policy

A distinct social process, immigration consists of both micro- and macro-social processes. At the microsocial level, immigrants have experienced another life in another country and culture, which they bring with them and which continues to influence them. At the macrosocial level, the state in

---

Figure 7.1 (*facing page*) While the *balseros* lived in the camps at Guantanamo Naval Base, they re-created society and sought ways to express themselves. Among these were the *periodiquitos* such as *¿Qué Pasa?* (What's Happening?) – the small tabloids full of news, advice, poems, comic strips, and cartoons. In the first cartoon, "Artiles" depicts a *balsero* rowing his *balsa* and towing his dog behind on a smaller *balsa*, arriving not in the United States but to a tent pitched in Guantanamo; in the second cartoon, "GMartínez" depicts the Statue of Liberty as busily laying out the barbed wire around the base of the *campamento* at Guantanamo.

197

two societies permits the immigrants to exit and enter. The state functions as a gatekeeper to regulate and direct migration through a body of law. Both the Cuban and U.S. governments shaped the exodus of the recent Cuban émigrés.

Ackerman and Clark argue that the 1994 *balsero* crisis showed the same pattern as past migration crises, during the chaotic flotilla exodus of Camarioca in 1965 and Mariel in 1980 (1995:42). The exit crisis built up, which the Cuban government amplified by allowing increasing numbers of rafters to go, giving vent to the popular desire to leave. In so doing, Fidel Castro transferred the crisis to the U.S. government, attempting to shift responsibility for the exodus away from the social and economic conditions in Cuba to the United States, and creating a domestic crisis there. Castro has repeatedly called the Cuban Adjustment Act "a diabolic machine intended to kill" – an incentive for Cubans to risk the dreaded passage, risking their lives (Ferreira 1999). Failure on the part of the United States to rescue the rafters would have been unacceptable, in humanitarian terms. Yet rescuing them made the crisis a domestic political issue for the United States, which created conflicting demands from various constituencies. Thus, it forced the United States to the negotiation table (cf. LeoGrande 1998). The cover of *Time* magazine on September 5 depicted it well: against the background of a dark, raging sea, with a raft of *balseros* sailing away, Castro defiantly asked: "Ready to Talk Now?" (*Time* 1994). Only the wish to avoid another domestic disaster, such as that created by the Mariel exodus, could, indeed, bring the United States to the negotiation table. Both countries agreed to take steps to bring the migration to an end by mid-September. Both countries moved to regulate the migration.

Through the accords reached in September 1994 and May 1995, the U.S. and Cuban governments drafted a new Migration Agreement, yet another instance of what Domínguez (1992) called "cooperating with the enemy." As mentioned earlier, the United States now promised to give visas to fully 20,000 Cubans a year, to be claimed by their immediate family members in the United States. This was a significant change from the previous agreement, which specified that up to 20,000 visas could be given a year, but in practice only around 2,000 or 3,000 were given. Moreover, as part of the total, it added a lottery, such as other countries had in place, of 5,000 visas for those who did not have immediate family in the United States to claim them. The lottery had an impact on the migration of black Cubans who lacked family networks in exile (cf. Aguirre and Bonilla-Silva 1999). The "special period" affected black Cubans in particular, because the lack of such family networks meant they received fewer remittances (Blue 2004; de la Fuente 2004). Even more, *balseros* in Guantanamo were to be gradually released and resettled throughout the United States.

The new Migration Agreement, generous as it was regarding the total number of Cubans to be admitted, did entail an abrupt change of policy, popularly known as the "wet foot/dry foot" policy. The 1980 Refugee Act changed the operating criteria for refugee admissions to the United States from one that, in effect, granted asylum to all immigrants from communism and from the repressive governments in the Middle East to one that considered each claim to asylum on an individual basis by the strict test established by the United Nations' Convention (1951) and Protocol (1968) on the Status of Refugees. As such, a refugee became a person who is unwilling or unable to return to his or her country of nationality or habitual residence because of "a well-founded fear of persecution on account of race, religion, nationality, membership in a particular social group, or political opinion." With this new definition, the Refugee Act attempted to assure greater equity in the treatment of refugees (Edward Kennedy 1981:143). In practice, however, the evidential burden placed on individuals who claim asylum is rather onerous. Moreover, the approval rates for asylum cases granted to particular nationalities continued to reflect that country's distance from U.S. foreign policy concerns (U.S. Committee for Refugees 1986; Wassem 1992).

Moreover, the strict standard that judged one individual at a time could not serve a mass exodus resulting from a crisis, what E. F. Kunz (1973) called an "acute" refugee movement, rather than an "anticipatory" one. Thus, all *Marielitos* as well as the Haitians who washed ashore in 1980 received the status of "entrants." While the domestic trauma created by the Mariel exodus made the U.S. government reluctant to open up its arms to more Cubans (Masud-Piloto 1966), the *balsero* crisis prompted it to negotiate so as to find a way to promote a legal and orderly departure for those who wanted to leave Cuba and to give it a chance to review those seeking U.S. admission. But the change meant that for the first time Cubans at sea who had not reached the shores of the United States ("wet foot") would be interdicted at sea and returned to Cuba, unless they could prove they suffered from outright persecution. Only those Cubans who did manage to land on U.S. shores ("dry foot") were to be welcomed as legal entrants. Indeed, in the decade of 1995–2004, 8,675 Cubans were interdicted by the U.S. Coast Guard at sea and returned to Cuba, despite the protests of Cuban Americans on the streets of Miami. At the same time, the new migration accords of 1994–95 did lessen the number of Cubans who put out to sea on a *balsa* considerably and achieved the safe, orderly departure of Cubans who were also screened prior to arrival. In the decade that followed, only 10,314 who put out to sea arrived on U.S. shores. Both interdictions and arrivals together numbered close to 19,000 over a 10-year span (U.S. Coast Guard 1995). Nonetheless, in the same decade, the number of *lancheros* or *boteros* increased dramatically, as migrants began to rely increasingly on expensive speedboat operators who swiftly make the illegal crossing (Henken 2005).

Henken argues that while this new policy of interdiction applied to Cubans seems like an abrupt change in policy, ultimately it is not, as Cubans continue to benefit from the special treatment accorded them by the Cuban Adjustment Act that has been in place since 1966. The act means that Cubans who arrive in the United States legally can solicit their residency after one year and one day. To Siro del Castillo (2005), the Cuban Adjustment Act was intended simply to allow Cubans already in the United States to adjust their immigrant status. To José Basulto, however, the act resulted from the role the United States played in compromising Cubans' freedom at the Bay of Pigs. Legally, at present, the act provides for Cubans who arrive with visas (obtained via family reunification or by winning the lottery); and by sea, if they land on U.S. shores as "dry foot;" or through the Mexican frontier. To Lisandro Pérez (1999), the new immigration policy constituted "the end of exile," as the door, indeed, began to close, once a hardening of the policies had taken place. Cubans, however, were still treated in a preferential manner, in comparison to other immigrants, not only in that anomalies exist, such as the Cuban Adjustment Act, but also in that asylum is granted much more often. Max Castro (1999) also underlined that exile cannot, in fact, come to an end for as long as it is not possible for Cubans who left to return to Cuba. Moreover, for the first time Cubans began to be treated like other immigrants. As Max Castro (1999) also pointed out, *both* governments use immigration policy as a weapon and think about immigration from the point of view of security, failing to see it as a right.

In my view, the interdiction policy for the "wet foot" does constitute a dramatic change in policy. This can be seen in how it changed the role that Los Hermanos al Rescate could play, flying over the Caribbean looking for *balseros* lost at sea. Raul Martínez, who flew for 10 years with Brothers to the Rescue, explained that, after the change in policy, they remained helpful to any *balseros* they sighted. From their small Cessna planes, they continued to throw down a bag with maps, food and water, an emergency aid kit, a couple of t-shirts, and a message. However, they could no longer be instrumental in rescuing the *balseros*, as they had been for so many years, when they could notify the U.S. Coast Guard of the *balseros'* location at sea and could also count on their being rescued. Prior to the massive exodus of 1994, Hermanos al Rescate sighted and contributed to the rescue of 4,100 *balseros* and around 1,600 during the crisis itself. Thereafter, until their operations ceased in mid-2002, they were instrumental in rescuing only 200. After the new Migration Agreement, the message the Brothers gave to the *balseros* was that if they were rescued by the Coast Guard they would be returned to Cuba. If their lives were in danger, or they wanted to be rescued, they should signal them by waving their arms. If not, they would leave, as if they had not seen them. Only once did a *balsero* signal.

The problem at stake, however, is larger than the peculiarities of the Cuban case. As I pointed out in my essay "American Paradox" (Pedraza 1996b), what is unique about the American experience is the nearly unceasing nature of immigration (voluntary and involuntary both) over the course of U.S. history. This enabled race and ethnicity to become so deeply intertwined with American history as to produce a distinct set of contradictions in the American fabric. One of these contradictions comes from the role that immigration has played in American history. As Muller and Espenshade (1985) expressed it, the United States is now experiencing only the most recent of its four major waves of migration. Because immigration has been coterminous with American history, one should not be surprised at the truth of Oscar Handlin's (1973 [1951]:3) encounter when, seeking to write a history of the immigrants in America, he discovered "that the immigrants were American history."

Because the history of America is also the history of American immigration, then, immigration is also a part of the American identity – of its definition of self. In *A Nation of Immigrants*, President John F. Kennedy himself expressed it well: "three large forces – religious persecution, political oppression, and economic hardship – provided the chief motives for the mass migrations to our shores" (1964:6). This American tradition of providing not only an opportunity for a better life but also a refuge from tyranny was nowhere else so well expressed as in that poem every school child learns – Emma Lazarus's poem (1883) written for the Statue of Liberty. Hence, for the United States, immigration is not only an economic issue or even a political issue, but also a moral issue. Yet both the controversies over the massive arrival of Southern and Eastern European immigrants at the turn of the 20th century as well as the recent controversies over the arrival of illegal aliens from Mexico and Central America at the turn of the

Table 7.1. *Typology of Migration*

		Legal and Political Status	
		Conferred	Not Conferred
Psychology and Motivation for Migration	Economic	Legal immigrants (e.g., Koreans, Indians)	Undocumented labor (e.g., Mexicans)
	Political	Legal refugees (e.g., Cubans, Vietnamese)	Undocumented refugees (e.g., Salvadorans, Guatemalans)

21st century betray a profound nativism. Such nativism consists of the desire to define "the real Americans" (those descended from yesterday's immigrants) as "us" versus "them" (today's immigrants). As Georg Simmel insisted, the stranger is not the man who comes today and goes tomorrow, but rather "the man who comes today and stays tomorrow" (1971 [1908]:143–44).

Amid the xenophobia generated by World War I, nativism led to the closing of the door to immigrants from Southern and Eastern Europe and became embedded in the discriminatory national-origins quotas of 1924 (Higham 1978). When the 1965 amendments abolished them, Edward Kennedy (1966:149) expressed that the national-origins quota system "was conceived in a radical period of our history – a period when bigotry and prejudice stalked our streets." Most recently, at the turn of this century, that nativism has again become expressed in attempts to curtail illegal aliens, such as California's Proposition 187 and the recent attempts by the Arizona Minute Men to patrol the border with Mexico.

The contradiction between the definition of America as a nation of immigrants and particularly its tradition of extending a hand to those who flee from tyranny and oppression has never been more vivid than in the U.S. government's recent treatment of Cuban and Haitian refugees. Table 7.1 shows the typology of migration that defines the types along two different axes: on the one hand, the immigrants' own motivation for migration (whether it is predominantly economic or political) and, on the other hand, the government's response (whether it grants or denies) the immigrants' claim through its legal system.

Of the four types this typology yields – legal aliens, undocumented aliens, legal refugees, and undocumented refugees – the most embarrassing and disputed is the last. One can deny legitimate claims to a grant of legal immigrant status on the simple basis that the nation lacks the capacity to absorb any more such immigrants. Regrettably, "the boat is too full." But denying claims of political asylum to those seeking to be considered as refugees involves denying their motivation. It is not that "the boat is too full," but that "they do not belong on the boat." Ultimately, that wounds not only the persons whose claims to fleeing oppression are thereby falsified but also the nation that has consistently claimed to be a refuge from tyranny. The United States' refusal to accept Haiti's refugees and the recent Cuban refugees interdicted at sea has eroded the belief of many in what America has always stood for, tarnishing its national image and hurting its credibility.

Peter Rose (1993:15) emphasized the situational nature of the politics of rescue: "It is no exaggeration to say that, when it comes to American refugee policy, the quality of mercy has long been strained by overriding economic, social, and political considerations. Our reception and treatment of would-be asylees is – and has long been – a textbook example of situational morality." With the end of the Cold War and the collapse of communism in Eastern Europe, refugees from communism lost their symbolic value. Thus, the most recent exodus of *balseros* from Cuba was met by the interdiction of the U.S. Coast Guard that routed them to the camps of Guantanamo Bay, insisting they were trying to enter the United States illegally. Since then, desperate *balseros* who are unable to reach the shore, "wet foot," are also interdicted at sea.

Moreover, the criteria for admissions imposed by the 1980 Refugee Act of a "well-founded fear of persecution" should be closely scrutinized. For while it undoubtedly was well intended, seeking to bring greater equity to the process of decision making, it recognizes only one type of refugee – namely, those who are *targets* of violence specifically directed at them (cf. Zolberg et al. 1989). Not all refugees, however, are targets. Some are *victims* of the cruel social processes they have lived through but scarcely participated in. As Zolberg et al. put it, victims are "persons displaced by societal or international violence that is not necessarily directed at them as individuals but makes life in their own country impossible" (1989:30). As victims, they live lives marked by fear, although they themselves may not belong to a social category that is persecuted, nor would they dare to act in such a way as to incur the attention (much less the wrath) of others. In Cuban slang, those who hide their political disaffection and live as if they were loyal supporters of a regime in which they no longer believe but still fear are called *tapaditos* – those who live under a cover, under a daily dissimulation (cf. Pedraza-Bailey 1982). As a nation, we should question whether we have imposed standards that perhaps hark back to the European reality of fascism in midcentury (whose targets were also its victims, such as all Jews) but that do not recognize the nature of victims' lives in the Third World today.

The United States has yet to develop a realistic and humane immigration policy. It should be realistic in the sense that the numbers of immigrants who can legitimately get on the boat should be delimited by its capacity as a society to absorb them and by its need to protect other poor Americans – immigrants and native both, black, white, Hispanic, all – from the labor displacement that excessive immigration can lead to. But it should be humane also in that it should consider the plight of people who flee economic and political oppression as well as the self-definition of this nation as a nation of immigrants, its tradition as a haven for the oppressed. To provide safety for people who flee in fear is a human rights issue, a duty as old as human history – "You shall not oppress a stranger; you know the heart of a stranger, for you were strangers in the land of Egypt" (Exodus 23: 9). It is also an American tradition, a cornerstone of this nation. George Washington expressed in 1783 that he sought to "establish an asylum for the poor and oppressed of all nations and all religions" (Flexner 1974:176). A realistic and humane immigration policy that, in a consistent manner, expresses the best American values *is* in our best interest.

8

The Last Wave

Tan luego como el hombre siente en sí el poder de producir y evitar un acto, es decir, su libertad, ya se juzga, y juzga a los demás, responsables.

When a man feels in himself the power to act or not to act, that is, his freedom, he judges himself, and judges others, responsible.

José de la Luz y Caballero, "Aforismos" (1840)

Political or Economic Migrants?

In *The Transplanted*, John Bodnar (1985) analyzed the European immigrants who poured into America at the turn of the 20th century. He called them "the children of capitalism" because they had encountered capitalism twice. First, they encountered it in the Old World, as the transition from feudalism to capitalism was taking place, and then in the New, in America. So, I wonder, of the recent immigrants from Cuba, are they "the children of communism" because most of them knew no other society than Cuba in communism? Many also met communism twice, once in Cuba and again in Eastern Europe and the Soviet Union, where they lived and studied or worked during the transition from communism to democracy and capitalism.

The crisis of "the special period" that resulted from the collapse of communism was not only an economic crisis but also a political crisis. The government's attempts at political reforms were quite weak. Cubans on the island put a lot of hope in the *llamamiento*, the calling that took place before the 1991 Communist Party congress. As Susan Eckstein pointed out, "over three million people participated in national 'kvetching' sessions. Over a million opinions were voiced on fifty topics. Citizen complaints centered on problems of 'everyday life': on transportation, education, housing, recreation facilities, the food supply, services, excessive nonwork-related meetings, and crime, as well as on disillusion with the mass organizations and bureaucratism. . . . The *llamamiento* gave islanders a chance for democratic input at a time when their former Soviet-bloc comrades brought Communism to its heels" (1994:115). But disappointment set in when Cubans realized their input would not lead to substantial reforms in the political sphere. For many, the *llamamiento* was the last time they had hope that substantial political reforms could be accomplished within the system. Still, about half of the party's 225-person Central Committee and the 25-member Political Bureau was replaced, a generational turnover that, according to Eckstein, "was designed to counter growing political disinterest and disquietude among youth who never experienced first hand the Old Order and to allow for intergenerational political continuity" (1994:115).

As Mesa-Lago summed it, this time "there was no foreign power capable and willing to help; hence, the only alternative open to Cuba was to integrate into the world capitalist market. A new, pragmatist cycle was launched and labeled 'the special period in a time of peace,' a euphemism for an emergency structural adjustment program to save the economy and the regime" (1994:115). Domínguez emphasized that Cuba's economic transition began when it sought to attract the confidence of foreign investors, cooperating in joint ventures because this "cast aside one of the foundation stones of Cuban socialism's political economy, built on the expropriation of foreign property. The promotion of international tourism was another shift" (2004b:17).

The desperate situation forced the introduction of domestic market reforms. A constitutional amendment allowed private and mixed property of the means of production. State farms were transformed into cooperatives. Free peasant markets, self-employment, and artisan markets were reauthorized. *La libreta*, the rationing book, was largely replaced by market prices. Material incentives were, once again, emphasized.

From 1994 to 2004, the "dollar economy" dominated, and many Cubans invested considerable energy in developing ingenious schemes and crafts to earn dollars, so they could feed their families. Cuba's effort was to make tourism the number one industry, to make up for the loss of the Soviet subsidy and trade with the Eastern European countries and the decline of the sugar industry. The sugar harvest reached the lowest point in the century. From a high of 8.1 million tons in 1989, the sugar harvest fell to

4.1 million tons in 1999 (Pollitt 2004: tables 5.1 and 5.3). In 2006, it is reported to be down to 1.3 million tons, the worst since 1908.

A modest economic recovery took place that saved the regime from the crisis of 1993. Feeling secure, the Castro brothers decided to halt the reform process – economic and political both – to avoid further decline in their power (Mesa-Lago 2004:37). Raúl Castro's speech and actions in March 1996 began the cycle, when he destroyed the Centro de Estudios Sobre América because he thought the researchers there were no longer acting as organic intellectuals of the party but resembled other foreign academics. In addition, Raúl Castro strongly criticized the negative effects of the market policies introduced in the early 1990s. The tightening of the U.S. embargo through, first, the Torricelli Law in 1992 and, thereafter, the Helms-Burton Act in 1996 also fanned the flames of an anti-American nationalism and strengthened the hard-liners in Cuba.

To this equation, one needs to add the growing presence of the dissident movement in Cuba. While the government insists that the dissidents are only *grupúsculos*, a contemptuous term for "the smallest of small groups," they were able to reach the larger Cuban population and to articulate an alternative vision of society. In the efforts of the dissidents, one can see a notion of rights as universal – belonging to all, including Cubans – as well as historical – part of Cuba's tradition and quest to become a constitutional republic.

As was to be expected, the economic reforms resulted in greater inequality in Cuba, what Mayra Espina (2004) calls a restratification and greater complexity. In addition, the dollarization of the economy and the development of legal channels through which to remit money from other countries, especially the United States, to Cuba made remittances one of the pillars on which the Cuban economy rested. A 2001 survey of the Inter-American Development Bank showed that 67 percent of Cuban respondents living in the United States sent money to their families in Cuba. Approximately 46 percent sent it through formal channels – Western Union or other services. The remainder is transferred through friends traveling to Cuba (Orozco 2000, in Barbería 2004). The World Bank estimated the flow of remittances in 2001 at $813 millions. Sarah Blue's (2004) survey of Cuban families in Havana who received remittances from their relatives abroad showed that the remittances were relinking the family that both the Cuban government and the exile community had torn asunder; and they certainly provided some measure of material comfort for those left behind, improving their lives; however, they also served to exacerbate racial inequality. Because the first two waves of the Cuban exodus were predominantly white, black and mulatto Cubans on the island have fewer immigrant networks abroad they can rely on to send remittances.

Tourism has, indeed, become the number one industry. Canadian, European, and Spanish tourists predominate on the island. However, the luxuries afforded to tourists – good accommodations, meals, and medicines – are not available to Cuban citizens, who oftentimes are not even allowed to enter the hotels. The situation has become known as the Cuban apartheid. While those excluded are all Cubans, the growth of tourism has racial implications because jobs in this sector often go to white Cubans, the thinking being that tourists will prefer them. Other social problems emerged, such as teenage prostitutes: the *jineteras* and *jineteros* who promote sexual tourism. While the return of tourism and prostitution remind one of the years under Batista, *jineterismo* as a way of life has spread to social groups that in the past never knew prostitution – for example, university students, as I repeatedly witnessed. The talents of well-educated Cubans also began to go to waste. For example, Cuba has many well-trained doctors, and due to its advances in public health during the early years of the revolution, Cuban medicine was once a model for other Third World countries. But in recent years, the medical infrastructure has decayed to the point where doctors work without medicine. Hence, doctors can diagnose, but they cannot cure.

The Cuban economy remained stagnant, even with substantial foreign investment from the European Union, particularly Spain and France, as well as Canada. The trend toward the market in the beginning of the decade was checked in the latter part of the decade (cf. Ritter 2004). Self-employment gave rise to a vast informal sector, where people hired themselves to do whatever their skills allowed them to do, such as repairing very old cars; entertaining children as *payasos*, clowns for their birthday parties; selling paintings that depict Cuba's beauty; and selling small pizzas on the street. In recent years, the number of occupations that can be practiced as a form of self-employment has been dramatically reduced. Professionals take other jobs that are more likely to be paid in dollars, such as cab drivers. A profound "mismatch" exists between the high educational levels attained by the population and the lack of industries that can make the best of these skills. Looking to Cuba's future, Pedro Monreal (2004:96) argued that a development plan should emphasize an export-oriented reindustrialization, for which the work force employed in industry and productive services is the

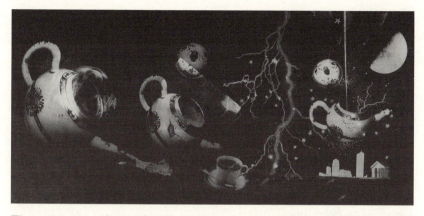

Figure 8.1   As author, in this photo collage about her adolescent daughter's growing up, "Letting Her Go with Difficulty," Joanne Leonard wanted to capture the tensions and pain of family life, along with the love. Here the tea service symbolizes both companionship and solitude. As the china teapot broke, from which her daughter issued, hearts also broke amid their anger and sadness, part of the struggles both mother and daughter waged over self and identity.

As viewer, I added another layer of meaning. In the Cuban revolution and exodus, the greatest pain was in the family break: people who loved each other but chose different political sides. Neither the pain nor the love ever left them. Also, in the beginning, the revolution had a strong class thrust, signified by the fine china teapot and the cups. But over time, those fine china plates taken from the upper middle classes broke, as everyone progressively became quite poor. (Joanne Leonard)

principal asset. Domínguez concurred that Cuba's macroeconomic strategy must harness "more effectively its people's human capital" (2004a:13).

Because the economic crisis of "the special period" was so profound, many interpret those who left as predominantly economic immigrants, as the Cuban government also consistently portrayed them. However, this ignores the depth of the political crisis that also took place. Moreover, the Cuban revolution is now nearly half a century old. Thus, the generational differences in experiences and attitudes between adults, who made the revolution and felt affirmed by it, and their children, who only inherited its problems, are profound. They result in very different reasons for the exodus. Always, the pain and the anger were lived *in* the family, as people who loved each other chose different political sides. Neither the pain nor the love ever left them (see Figure 8.1).

Regarding their motivation for leaving, my interviews fell into three types: those who had no real political motives for leaving, but left due to family considerations; those who had very real political motives for leaving, as they sought to overcome the authoritarian nature of the society in which they lived; and the vast majority, for whom the political and the economic were profoundly intertwined. In any society, there is an inextricable relationship between the political and the economic, but it is all the more pronounced in a communist society, where the same actors make the major political as well as economic decisions. To demonstrate this, I rely on interviews with Felix Fojo, Tomás Medina (pseudonym), Lázaro Santamaría, Wilfredo Cancio, Georgina Mestre (pseudonym), Kenia González, Alejandro Ríos, Joel Brito, Eva Zaldívar (pseudonym), Oscar Aguirre and Natalia Goderich, Enrique Patterson, and Rolando Prats-Páez.

Familial or Economic Motives

Felix Fojo, a surgeon who was well respected in Cuba, left at the age of 47, primarily because he wanted to be reunited with his daughter. This is not to say that Felix Fojo had no political differences with the society in which he lived; rather, he had adjusted to those and carved out a life in Cuba that satisfied him. In the beginning, his identification with the revolution was quite profound. Two of his uncles had fought together with Frank País, in the uprising of November 30, 1956. When the revolution triumphed in 1959, he was rather young, only 12 years old, but he felt it in a very personal way, because family members died fighting against Batista. His identification, however, like that of most who fought and risked their lives for the revolution, was with being a *revolucionario* – a revolutionary – not a communist. Therefore, as the revolution progressively became communist, his doubts increased and he increasingly felt he had to convince himself that the truth lay with Fidel and communism, as he tried to justify policies, such as the October Missile Crisis. Yet he lived within the system, as he put it: as a *miliciano*, who guarded against possible invasions; as an *alfabetizador*, who went to the rural areas to teach the peasants to read and write; as a participant in public acts where he sang the "Internationale"; as a *becado*, on a fellowship, who attended military schools and who went to the countryside nine times to cut sugarcane while studying medicine.

As the revolution was consolidated and the "effervescence" of those early years – what could be called the revolutionary moment, properly speaking – subsided, a new stage began that proved stable for many years, in which Cuba was part of the communist bloc that comprised "one third of mankind" and social inequality was not very great. Those who remained behind had to adjust to life "as is." In Cuba, Fojo said, people had three options: they could leave the country, in whatever way; they could become integrated to the revolution, whether or not they really believed in it, and climb with it professionally, as far as it took them; or they could do what the vast majority did: become passive observers and concentrate only on their work and their family. He chose the second option; his father, also a doctor, who to this day lives in Cuba, the third. He put all his energy and talents into becoming a good doctor and became a surgeon. He took pride in helping to create the first coronary unit within a hospital in Cuba, the second one in all of Latin America. Doctors came from everywhere in the world, he said, to see what Cuba had done in public health. Today, in Cuba, he said, to concentrate on creating something of value through your work is no longer possible; in the "special period" the aim has become to survive in any way possible.

The collapse of the Berlin Wall and Eastern European communism was a turning point, he said, making it clear to him and to others that "one no longer had to adjust to life under communism" and, in addition, that life would no longer be worth living in Cuba. Felix described himself as an economic immigrant because he adjusted to life in Cuba for many years, including its lack of liberty; he succeeded in his medical profession and lived as well as he could there; but he sought to leave to reunite with his daughter and to help his parents back in Cuba.

Although he worked as a doctor in the United States, he was not able to regain the medical prestige he had once enjoyed in Cuba, and after a few years he left the medical profession altogether. Eventually, he started another business with his daughter and son-in-law in Puerto Rico that relies on their medical know-how, selling artificial limbs. After he married Isis María, an executive with State Farm who was also a singer, they went on to found Viva Records, which produces and sells new CDs of romantic melodies based on the ever-present nostalgia for Havana's tropical nights filled with music and entertainment.

Tomás Medina also lived well and adjusted to life in Cuba. He came from a family that had quickly gone from being poor to being very rich in Cuba – "from going places by bus to being driven by a chauffeur," he remembered. His father was a boxer, who learned to read and write at the age of 40, when he was already a rich man. His social rise was thanks to the help he gave former presidents Grau and Prío, gathering votes for them at the local level. At the beginning of the revolution, he held a very important post in a ministry. However, he was viscerally anticommunist, so he resigned. He helped many people in Cuba leave, securing passports for them, a very lucrative business, until he was accused of being a counterrevolutionary

211

and was imprisoned. As a result, though Tomás believed in the revolution, he was never fanatical. He had risen quite high within it, "as high as is possible, when you are not a party militant, come from a bourgeois family, and have close family in the United States." He worked hard as a well-qualified economist and accountant who was involved in central economic planning in Cuba, JUCEPLAN, in the import and export of agricultural products. A mulatto, the son of a Spanish Gallego and a Cuban mulatta, he had never wanted to leave Cuba, both because he was quite financially comfortable and because he knew firsthand the problem of race in the United States. In the 1950s, he had lived in Miami and New York as a student. As an adult, he became a member of the *tecnocracia* – the technical aristocracy, as it is called in Cuba – and had lived well in a penthouse overlooking the seaside avenue of *el malecón;* he had traveled throughout the world representing Cuba and had no real economic problems. He also witnessed what he thought was Cuba's greatest problem: "the corruption and the moral degradation of its leaders," leaders who did not differentiate between personal property and state property and at times used the latter as the former. Medina had often seen how gradually a leader who initially led an ascetic life became transformed and began to live "the finest of lives," eating and drinking only the best, corrupted by the power he exercised. He then ceased to be the exemplary leader others believed in. "As you rise in the system, you yourself begin to participate in *el festín,*" in the grand feast, as he contemptuously expressed it. Moreover, those in positions of leadership were often chosen for their revolutionary fealty, not their intellectual capacity, so the incompetent led the competent. Gradually, a new class was born.

While Medina had no economic problems, his family problems loomed large. On several occasions he requested permission to leave Cuba to come to the United States to see his father and mother, who left Cuba in 1965, but permission was always denied. Moreover, when the *balsero* wave peaked in the 1990s, his sons threatened to leave the country on a *balsa*, risking death. None of his three sons were able to find work in their profession. Thus, his children entreated him to stay on his next trip overseas, not to return. Tomás, therefore, made the choice to desert in 1996, at the age of 59, while working overseas on a foreign mission, thinking he would later be able to bring his children and wife. Once he saw his father and mother again in Mexico, he knew he would stay, the longing to be reunited with them being so strong. When his wife applied to leave Cuba after he left, Raúl Castro called him a traitor. Although neither he nor his wife were members of the party and their positions were as administrators, not political posts, they still demanded "loyalty to the system and a certain level of integration." In the end, Medina was able to be with his father for some time and was by his side when he died.

Lázaro Santamaría came from a different social background. Born in 1962, he was a child of the new society. Descended many generations from Africa, he was raised in a family that practiced the religion of Santería in Cuba, and he continued to do so in the Bronx, where I interviewed him. He and his mother lived in an apartment where each of the major *orishas* had an altar and the many porcelain statues and shrines gave evidence of their profound religiosity.

In Cuba, his parents had been extremely poor. His father had been born in a *solar*, an urban shanty town in the neighborhood of Jesús María, so poor that to attend school he even wore women's shoes. As an adult, he made shoes. His mother was not able to finish her training as a *comadrona*, a midwife, due to lack of money to pay the last year's fees. She was a maid in the homes of many whites who humiliated her and paid her minimally. She lived in *un cuartico*, a small room. His family had benefited from the revolution initially. Hence, his parents "were grateful to the revolution because they were not among those who lost; they were among those who gained."

His father, in particular, was very enthusiastic about the revolution. Thanks to the Urban Reform Law, they were able to have their own home for the first time. His father also gained good, steady employment. He worked for the Ministry of Justice, in the Archives where penal records were kept, and he belonged to the labor union, so "he felt important, he felt well." Fidel opened up opportunities for them, so they would not speak ill of him, Lázaro informed me. Yet his father had never joined the party because he was a *santero* and he did not want to give up his religion, as required. Lazaro came from a long line of *santeros* and *babalaos* who were initiated in Santería. They were also Catholics, as their religion required a Catholic baptism – "God's blessing."

Lázaro was grateful to the revolution for the education it gave him – "Who would have taught me to read and write otherwise?" As a young man in Cuba, Lázaro was a good citizen in every way. He was a member of the UJC; he had engaged in volunteer work of all sorts; the family had been *Cederistas* (members of the CDR); his older brother fought in Angola, as an *internacionalista* serving overseas. In truth, his family had not been communists – they lived "at the margin of politics," as it is expressed in Spanish. But they participated politically because "it was a passport to a

213

good job; a passport to not being persecuted for other reasons; it was a credit before society." He added: "If you had some level of integration, everyone received you with open arms." Thus, he was able to practice his religion, the aim of his life. He practiced Santería part-time, as he was a primary school teacher and also a tailor on the side. Despite the economic problems in Cuba, he had none, as he had "so many ways to earn a living honestly." In addition, his family in the United States sent them U.S. dollars. His uncle, Ramón ("Mongo") Santamaría, was quite successful in the Latin jazz circles in the United States, known as an excellent percussionist in the Afro-Cuban tradition.

Prior to the revolution, Santería was mostly concentrated among blacks, especially the poor, with minimal participation from whites. After the revolution, Santería expanded to encompass all the races, across a broad social spectrum. For a period of time, Castro's government repressed it because, Santamaría said, "Fidel associated it with marginality, with obscurantism." Throughout the mid-1970s and early 1980s, when Lázaro became initiated at the age of 12, his mother could have been sent to prison for it. Despite the repression, Santería continued to expand. In my view, it grew in part because it could be practiced without temples and associations. This was especially important at the time when the Catholic Church was silenced, Cuba defined itself as an atheist nation, and few Cubans practiced any religion openly. Many Cubans practiced it in hiding, behind the atheist front they gave to the world. Santería also expanded due to its stress on solving the daily problems of living (cf. Sandoval 1986; 1975) – problems that loomed ever larger during "the special period." "People come to our religion," Lázaro noted, "out of need" – for reasons of sentiment, for health reasons, or looking to overcome difficulties, seeking peace. Now that Santería can be practiced openly, many people from all over the world go to Cuba to *hacerse el santo*. Today, Santería is no longer in danger of extinction; rather, it is in danger of becoming commodified, encouraged as it is as a tourist draw.

Lázaro's oldest brother left Cuba through *el Mariel* in 1980 – the same year Lázaro became initiated as a *santero* – and later claimed the family. Lázaro, his mother, and another brother left Cuba in 1989, first for Panama, then for the United States. In the Bronx, Lázaro practiced Santería full-time, as many people sought his advice. In Santería, the West African deity becomes expressed as a Catholic saint with whom it shares some traits – for example, *Babalú Ayé* became *San Lázaro*, *Changó* became *Santa Barbara*. To be a *santero* is a step toward becoming a *babalao*; still higher is the *oriate*

214

(or *eriate*), who has the power of divination, reading oracles from cowry shells. Lázaro was an *oriate*.

Lázaro and his family left for no other reason than the wish to be reunited with their family in the United States, hoping for a better future for the family. Only after leaving Cuba, when he was able to compare life in Cuba to life in other places, did Lázaro grow politically disaffected. He thought it was time for Fidel to give way to other leaders; other ways of thinking; other cultures that can bring in new influences; and free elections for the people. Lázaro did not think he would ever return to Cuba, despite his longing for his *patria*, because "Cuba is a nation that has been damaged." Despite the high level of education of the people, it is lacking in the advances of civilization. His heart still remained with the poor people of Cuba – with *la masa humilde*, the mass that suffers.

Both Political and Economic Motives

While political motives were largely absent in the experiences just described, for most Cubans who left in recent years, political motives weighed heavily in their decision. Given Cuba's enormous isolation from the Western world, especially the United States and most of Latin America, it is instructive to see how these young people changed their political attitudes. From their interviews, I learned three factors that stood out as decisive in promoting their political disaffection: growing to love and admire those whose ideas and values differed from theirs; living abroad, breaking the isolation under which Cubans live, and coming to know other worlds, other ways of living; and being exposed to new ideas and values, to other ways of thinking, through books or teaching. For the vast majority, the political and the economic were deeply intertwined.

Wilfredo Cancio left in 1994 by plane, so he called himself a *balsero aéreo*, an airborne *balsero*. Today a journalist for *El Nuevo Herald*, he was then a professor in the Journalism Department of the University of Havana. Twice he left Cuba for conferences in the early 1990s, but when he returned, he "no longer felt he was part of Cuba." He started working on a doctorate in 1993, in the Canary Islands, Spain. Being outside of Cuba for a few months was a decisive experience, because he felt like a human being who could enjoy life, travel, and make personal decisions. He returned to Cuba in August 1993, just when the dollarization of the economy began. He worked in the university for 12 years, directed the cultural section of the magazine *Revolución y Cultura* of the Ministry of Culture, and also wrote for *La Gaceta de Cuba*, another leading intellectual magazine. Despite all this, he still did not have enough to live with, though his monthly salary of 600 or 700 pesos a month was way beyond the median salary in Cuba then. Due to the dollarization of the economy, however, it soon became worth very little. Moreover, a steep economic decline from 1991 to 1994 resulted from the Soviet collapse, and the direction of the country was unknown. "Now," he emphasized, "it is clear: the country is moving toward a state-led capitalism" that will result in dramatic contrasts among the social classes, "the worst of capitalism and the worst of socialism."

Born in 1960, at the dawn of the revolution, Cancio was 34 years old when he left – a product of the revolution in every way. He was educated in Sancti Spíritus and participated in the schools in the countryside, until in 1977 he earned the only scholarship awarded to study journalism in his province. After finishing his thesis in Havana, he completed eight months of obligatory service in the military. After that, he worked in the university in the Journalism Department. His greatest satisfaction there was the work he did, for seven years, with the admissions committee, which sought to depoliticize the admissions process by choosing students not on the basis of their loyalty to the system but on the basis of their intellectual promise. This resulted in numerous conflicts with the party, as did the committee's efforts to protect gay candidates who qualified. But at the same time, they created a curriculum in journalism that was less political, more technical, and more humanistic. It included major Cuban and Latin American writers who were excluded due to their not toeing the party line. Cancio and others in the admissions committee sought to preserve a certain independence.

Cancio had taken on the revolution, initially out of fear and then out of conviction. His parents never became politically integrated to the revolution. His mother was a teacher; his father, an accountant for the rice industry. Their lack of political integration became a cost to him when filling out applications where he could not write that his parents were part of the CDR or his mother part of the FMC. His mother's religiosity was also a problem, so in 1963 the government took her teaching job away from her and left her to only fill out forms, a task that she performed with gusto. Even so, his father retired with honors due to his exemplary work. When the *Mariel* exodus took place, his family in the United States offered to come and get them, but he refused to go. He was studying at the university then, and he still believed in the revolution. Later on, he came to see his belief as a mixture of commitment and fear. A turning point came for him in 1983. In the army then, he was on the way to Angola, with his suitcase packed, when the U.S. invasion of Granada took place. It kept him from going to Angola, but it was also the last time he went to the Plaza of the Revolution to greet the arrival of the heroes and martyrs. To him, the falsity of what had taken place became evident. On the radio, the report said the young Cuban soldiers had died with the flag wrapped around them, but when he went to greet the returning soldiers, he could see them descending from the airplane with bags full of household items. "Everything was a lie.... Everything began to seem false to me," he remembered.

The *Mariel* episode, when he was 20 years old, also marked him, despite his refusal to leave. He sided with the government that called those who left *escoria*, scum. Though he did not participate in the *actos de repudio*, throwing eggs at those who left and the like, he did wear a T-shirt that said *Que se vaya la escoria* – let the scum go. At the time, he did not realize the gravity of *el Mariel*: the first exodus of the young raised under the revolution. Moreover, the very way in which the stampede developed gave the lie to the revolution. The very people who shouted *Abajo la gusanera!* and marched against the *gusanos* – the worms who were leaving then – later asked for their exit permit and left. Even more, during *el Mariel* "the repressive forces were turned against *el pueblo*," the people. Hence, while he did not realize it at the time, the impact of Mariel when he was 20 spurred his political disaffection, which other events deepened.

Among the worst incidents in his life took place when he served on military duty as a lieutenant, in the military unit at Quemado de Hilario. Twice he was asked to keep watch over the prisoners at a prison in a suburb of Santa Clara, where the military men who deserted or in other ways infringed upon their military duty were kept. On one occasion, he was asked by his superior, a sergeant, to put on brass knuckles to beat up a defenseless prisoner who was reputed to be dangerous, as he was about to come out of solitary confinement in a dark cell. Despite his lower rank, he refused to do so, or to allow either of the recruits under his charge to do so.

Finally, his work with the admissions committee and teaching at the university also proved important in changing his political views. His desertion while on a trip to Chapel Hill, therefore, came as no surprise. Many of his friends thought he should have left earlier, his ideological clashes were so strong. On that trip, he particularly clashed with his dean, a woman who went out of her way to defend the press in Cuba, while he made it clear to all that the press functioned as an ideological instrument and, thus, could not progress as a press. His generation and many younger Cubans expected *glasnost* and *perestroika* in Cuba, but it did not happen.

As he was an only child, after he left Cuba, every month he sent his mother an extremely expensive medicine she depended on for the last three years of her life. But when she was dying and he asked Cuban government officials for permission to return to see her, they denied him the permission until after she died. As a journalist for *El Nuevo Herald* today, he strives as much as possible to be an objective journalist; as a human being, he strives to overcome the hatred both the revolution and the exile engendered – "not to forget, yet not to hate."

Georgina Mestre's story shows the impact of the economic conditions as well as the profound generational differences that now exist in Cuba between the protagonists of the revolution, who felt affirmed by it, and their children, who inherited its problems. Georgina is a tall, impeccably well-mannered and lovely woman who left Cuba when she was 30 years old. She was born in the Soviet Union while both her parents finished their college education there. She described her father, a convinced communist to this day, as being very grateful to the revolution because, coming from a very humble family – his own father had made and sold brooms – the revolution made it possible for him to study and to become "someone," to have a career. Her grandmother ran a boardinghouse to supplement her husband's meager earnings cutting sugarcane. Georgina's father was only 14 years old when the revolution triumphed, so was too young to fight for it, but he and his wife enthusiastically became integrated to the Jóvenes Rebeldes (Rebel Youth). Moreover, the government gave him a nice house and a car, enabled him to travel, to become middle class. He was manager for several major industries involved in machinery. Coupled with studying in the Soviet Union, Georgina's parents became fervent believers in the revolution, unwavering to this day. "My father and I respect one another," she said. Still, in his letters he invariably found a way of pointing to the revolution's accomplishments; whatever was wrong with Cuba he always blamed on the U.S. embargo.

Georgina, however, underwent a process of profound political disaffection that – as was usually the case with most people I interviewed – was gradual and cumulative, "until one day you suddenly see it differently," she said. In the 1970s, when Georgina was in her teens, there was also no freedom of expression, no civil liberties; but because in her circle of family and friends at that time she knew no one who thought differently, she did not miss them. Wherever she turned, the *consignas* on the billboards, the radio, or the television read *Viva Fidel!* or *Patria o Muerte!* (Fatherland or Death!). And in the preuniversity years, she took a leading role organizing the students.

The change in her attitudes came about in the mid to late 1980s, when she began studying electrical engineering and met people of all persuasions. Although she became a member of the UJC because of her convictions, she began to exchange opinions and to have discussions with people who were not in favor of the revolution. These students' parents had tried to leave Cuba and suffered a great deal there – either because they had been political prisoners or because they were the objects of violent *actos de repudio*. "Then they began to explain all that to me," she said, "and I began to know a world I had not known existed." She herself had participated in those *actos de repudio* in her school when she was only 11 years old, and her teachers and principals had given her tomatoes and eggs to throw at those who were trying to leave through the port of Mariel. Like all the young girls then, she sang and danced the insults of *gusanos* and *escoria*, not understanding why those people wanted to leave, simply believing what she was told: that they were counterrevolutionaries and bad people. She never heard anything good being said about capitalist societies but only about the seamy side: the poverty and inequality that reigned there. To her, the fundamental tenet of socialism was equality. Yet her new friends at the university pointed out that not everyone in Cuban society was equal – that the party elite and their children had many privileges others lacked. "When I met people whose opinions were different, I realized for the first time what freedom of expression meant." And she also learned that some people had been jailed only because their opinions were different.

She transferred to the University of Havana to pursue law as a profession and soon began to chafe under the excessive control there, when the leaders of the UJC would tally whether or not their members attended certain political activities. Up until then she had thought the CDRs were intended for neighbors to get together and solve their problems, such as the need to paint the building they lived in, but then she began to realize that the purpose of the CDR was also to exercise control over persons. In addition, Cubans who had left and lived elsewhere began to arrive: "Everyone had someone," she said, "an uncle, a grandfather, some relative. And we could then see all the material things that were possible, and we did not have them." And then, at the end of the 1980s, the communist world in Eastern Europe collapsed. In Cuba, she recalled, people began to speak more freely. And she realized the equality she had thought was so critical was not so equal

219

after all: "The equality that existed was among all of us who were poor – we were all poor," but not among the upper class of the political leaders – "they had everything and lived well, living in the huge mansions that they took over from those who left, the rich who left."

Moreover, when she began studying law, she tried to hold an open discussion in the classroom regarding why Cubans who wanted to form another political party were not allowed to do so, and the professor and other students insisted she should not express herself in that manner because Fidel had said these people were nothing other than a *grupúsculo* maintained by the Cuban American National Foundation, whose intent was only to sabotage the revolution. And then she fell in love with a young man who was a dissident. At first they fought a lot, because their points of view were different, but they always came back together. As a result of her love for him, a new world opened up for her in Cuba – that of the dissidents – that she had not known existed. "And then he began to change me," she realized. Though this boyfriend was not the man she would later love and marry, his impact on her feelings and attitudes was decisive. Indeed, most people I interviewed showed the impact of the political commitments of those they loved deeply and admired – whether a boyfriend, father, sister, or friend – on their own.

Thereafter, the economic problems in the 1990s dealt yet another blow to her profound process of political disaffection. For her husband worked as a doctor in the tourist industry and therefore had access to dollars. In addition, his family in the United States regularly sent remittances. Thus, very soon she began to live a life very different from that of her sister and family, who had no access to the dollar economy, becoming part of a new social class that has grown in Cuba recently. This new social class that has emerged is rather ostentatious in its economic behavior and, though hardly supportive of the government, is mostly apolitical. Georgina and her husband had a car, could travel to the beautiful tourist spots of Varadero and Soroa. They could throw a birthday party for their one-year-old with a clown, *piñata*, favors for the children, soda pop, cake, and beer for the adults. She and her husband ate well, so they invited the rest of her family for a nice dinner every Saturday – often the only time of the week her family ate meat. "In my apartment building," she said, "they began calling us *los millonarios*." However, that also became a reason to leave, because they feared for her husband's safety, as they were becoming *señalados* (noted). "It was the economic problems that opened up the eyes of the people," she emphasized.

When I interviewed her, Georgina worked in an old folks' home in Los Angeles, trying to learn English while she cared for an old man in a wheel-chair, care that she gave with a lot of affection while also being a mother to a four-year-old. She hopes that in the future she can study for a career other than law. She corresponds with her father, whom she still admires: "He never harmed anyone nor was opportunistic," she said. They both try to avoid a political confrontation, though they each tell the other what is good about the system in Cuba and in the United States.

Kenia González arrived in August 1994, but not as a *balsera*; rather, her father claimed her. Kenia's parents were divorced when she was a child, and she went to live with her father until she was 15, while her mother began working as a maid. Her father's family worked in the factory of the famous tobacco company, H-Upman. Her father decided to leave Cuba in 1967 because the police repeatedly harassed him and interrogated him. It was *una zozobra*, a constant anxiety. "We could not go on living in that way." So he left for Spain, and gradually the whole family left.

Around 13 years old when the revolution triumphed, Kenia attended both Catholic and public schools, and attained a ninth-grade education. Because her marriage failed when she was fairly young, she worked from an early age. She learned to use IBM machines and worked in data pro-cessing. In her 20s, she was able to get a good job in Camagüey, working for the civil registrar of births, deaths, and marriages. After a few years, she managed a transfer back to Havana, to live with her mother's fam-ily. Cubans cannot move freely from one town to another, she explained, because such transfers entail having *la libreta* transferred to a new fam-ily unit, without which one cannot obtain the rationed food and cloth-ing. For the next 20 years, she lived in Centro Habana, worked in the "Polar" factory, where they made beer and malt, and in the accounting department, processing the data on the employees' work effort. She stud-ied *bachillerato* in the evenings, in the old Escuelas Pías, until she obtained her diploma. As a result of her father's exile, she never acquired affection for the revolution and participated only in the organizations in which it was essential she participate to obtain a decent job: the CTC, the FMC, and the CDR.

After her mother died, she remained alone. Her father had invited her to visit him in 1992, but the U.S. Interests Section denied her the visa, as it did to so many who applied then, on the basis that their "family ties in Cuba seemed insufficiently strong" for them to return. Thus, her father decided to claim her definitively. When she finally arrived in 1994, she was 48 years old. Her father had only 21 days left to live. A week after she arrived, he was hospitalized.

She arrived on August 23, a couple of weeks after the massive riots that took place on *el 5 de Agosto* down her street. "It was a rebellion," she said. "The police beat up those who rebelled. They threw rocks at the stores' windows, shattering them, then went inside and looted the money and goods." The Rapid Response Brigades "beat up the participants," she remembered. She remained uninvolved, afraid something could happen to her departure plans. Informing against others is so common in Cuba, she explained: "You never know who is who. People pretend to be *gusanos*, complain about the social conditions, so that you will speak freely. Then that person *lo echa a Usted para delante* – a phrase that means they betray you to the police, the government.

Kenia's religious beliefs were profound: a mix of Catholicism and *espiritismo*, which her mother practiced. "My mother was able to bring someone's spirit forth; she had that grace," and she could cure the sick with prayer. *Espiritismo* differs from Santería in that it lacks the African religious base, but in Cuba some people engage in both. Kenia particularly liked the saints. In the years when the temples were largely empty, she still went to church. To her, religion was a refuge.

Before she left Cuba, she went to Rincón again, to bid the saint San Lázaro farewell. "Public transport is an enormous problem in Cuba," she emphasized. So much so, that when a letter from her father came to her cousin's house, she decided to go on foot to get it. It took her four hours, walking under the hot sun, and four hours to walk back. Such were the conditions in Cuba during "the special period," as Eckstein (1994) has documented.

In the beginning, her family was enthusiastic about the revolution, thinking it would benefit *el pueblo*, but when they introduced *la libreta* to ration food and goods, the disappointment began to set in. They realized the elite government class did not suffer in the same way because it had its own stores. Old enough to remember *la Cuba de ayer*, she remembered going to the *bodegas* to buy ham and such. "The *libreta* was an enormous frustration for the Cuban people," she underlined. "Can you imagine eating a quarter pound of meat a month, when there was some?" In the 1990s, the situation worsened with "the special period." "It then became a quarter pound of soy sausage; one onion per person; a few pieces of garlic. This was not enough to make a *sofrito* to flavor food with, especially since very little oil was given. The diet was so meager: a small roll of bread a day; a few vegetables; a couple of bananas, when they arrived; one bottle of beer every six months; two ounces of coffee every 15 days – "And Cubans are *cafeteros*; they really like coffee." Oftentimes, dinner consisted of a roll of bread with oil and a little garlic, a scrambled egg.

The lack of religious freedom cut deep, as did the political obligations, but the economic crisis of "the special period" had a particularly great impact on her. Kenia's salary was so low – 200 pesos a month, plus 99 pesos for her mother's widow's pension – it was impossible for her to make ends meet. Thus, beginning in 1990, she participated in the black market. She sold liquor, deodorant, shampoo, cigarettes, soap, toothpaste – whatever she could get that had resale value. With the profit she turned, she bought what she needed in the dollar stores to feed her mother well – perhaps *un bistecito* (a small steak) or *un pollito* (a small chicken). Getting these entailed enormous sacrifices. "I was never in a prison," she emphasized, "but I felt like I was in a prison.... When I went out with the liquor or the cigarettes in a *jaba*, I felt the police watching me."

A tall, attractive, and strong *trigueña*, when she arrived in Miami she went on to study at night and obtained a certificate to work as a security guard in places like condominiums. Yet Kenia was baffled by how much she missed Cuba, when she had suffered so much there.

Alejandro Ríos's family were among the *repatriados* who lived outside of Cuba but, enthusiastic about the revolution, repatriated. His family was lower middle class, working in its own printing press business. His father had decided "to search for better luck" as an economic immigrant in the United States. They returned to Cuba from Hialeah in 1962, when Alejandro was 10.

Both his parents were extremely enthusiastic about the revolution. His mother wrote a letter to a dear friend, Hilda, in which she exhorted her to return to Cuba because "there is where hope and a future for the children lies." Alejandro emphasized that his mother had many *ilusiones*, which in Spanish means both real hope and unreal expectations. When they returned in 1962, his family went to live in the neighborhood of Habana del Este. From the United States, the family brought household goods not common in Cuba then, such as a washing machine and a record player, and people looked up to them as "the repatriated."

For Alejandro, however, the return was traumatic. He felt alienated, lost, in the new system that organized social life collectively, as a mass, and did not respect one's privacy. Even as a child, he minded the constant intrusion in his life. His teachers shamed him in public, calling him *apático*, one who did not participate, "as a revolutionary must." Moreover, he was frightened by the way students treated each other, the vulgarity of *la guapería*, rather than the discreet courtesy he was used to. The old, black urban slum of Las Yaguas was destroyed, and many of its inhabitants were relocated to Habana del Este, which became a socially marginal neighborhood. The case of a neighbor who kept a horse in a fourth-floor apartment became a legend. Rather than losing political faith, Alejandro never acquired it. Yet he lived in Cuba for 30 years.

Throughout all these years, the feeling was that everything in Cuba *se estaba derrumbando*, was falling apart. Their car, an Austin made in Britain, which his father purchased with the savings from his work in the United States, broke down. With his mechanical expertise, Alejandro's father kept it going, replacing its parts with parts from Russian jeeps and trucks. It became "a Frankenstein," he said – British outside, who knows what other country inside.

His father responded, however, by becoming more incorporated to the revolution. He did everything he was expected to: he went to the country-side to cut sugarcane; he went to Angola as a civilian; he was elected as a "vanguard worker." While his father *asumió*, took on the revolution well, his mother was bothered by the demands to participate: to be a member of the FMC, to *hacer la guardia*, to keep watch for the CDR. For him also, the constant participation grated.

The economic scarcity also weighed heavily. He remembered days when he drank water with sugar. The butcher gave his father the broken eggs to make a *tortilla*, an omelet. In Cuba, he emphasized, "people joke there are three problems the revolution has not solved: breakfast, lunch, and dinner." These are the first human rights that need to be respected, Ríos stressed. "It does not have to be a banquet, but neither should it make your life an agony, as it is in Cuba."

The compulsory military service at the *pre-Universitario* called Héroes de Yagüajay beginning at 15 was also traumatic. Afterward, he joined the youth counterculture that developed in Cuba then – young people with long hair and tight pants, who enjoyed the music of the Beatles and Bob Dylan – "the fascination with American culture that has never ceased to exist in Cuba." During the massive mobilization in 1970, he became part of a countercultural brigade called *Venceremos*. This cost Alejandro a delay of several years in admission to the university.

Until he left Cuba, Alejandro worked at the Instituto Cubano del Libro as a film critic, and in public relations, promoting writers and artists. While he never became a dissident, he was quite liberal – *inconforme*, a rebel. He had a radio program, a television program, and he wrote for *La Gaceta de Cuba*. He grew to know well a young generation of artists, film makers, and writers in the 1980s who, through their art, questioned the system. Later on, they became dissidents – though, in Ríos's judgment, they lacked a political vocation. Among them were Juan Sí and Juan Vega, in film; Arturo Cuenca in art; Senel Paz in literature. Paz's short story crossed over into the mainstream when it became the screenplay for the internationally popular film, *Fresa y Chocolate* (Strawberry and Chocolate) (Gutiérrez-Alea and Tabío 1994). "Many interesting things were done then; it was a curious time," Alejandro stressed, "and I am glad to have lived through it."

Ríos today works at Miami-Dade College as a media relations specialist, who strives to teach the public about all aspects of Cuban culture, including writers and film makers on the island and in the diaspora. Ríos emphasized his parents were not *pancistas* – what they call in Cuba those who left looking for *pan*, for bread, due to the economic problems. They left because they got tired of the madness, the utopia of a socialism that was always constructed in the future, like the horizon that never arrives. They lost hope; they felt betrayed.

Though young, Joel Bito had risen to become a labor leader. As an adolescent, he had studied in the German Democratic Republic, from where he returned to Cuba at the age of 19, in 1983. He had studied economics, specializing in finance, in Gotha. A few months after returning to work in Cuba, he began working for the Central de Trabajadores Cubanos (CTC), the national labor union. Joel started out working in the national *sindicato* of workers in light industry, in the Sección de Revisión, where he was the head of accounting and financing, reporting to the Central Committee of the Communist Party. After six years, Brito became the head of the CTC's National Accounting Department – an extremely high position in which he handled and audited the national accounts. In communist societies, labor unions are "transmission belts" of the party, Brito also noted, because they are not independent from the government – "whoever has an important position in the one has an important position in the other."

Brito fervently believed in the communist system. At the age of 15, he was a member of the UJC; at 18, a member of the party. As he put it: "I grew to love the system, to think it was the best there was. I saw it as a model for Latin America, and I defended it as such." Like Brito, many leaders had studied in the socialist countries, and they were aware that the CTC was falling behind, in the years after the Eastern European countries collapsed.

Thus, they instituted new measures that would make the economy more open, such as the *parlamentos obreros* – the workers' parliaments. There, open discussions took place that allowed workers to bring problems to the fore that were hidden for many years, and to express their concerns, such as the extremely low salaries workers received and the increase in the number of *trabajadores disponibles* – available workers, a Cuban euphemism for the unemployed.

Brito was elected to be a member of the national executive committee of the CTC. He oversaw the department that organized jobs and salaries, as well as engaged in worker protection. "To rise to the highest positions, to be part of the *nomenklatura*, one has to be competent – personally and politically," Brito said. But in 1998 he left Cuba, at the age of 35. As with most people I interviewed, the causes of his disaffection were multiple. First, as head of the accounting department, he began to see the corruption and the privilege in the CTC itself. When he traveled to another province for his job, he did not stay in a regular hotel but in a hotel for the party, or *la casita*, that belonged to the party, where one was treated quite well, with good accommodations, good food – "what is normal anywhere in the world, but in Cuba constitutes a privilege." Another source of his disaffection was his training as an economist – his knowledge that Cuba faced a situation from which there was no exit. "The economic crisis is created by the political system. To solve it, they have to open up the political system," Brito emphasized. When Cuba opened itself up modestly to the market – such as when it allowed the self-employed to buy and sell on their own, or when the agricultural cooperatives were able to regulate themselves – the results were successful. Yet, once again, the government is restricting the number of self-employed occupations it allows, the *cuenta propistas*. "It is impossible," Brito claimed, "for a country with the level of centralization Cuba has to progress." Professionals in Cuba know this: "They are enterprising people, but the system does not allow them to be so. They know they cannot advance professionally in Cuba, and they also know that you cannot go against the system and prosper."

Like many who studied overseas in the socialist countries, Brito had expected a *perestroika* to take place in Cuba. But progressively it became clear that the leadership of the Castro brothers would not allow it. "Professionals in Cuba know that the economy is ill and the problem has spread beyond containment," he explained. "The problem is the centralization of the system, in substitution for the market. It has no solution." Brito's very centrality allowed him to reach this conclusion. Thus, to him, the government's efforts to deal with the crisis of the "special period" by policies such as *la estimulación con divisas* (stimulating the worker by paying him in dollars) or rewarding the workers' extra efforts with a *jaba*, a bag full of food and other necessities, were false substitutes for what workers should have: an adequate salary, in Cuban pesos, with which to buy what they needed in the marketplace.

Brito's process of political disaffection was also the result of his relationship with the International Labour Organization, when it started to visit Cuba, bringing materials, and he grew to know well the notion of labor rights. Today, there are no labor rights in Cuba, he stressed, not even the right to strike, *de la huelga*.

When he left Cuba, Brito received political asylum right away, but the government retained his wife, Marilyn Mosquere, and their daughter in Cuba for five years and nine months. He suffered so much that "whatever good he once saw in the revolution," he admitted, he "could no longer see." In the United States, Brito eventually went on to become director of the Federación Sindical de Plantas Eléctricas, Gas y Agua de Cuba en el Exilio (the labor union for electrical, gas, and water workers in exile) in Miami, which represents the Cuban Independent Federation of Trade Unions (CONIC). They are funded by the U.S. Agency for International Development and by the National Endowment for Democracy. Their work consists of itemizing and denouncing Cuba's labor violations before international bodies, such as the International Labour Organization, and of supporting the *sindicalistas independientes* on the island, who try to promote labor rights. They publish the magazine *Lux*, sending more than 10,000 copies to Cuba each year.

Brito estimated there are around 10,000 *sindicalistas independientes* in Cuba today, in 109 independent labor organizations throughout the island as well as the CONIC. Clearly, they are penetrated by government spies who inform on their work, as are all dissident organizations. The case of agent "Vilma," recently uncovered in the Cuban newspapers, gives the evidence (Tamayo-León 2003). "Vilma" was Aleida Godínez-Soler, the secretary-general of the CONIC. She gained the confidence of the U.S. Interests Section, where she was often welcome. She talked to Joel Brito on the phone constantly, as he sent her substantial amounts of money and medicines (Marx 2005; Godínez-Soler 2005). "Vilma" was unmasked when the government cracked down on the dissident movement in 2003. Among *"los 75"* sent to jail, seven were *sindicalistas independientes*.

Contrary to many others in Miami, Brito expects that the process of transition to a democratic society in Cuba will be shaped not only by the *sindicalistas independientes* and the exiles but also by many Cubans still on the island and still inside the CTC. They would be "recyclable" because they worked with the best intentions toward the workers.

Political Motives

For some who left, the economic problems were largely irrelevant, while the impact of living abroad, seeing other ways of living, and learning other value systems, as well as growing to love those who held different values, promoted their disaffection.

Eva Zaldívar went to The Netherlands to work as a research scientist. The only child of parents who "had given all for the revolution," she had grown up with strong revolutionary convictions. She had seen her parents always busy, trying to go the extra mile for the revolution, yet never properly rewarded. They had never been invited to join the party, for example, or given a car or a trip overseas. "Others who had done less had been able to cut a larger slice from the side of the revolution," she realized.

Eva had been a member of the UJC and part of the student government at the University of Havana. After graduating, having specialized in physics, she started working in one of the centers dedicated to biotechnology and medical research, located in *el polo científico*, as Fidel called all the new research centers located in the east of Havana. With her research team, she hoped to find new products that could be marketed for profit – that might have application in the treatment of cancer, for example. Cuba has placed an emphasis on tourism and on medical and biotechnological research in recent years, expecting that "these would lift Cuba out of the hole it had fallen into." To continue the research, she was sent to The Netherlands to work for two years in a project sponsored by the United Nations. In her case, like that of most young people who grew up within the system, change came about gradually, in a cumulative manner. She watched instances of the arbitrary misuse of power, felt coerced to participate in "voluntary work," and saw the costs of dissidence when young people were expelled from their workplace for their political ideals. She grew tired from the constant surveillance, the feeling of always being controlled, and the sense that people were betraying one another so they might benefit. Though Eva and her mother were extremely fair, they developed an attraction for Santería, to help them with the hardships of daily living in Cuba.

While she was working in The Netherlands, Eva had told her boss back in Cuba that she would not be returning. He was furious and nearly called her a traitor. Without doubt, he felt betrayed by her, as he had fought for her to be able to remain there, working for a second year. Yet, in truth, she had not gone to The Netherlands with the idea of deserting; nor did she think she would have done so had she not had that second year, the time for her experiences to add up to the decision not to return. Had they allowed her to remain outside Cuba to do her doctorate, this would have been her choice. Because they did not allow her to stay abroad, in effect they forced her decision to not return. But living in Europe for two years gave her the space to feel what it was like to live without being controlled, coerced, watched. Emotionally, the decision was costly. Her parents remained in Cuba. Her grandfather, an idealistic communist, expressed his hurt and anger: "Does she not realize that the sacrifice of a whole people went into her studying abroad?" he wrote in a letter.

Asked whether the economic problems in Cuba played a part in her decision to leave, she replied frankly that in her lifetime in Cuba they had never had much of anything, but like most Cubans, she had grown used to it and knew how to live with the little they had. After the two years in Europe and nearly a year in Latin America, she and an Argentinean student she met in The Netherlands got married. She came to the United States to accompany him, as he studied toward a Ph.D. in computational biology. Their conversations often revolved around what they had in common: growing up under an authoritarian regime, she of the left, he of the right. The stress of the constant political participation she grew under resulted in her political apathy. "Now I don't want to participate in anything other than my work and my family. I don't want to belong to anything. I don't want to join any group. I want to live in peace, without politics."

Living abroad in Eastern Europe when communism collapsed made even more of an impact. Oscar Aguirre and Natalia Goderich, a young married couple with three beautiful children, were both students in the Soviet Union who eventually became what Castro called *gusanos rojos* (red worms) when they failed to return to Cuba. Natalia is the daughter of a Russian mother, who taught Russian history to students who were going to study in Russia, and a Cuban father, while Oscar is all Cuban. Both were born in 1966, and grew up fully within the revolution. In the years during which they were reaching adulthood, both were studying in Russia, as were approximately 10,000 other Cuban students. But they arrived there at a time when young Russians their age were living through the processes of change that we came to know as *perestroika* and *glasnost*. Oscar grew up around family who thought that Cuba was nothing other than a disaster: "We were always *gusanos*," he said.

Natalia, by contrast, grew up surrounded by family who were true believers in communism, as she had been, until they grew disillusioned. In the case of her father, an economist working on central planning, the arbitrary use of power in the case of the trial and execution of General Arnaldo Ochoa in 1989 was "the drop that made the cup overflow." In Natalia's case, her love for Oscar had been decisive, coupled with her experience in Russia when they went there to study and live for eight years. Suddenly, due to *glasnost*, there was no longer censure, and all the literature in the world was available for them to read and consider. Moreover, Russian students were deeply engaged, and the dorms where they lived were hotbeds of discussion lasting late into the night.

After the first two years of studying there, Oscar and Natalia married and moved to married-student housing, away from the ideological control most Cuban students were under then, and close to students from many other countries. Worried that the Cuban students would catch the flame of *perestroika*, Cuba sent some representatives to explain to the students that Cuba's process was different, not a *perestroika*, but a process of Rectification of Errors. But the Cuban students had already begun to discuss the situation quite freely and had openly debated the extent to which in Cuba there was a personality cult. Ultimately, Oscar's open criticisms regarding the extent to which Cubans were not allowed to speak freely, to travel, and to be masters of their lives cost him his career. He was only one semester short of graduating with excellent grades when he was "expelled by the request of the Cuban embassy," as his transcript reads. Natalia was saved from a similar fate because she could remain there on her Russian passport and because she also had the backing of her dean, "a man of new ideas," as she put it. Oscar also went to Germany and actually witnessed the fall of the Berlin Wall in 1989. He returned to Russia and told Natalia they would not be returning to Cuba. She finished studying, and they went on to found the Unión Cubana, an organization that aimed to help the more than 100 other young Cubans in their situation who were illegal and could neither return to Cuba nor gain political asylum in Russia. They came to the United States in 1993, thanks to Jorge Mas-Canosa's "Program Exodus," organized by the Cuban American National Foundation. They were then 27 years old, young enough to remake their lives and have two more beautiful children and have her parents join them. With a large family to be responsible for, Oscar never finished studying metallurgical engineering, but he makes a good living as a self-employed electrician, while Natalia first taught Russian and Spanish and now teaches high school physics.

By contrast, Enrique Patterson's experience was eminently political, yet he never lived anywhere else. He was nine years old when the revolution triumphed in 1959. A black Cuban from Oriente province, he remembered how after Batista's soldiers abused the villagers, everyone was on the side of the rebels. The rebels came at night to eat in people's houses, like his family's.

When Patterson was a child, prior to the revolution, his father had a prosperous small factory, where they made shoes, especially boots for the peasants. Patterson placed himself in the petite bourgeoisie, as *un negrito que tenía manejadora*, a small black child who had a nanny. But then the business failed, and they moved to Camagüey, where his father went to work in the construction of the Central Highway, while his mother went to Havana to become a domestic. His mother went from having servants to being a servant, he emphasized. When the revolution triumphed, his father was working in a shoe factory and had become the secretary-general of the *sindicato* for shoemakers. While his father was a black Cuban who was an independent small businessman, he was also an old communist and an activist in the *sindicato*.

Patterson's process of political disaffection was gradual and cumulative. As an adolescent, he was a *miliciano*, as well as leader of the High School Students League (Unión de Estudiantes Secundarios), then a member of the UJC. But the Soviet Union's invasion of Czechoslovakia entailed a serious "political shock." He expected Castro to support Czechoslovakia, given how often the government insisted it was a small island assailed by a major superpower. But Castro supported the Soviet Union. The UJC asked those who were in favor of Czechoslovakia to engage in autocriticism. Patterson refused and was expelled from the UJC, for "ideological problems."

Patterson's interview gives plenty of evidence for what James C. Scott (1990) called cultural patterns of resistance to domination. Despite his excellence as a student, he developed a reputation that followed him. At the workplace, they called him in for coming to work without wearing socks, noting it was evidence of an "ideological problem." He replied that there were no socks in Cuba, but they still insisted he had to wear socks. One day he came in to work *descalzo* – without shoes. Asked why he insisted on doing that, he replied that he did so because in Cuba there were no shoes. He was expelled from the workplace.

With the help of a former teacher from the *pre-Universitario*, he was able to obtain a job teaching history at the School for Party Leaders, in La Coronela, on the outskirts of Havana. At this time, blacks in Cuba were deeply influenced by the assertions of blackness – *Negritude*, as it was called by Aimé Césaire –with figures such as Malcolm X and Leopold Senghor. As a result, black intellectuals in Cuba started using hairstyles such as the "Afro" or "dreadlocks," which the government saw as a protest against the system. Patterson was called in by the political section of the school and told he had to get a haircut, because they could see that he was having serious ideological problems. To get back at them, Patterson had the barber shave his hair off completely. For his disrespect, they expelled him, escorting him out of the school with soldiers bearing rifles.

Patterson felt these expressions of cultural resistance were linked to the problem of race in Cuba. Many black Cubans felt oppressed because, on the one hand, from the beginning the revolution told them they were equal and had access to schooling and jobs, but, on the other hand, it did not allow them to express themselves culturally as blacks. Moreover, he felt used by the racial equality leitmotif of the revolution: "The problem of race in Cuba was cultural and historical, and the triumph of the revolution was unlikely to bring it to a sudden end."

Ultimately, those acts of rebellion led him to become intellectually critical and prompted him to study Marxism as a philosophical tradition. On his own, he read Marx, Engels, Lenin, Lucas, the Frankfurt school. When he entered the University of Havana in 1973, he studied the history of social thought. The old Department of Philosophy had folded in 1968, due to the political controversy created by the journal *Pensamiento Crítico*. In 1975 Patterson became part of the new department, where he taught the history of philosophy, specializing in classical German philosophy of the 19th century prior to Marx, so he "could avoid repeating the dogma they wanted to teach." He was quite popular among the students.

Irreverent in his ways, he refused to participate in the *actos de repudio* around the Mariel exodus. He was expelled again in 1981, accused of being a "counterrevolutionary," "a dangerous enemy of socialism," and was barred from teaching in any university. He became a laborer in the port of the bay, where he had to survive like the average Cuban. When he could not get work, he made a couple of pairs of shoes and sold them. Wherever he went in the city, he felt watched. He sought to start a new life and be as far away from the reach of the government as possible. He got married and went to live with his wife's family. Thanks to the racial solidarity that existed among black Cubans, a good friend who was a party member helped him get hold of the file that was kept on him (as on all Cubans), where his clashes with the political authorities were recorded. He told others he had lost it, though in truth he kept it well hidden. After working in the bay of Havana, he asked for an evaluation from the labor union and the party representative there, who gave him a good evaluation. Thus, he created a new work file, a new reputation.

With this new work file, he was able to go back to teaching literature at a *pre-Universitario* in Batabanó. Together with Francisco Morán (today the editor of *Habana Elegante*), they won three prizes, at the municipality, provincial, and national levels, for the best way to teach literature in the *pre-Universitario*. Unfortunately, the prize made him visible and the government detected him. They now barred him from teaching anywhere, as they reconstructed his former life and his old file. Calling him a counterrevolutionary, they pushed him to become a dissident. Patterson decided to "come up to the light" and joined the emerging dissident movement.

This new form of opposition that began to develop in the mid-1980s was philosophically based on the notion of nonviolent resistance. It gained force in the 1990s, spurred by the collapse of communism. It patterned itself after world leaders such as Mahatma Gandhi, Martin Luther King Jr., and Cesar Chavez, and it stressed its belief in human rights, as expressed in the United Nations' Declaration of Human Rights (1948). Moreover, its leadership incorporated young Cubans who grew up under the revolution and even benefited from the social mobility the revolution's emphasis on universal education facilitated. An early movement was called Tercera Opción – the third option – and was founded by Rolando Prats-Páez, César Mora, Omar Pérez, and Jorge Crespo. As Rolando Prats-Páez explained, it issued from the left, inspired by the work of Antonio Gramsci and the critical theory of the Frankfurt School. They saw themselves as an alternative to the counterrevolutionary restoration they perceived the Cuban exile to espouse and also an alternative to the imposition of a Soviet, Stalinized version of socialism at a time when the Cuban revolution had reached a deep ideological, economic, and institutional crisis.

Both Patterson and Prats-Páez helped to found the first fully developed embryonic political party of opposition in Cuba – the Corriente Socialista Democrática Cubana (Cuban Democratic Socialists). Later, the CSDC became closely allied with a human rights group led by Elizardo Sánchez–Santa Cruz, the Comisión Cubana de Derechos Humanos y Reconciliación Nacional (National Committee for Human Rights and National

Reconciliation). The latter was a social democratic group that attracted other impressive figures, such as Vladimiro Roca, former pilot in the armed forces and son of the well-known old communist Blas Roca.

Underground, in the university, Patterson helped found a new Directorio Estudiantil that wanted autonomy for the university and democratization for the society. He was detained, harassed, interrogated – clear forms of persecution. To cope with the stress, he relied on family and friends he could count on totally, as well as his sense of humor. He no longer suffered internal conflicts, as his rejection of the government was now total, because he no longer believed in it. "When you reach that point," he stressed, "it's you versus them." He decided to leave Cuba during an interrogation at Villa Marista. Seguridad del Estado threatened him with imprisonment and pointed out that he would not be provided with the asthma inhaler he needed. He sent the U.S. Interests Section office his original file, which he had kept, and requested political asylum.

Today Patterson teaches at Charles R. Drew Elementary School in Miami. In addition, he occasionally writes for *El Nuevo Herald* and has a radio program on Radio Martí. Years later, Patterson (1999) reflected on race and dissidence in Cuba, seeing that Cuban blacks and mulattoes participated in large numbers in the dissident movement. He realized that history repeats itself. Antonio Maceo in the 19th century and Oscar Elías Bisset in the 20th, both mulattoes, led the social movement of their time. Bisset, founder of the human rights organization Fundación Lawton, however, has a Gandhian commitment to nonviolent resistance, whereas Maceo was a general armed with the *machete* of the time. In the same vein, Patterson pointed out, the authors of "La Patria es de Todos" (Our Nation Belongs to All) (Bonne-Carcassés et al. 1997) are black, mulatto, and white. Patterson asked: Are they in the leadership of the dissident movement because they were pushed to the dangerous front of the line by their white colleagues (cf. Cuesta-Morúa 1999)? Or are they in the leadership of the dissident movement because of their commitment to the principles of civil and human rights?

Prats-Páez ("Cayo" to his friends) helped write the original program of the Corriente Socialista Democrática (1991–92) and a statement of its principles (1992), both of which stressed the conditions to achieve a transition to a democratic state in Cuba, allowing Cubans the freedom to dissent. Even before leaving Cuba, in the summer of 1994, Prats-Páez (1993a; 1993b) repeatedly stressed that if the United States were to lift at least parts of the embargo, it could help bring about a climate in which Cuban leaders were more likely to initiate real reforms. As he put it, "No one who is politically honest can deny that in the last three decades Cuban society has made substantial progress in the area of social rights." But neither can such a person, he emphasized, deny the Cuban government's "gross daily human rights violations. . . . In Cuban law, an individual's liberties matter only when they don't go against the interests of a state power unrestrained by civil society" (1993a).

In sum, some of Cuba's most recent émigrés were motivated by family reunification considerations above all. They had already made an adjustment to living in Cuba "as is" and carved out a satisfactory life for themselves, until their children "pushed" them to leave. Some Cubans also left for purely political reasons, irrespective of the economic conditions on the island, because to them the central issue was the Cuban government's systematic violations of civil liberties and human rights. And most Cubans left because, for them, the profound economic and political problems Cubans lived through in the 1990s led to their political disaffection.

PART III

Civil Society Returns

9

The Church and Civil Society

Diles que ellos son la dulce esperanza de la patria, y que no hay patria sin virtud, ni virtud con impiedad.

Tell them they are our nation's sweet hope, and there is neither a nation without virtue, nor virtue without piety and compassion.

Father Félix Varela, *Cartas a Elpidio* (1996 [1835])

The Church in Cuba

Cubans are now beginning to build a civil society that is independent of government. Weak and fragile as it may be, it is real. One of the pillars that upholds this new civil society is religion. As Ariel Armony noted, "religion has emerged as a key source of associationalism in Cuba. Catholicism, Protestantism, Spiritism, Judaism, and other manifestations of religious activity provide fora where people congregate and engage in social interaction. In a context in which the state attempts to penetrate most arenas of social life, religious groups provide an opportunity for individuals to associate with a degree of independence from state control" (2003:21). In Cuba in the 1990s, during "the special period," a significant religious revival took place, as the churches and synagogues that were nearly empty for years filled with people. To illustrate the changing roles religion plays in Cuba and the exodus, I rely on interviews with Graciela Relloso, Moisés Asís and Teresa Hernández, Ivanna Martín, Amelia Sosa (pseudonym), Enrique Naranjo and Ildelisa Rivera, Mariana Torres (pseudonym), José Conrado Rodríguez, Fernando Roa, Rafael Diéguez, Wilfredo Beyra and Zaimar Campins, Emma Tejera (pseudonym), and Luisa Suárez (pseudonym).

When the revolution was fought initially against the dictatorship of Fulgencio Batista, the church strongly supported the revolutionary effort. But when the government showed its communist hand, church and state found themselves locked in a confrontation that culminated in the silencing of the church: the nationalization of the Catholic, private schools and the University of Villanueva; the expulsion of many priests and nuns; and the departure of most of the religious congregations from the island (Collazo 2001). Around 300 priests and nuns were expelled from Cuba aboard the steamer *Covadonga*, bound for Spain. For months later, entire religious orders left the island. An antireligious climate then took hold that lasted for more than 20 years. The Catholic Church became what Ondina Menocal (2003) calls "a church in silence." That phase lasted throughout most of the 1960s and well into the 1970s. By the mid-1970s, Menocal notes, the church was still turned inward, as the church of the few faithful, but was undergoing a period of modernization that resulted from the reforms of the Second Vatican Council and internal strengthening. This culminated in 1986 with the Encuentro Nacional Eclesiástico Cubano. The ENEC changed the posture of the church: it turned it outward again, helping it become incorporated in the society. Menocal describes the church in the 1980s as a church seeking its identity through its good works in the society.

Throughout this period, however, Cuba defined itself as an atheist society guided by a philosophical doctrine – the materialism of Marxism-Leninism – that was antithetical to a spiritual understanding of life. Hence, Cubans who were religious – of any faith – and practiced their religion paid very real prices for their convictions: social ostracism in the neighborhood, loss of promotions at work, no admission to higher education or the careers they sought. Because attending a church or synagogue was declaring oneself to be against the mainstream and young people no longer received instruction in their faith, few Cubans were found inside the temples. As a result, the church faithful became minimal in number, although those who remained often underwent a deeper mystical experience and gained a clearer significance regarding the meaning of their religious commitment (Suárez-Cobián 2002).

Such was the case for Graciela Relloso, who described herself as a *guajira* who came from a very small town in the countryside, San José de los Ramos. She came from a poor family where eight people lived together, five of them children. The house was quite old, and the floor planks were so rotten that her feet at times fell through. They had only two electrical appliances: a radio and an iron. A neighbor kept the meat for them in his refrigerator. Yet she remembered her family life with happiness, as her parents got along very well and she was quite close to her mother, like a friend. She remembered how people stopped going to church, including her adolescent friends in the choir: "They were young, beginning to work, and they wanted to study, so it was not convenient" to be known for participating in the church. She too would have liked to go on to study, as she was always the best student in her class, but she sacrificed pursuing a career for her deep religious beliefs and, instead, she specialized in sewing and embroidery. She sometimes went to give a catechism class that no one was there to receive. "In the end, I was alone," she emphasized. She assisted the priest in every way when he came to the church, only twice a month. He had so many parishes to take care of, with so few priests. While in 1960 there had been 723 priests and 2,225 nuns in Cuba, by 1980, though the population had grown much larger, the numbers had shrunk to 213 priests and 200 nuns (Fernández 1984:184–85). So Graciela did nearly everything: she took care of the accounts, prepared the baptisms, rang the bells, and even gave a service with the consecrated host the priest left behind. "People did not stop believing in God, but they left because they were afraid, that is the truth." Such was the situation until she left Cuba in 1975.

Equally difficult was the life of many Jewish Cubans. Moisés Asís, a Cuban Jew of Turkish ancestry, also held deep religious convictions. In 1972, when he applied for admission to the university, those convictions barred him from access to the career he most wanted to pursue – psychology – despite his excellent test scores. Not only the university, he stressed, but also many of the work centers had rules in place that impeded those who believed in God from joining them. Moreover, such beliefs were sufficient cause to expel them from work. Teresa Hernández, Moisés's wife, recalled that all the employment applications asked whether the person had been in prison, had religious convictions, or had maintained a relationship with Cubans who emigrated. Moisés could answer yes to all three.

Initially imbued with revolutionary enthusiasm, at the age of 14 he volunteered to join the army. But only three years later he attempted to leave the country. A number of experiences spurred his disaffection. Chief among them was the profound family conflict that developed when most of the family left Cuba, while his father, instead, dedicated all his time and efforts to the revolution. He slighted the family, resulting in his parents' divorce. Moisés also minded the lack of freedom of information, the lack of freedom to travel. Moreover, he disliked seeing how the revolutionary government fanned the flames of envy and hatred toward other social classes and groups. Early in 1970 he tried to leave Cuba on a small boat, but it capsized near the coast. Illegal exit, as it was deemed to be then, was a criminal offense in Cuba that landed him and his friends in jail; as a minor, he was sentenced to a year, while the others served two years. During that time, he was forced to work in the construction of the Parque Lenin.

His religiosity also marked him. As a Jew who sought his ancestral past, this mark of difference may have become more salient because so few Jews remained in Cuba. Around 90 percent of the Jewish community emigrated in the early years of the revolution. Left behind were those imbued with hope in the revolution; the elderly; and the poor. While there was no explicit anti-Semitism in Cuba after the revolution, Moisés stressed that the government's antireligious campaign, as well as its anti-Israeli, pro-Palestinian posture, did create some anti-Jewish feeling in Cuba. Moisés remembered that in Cuba no one ever mentioned the Nazi holocaust of 6 million Jews, though the 20 million Soviets who died during World War II were always mentioned; likewise, *The Diary of Anne Frank* was not published.

In general, the revolutionary government enjoyed better relations with the Protestant churches (Ham 1977; Ramos 1989). While numbers are lacking, they seem to have grown vigorously in recent years. Protestantism became well established in Cuba after the war of independence from Spain. John Kirk pointed out that, with true missionary zeal, the mainline Protestant denominations took up the task of "saving" Cubans from Catholicism and showing them "the true way" (1989:54). Like the Catholic Church, they accomplished their mission by establishing numerous schools in the cities, though neglecting the rural areas.

Perhaps no other group suffered as much for its religious convictions as the Jehovah's Witnesses. Pacifists as part of their deeply held religious convictions, Jehovah's Witnesses refused to join the army in Cuba, despite the forced army conscription; they refused to salute the flag; they refused to fight in Cuba's overseas ventures. These refusals landed them in jail. "But we are neutral with respect to *all* governments, everywhere, not just Cuba," said Ivanna Martín, today a manicurist in Miami whose father and uncle both were jailed for their refusals.

The situation began to change when Frei Betto, a Brazilian Catholic priest who came out of the liberation theology perspective in Latin America, interviewed Fidel Castro regarding his views on religion. Betto's (1985) interview became an immediate best seller and was widely read. As Kirk emphasized, because it was published by the Council of State, the book represented not only "a major olive branch extended to the church by a sector of the Communist party hierarchy, but also an extraordinary personal appeal by the Cuban President himself" (1989:164). Kirk noted that both the political and church leaders "warily edged toward a more meaningful relationship," with Fidel Castro being "of paramount importance in laying the groundwork for their mutually beneficial dialogue" (1989:162). Gradually a new government posture developed that allowed more religious expression and tolerance. In 1991 it was decided that believers could become members of the Communist Party; in 1992 a constitutional amendment changed Cuba's definition of itself from an atheist to a secular state (Prieto 2001). Such a redefinition allowed the practice of religious beliefs. Together with the new search for meaning prompted by the collapse of communism in Eastern Europe, many Cubans returned to or joined the churches and synagogues. Arturo López-Levy (2003) noted that in the 1990s there was a renaissance of Jewish life, a revival that was assisted by these changes. As I witnessed, many churches and synagogues, once nearly empty, gradually filled with parishioners. Many congregations now conduct a lively religious life, and the churches play numerous roles, in Cuba and in exile.

Providing Spiritual Sustenance

The spiritual sustenance the church provides people in Cuba, giving direction to their lives, is important. Prior to the revolution, Catholicism exerted great weight in the culture, but its observance by the people was minimal (de Céspedes 1995). During the revolution, Cubans who became politically integrated were ardent believers in the revolution's promises, and their children grew up without any religious instruction whatsoever. As adults, many went on to become politically disaffected and left Cuba, feeling the absence of religion in their lives. As Amelia Sosa put it to me, "I wish I could pray...but I do not know how." For those who did not receive religious instruction as children or who underwent a conversion as adults, this basic role that any set of spiritual beliefs plays is, thus, rather important. After the collapse of communism in the Soviet Union and Eastern Europe, the church also provides an alternative vision of society – one where social classes and races are not pitted against one another, but where the social message is about justice with mercy – helping others through compassion.

Solving Problems

For many Cubans, the church also provides assistance for solving life's problems – for those who are lonely, hungry, ill, suffer from alcoholism, and the like. And while these are problems churches everywhere strive to solve, in Cuba they are not unrelated to the massive exodus that took place over the years. The exodus severed the complex, extended family that in the past had characterized Cuban culture – an extended family that in the past served as a "safety net" for coping with life's most extreme circumstances. Moreover, it was only in 1986, as the result of the Encuentro Nacional Eclesiástico Cubano (1987), the largest such gathering to ever take place in the history of the church in Cuba, that a new commitment to being a missionary church developed. Deciding to fully utilize its lay members, the church sought to create vibrant local communities where the religious message takes life in helping the actual lives of its people (Collazo 2001; Suárez-Cobián 2002). Along with this change came a new generation of young Cuban priests. The church also relies on its transnational ties to accomplish its mission (Quigley 2003; Hansing and Mahler 2003). Thereafter, the Cuban church began to work with Caritas (the international Catholic charities) to assist in delivering food and medicine to those most in need, such as the imprisoned and the elderly. The pope's visit a decade later affirmed and strengthened this new missionary church.

The massive exodus left many old people alone in Cuba. Given the economic crisis, they have little to eat and are often quite ill; despite their frailty, they have to fend for themselves. Many of the churches and synagogues stepped in to try to help. Certainly the Jewish community in Cuba looks out for its elderly, conscious that many go hungry. In this effort, it is aided by international organizations, such as the Canadian Jewish Congress, and other self-help groups, such as the Jewish Solidarity group formed by Eddie Levy and Xiomara Almaguer in Miami, who regularly travel to Cuba.

The Catholic Church also considers such assistance to the elderly part of its mission. For example, the Church of Santa Teresita in Santiago de Cuba, which I visited, feeds its old parishioners by making an *ajiaco* (a traditional Cuban vegetable stew) that feeds approximately 70 old persons once a day. That *ajiaco* became possible thanks to the culinary expertise of Enrique Naranjo, a parishioner who for many years was the chef at the Hotel Seville in Havana. Though he eventually left for Spain, he and his wife, Ildelisa Rivera, institutionalized the making of this meal as one of the church's projects of social assistance. Many parishioners who initially entered the church looking for this kind of material assistance progressively became drawn to its religious message. Moreover, the church provided them with a new social network on which to rely for solving life's problems and others with whom to share their feelings. This enabled many Cubans to cope with the hardships of life and remain in Cuba.

Giving Refuge

Many Cubans who became profoundly disaffected from the government and its politics turned to the church seeking *amparo* – refuge. Mariana Torres was the daughter of a working-class woman who, more than revolutionary or communist, was a *Fidelista*. From the beginning of the revolution, she was imbued with Fidel's charisma and followed him in everything he did and said. So much so, that their house was used as what was called a *casa de confianza* – literally, a house that could be trusted, where informants could meet with members of the state security to give their reports on the dissident groups they had penetrated. But Mariana herself went to the university and became extremely well educated and progressively more and more disaffected from the revolution, feelings she shared with her father. When she lost her job working in a laboratory, she desperately wanted to leave Cuba. She did not tell her family that she had lost her job or that she hoped to leave. Every day, she pretended to leave home for work and, instead, went to a church in Centro Habana. There she sat in a pew for hours to think and pray, caught between her deep love for her mother and her profound disaffection. After some months, she made a promise to the Virgin that she would fulfill if she was able to leave Cuba – as, indeed, she did. To her, the church was a refuge, both physically and spiritually – a place that gave her *amparo* when she was most in despair, enabling her to cope with life in Cuba, and it also gave her the spiritual strength to pursue her own path, despite her family background, and leave.

Building Democracy

To some church leaders, among them the current cardinal Jaime Ortega, the mission of the church should be strictly religious, not political. To many in the exile community, such a stance seems too weak. Agustín Tamargo (1997), a leading voice in Miami, asked that a cardinal with the valor of Miguel Ovando-Bravo, in Nicaragua, be lent to Cuba, to be its conscience. Upon Archbishop Pedro Meurice's retirement, Adolfo Rivero-Caro (2007) called him "the people's bishop," for being the sole member of the church hierarchy to play a combative role.

Yet in recent years some church leaders consciously sought to use the church to build a democratic future, trying to enable Cubans on the island to make the effort to solve the profound political and economic crisis that Cuba was living through by themselves. Perhaps no other priest has played this role as publicly as Father José Conrado Rodríguez did on the heels of the dramatic *balsero* crisis of the summer of 1994, a crisis that emboldened him to act. On September 8, the day Cubans celebrate the national feast day of their cherished patron saint, la Virgen de la Caridad del Cobre, in his church in Palma Soriano, Oriente province, that day's homily consisted of his reading a letter he had written to Fidel Castro. It read:

My deep concern for the situation our people are living through moves me to write you.... For over 30 years, our country engaged in a politics at the base of which was violence. This politics was justified because of the presence of a powerful and tenacious enemy only 90 miles away, the United States of America. The way in which we confronted this enemy was to place ourselves under the power that for years confronted it, the Soviet Union....

While the Soviet Union gave massive assistance to our economy and our arms race, Cuba gradually fell into a state of internal violence and profound repression.... The use, within and without our country, of hatred, division, violence, suspicion and ill will, has been the main cause of our present and past misfortune.

Now we can see it clearly. The excessive growth of the state, progressively more powerful, left our people defenseless and silenced. The lack of liberty that would have allowed healthy criticism and alternative ways of thinking caused us to slide down the slippery slope of political volition and intolerance toward others. The fruits it bore were those of hypocrisy and dissimulation, insincerity and lying, and a general state of fear that affected everyone in the island.... We are all responsible, but no one is more responsible than you. (Rodríguez 1995)

The letter also called for a peaceful, negotiated agreement through the process of a national dialogue among the major political actors – the Communist Party, the dissident movement, as well as Cubans in exile – and called for a popular referendum. To date, that meeting of the major political actors has not taken place. Father José Conrado's letter was widely circulated in Cuba as well as in the exile community. To many Cubans on both shores, it was "a clarion call," as Fernando Roa, former Cuban magistrate in Miami, put it. Inside and outside of Cuba, many began calling him *el Cardenal del pueblo* (the people's cardinal).

To Father José Conrado, the bishops' statement (Conferencia de Obispos Católicos de Cuba, 1993) a year earlier, "El Amor Todo lo Espera" ("Love

Hopeth All Things") simply did not go far enough. The depth of the crisis and the felt oppression made him take this responsibility to act. In his work as a priest for eight years in the two parishes of Palma Soriano and Contramaestre, Father José Conrado also engaged in a traveling ministry throughout the island. He regularly visited and said mass in numerous towns – as many as 43 in the year of 1991, when I first met him. I visited him in his parish of Palma Soriano in July 1996 and accompanied him on his many visits to the townspeople, as he tried to help everyone, the powerless and the powerful both (see Yero 1996). In some, such as the town of Aguacate, his was the first mass held there in 30 years. In his travels and visits, he spoke with hundreds of families, thousands of persons, from the poorest to the powerful, communists and noncommunists alike; many confided their problems in him. Hence, he became their voice: "I felt that the situation was a real challenge, not only for my parishioners but also for me, as their suffering was my suffering.... That was when I decided to act, to try to solve the situation with the means I had." Thus he wrote the letter he read to Fidel Castro from the pulpit.

José Conrado had the opportunity to leave Cuba on a number of occasions as a young man. Each time, he decided against it, and his parents and grandparents chose to remain behind to accompany him, though everyone else in the family was leaving. Father José Conrado's position was that it is in Cuba that Cubans must carry the cross of serving *la patria*; that the *compromiso* (commitment) with Cuba needs to keep those who care about its future in Cuba, not in exile – even at the cost of their lives. He maintained this position even when the church, afraid for his safety, pulled him out of Cuba and sent him to study in Spain for a couple of years (see his letter "Adíos Hermanos" [Goodbye, My Brethren] 1996).

A few weeks after he read the letter to Fidel Castro from the pulpit, a plot by the state security to kill him was uncovered. When José Conrado learned of this plan, he quickly communicated it, via a taped telephone call to a close childhood friend who was working as a lawyer in Miami, so that if anything in fact happened to him, the real reason for his death would be known. This very action also protected him because afterward the state security changed its attitude toward him. Wanting to avoid a scandal, the officials greeted him warmly in public.

Due to the vow of obedience he took as a priest, he left Cuba to study both theology and journalism at the Universidad Pontificia de Salamanca, in Spain, where I also visited him. While there, both in a television and press interviews, he asked others not to call him *el Cardenal del pueblo* (the

247

people's cardinal). Cuba's cardinal is called Jaime, he stressed. Accused of politicizing his masses in Cuba, Padre José Conrado defended himself by noting that "the Church is not an alternative to the political power, nor does it wish to be. But it should realize the duty of its prophetic mission: to denounce injustice" (Correa 1996). While studying overseas, he began to add the communities of Cubans in the diaspora to his traveling ministry. Father José Conrado returned to Cuba, to "accompany *el pueblo* [the people] in their process of change." There he has continued to serve the Cuban people, though in a quieter manner.

Sustaining Identity

Because for several decades religion played no part in the life of most Cubans and young people grew up without any religious instruction, a major task of the churches and synagogues at present is that of sustaining the identities nearly lost. Perhaps for no other group is this as true as for Cuban Jews. Of the approximately 10,000 Jews who lived in Cuba in the 1950s, by 1965 only 1,900 Jews remained in Havana, while another 400 lived in the provinces. After the Mariel exodus of 1980, less than 800 Cuban Jews were left on the island. Approximately 85 percent of the Jews who fled Cuba moved to Florida, particularly Miami Beach, where the transfer of the Cuban Jewish community to Miami was accomplished. Symbolically, this was commemorated during the High Holidays of 1980, when Cuban Jews in Miami dedicated their Cuban Hebrew Congregation, worshiping with the Sifrei Torah that Bernardo Benes had personally brought to Miami from Havana (Kaplan et al. 1990).

In part, the massive exodus of Cuba's Jews was due to the government's nationalization of the business sector. As in the European past, Jews in Cuba were a "middleman minority" overwhelmingly concentrated in commerce and trade (cf. Bonacich 1973). In Old Havana, the street called Muralla was totally identified with Jewish commerce, particularly the garment industry. Indeed, in the 1950s the Jewish community in Cuba had reached its economic apex together with social freedom, experience that contrasted sharply with their European past (Levine 1993). Hence, the government's takeover of the commercial trade sector hit the Cuban Jewish community hard. So much so, that it is easy to derive an interpretation that they left solely due to economic reasons, as they lost their modus vivendi. This is the interpretation put forth by José Miller, president of the Patronato Synagogue in Havana, and Professor Maritza Corrales, history professor at the

248

University of Havana, in the filmed interviews of the documentary *"Havana Nagila": The Jews in Cuba* (Paull 1995). To Asís and others in the Cuban Jewish community, however, this interpretation misses the fact that many in that community were already well acquainted with communism from their Eastern European past; hence, they rapidly perceived what was coming and left Cuba.

The result, emphasized Asís, was that "the community became like an orphan. Those who had the most economic power left; those who had the strongest Jewish identities – the rabbis, the teachers – left." Not a single rabbi remained. Jews were no longer immigrating to Cuba, and a large part of the very small community that remained became assimilated to the new communist society. Thus, by the mid-1980s, when Moisés was in his 30s, he was faced with the virtual extinction of the Cuban Jewish community. He then founded a school (popularly called *la escuelita*), where he taught the children Hebrew, Jewish history, religion, and identity – what it means to be Jewish. Gradually, both the number of students and the number of teachers grew and the school became a center of the community (Asís 2003). To Moisés, the school was the future, so he devoted himself to the school from 1985 to 1993. He finally left shortly after the completion of the filmed interviews for *"Havana Nagila": The Jews in Cuba*, in which he played a central part. He left overwhelmed by political circumstances and his sense of being very alone. "I wanted to save the Jewish community," he stressed. "It was in danger of extinction."

The situation with the Catholic Church was vastly different in that even in the years when there were few practicing Catholics inside the church and Cuban history was written without the church being part of it, Catholicism still exerted a weight in the culture (see de Céspedes 1999b). Precisely because of this, the effort in Cuba today is to put the church back in the history of Cuba, where it belongs, as Estrada (2005) has sought to do.

The most obvious "sign" of the impact of the Catholic Church on Cuba's culture and identity has always been the devotion to la Virgen de la Caridad del Cobre. Like the story of the Virgin of Guadalupe's appearance to Juan Diego, a poor Indian in Mexico, shortly after the Spanish conquest, the story of the appearance of Our Lady of Charity symbolizes the origins of the Cuban people. A Spanish Catholic Virgin, she appeared in the early 1600s to three Cuban fishermen who were caught in a tempest at sea in the Bay of Nipe, Oriente province. One was a young, black slave only 10 years old (who in his old age told the story), and the other two were Indian brothers. In their fear, they fervently prayed for help and protection. When

249

her image appeared, floating on a wooden tablet, the sea and sky became calm (in Marrero 1976). Religion and nationalism became deeply welded in the figure of *la Caridad* during Cuba's struggle for independence in the 19th century. Cubans who fought in their long struggle for independence from Spain, such as Antonio Maceo and Carlos Manuel de Céspedes, prayed to her as a symbol of nationhood before taking up arms and going into battle (Díaz de Villar 1986).

In recent years, amid the far-ranging religious revival that has taken place in Cuba, the devotion to la Virgen de la Caridad del Cobre has gained enormous popularity. The devotion to *la Caridad* structures meaning for many in Cuba today. This can be seen in the way Cubans express their present plight in Cuba in numerous paintings that depict her in the traditional manner yet substitute the *balseros* of the 1990s for the traditional rowing boat with the three fishermen. One work that stands out as particularly memorable to me is a pen-and-ink drawing by Rafael Díeguez: as the sea rages under a black sky at night, a delicate Virgin oversees an empty *balsa*, buffeted by tall waves (see Figure 9.1)

Opening Society

The pope's visit in 1998 was a watershed moment in the history of the church during the revolution, spurring the return of religiosity to Cuban society and culture. For some Cubans, it was also an opportunity to express their dissent and hope for a democratic future.

More than any other pope, John Paul II traveled far and wide. Few of his visits, however, captured the imagination as much as his visit to Cuba. When he arrived in Cuba in January, the country had been under the communist rule of Fidel Castro for 38 years. This international drama was played out alongside many personal dramas, such as my own (see Morello 1998). Many Cubans who left the island as exiles, or the children of exiles, returned to Cuba – some for the first time – to share this dramatic event on Cuban soil. Prior to the pope's visit, I had made eight trips to Cuba since 1979, but no other trip was as thrilling as this one, as it showed the most change in Cuba.

Even before he arrived, Cubans prepared a warm welcome for the pope. All over the city, posters of the pope against a true blue sky were pasted on the walls. They said: *¡Juan Pablo II, Te Esperamos!* (We Await You!) or *¡Bendícenos!* (Bless Us!) When he arrived, the response of the Cuban people was joyful, as was evident on television. Thousands of people lined the streets, waiting for him to pass by; attended the masses; waved

Figure 9.1 In recent years, a religious revival took place in Cuba, spurred by the deep economic and political crisis of "the special period." The devotion to la Virgen de la Caridad del Cobre gained enormous popularity. Through paintings of her, Cubans express their plight. Here is a work by Rafael Díeguez, a young artist overcome with grief when he found out his best friend had left Cuba on a *balsa* but never reached another shore – a common tragedy in the summer of 1994. Rather than the traditional three fishermen in a boat under the patron saint, his pen-and-ink drawing depicted Our Lady of Charity over an empty *balsa*, expressing the tragedy that Cubans continue to live today. Díeguez left Cuba for Spain in 1996. (Rafael Díeguez)

flags; chanted their support for the pope in unison; and expressed their happiness. Young men from the Rapid Response Brigade charged with keeping order on the streets were standing next to me for hours waiting for the pope, and even they shouted and jumped with joy when they saw him pass by in his *papamobile*.

The pope offered four masses while in Cuba, two of which I attended – the first one in Santa Clara, a small provincial city, where both sides of my family, the Rodríguez and the Lubián, were among its founding families. I also attended the last one at the Plaza of the Revolution in Havana. The other two (in Camagüey and Oriente) I watched on television, along with millions of Cubans on the island, while I stayed with my family in Santa Clara, meeting my cousins for the first time. People really came out for these masses, something no one could have predicted. Posters, banners, and flags welcoming the pope went up everywhere. And Cubans who came out to the masses in support of the pope were of all social classes, all races, all ages – truly *el pueblo*.

At the masses, people waved the Vatican and Cuban flags together with enormous joy. In Cuba, there is a culture of mobilization, where people come out on the streets and plazas and express themselves in chants and songs. Like much else in Cuban culture, it has both Spanish and African origins. It is the culture of people who for centuries went out on the streets, *arrollando* – singing and dancing in unison – during Carnival, as well as during religious processions. During the revolution, Castro used this same culture of mobilization for political purposes, as during his speeches he would elicit this same response from the masses of people around him. During the pope's visit, Cubans used it to express themselves. The crowds chanted, rhythmically, their support for the pope and his message, with rhymes such as:

Juan Pablo, amigo,	Juan Pablo, our friend,
el pueblo está contigo.	the people are with you.
Se ve,	We can see it,
Se siente,	we can feel it,
el Papa está presente.	the Pope is with us.

The mass in Santiago de Cuba was particularly moving in a number of ways. The archbishop of Santiago, Pedro Meurice, spoke loudly and boldly in defense of human rights when he emphasized that the Cuban nation lives both on the island and in the diaspora, and Cubans "suffer, live, and hope both here and there." The church's commitment, as affirmed in Puebla, is with the "poorest of the poor." He added, "And the poorest among us are those who lack liberty."

Moreover, because Santiago de Cuba is very near El Cobre, the shrine next to the copper mines where Cuba's patron saint resides, at the Santiago de Cuba mass the pope symbolically crowned her. The Cuban people accompanied him in song, to the tune of "Virgen Mambisa" – the Lady to whom Cuba's patriots who fought for independence from Spain in the 19th century prayed. The *Virgen's* crowning, therefore, constituted a deeply moving *rencuentro* of the Cuban people with themselves – a newly found tradition.

When the last mass took place in Havana, Cubans came out massively – running to the Plaza of the Revolution, where it was held (see Figure 9.2). In the middle of the mass, repeated shouts of "Liberty!" could be heard. A sign that read *La Patria es de Todos* (Our Nation Belongs to All), the name of a document written by dissidents, was held high above. The pope's visit was a meld of religious and political purposes. As he has for many years, the pope both critiqued the U.S. embargo of Cuba as a form of violence against a poor country that hurts the poorest there the most *and* Castro's human rights violations as a denial of individual human dignity. Pope John Paul also exhorted Cubans not to leave the island but to remain in Cuba and to become protagonists of their own future. The direction he gave to that future – "Let Cuba open itself up to the world, and the world to Cuba" – is one that many Cubans, on the island and in exile, today take very seriously.

The Catholic Church does not acknowledge Santería as a faith on the same footing as Christianity or Judaism (de Céspedes 1999a). Hence, the pope refused to meet with its religious leaders. To the Catholic Church, those practices are a form of magic, of folklore, rather than a well-structured religion. But to many Cubans, Saint Barbara is Changó, and Changó is Saint Barbara; Our Lady of Charity is Ochún, and Ochún is la Virgen de la Caridad. This syncretism could be seen and heard during the pope's visit.

One should not expect the pope to have in Cuba the impact he had in Poland. Cuba was not a deeply Catholic country, as Poland was. Moreover, the pope was a Polish pope, who spent all his life accompanying his people, not a Cuban pope. But his visit left an indelible mark that holds various meanings for Cubans. One is that which John Paul II himself intended, as expressed in one of his homilies: to defend a larger space for the church and, along with it, a larger space of liberty for all Cubans. It is part of the process of the return of civil society, a process that is underway in Cuba

Figure 9.2 During the early years of the revolution, a profound conflict developed between the church and the state that led to a silencing of the church. In recent years, however, there has been a religious revival in Cuba, part of the return of civil society. Pope John Paul II's visit in January 1998 strengthened this new era. Here Cubans turned out with enthusiasm, chanting and cheering, to the last mass the pope held in Havana at the Plaza of the Revolution. The symbols of the past and the present – support for Che Guevara and for the pope's message – are found side by side in Cuba. (Silvia Pedraza)

and which the experience of other countries tells us constitutes the sine qua non of successful democratic transitions. Second, because the pope himself called "for Cuba to open itself to the world, and for the world to open itself up to Cuba," within the United States it reopened the debate and controversy regarding the U.S. embargo of Cuba and sparked efforts at humanitarian assistance with food and medicine. Third, Cubans on the island came out clearly and massively in support of the alternative values the pope articulated regarding the central importance of family, school, and church as independent social institutions that need to play leading roles in society not totally usurped by government. In so doing, they issued a call for change. And, as if that were not all, for me personally, as for so many other Cubans, his visit prompted a family reunion and reconciliation. A month after I returned, I received a letter from my cousin in Santa Clara that said, "The best thing about the Pope's visit was that he brought you to us."

Promoting Human Rights

Due in part to the crisis of "the special period," the 1990s witnessed the rapid growth of a new dissident movement, nonviolent in strategy and approach. Some of it has Christian roots. For example, the Proyecto Varela was spearheaded by Oswaldo Payá, founder of the Movimiento Cristiano Liberación (Christian Liberation Movement). The magazine *Vitral* was founded by Dagoberto Valdés. The very title was chosen to mean that a stained-glass window filters the light through a many-colored prism; its subtitle, *La Libertad de la Luz*, is indicative of its content, as it denotes the freedom of light as it passes through stained glass, refracting multiple colors. Both Payá and Valdés were young men who participated in the Encuentro Nacional Eclesiástico Cubano in 1986 and drew inspiration from it. Their efforts at building a democratic future are different – Payá's through creating the conditions for representative democracy from a political movement, Valdés's through creating independent ways of acting and thinking (see Valdés-Hernández 1997). But both share the principle that Cubans should remain in Cuba and help build the future there. Though *Vitral* is a lay magazine, it was made possible by the assistance and the printing press of the church in the Arzobispado de Pinar del Río. As Valdés put it, "without the help of the church, it would not have been possible" (personal communication, September 2001). Payá's political vision is also religious; his Movimiento Cristiano Liberación is part of the international Christian Democratic movement.

255

Creating Leaders

To build institutions, one necessarily has to build leaders. Wilfredo Beyra, a young man who knew no other world than Cuba in revolution, became a member of the UJC at a very young age. The UJC always sought out the best young people like him (in grades, looks, political commitment, popularity) for this organization, to prepare them to be the leaders of Cuba's tomorrow. The son of a father who was a veterinarian and a mother of peasant origin, as a child he grew up partly in the countryside, schooled in a rural school the teachers did not often attend. From his father's side he learned to respect democracy, because his father turned against Batista after his coup. From his mother's side, he learned respect for Christianity, because his grandmother was Baptist and taught them to read the Bible. A top student in his class, Wilfredo became a doctor, a profession for which he felt a real devotion. He was grateful to the revolution for having given him and others of his class background the opportunity to study, to make something of themselves. He sincerely believed in the social gains of the revolution – in education, in public health, as a system that existed for the benefit of the people. But he became profoundly disaffected from the communist society when, as a militant communist, he began to perceive its dishonesty, noting, for example, that promotions were due to politics rather than competence. For Wilfredo, a critical experience took place in 1991, when the secretary-general of the party in Palma Soriano, his hometown, gathered all the Young Communists at the party headquarters and said to them: "The socialist world is crumbling, the situation is extremely difficult. We have to defend this because the first heads to roll will be ours." To Wilfredo, that was a terrible blow because he realized the party leader was not saying they had to defend their system because they believed in it, because of their ideals, but because they would be in danger. Nonetheless, he joined the Communist Party a year later, becoming a dual militant.

Progressively, however, he began to realize all the sacrifices he had made – cutting sugarcane though he was a doctor, for example – were in vain: they benefited neither the poor, the old, the sick, nor those who worked the hardest; rather, they benefited those who were in power. Moreover, his efforts to reform the system from within failed, as the party was unable to absorb his criticism constructively. In 1994, the summer of the *balsero* crisis, he achieved his political self-definition. Right after the tragic incident involving the *13 de Marzo* tugboat, in which 41 adults and children died trying to leave the island, the secretary of the Young Communists in Palma

Soriano came to see him. Wilfredo said to him: "Have you heard the news? They have assassinated more than 25 persons." To which the secretary replied: "They have not assassinated them. It was necessary, so that it would serve to deter others." For Wilfredo, that was the last straw. He applied to the party to leave Cuba with his family and turned in his party card. As a result, the government kept him from finishing his career, though he had a brilliant record and was quite close to finishing. They gave him five days to move out of the clinic where he both lived and worked, and left him without work. He and his wife and small child went to live in his in-laws' garage.

Wilfredo realized he needed to leave the party. With the help of his wife's family, who had always been Christian, he went to find the priest at the church in Palma Soriano – after José Conrado read the letter to Fidel Castro from the pulpit. There he began attending classes for religious instruction and became baptized. He became one of *los muchachos* (young men and women) who often surrounded Father José Conrado in a *conversatorio* (a discussion group), while seated on rocking chairs placed in a circle of eight. I first met him in July 1996 (see Yero 1996 for a description of my visit then). Father José Conrado's effort was to form, to mold these young people to have a consciousness different from the communist consciousness: to be giving through compassion; to stand up for their rights and those of others; to know world history and to study the lives of those who had given their lives to others through their faith, like Mahatma Ghandi, Monsignor Oscar Arnulfo Romero, Mother Teresa of Calcutta; to learn Cuba's history, especially those parts that were silenced by the government; not to hate, not to use violence, but to have mercy; in short, to mold them so that in a future Cuba they would be able to exercise a moral leadership.

For Wilfredo, Father José Conrado became a spiritual father. Once inside the church, he began to know other dissidents, *opositores* (those in opposition to the communist system) who defended democracy as a system. Then he learned of the origin of democracy in Greece, read the Universal Declaration of Human Rights, understood the notion of citizenship and human rights. As a result of this relationship, he established with the priest and others, however, the state security came to speak with Wilfredo's family and threatened him. Nonetheless, he became very active in the church, and in 1997 he founded, together with others, a human rights movement: Movimiento Pro Derechos Humanos, Carlos Manuel de Céspedes. They participated in a public act in the park of Palma Soriano, placing a wreath of flowers on the bust of José Marti, Cuba's revered leader of the independence movement, while Wilfredo read a statement that emphasized Marti's democratic ideas. Immediately the state security called out the Rapid Response Brigades to beat them up. During the pope's visit to Cuba in 1998, he gave interviews to Univision, the Spanish-language television channel, that were broadcasted throughout the United States and the Spanish-speaking world. As a result, his situation became unbearable, and he decided he needed to leave Cuba. By then, he and his wife, Zaimar Campins, who stood solidly behind him, had two small children, who were going to bed hungry every night, eating whatever others gave them. On various occasions, the state security also detained and interrogated him. On the last occasion, they used his children's safety as a threat. A good friend of his still in Cuba later told me: "It was too much to bear."

Even so, Father José Conrado did not want Wilfredo to leave Cuba and could not agree to Wilfredo's departure. Nonetheless, he expressed that he loved him as a son and would wait for him there. On the day Wilfredo and Zaimar left, the streets of Palma Soriano were packed tight with people who came out to bid them farewell, in solidarity with them. The United States granted Wilfredo political asylum, and he was resettled to Arizona in 2000. In Phoenix, his family made tremendous progress in a short time, due to their hard work and family unity. While he began working as a butcher in the meatpacking industry, he soon began to work as a medical assistant. In exile, together with others, he sought to help those left behind through the Catholic Church. Two years after Wilfredo's departure, Father José Conrado traveled to Spain and throughout the United States. Reunited again briefly in Phoenix, they achieved a measure of reconciliation.

Accompanying the Journey

Once the decision to leave was made, for many Cubans the journey itself was perilous and arduous. Their religion accompanied them. Emma Tejera was the granddaughter of Spanish immigrants from Asturias and Castilla. Both her grandparents and parents worked in the cultivation and processing of tobacco and making cigars in Pinar del Río. Though of humble extraction, she attended both a Baptist school initially and, thereafter, when the family moved to Havana to work in construction, a Catholic school as a child. There she had become very close to *mis monjitas* (my dear nuns), as she put it, and never separated herself from the church, even in the lean years.

When she married, her husband was a Sears employee, so the wave of nationalizations at the beginning of the revolution impacted them greatly. Her daughter, Luisa, left on a *balsa* with 13 other Cubans, and it was 13 days before she had any news of her. Every day she went to the church to see the names of those who had arrived in Guantanamo posted there. When she finally heard Luisa's name mentioned on Radio Martí, her joy and relief were such that she could not sleep and only wanted daybreak to arrive so that she could go to *el Rincón* – the shrine of San Lazaro in Rincón, a leper colony on the outskirts of Havana. On his feast day, December 17, when quite a large and festive gathering now takes place in Cuba, she had gone to make a *promesa* for her daughter and "for everything, for Cuba." It took two years before she was reunited with her daughter, however. She and her husband left Cuba for Venezuela, hoping to join their daughter in the United States, but while in Venezuela her husband died. Eventually she did come to the United States – crossing the Rio Grande near Matamoros, Mexico, with the help of a *coyote* whom her daughter had paid for. As she crossed the river, the water reached all the way to her waist. Above that she kept her purse. In it, she had two Virgins with her, la Virgen de la Caridad and la Virgen de Regla, that a friend had given to her husband on the very day they learned Luisa was alive and safe. They accompanied her in the crossing – full of mud but enormously relieved – during her perilous journey.

The Church among the Immigrants

Maintaining Culture

Religion has always played many roles in the lives of immigrants, as they both longed for the homes they left and adapted to radically new and baffling circumstances. Moreover, the newly arrived undergo a process of assimilation, both cultural and structural (see Pedraza 2006), that often threatens their culture. Hence, the church plays an important role among immigrants as it helps them maintain that culture. Thomas Tweed's (1997) *Our Lady of the Exile: Diasporic Religion at a Cuban Catholic Shrine in Miami* documents this well, focusing on the meaning the devotion to Cuba's patron saint holds in the lives of Cubans in exile. Tweed argues that Cuban exiles come to the shrine to express their diasporic nationalism, to make sense of themselves as a displaced people. Through rituals and artifacts at the shrine that transcend time and place, "the diaspora imaginatively constructs its collective identity and transports itself to the Cuba of memory and desire" (1997:10).

In their popular religious tradition, many Cuban women hold a particular devotion to this Virgin, as Robert Orsi (1985) explained was also true for Italian immigrant women at the turn of the previous century. In Italian Harlem, women were its main participants because "it emerged out of and reflected the special role and position of women in Italian culture" (1985:204–5). These women turned to the Madonna with petitions for help with the hardship and powerlessness of their lives – as women bound by a strong, patriarchal tradition, and as immigrants mired in poverty, toil, and trouble. That private relation became public at the annual *festa*, when both men and women celebrated as a community, regenerating their culture and consoling them for the physical and spiritual trials of immigration. Every September 8, the annual *fiesta* of Cuba's patron saint has been held in Miami since 1961, when a replica of the Virgin was brought to Miami from Cuba by the exiles (Jované de Zayas 1968). A few years later, the national shrine of *la Ermita* was built symbolically facing Cuba. It is shaped like the cape the Virgin wears, under which there is room, it is said, for all Cubans. In the shrine, the mural painted by Teok Carrasco tells the history of Cuba as a colony, its struggle for independence, the achievement of the republic, and the expulsion of the religious leaders from revolutionary Cuba. All of these surround the Virgin and Child – yet another expression of the meld between religion and nationalism that is characteristically Cuban.

Expressing Patriotism, Healing Pain

Religion also serves to express the émigrés' patriotism and to heal the pain of exile. As Marill (2000:44), who lives and works in South Florida, pointed out, a refugee community is made up of people who carry scars: "South Florida is a place where one is greeted by an exilic population of people who have had to give up their homeland, their possessions, and, most importantly, their world of affections. This is also a place where there is great evidence of a people's effort to protect their identities and memories: Little Haiti, Little Managua, and of course, Little Havana." Memories of victimization, torture, oppression, as well as heroic acts in defense of family and justice, are all part of the exile narratives.

Precisely because it is situated in the context of such a wounded community, to many in Miami *la Ermita* is both a spiritual and patriotic center. For example, shortly after the tragedy of the tugboat incident in the summer of 1994, at *la Ermita* a deeply moving service was held in which many of those who attended were given a white rose wrapped in a tricolor bow with the colors of Cuba's flag. To pray for the dead, each rose bore the name of one of the people who died. Likewise, when the Cuban air force downed three of the planes flown by Hermanos al Rescate, killing four young men, on February 24, 1996, another service was held at *la Ermita*. Their relatives folded the Cuban flag in the manner it is folded for soldiers who die for their country. At the huge service that took place in Miami's Orange Bowl commemorating this tragedy, Monsignor Agustín Román seemingly gathered all the pain of the thousands who mourned there onto himself, as he spoke and prayed while four riderless horses galloped across the field.

Those expressions of patriotism have not always been so positive, however. Prior to the pope's visit to Cuba in late January 1998, the leaders of the Cuban community in Miami pressured the Catholic Church there not to allow its priests to travel to Cuba to participate in the event. The Miami Catholic Church had planned to travel to Cuba on a cruise that was to anchor in Havana for only one night, so that hundreds of Miami Cubans could attend just the last mass held by the pope in Havana. Leaders of the Miami community insisted that such a trip ignored the thousands of people who died in those 90 miles of sea along the way. The pressure exerted by a large part of the Miami exile community won the day, and the trip was canceled. As a result, Monsignor Román watched the pope's visit to Cuba on television, in *la Ermita*, surrounded by his parishioners.

By contrast, Monsignor Boza-Masvidal, who lived and worked in Venezuela, did return to Cuba. Like Monsignor Román, he was expelled from Cuba in the early years of the revolution, but his Venezuelan community did not demand his absence from Cuba. As a result, he was present, and I was able to see him there. When he visited his church in Havana, 38 years after his expulsion, the oldest parishioners there knew him and received him with tears of joy. For him, the return was visibly a moment of great joy. Boza-Masvidal died in Los Teques, Venezuela, in July 2003. He had lived and worked as vicar and rector of the Cathedral there for 42 years, a community to which he was just as dedicated as he had been to the one in Cuba. The outpouring of sentiment, from both Cubans and Venezuelans, was enormous. As they lowered his casket, wrapped in both the Cuban and the Venezuelan flags, they threw earth from both Cuba and Venezuela onto it (Aranguren 2003). While the church in Cuba was silenced for about a quarter of a century, over the years in exile Boza-Masvidal's message, with which I concur, never wavered: neither Marxism nor neoliberalism (Boza-Masvidal 1997).

In sum, an intricate relationship exists between religion and exodus in this contemporary period, helping many Cubans to remain steadfast on the island, while also helping others to leave, becoming immigrants and exiles in another land. Nowhere is this more apparent than in Cubans' devotion to their major national symbol – la Virgen de la Caridad del Cobre – as Cubans on both sides of the ocean pray to her for help and protection from the hardships of their lives in Cuba and in exile. On both sides of the ocean she represents a welding of religion and national identity.

This welding of religion and national identity symbolized by a national Virgin is particularly strong in some Latin American countries, such as Cuba and Mexico, where those traditions are deeply held. They follow their emigrants to other lands, where they root in new immigrant circumstances that bring new forms of hardship with them – the pain of exile for Cubans, the exploitation of farm work for Mexicans. Both on the island and in exile, Cubans' devotion to their patron saint as a national symbol remains the same. It is only the nature of the hardship that has changed.

While the leadership of the Cuban church insists that the role and the mission of the church is and must remain strictly spiritual, for many Cubans today the church is not just a church, a religious vision, but also an alternative to the communist vision – another way to think, feel, act, live. Hence, religion and politics are linked in Cuba, as they were in Poland during the years of Solidarity's anticommunist struggle. That does not mean that one should expect the Cuban Catholic Church to be the fountainhead of a large, popular, anticommunist social movement. Indeed, as Crahan (2003) argued, what happened in Poland is unlikely to happen in Cuba. Yet, in truth, what happened in Poland in its exit from communism also did not happen elsewhere in Eastern Europe – neither in Czechoslovakia, Rumania, Yugoslavia, nor the Soviet Union. To date, the experience of Poland is that of an outlier – unique. Analyzing *exit-voice* dynamics in the collapse of East Germany, Steven Pfaff notes that the role of the Lutheran Church was crucial in the birth of *voice* there, giving an honest refuge to those who needed to retreat from the larger society. Yet, it "did not embody the national, cultural, or spiritual ambitions of the people, as did the Roman Catholic Church in Poland" (2006:105), nor did it serve to link activists, intellectuals, and the broader public. However, "it did provide a niche in

262

which political subcultures could survive" (2006:105). In my view, this last is the role that the church – all denominations – in Cuba has recently played. For a large part of the population, the church is a source of help, as well as an alternative in the quest for meaning that, at all times everywhere, men and women inevitably grope for. For those Cubans who strive to create a democratic future, the church has been a vital source of support.

10

Democratization and Migration

Adíos, isla florida, donde fui tan feliz, tierra fragrante que casi no eres tierra.... Que los dioses te guarden y te dejen recordar algún día a la viajera.

Farewell, island in bloom, where I found such happiness, island so fragrant that you are almost not land.... May the gods guard you and allow you to someday remember this voyageur.

Dulce María Loynaz, *Un Verano en Tenerife* (1958)

Exit-Voice Relationships

In the "special period," we witnessed the emergence of civil society in Cuba. At the same time, the 1990s and the present have been a period of massive emigration out of Cuba, both legal and illegal: the migration of *balseros*, *lancheros*, third-country arrivals, asylum recipients, visa recipients, and visa lottery winners. The question is whether this new, massive exodus is a hindrance or a help to the development of civil society in Cuba.

The question can also be framed with the analogy that Albert O. Hirschman (1970) first introduced in his *Exit, Voice, and Loyalty: Responses to Decline in Firms, Organizations, and States*. Firms, organizations, and states provide benefits or services. As Hirschman argued, when the quality of the benefits or services they provide deteriorates, the *loyalty* of its members is threatened. The members can then express themselves by using one of two options: they can choose to *exit* – simply leave – or they can use their *voice* – organize, protest, and call for change. The pattern could be characterized, according to Hirschman (1986), as a simple hydraulic model: deterioration generates the pressure of discontent, which will be channeled into *voice* or *exit*. The more pressure escapes through *exit*, the less is available to foment *voice*. Moreover, as Hirschman noted, those who exited cannot promote recuperation. Hence, the question becomes whether the new Cuban exodus, massive and seemingly unabated, constitutes the use of the *exit* option to such an extent that it will serve to impede the use of *voice*, which is necessary to develop civil society. To illustrate the exit-voice relationships, I rely on interviews with Armando Añel, José Conrado Rodríguez, Moisés Asís, and Amelia Sosa (pseudonym).

Because civil society is a somewhat ambiguous concept, I follow Víctor Pérez-Díaz's (1993) definition in his analysis of the return of civil society to Spain. It entails the existence of associations (whose ends may be political, economic, or purely social) that were created by the voluntary participation of its members. Such associations – for example, the press, media, labor unions, churches, and professional societies – occupy an intermediate position between the individual and the state. As Pérez-Díaz (1993:57) summed it, civil society "denotes a *type* of society that combines, to one degree or another, markets, voluntary associations, and a public sphere which are outside the direct control, in a full or mitigated sense, of the state." This civil society is what Vaclav Havel (1986) called the "independent life of society." In Cuba, those intermediate associations effectively ceased to exist as they were either abolished or silenced by the government in the beginning years of the revolutionary process. Due to the enormous popularity of the revolution initially, as well as his charisma, Fidel Castro succeeded in making the state the sole arbiter, the sole owner, the sole administrator, the sole judge, and the sole political party, excluding all others from participation. Thereafter, that same government went on to organize some of the intermediate associations – such as the professional societies, the press, the labor unions – but these lack independence from government; hence, they do not qualify as part of what is here defined as civil society.

The economic and political crises of the "special period," however, spurred the return of civil society in Cuba. Along with the religious revival, today we witness in Cuba an increase in independent professionals and associations. *Independientes* is the term used in Cuba to mean free of government control and organization. Independent journalists, economists, lawyers, trade unionists, publications, and grass-roots organizations aim to solve social problems at the local level of family and town. Cubans who founded these organizations are involved in the deliberate effort to reconstruct civil society. This entails what Dagoberto Valdés-Hernández (1997:104) called moving along two paths: renewing the hearts and the minds of the people – *una renovación de los espíritus* – and reforming the social structure of the society. To Valdés, this social project of reconstructing civil society issues from, or is accompanied by, a Christian humanism. Others who lack religious beliefs participate due to their ethical and philosophical convictions. To all in Cuba today who consciously participate in reconstructing civil society, civil society is the sine qua non of a democratic transition and is also the warranty of a democratic future in which Cubans of all political convictions can participate (Valdés-Hernández 1997:130).

The new Cuban exodus has been both unregulated and regulated. The unregulated exodus consisted of the *balseros*. As a consequence of this crisis, the United States and Cuba signed a new Migration Agreement, which allows for the regulated and orderly departure of Cubans from the island, at the rate of 20,000 Cubans a year. An unknown but also rather sizable exodus left for other countries – particularly Spain, Venezuela, Canada, and Costa Rica. While the regulation of the exodus certainly contributed to a decline in the number of *balseros* who risked their lives in the crossing, some continue to leave Cuba and try to enter the United States illegally, occasionally as *balseros*, often as *lancheros*, and through third countries. The new Cuban exodus is rather massive: roughly 25,000 Cubans leave Cuba now every year, or 100,000 persons every four years. And it shows no signs of abating. Sergio Díaz-Briquets (2006) used the 2000 global census recently compiled by the University of Sussex's Development Research Center on Migration plus the recent official Cuban statistics on emigration to arrive at an estimate of the number of persons born in Cuba residing abroad around the year 2000. Of course, the largest concentration is in the United States, with 885,970 Cuban immigrants, followed by Spain (50,765), Italy and Germany (each with close to 8,000), Mexico (6,647), Canada (5,410), Chile (3,290), the Dominican Republic (2,255), the Netherlands Antilles (2,046), and other countries with more than 1,000 (France, Sweden, Panama, Switzerland, and the United Kingdom).

Comparing this new Cuban exodus to the former waves of the Cuban exodus will show its proportions. Table 1.1, based on the 1990 and 2000 censuses of the United States, shows that until now the largest wave of immigrants after the revolution was the second wave – the quarter of a million Cuban immigrants who left the island during the nine years from 1965 to 1974. They constituted 41 percent of those who immigrated from 1960 to 1990 and 30 percent of those who immigrated from 1959 to 2000. The second wave and the contemporary exodus resemble each other in several ways. Both migrations are an exodus of massive proportions. Both migrations were regulated and administered by both the Cuban and the United States governments. Both times, a migration crisis spurred them to collaborate: the flotilla exodus from Camarioca in 1965 and the *balsero* crisis of 1994. Both times, family reunification was the criteria used to allow those in Cuba to leave when their relatives in the United States claimed them. However, the family reunification criterion used now is extremely stringent, compared with the more inclusive definition of family used in the past. At present, parents residing in the United States may claim their children who remained in Cuba – but only if, when older than 21, they are still unmarried. As a result, in recent years a visa lottery was introduced to allow those who do not have close family in the United States to apply to leave Cuba. The difference between the two migrations is that they take place at a very different moment in the history of the Cuban revolution. The second wave took place at a time of revolutionary consolidation. The fourth wave is taking place at a time when Cubans are beginning to build a civil society independent of government.

Four Theses

To assess whether the *exit* option impedes or facilitates the use of the *voice* option, I assess four different theses in the literature in the light of the research presented in this book: a massive exodus impedes the use of voice; those who exited helped voice to develop; those who exited became the voice; and both exit and voice increased in tandem.

A Massive Exit Impeded the Use of Voice

The first thesis is that which Dagoberto Valdés-Hernández (1997) stated in his *Reconstruir la Sociedad Civil: Un Proyecto de Educación Cívica, Pluralismo, y Participación para Cuba*. Valdés clearly sees the Cuban exodus as a hindrance to the development of civil society in Cuba: "One of the causes of the impoverishment and the near disappearance of a civil society in Cuba has been the massive and permanent exodus of Cubans." To him, the exodus is the result of the lack of political liberty, which does not allow Cubans to participate freely and responsibly in the polity, and the lack of economic initiatives Cubans can undertake, which result in dismay and civic irresponsibility (Valdés-Hernández 1997:118–19). Phrased in Hirschman's terms, the use of the *exit* option becomes an obstacle to the development of *voice* in the country – the thesis he first postulated (1970).

Valdes' thesis is in line with what I wrote in the past regarding the functions of political and economic migration to both the societies involved (see Pedraza-Bailey 1985). Analysts of labor migrations argued that the exodus of migrants performed a "safety valve" function for the societies they left (e.g., Spain, Mexico, Turkey) as it externalizes the material discontent their society could not alleviate. In the same vein, I argued, a political exodus also externalizes the political discontent, the dissent, to which their society could not respond. Thus, the Cuban exodus always contributed to strengthening the Cuban revolution in the political sense. At the same time, however, it proved erosive to the development of the society because the exodus also represented an enormous "brain drain" of the professional and middle classes whose resources and talents the society needed.

This thesis is quite common in Cuba among people who, like Valdes, are struggling to help build the new civil society in Cuba, whether through the development of intellectual alternatives, such as his own effort with the magazine *Vitral*, or through the strengthening of an institution, such as a church or synagogue, as a viable alternative to think, feel, live. A vivid example came to me a few years ago in Cuba when I visited a friend, Father Mario Delgado, a priest in San Antonio de los Baños, a community that I had visited on occasion in the past. As we drove through the small town where everyone knew everyone else, he pointed to each house where a family left, and said "They left," then "They also left," and "Do you remember them? They are no longer here." I felt his sense of desolation when he said, "*el país se está desangrando*" (the country is bleeding to death). To those on the ground who are struggling with the renewal of the minds and hearts of the Cuban people, the exodus feels like a vital loss of people who could help develop the new civil society.

Yet I think one has to distinguish between those who left "in the first instance" and those who left "in the last instance." Those who left Cuba recently "in the first instance" were those who could not translate their evident dissatisfaction into an active search for a new political alternative, or at least another way of living and thinking. Without doubt, these are people who were disaffected from the political and economic conditions in Cuba and whose minds and hearts grew tired of the government's promises that no longer held out any hope for them. But they held their dissent close to their chest and shared it with very few intimate friends (sometimes not even with their closest family members). They either publicly assented to the conditions there – what Cubans call *la doble moral* – or they sought to live as uninvolved in the political process there as possible.

Some analysts have pointed out that Hirschman forgot the fourth option – *neglect*. Most of these Cubans exercised either the option of a false *loyalty* or the option of a lived *neglect*. Either way, they were unlikely to become involved in the development of civil society, even if they remained in Cuba. Using Wright's (1976) terminology, they were *assenters* – spectators to someone else's game. By contrast, those who left Cuba recently "in the last instance," were *dissenters*, who left Cuba only after exercising the *voice* option; for example, involving themselves in the dissident movement, or founding a new human rights organization, or participating in the development of a new alternative through their church or synagogue, or becoming an independent journalist. Doing so, they suffered its costs: lost their jobs and many of their friends and saw doors closed behind them until they ended up in prison or living in intolerable conditions that pushed them to leave. They left after giving to the development of civil society in Cuba all they could. Their efforts to bring a democratic polity to Cuba and a sense of human rights as just that – rights – were perceived by the government and its allies as illegitimate forms of opposition, as criminal acts. Pushing them into a corner certainly served as an example to many Cubans of the futility of going against the powerful government. Yet they also became heroes to many who remained behind. Armando Añel, for example, was a young, well-educated mulatto, who joined the independent journalists and worked in that capacity for two years before leaving for Spain. He explained:

When you become an independent journalist, you die socially. People in your same block look at you differently. You lose friends; you develop problems with your father in-law; you have to worry about with whom you talk; young people who hate the government viscerally come and tell you 'You're young! Why are you going to do that? They'll put you in prison!' It's the result of the control they have over the society, the fear people have inside of them, the political apathy of the young. But at the same time, it is contradictory. You feel actualized in your self, morally, as a human being. Because once you get into it, people admire you, they care for you.

Those Who Exited Helped Voice Develop

In his analysis of the transition to democracy in Spain after Franco, Víctor Pérez-Díaz (1993) espoused the opposite thesis. From the early 1960s to the mid-1970s, Spain was changing from a predominantly rural, agrarian nation to a predominantly urban, industrial nation. As a peripheral country in Europe, Spain lent its labor – via a massive labor exodus – to the core European countries of Germany, France, England, Switzerland, and

Belgium. The émigrés labored in the industrial sector (working in factories) or the service sector (working in hotels and restaurants) in these developed countries. In Pérez-Díaz's assessment, this Spanish exodus was part of the massive shift of capital, commodities, and people that began to flow across the Spanish borders for at least 15 years, bringing with them all sorts of institutions and cultural transformations: "Millions of tourists invaded the coasts of Mediterranean Spain, while millions of Spaniards emigrated northward, often to spend years living and working in Germany, France, Holland, or Switzerland; thousands of students and young professionals went abroad to study; entrepreneurs imported machines; foreign investors poured capital into the Spanish economy; and consumers became accustomed to buying foreign-made goods." As the migration increased, he continued, "It could be summarized as a massive, all-pervasive learning experience." Spaniards were exposed to institutions and cultures, ways of accomplishing things in all spheres of life that were more efficient than their own. They also rapidly learned to appreciate a more comfortable standard of living, increased freedom of movement, more opportunities to prosper, less subjection to authority, and "more varied ways of relating freely among themselves" (1993:12–13). As a result, Spaniards learned from, imitated, and identified with the people of Western Europe, their institutions, and their culture.

In this analysis, the exodus was a midwife to the development of civil society because the émigrés lived and worked for many years in societies that were politically democratic and pluralistic, where groups of people were organized in institutions they created to defend themselves. Living there, the émigrés underwent an *aprendizaje democrático*, a democratic apprenticeship.

For this to influence their homeland, however, the émigrés had to return. Spaniards, indeed, returned to Spain and, with this know-how, contributed to the development of the peaceful transition out of Franco's Spain, as well as to being governed in a pluralistic fashion in the years that followed, when democracy was institutionalized and consolidated. To Pérez-Díaz, these processes went hand in hand with "the invention of a new tradition and a new identity: that of a democratic Spain in contrast to a Francoist Spain, connected in a problematic way with pre-Francoist history, from which it is cut off by the trauma of the civil war" (1993:20). Phrased in Hirschman's terms, those who first used the *exit* option underwent a democratic apprenticeship where they lived and worked; when they returned, they brought back what they had learned about the *voice* option, influencing the development of a new political culture and civil society there, at a time when Spain was growing economically and becoming part of the European Union.

Eastern Europeans also migrated to Western Europe in large numbers to work. Ewa Morawska (2001), a Polish sociologist, studied the recent exodus of Eastern European immigrants who went to work in Western European societies. She concluded that for the vast majority of those émigrés that democratic apprenticeship did not take place because their stay in those countries was very brief and their participation in the economy and the polity as "guest workers" was very delimited. Morawska did find a more substantial change among the educated Eastern European immigrants who traveled overseas for professional work because, though their stays were brief, the very nature of their professions allowed them greater access to the new society, from which they learned a great deal. Because these Eastern European migrations – both the labor migrants and the professionals – were brief, the social class of the émigrés had a decisive impact on whether or not they could realize such a democratic apprenticeship.

From the work of both Pérez-Díaz and Morawska, we can learn the conditions of the exodus on which such a democratic learning depends: the social class of the émigrés; the length of their stay abroad; the access to the polity they had in the countries where they lived and worked; and – crucially – whether they returned, bringing their newfound political culture back with them.

In the Cuban case there has been such a democratic learning, but the passage of time – now close to 50 years – as well as the economic success of a large part of the Cuban exile community actually go against the grain of facilitating the development of civil society in Cuba. My interviews lead me to conclude that few Cubans would return to live and work in Cuba. When I asked my respondents whether they would return to Cuba if there were to be a new democratic opening, the early exiles' and the recent exiles' answers contrasted sharply. Those who left in the early years of the exodus and were adolescents or older in the 1950s cherish the warmest memories of the life they led in Cuba, especially in Havana, a city whose beauty, sounds, aromas rendered it "the Paris of Latin America." Nowhere is this captured better than in the interviews in the documentary *Havana: Portrait of Yesteryear* (Cardona and de Varona 1998), where many prominent Cuban Americans remembered their lives then, such as Fausto Miranda, Guillermo Alvarez-Guedes, Guillermo Cabrera-Infante, Teresa and Bobby Betancourt. Their memories were of a colorful, beautiful city full of fun and passion. At night, this meant the dancing rhythms of the nightclubs, the extraordinary nightlife that artists from all over the world became a part of, the new drinks at the bars (such as the Daiquiri from Hemingway's favorite bar, El Floridita). At daybreak, there was the smell of *café con leche* and fresh-baked bread everywhere. During the day, even the street vendors sold their wares – peanuts, mangos, pineapples – in song, with *pregones*, in high and low notes. Havana then had a beauty, a vitality, and eroticism few cities in the world could match. The nostalgia for the life the early exiles left behind can also be seen in Miami today in restaurants, such as La Habana Vieja, where various oil-relief paintings by Haydée Scull hang on its walls, depicting these memories, the color, and sensuality of Old Havana. They are the memories of *la Cuba de ayer*, the memories of people who led a very comfortable life in a society known for its splendor. The early exiles never tire of telling and retelling their stories of those days. Surely, if they could, they would return to Cuba. But they will not be able to. Too much time has passed – nearly half a century. Those who left as adults will most likely die in exile.

Moreover, despite those glowing memories, with the passage of time these exiles already put deep roots in other lands, where another culture, often another language, as in the United States, exert strong pressures to assimilate. At least one, if not two generations of their children were born in other countries. The new transnational diasporic citizenship that Michel Laguerre (1999) argued is the new form of immigrant orientation may well be true of the first generation of immigrants, but can seldom be true for their children (Pedraza 2006). For the most part, the second generation does not have an interest in returning to Cuba. They feel culturally inept in how they handle their parents' and grandparents' culture and find it difficult to understand and fit in that world. Even more, Cuban society became an odd amalgam of Third World poverty with Eastern European communism, complex in ways that many find too difficult to understand. Hence, while the Cuban government tells its people regularly that the Miami exiles will return to take their houses away (their former homes, that is), it is unlikely that this will happen on a large scale. I expect few of the early exiles will return, as they are now part of another world where they have put down new roots. Quite simply, their children and grandchildren grew up on other soil, in another culture. A partial exception may be Cubans who can be said to be "the 1.5 generation" (Rumbaut 1991) – my generation. Those who grew up in Cuba long enough that they acquired a deep attachment to its values, culture, and history, yet also came to the United States at a young age and were resocialized here. Their hybridity, their in-betweenness and attachments to both worlds, may allow them to serve as a bridge between them in a period of democratic transition. Gustavo Pérez-Firmat reflected on the quality of in-betweenness of this generation (also his). He does not plan to return to Cuba because it "would be tantamount to going into exile a second time" (1994:19). But he recognizes that, while those whose life is on the hyphen (Cuban-American, that is) are marginal to both their native and adopted cultures, they are also marginal to *neither* culture.

By contrast, the recent immigrants are more likely to return because much less time has passed, and fewer "roots" were put down elsewhere. However, their own memories may impede it. Contrary to the early exiles' nostalgia, the recent exiles' memories are often full of trauma. The trauma results from the lack of material comfort they endured in Cuba, the hunger and the poverty they experienced. It also comes from the marginality they experienced when their *loyalty* was questioned, the isolation they felt when their lives denied their real feelings and convictions (see Figure 10.1). Moisés Asís, who founded a school for Jewish children in Cuba so as to help them find their lost identity as Jews, expressed no interest in returning to Cuba: "I left so disappointed, culturally. For me, Cuba is a nightmare in my life." He went on: "I have never felt nostalgia for Cuba. Never. Twice I dreamed about Cuba, and they were two nightmares. I dreamed that I returned. I woke up startled in the middle of the night." Likewise, Amelia Sosa, who arrived in Florida on a *balsa*, quipped: "Return where?" She would like to return to Cuba to visit her mother, the family left behind, but she emphasized she could never return to a place where she had suffered such humiliation. For many of the recent exiles, their way of coping with a past that lacked dignity was to close the door on it forever. Many of them, though quite young, will not return to Cuba but will go on to make new lives, wherever they settle.

Moreover, Spaniards returned to Spain because, however stifling Francoism was to working-class organizations, it did deliver economic growth and modernization as Spain underwent a transition from being a rural, agrarian society to an urban, industrial society. By contrast, Cuba has never undergone such economic modernization, with or without the Soviet subsidy. Still, if a successful transition to a democratic society were to take place in Cuba, accompanied by international assistance (such as the Marshall Plan after the end of World War II), and economic growth could be achieved in their productive lifetimes, the more recent émigrés and some of

Figure 10.1 With these images superimposed on one another – an Orthodox Jew in Miami Beach behind the recognition that "This Isn't Havana" – Arturo Cuenca captured the sense of difference and isolation typical of the Jewish as well as the Cuban experience. To Cuenca, both the Jew and the Cuban are uprooted, not understood, alone. Finally, it also depicts himself. Cuenca left Cuba for Miami Beach and New York in 1994 (Arturo Cuenca).

the early exiles' children may return. With the democratic learning that living and working overseas – in the United States, Spain, Canada, Venezuela, or Costa Rica – entailed, they may influence the institutionalization and consolidation of democracy. Only then will a process similar to that which Spain underwent will occur.

Those Who Exited Became Its Voice

Michel Laguerre (1998), a Haitian social scientist who analyzed the role the Haitian immigration played in the United States, articulated a different thesis: that the Haitian immigrants themselves became the civil society that Haiti lacked. Through their exercise of what Laguerre called "a transnational diasporic citizenship," Haitian émigrés became the missing political center – between the government, on the one hand, and the atomized, inarticulate masses, on the other. As a result of their transnationalism, the diaspora, as individuals and as groups, crossed national boundaries to engage in productive informal interactions and dialogue, infusing "the country widely and deeply with its democratic views" (1998:170). With Haiti's long history of political repression, the diaspora may well be playing the role of the missing political center – between the army and the government, siding with the people, thus helping the development of civil society and democracy in Haiti. Incidentally, that is precisely the role that the Cuban diaspora has never been able to play with respect to Cuba, at least in part because both the American and Cuban governments have drastically curtailed its involvement with life in Cuba, its transnationalism, even more its diasporic citizenship. As David Hollinger noted, the new immigration, like the old, "displays a variety of degrees of engagement with the United States and with prior homelands, and it yields some strong assimilationist impulses along with vivid expressions of diasporic consciousness" (1995:153).

Transnationalism, however, had negative consequences for those in the Haitian American community because it diverted their energies toward their homeland, at the expense of their role and place in the receiving country. Nonetheless, Laguerre saw the role of the Haitian émigrés toward their homeland as a substantial help in the form of an informal diplomacy that civilians who traveled to Haiti engaged in. They spoke not on behalf of their government but on behalf of themselves or their organizations – *ambassadeurs du béton ou sans cravate*. They helped to establish civilian control over the military and funded cherished social projects back in Haiti, both of which strengthened the development of civil society there. Such informal diplomacy was not only an outcome of transnationalism but also was totally outside the control of both the United States and the Haitian governments, "effectively transforming the immigrant subject into a transnational citizen" (1998:xx). Phrased in Hirschman's terms, when the civil society in the homeland has effectively disappeared and the people there remain too atomized and marginalized to constitute it, those who first exercised the *exit* option may end up becoming the ones who constitute its *voice*.

Carrying out this "transnational diasporic citizenship" is a goal of many Cuban exile political organizations, even when situated at different ends of the political spectrum, as are the original Cuban American National Foundation and the Cuban American Alliance Educational Foundation. Certainly Cuban exiles, particularly in Miami, have sought to become this civil society – for example, through developing organizations and political parties that have ties to their homologous organizations in the dissident movement in Cuba. However, they can be effective only if they are in touch with those in Cuba, which both the Cuban and U.S. governments try to prevent. Nonetheless, Cuban Americans do have a sizable political representation in Congress – an effective lobby out of all proportion to their size, such as only a couple of other immigrant groups were able to achieve (notably, Jewish Americans and Irish Americans).

In assessing the role other exile groups played in other transitions to democracy – in Spain, Poland, the Czech Republic, Brazil – the historical record may well show that the exiles' role was rather delimited. It remains to be researched. Nonetheless, the Cuban case is different in that a much greater part of the Cuban population has emigrated – 12 to 15 percent of the population – and the time span is overwhelmingly long (now close to 50 years). Moreover, its concentration in southern Florida, so near the island, renders it potentially a more decisive political actor than other exile communities. But, in my view, the exile community could play a leading role in a transition only if its ties with the people on the island were strong, which, generally, they are not.

The recent incident involving the custody of the little boy Elián González makes the point. The *balserito* was rescued at sea, alone, on Thanksgiving Day in 1999. His mother, who made the passage with him, drowned at sea. The struggle for his custody that developed between his uncle's family in Miami, who looked after him for months, and his father, still in Cuba, made evident the gulf between the two communities. Cubans on the island did not side with the Miami community. Even those who were not supporters of the government felt he was a Cuban child who belonged with his father back home. Given the gulf in understanding that separates the two Cuban communities – nation and diaspora – the exile community can hardly become the missing civil society.

Both Exit and Voice Increased in Tandem

Yet another thesis comes from Hirschman's (1993) later work, when he applied his initial conceptual scheme to the case of the German Democratic Republic (GDR) in 1989, the year in which a series of social movements developed in rapid succession in Poland, Hungary, East Germany, Czechoslovakia, Bulgaria, and Rumania that resulted in the collapse of the communist world in Eastern Europe and the demise of the GDR. In his earlier work (1970; 1986) Hirschman had argued that a basic seesaw pattern existed between *exit* and *voice* – the more of one, the less of the other. But 23 years later, when he examined the GDR up close during *die Wende* (the turn, as it was called), he was forced to conclude that in the last year both *exit* and *voice* had "worked in tandem" and reinforced each other, "achieving jointly the collapse of the regime" (1993:177). This insight came from the work of the East German sociologist Detlef Pollack, who witnessed the events during 1989 at very close range.

Hirschman reformulated his initial thesis because he saw that the course of events over the 40-year-long life of that state (1949–89) "comprised a large variety of *exit-voice* relationships" (1993:177). While over the course of time, the easy availability of *exit* did undermine the development of *voice*, other relationships also obtained. For example, in 1961, with the building of the Berlin Wall, the authorities sought to repress both *exit* and *voice*. And in 1989, the last year, both *exit* and *voice* worked in tandem, reinforcing each other. In my view, in Cuba in recent years, both have also worked in tandem. And we can expect both to increase.

The cases of Cuba and the GDR hold many parallels, not the least of which was the constant availability of the *exit* option to another very near place where a measurably easier life, political liberty, and the availability of family exerted a strong "pull." In Cuba, this was especially true during the second wave of the exodus, when the violence of the counterrevolution came to an end and they had to lay down arms, defeated in a conflict for which thousands died and thousands more were imprisoned. Throughout those years, the use of the *exit* option did impede the use of the *voice* option because due to the consolidation of the revolution, Cubans no longer believed the use of the *voice* option could be an effective challenge to the government.

Moreover, the government itself (as in the GDR) was quite conscious of the basic seesaw pattern of *exit* and *voice* and chose to consciously manipulate the *exit* option to undermine the *voice* of dissent. Two examples make the point. First, the *Marielitos* were the children of communism, the people in whose name the revolution was made. Fidel Castro responded by repeatedly calling them *escoria* (scum) and *Lumpen* (from *Lumpenproletariat*), and emphasized that letting them go would be beneficial. *Granma*, the official newspaper of the Communist Party, explained the government's position in an editorial, just a few days after Cubans congregated in the Peruvian Embassy: "Let them go, the loafers, the antisocial, the lumpen, the criminals, and the scum!" (*Granma* 1980a). Cuba gladly opened the doors for them, as it had done before with all who opposed socialism and the revolution. A couple of weeks later, *Granma*'s editorial (1980b) explained the benefit of externalizing dissent: "The United States always wanted to take our best brains. Let them now take our *lumpen*!" In the same vein, in his May 1 speech before the enormous crowd that had gathered in the Plaza of

277

the Revolution, Fidel Castro contrasted the exodus at the beginning of the revolution with that leaving through Mariel harbor: "They used to take the refined bourgeois [mockingly called *refinadito*], the well-dressed landholder [also mockingly called *vestidito*], the doctor, the professional.... Now it is no longer the engineer, the architect, the professional, no." It is *el lumpen* (Castro 1980).

Second, the exodus of the dissidents in the 1990s was the result of the government's selective policy of forced *exit* that literally "pushed" certain critical *voices* out of Cuba and barred others from returning home. The result of this forced *exit* policy was palpable. In 1992 Amnesty International issued a special Country Report on Cuba titled "Silencing the Voices of Dissent," where many of Cuba's most prominent dissidents were featured. Just a few years later, virtually all those featured were living outside of Cuba, in exile. Oftentimes, the *voice* of the dissidents has been barely audible.

But the easy availability of *exit* was not the only reason why *voice* was less likely to emerge in East Germany than elsewhere in the Soviet-dominated Eastern European countries. Hirschman noted other major reasons, which have parallels in Cuba. First, East Germans had no independent institutions, like the Catholic Church of Poland, to sustain them in a struggle for some autonomy from the all-powerful communist state. That was also true in Cuba. Second, many East Germans initially embraced the ideology of the state "for reasons intimately connected with the catastrophic historical episode they had just lived through" – Nazism. That "ideological advantage," as Hirschman (1993:182–83) called it, was also the role that Batista's dictatorship played in the initial acceptance and popularity of the Cuban revolution. Third, East Germany played a different role for the Soviet empire in its contest with the West during the Cold War, as evidenced by the presence of Soviet atomic missiles there. That was equally true in Cuba, which played a similar role for the Soviet Union throughout the Third World. In exchange for this role of exporting revolution to Latin America and Africa and contesting the United States, the Soviet Union subsidized the Cuban economy very generously, mitigating the role of the U.S. embargo. In sum, until the 1990s one could arrive at the same conclusion regarding Cuba as Hirschman did regarding the GDR: "The direct obstacles to voice, that is, to any political movements of resistance or dissidence, were enormous. They must be added to the indirect undermining of voice by the real or imagined availability of exit to the West. Jointly these direct and indirect restraints on voice produced an exit-voice balance that was tilted far more against voice and in favor of exit" (1993:183).

Yet throughout the 1990s, during the crisis of the "special period," we witnessed the increasing use of both the *exit* and *voice* options in Cuba, as was the case in the GDR in 1989. For example, in the summer of 1994 *exit* and *voice* were expressed in multiple ways, reinforcing each other. The *exit* of the dramatic *balsero* crisis was the immediate result of *el Habanazo* – the largest *voice* event on record – when massive riots took place in central Havana, protesting the economic conditions in Cuba as well as the lack of liberty. The riots themselves were set off by another *exit* event: the detour of the small boat that regularly crossed the Bay of Havana for the town of Regla and on that day took a different course, seeking to leave Cuba. The riots were also preceded by the most tragic *exit* event: the tugboat incident in mid-July, when 41 adults and children died. As a result of these multiple ways in which *exit* and *voice* were expressed that summer, reinforcing each other in tandem, Fidel Castro announced that the authorities would not interfere with anyone who wanted to leave. This announcement led immediately to the massive outpouring of *balseros* to sea throughout the month of August, which in turn resulted in the signing of the Migration Accords that now regulate the massive, orderly departure of Cubans.

Even more, on September 8, when Cubans celebrate the feast day of their cherished patron saint, they witnessed yet another clear expression of the incipient use of *voice* in Cuba as Father José Conrado Rodríguez was emboldened to act by the crisis. His letter to Fidel Castro erupted exactly as Havel (1978) explained any sudden action that signifies a coming to live in the truth rather than the lie of the "post-totalitarian society": as an act of courage that places that person in real danger.

In recent years, a new dissident movement began to emerge. Its seeds were sown in the mid-1980s. Ricardo Bofill, a former member of the old Cuban Communist Party (the PSP), was a founding member of the Comité Cubano Pro Derechos Humanos, Cuba's first human rights committee. Upon Ronald Reagan's recent death, Bofill (2004) recalled the importance of the former president's support, at a time when Cubans who struggled for human rights did so in total isolation. Reagan championed their cause, strengthening the tie between a large part of the Cuban exiles and the Republican Party. Other expressions of dissidence, however, such as those of the Corriente Socialista Democrática, issued from the left and looked to the Democratic Party for support, which President Jimmy Carter gave.

279

Due in part to the crisis of the "special period," the 1990s witnessed the rapid growth of this *voice*. Contrary to the opposition that gathered force in the early years of the revolution, whose strategy consisted of fighting the government with military might, this new dissident movement was characterized by its being nonviolent in strategy and approach, following the social movements spearheaded by Mahatma Gandhi, Martin Luther King Jr., and Cesar Chavez. It takes its inspiration from the worldwide human rights movement that found its earliest expression in the United Nations' Universal Declaration of Human Rights (1948) as well as the Czechoslovakian intellectuals' Charter 77 (Havel 1986). That dissident movement not only grew in size – Concilio Cubano (Cuban Council), the umbrella organization that developed at one point, covered more than 70 different groups, notwithstanding the small size of some – but also grew in maturity, seeking to provide an alternative vision of a democratic society in Cuba. In recent years, among many documents two particularly stand out: "La Patria es de Todos" (Our Nation Belongs to All) and the Proyecto Varela.

Four of Cuba's leading dissidents, each of them representing a different group, came together to write "La Patria es de Todos," which criticized the Communist Party's sole monopoly of power in Cuba and called for a return to some of the principles of the 1940 Cuban Constitution. Arrested in July 1997, in March 1999 the four dissidents were tried behind closed doors and sentenced to three to five years in prison for acts of sedition and for being "counterrevolutionaries" (Alfonso 1999; Tamayo 1999). The four came to be known as El Grupo de los Cuatro. They also represented the full gamut of race and gender in Cuba. They were Vladimiro Roca, mulatto, son of Blas Roca, the prominent communist leader of the 1930s; René Gómez-Manzano, a lawyer, white, who represented the Independent Lawyers; Félix Bonne-Carcasés, black, an engineer who previously taught in the university; and Marta Beatriz Roque, an economist and woman, who represented the Independent Economists. Due to the pressure for their release exerted by Amnesty International, Americas Watch, Pope John Paul II, the European Union, and the governments of Canada, Mexico, and Spain (Cuba's major trading partners), three of them were released after serving three years in prison. Vladimiro Roca remained in jail longer, though eventually he too was released.

In May 2002 the Proyecto Varela handed the National Assembly of Popular Power more than the 10,000 signatures (11,020, to be exact, on the first round, and a similar number on the second round) that the 1976 Cuban Constitution said were necessary for citizens to introduce a real change. Though different, both projects called for a plebiscite in Cuba so that Cubans can freely elect their government. Spearheaded by one of Cuba's leading dissidents, Osvaldo Payá, founder of the Movimiento Cristiano Liberación, the Proyecto Varela called for a popular referendum of the Cuban people. It demanded five forms of change in Cuba: the right to free expression and a free press; the right to free association; amnesty for political prisoners; the right to form small, private enterprises; and a plebiscite – a new electoral law and general elections. As Oswaldo Payá expressed it: "Let no one else speak for Cubans. Let their own voices be heard in a referendum" (Payá 2001).

It is worth noting the name of the document and project that sought the signatures. It was named after Father Félix Varela, a Cuban priest who, in the early 19th century strove for Cuban independence from Spain. Forced to *exit* Cuba, he spent the rest of his life in the United States, in exile, working with Irish and Italian immigrants in a parish in New York. He also wrote prolifically, expressing his dissent, as a form of *voice*. Hence, Varela's very life holds within it the use of both the *exit* and *voice* options. Though he died in exile, long before Cuba achieved its independence, today he symbolizes the use of the *voice* option inside Cuba.

For his role as a human rights activist in promoting peaceful change within Cuba, the European Parliament awarded Payá the Sakharov Prize in 2002 – named after Andrei Sakharov, the late Soviet physicist, dissident, and Nobel Prize laureate. Payá went to Strasbourg, France, to receive the award in December 2002. It was only the second time in his life he traveled outside of Cuba. He accepted the prize in the name of all Cubans because, he stressed, human rights are universal. Afterward, he traveled throughout France, Spain, and the United States, meeting with government authorities and public figures.

Shortly after his return to Cuba, in March 2003, the Cuban government arrested and imprisoned 75 dissidents, around 40 of whom had collaborated with the Proyecto Varela and many others who worked as independent journalists. Among these was Raúl Rivero, who a year later was awarded a prize by UNESCO for his excellent journalism – a prize he was not able to receive in jail. Amnesty International adopted these 75 Cubans imprisoned as prisoners of conscience. They were jailed with extremely long sentences for their peaceful opposition and were sent to jails in places quite far away from their families. The incident began to be called the Cuban Spring, after its European counterpart. Cuban women amplified the echoes of their dissidence with another dramatic *voice* event – a quiet protest. Las Damas

281

de Blanco (the Ladies in White) are the wives, mothers, and sisters of the
75. They gather in a church or public plaza every Sunday. Dressed in white,
they often wear the photo of their loved one on their t-shirt. They quietly
set out for a walk along the streets of Havana, for all to see their peaceful
protest. Oftentimes, they hold a single flower. The women are white, black,
mulatto – every color that is Cuban.

With so many obstacles to the emergent use of *voice*, how is it possible for both *exit* and *voice* to have developed in tandem, reinforcing one
another? In Hirschman's analysis of Germany in the final, climactic year
of 1989, the seesaw of *exit* and *voice* suddenly turned into a joint act when
the inability of the government to prevent a large-scale flight of its citizens
out of the country "signaled a novel, serious, and *general* decline in state
authority" (Hirschman 1993:187, emphasis in original), a signal that proved
emboldening to others. The mass exodus of some citizens – a private solution to their troubles – did feel to many then in the GDR, as today in Cuba,
as a bloodletting of the country. But, as Hirschman argued, it "did suffi-
ciently impress, depress, and alert some of the more loyal citizens, those
who had no thought of exiting, so that they finally decided to speak out"
(1993:197) – a most public act. So it was also in the Cuban case. For example, it was the *balsero* crisis that provoked Padre José Conrado Rodríguez
to write the letter to Fidel Castro and emboldened many other Cubans
to join the dissident movement and to found new human rights organizations. Hirschman underlined that the collaboration of *exit* and *voice* in the
last phase can be explained by an appeal to the concept of *loyalty*. Loyalty
delays *exit* as well as *voice* when there is a decline in the performance of an
organization, party, or nation to which one belongs. But when the decline
passes a certain threshold, the *voice* of the loyal members tends to become
particularly vigorous. Hirschman, however, did not emphasize, as I think it
is important to do, that in this case the *loyalty* was no longer to the government but to the nation. For Cubans, that is precisely the symbolic meaning
of titling the call for a national referendum after Father Félix Varela, the
19th-century hero.

Examining the four theses shows that migration clearly bears a relationship to democratization, but it is a highly historically contingent one.
Ultimately, the question of whether the exodus is a hindrance or a help to
the development of civil society does not have only one answer. Rather, as
Hirschman found, in the GDR, over the course of many years, a number
of *exit-voice* relationships obtained. Such, I contend, was also true in Cuba.
There, at present, both *exit* and *voice* work together in tandem.

282

11

The Impossible Triangle

Mi madre decía siempre
que la patria era cualquier sitio,
preferiblemente el sitio de la muerte.
Por eso compró la tierra más árida
y el paisaje más triste
y la yerba más seca,
y junto al árbol infeliz
comenzó a levantar su patria.

My mother always said
your homeland is any place,
preferably the place where you die.
That's why she bought the most arid land
the saddest landscape,
the driest grass,
and beside the wretched tree
began to build her homeland.

   Belkis Cuza-Malé,
   "La Patria de mi Madre" (1987)

Cuba, the United States, and the Exiles

For the nearly half century since the United States began to provide
refuge to Cuban émigrés, a triangulated relationship developed between
the United States, Cuba, and the exiles that can best be understood with
Stéphane Dufoix's (2000) notion of an "impossible triangle" (see Figure 11.1). As a concept, the triangle has appeal because it has to do with
whose side one is on, as well as with the loyalty or treason that results from

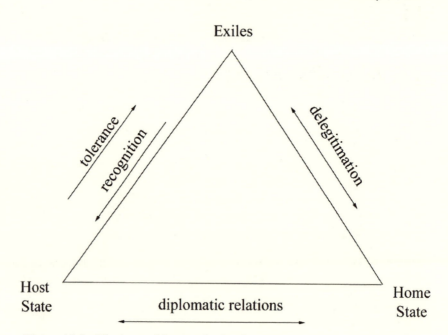

Figure 11.1   The impossible triangle. (Dufoix 2000)

belonging to different political communities. Because the triangle that develops is so conflictive, both the home and host societies are involved in intelligence, counterintelligence, and espionage – all activities that involve the exiles. Thus, as Dufoix points out, a great deal of uncertainty exists in the exile community regarding, as Cubans say in Spanish, *quien es quien* (who is who). Little trust exists even among collaborators, who often see one another as possible traitors.

Dufoix called the relationship that develops between the home regime (Cuba), the host regime (the United States), and the exile community (Cuban Americans) an impossible triangle because it is impossible for the host state to recognize the exiles within – to tolerate them or encourage them, thus legitimizing their existence and their political goal – and at the same time to pursue diplomatic relations with the home state. The host state has to side with the one or the other, but cannot side with both at once. Only when there is an actual war between the two states does the impossible triangle disappear, as the host state and the exiles stand together against the home regime (e.g., during the planning of the Bay of Pigs 1961 exile invasion of Cuba). At such times, governments in exile are recognized.

Such is also the case at those times when the war is not an actual war but a war by another name (e.g., the U.S. economic embargo of Cuba).

Because it is impossible to satisfy all elements of the triangle most of the time, the exiles have often felt betrayed by the host state when its relationship with the home state becomes more important than its relationship with the exiles. The first betrayal that affected the Cuban exile community was the actual Bay of Pigs invasion, when the promised U.S. support was withdrawn by the Kennedy administration.

Due to the Bay of Pigs betrayal at the hands of a Democratic administration, many Cuban exiles reacted by turning massively toward the Republican Party. Electoral data are not available to support this point, because in the early 1960s Cuban exiles had not yet become citizens, nor did they aspire to become so, still imagining exile to be temporary and the return to a democratic Cuba imminent. However, my participant observation among the Bay of Pigs' veterans confirmed it. The relationship that developed then between the early waves of the exiles and the Republican Party was cemented later when Ronald Reagan, partly through his anticommunism, strengthened the modern, conservative movement.

More recent accusations of betrayal by the host country have centered around Castro's downing of the airplanes manned by the exile group Hermanos al Rescate in 1996 and the Elián González case in 2000, both of which occurred during Bill Clinton's Democratic administration. The U.S. responses to both cases have caused many in the exile community to question the reliability of the Democrats in advancing the interests of Cuban Americans and have tended to reinforce their identification with the Republican Party. In this chapter I consider these two later betrayals and also trace how such betrayals have affected the Cuban exiles' political attitudes over time. In doing so, I rely on interviews with José Basulto, Liana Blanco, Andrés Vargas-Gómez, José Ignacio Rasco, Oscar Aguirre and Natalia Goderich, and Mariano Pérez.

On February 24, 1996, Cuban MiG airplanes downed two of the three Cessna planes piloted by exiles from Hermanos al Rescate that were flying over Havana, with the aim of distributing leaflets with the articles from the Universal Declaration of Human Rights. To José Basulto, their leader, this was a form of nonviolent resistance, similar to that promoted by Martin Luther King Jr. Two planes were downed, but one escaped, piloted by Basulto. The deaths of the four young men piloting those two planes – Carlos Costa, Pablo Morales, Mario de la Peña, Armando Alejandre Jr. – cut the exile community deeply. Hermanos al Rescate also blames the U.S.

government because it had prior knowledge of Castro's intentions but did nothing to prevent the crime or to warn Brothers to the Rescue ("The Shootdown of Brothers to the Rescue..." 2006). To José Basulto, the United States betrayed Cubans whose cause was to restore liberty in Cuba three times: the Bay of Pigs in April 1961, the Missile Crisis in October 1962, and the downing of the Hermanos al Rescate airplanes in February 1996. After the downing of the airplanes, however, President Clinton agreed to tighten the trade embargo by signing the Helms-Burton Act, legislation the Cuban American National Foundation, under Jorge Mas-Canosa's leadership, lobbied through Congress. Three years later, however, when the same Cuban American National Foundation rallied behind the cause of keeping six-year-old Elián González in the United States and not returning him to Cuba, the Clinton administration withdrew its support from the exiles.

Elián González arrived in Miami on Thanksgiving Day, 1999, when I was visiting there. He was five years old, when he was found at sea, alone, floating on an inner tube. In the days and months to come, the little *balserito* was featured daily in the news. Elián had left his home in the small town of Cárdenas, Matanzas, on the north coast of Cuba, on November 21, on a small boat with 14 persons. The boat capsized off the Florida Keys, and all but two adults and Elián drowned, including his mother, who first tied him to the inner tube. After a couple of days drifting alone in the ocean, on Thanksgiving Day two fishermen out at sea spotted him and rescued him. The Immigration and Naturalization Service (INS) gave temporary custody to the boy's great uncle, Lázaro González, who lived in Miami, in a small home in Little Havana. Soon the boy's father, Juan Miguel González, demanded Elián's return to him in Cuba. Thus, a saga began that made the little boy the center of a struggle between Cuban exiles in Miami and the Cuban government on the island.

The Cuban exiles seized the opportunity to politicize the event (see Figure 11.2). They sought to keep Elián in the United States, to save him from being brought up under communism. To this end, they emphasized that his mother, Elizabeth Brotons, did all she could to save him, to bring him to a land of freedom. Moreover, strong bonds of love developed between the child and his Miami family. In Miami, Elián became a symbol of communism's harm, a standard borne by the opposition to the Castro regime.

The Cuban government also politicized the event (see Figure 11.3), insisting that the child was Cuban and that his father had the right to claim him so that he could grow up in Cuba with him. Elián's two grandmothers

Figure 11.2 The case of the little *balserito*, six-year-old Elián González, drew protests in Miami as well as Cuba. Elián was found floating alone at sea on Thanksgiving Day, November 1999, after his mother died in an attempt to reach the United States on a boat that capsized off the Florida waters. Elián was given to the custody of his Miami family, who loved him and wanted to keep him in the United States, despite his father's objections back in Cuba. To the Miami exiles, he became a symbol of their plight, of the families divided by the Cuban revolution and the exodus. Here the Miami exiles protest in front of the boy's Miami home, holding photos of Elián and his mother, Elizabeth Brotons, who gave her life to bring him here. (AP Images)

came to the United States in January 2000 to personally deliver that message to Congress. That fall, I was able to see the events in Miami unfold, as they reached an emotional and political crescendo.

In March, I traveled to Cuba and was able to witness the emotional and political crescendo there. I saw the crowds of people marching in Havana, in front of the U.S. Interests Section, in protest against the retention of the boy. As is the usual case, some Cubans joined these marches freely, while others told me they felt obliged to join them. Fidel Castro demanded the mass mobilization, and Cubans were rounded up to participate at their workplace and at their neighborhood. In Cuba, Elián became a symbol of the inhumanity both the United States and the "Miami mafia" (as Castro repeatedly called the organized exiles) were capable of toward Cuba. Throughout the island, one could see posters depicting Elián's plight. One

Figure 11.3 Thousands of Cuban university students protest the Elián González case outside the U.S. Interests Section in Havana on December 20, 1999, wearing t-shirts with his portrait. In these, Elián looks angry and upset. Fidel Castro called for resumption of street protests, pressing for a rapid decision on the six-year-old's fate, who was "a Cuban child" who belonged with his father in Cuba. (AP Images/ José Luis Magana)

showed him behind polka-dot bars, reading *Salvemos a Elián* (Let us Save Elián); another showed him looking upset and sad, reading *Liberen a Elián* (Free Elián). Elián was said to be *secuestrado*, kidnapped (e.g., López-Blanch 1999). As Dufoix pointed out, both the exiles and the home country engaged in delegitimation of the other.

Having seen both sides of this conflict, I immediately wrote a letter to the Miami exile community when I returned to the United States (Pedraza 2000). I pointed out that the position taken by a large part of the Cuban exile community was not only wrong but also counterproductive. I agreed that Elián would have a decidedly better life in the United States. I also underscored the importance of the argument that his mother had risked all, including her life, to have him come to a land of freedom. Moreover, I stressed, it was eminently clear that his Miami family loved him. Yet I exhorted them to return the child to his father because he was still the boy's father, and he claimed him. Cuban parents of the more than 14,000 Cuban children who had come to the United States alone, during Operation

Pedro Pan in the early 1960s, made the same claim. Cubans then felt that the right of parents over their children took precedence over the right of the state. I also stressed that Fidel Castro, always an astute leader, was utilizing the incident to fan the dying embers of nationalism and anti-imperialism in Cuba, nearly extinguished by a decade of "the special period." I closed by asking Cuban exiles to return the child to his father and expressed the hope that in the future Elián would understand why we had done so. Neither that reasoned plea nor any others made any difference. By that time, Cubans on both sides of the Gulf had built themselves into an emotional and political frenzy that swept everyone along the way. Amid the loud protests, both on the streets of Miami and Cuba, other voices could not be heard.

Miguel de la Torre (2003) analyzed the Elían González episode from the perspective of *la lucha* – the struggle against Fidel Castro's regime, a struggle that wove religion and politics together. He highlighted that as a sacred symbol Elián merged the religious and political hopes of the Miami Cuban community. Elián, it was said, came to speak to those who had been wandering in exile for more than 40 years, as in the biblical tradition, and who sought deliverance. Elián was also depicted as the child of Ochún, the West African deity of the waters, whose syncretic expression is *la Caridad*. Elián was also said to be "the Cuban Moses" (Robaína 2000). Clearly, Elián was a miracle.

Religion and politics were tightly woven in the rituals the exiles created. Cuban women dressed in black to symbolize mourning and gathered outside Elián's house in Miami to pray a rosary. Among them was Liana Blanco, who did everything she could to keep Elián in Miami. "They will not give him a real education," she said. "It will be an indoctrination." Silvia Iriondo, president of Mothers against Repression, expressed the community's sentiment well: "In that child, we saw all the pain and all the suffering of 41 years. Elián symbolizes the pain of the Cuban family, the Cuban families that throughout 41 years of oppression have been divided by one man and one system" (Bikel 2001).

Whereas the exiles had made the cause of the *balserito* a political cause about not returning a child who escaped communism at the cost of his mother's death, President Bill Clinton, Attorney General Janet Reno, and Immigration Commissioner Doris Meissner failed to recognize the exiles' claim. Instead, they sided with the Cuban side of the triangle. They insisted that the issue had to be depoliticized because it involved only the return of a child to his father. Clinton said the case spoke to "the importance of family and the bond between a father and son" ("Appeals Court Denies..." 2000). On April 22, INS officials and armed federal agents stormed into the Miami relatives' house at dawn and forcefully grabbed the child, who was hiding in a closet in the arms of his friend, Donato Dalrymple, one of the fishermen who had rescued him. A photo captured the agent pointing his gun at them and the fright on Elián's face. A woman who was a special agent whisked Elián away. Later that day, the boy was returned to his father, who was waiting for him in Maryland. Shortly thereafter, Cuban exiles in Miami rioted in protest over this latest betrayal.

Elian's case had a number of consequences. The American people grew sympathetic toward the plight of the Cuban people on the island, their poverty and want. For the first time, the trade embargo was softened, allowing the sale of food and medicine to Cuba. The agreement made by the House of Representatives during the very last days Elián was in the United States marked a fundamental shift in U.S. policy, as it permitted the first U.S. agricultural sales to Cuba in 38 years. In 2001 Cuba bought 28,200 tons of food from the United States, worth $4.4 millions; in 2005 it purchased 1,861,000 tons, worth $540.8 millions (Agence France Presse 2006).

Another consequence was the massive flight of Cuban Americans away from the Democratic Party. This impact can be seen contrasting the results of the 1997 and 2000 polls in Miami conducted by Guillermo Grenier and Hugh Gladwin at Florida International University (FIU). The polls showed that, of the registered Cuban voters, 33.5 percent had voted for Bill Clinton for president in the 1996 elections; in 2000 that percentage dropped sharply, down to 14.9 percent – the *voto castigo* (revenge vote) that was a consequence of the betrayal involved in the Elián González case. George W. Bush's campaign benefited from this electoral shift, with 63.8 percent of the Cuban vote in the Miami area going to him. Sergio Bendixen, a Miami-based pollster, said the 2000 presidential election will be remembered not only for "being the closest one in U.S. history" but also for "finally establishing the importance of the Hispanic vote." Bendixen also added that Bush captured about 50,000 more votes than the former Republican presidential nominee, Robert Dole, in 1996. Bendixen pointed to the Elián González revenge vote as the main reason for the increase (in Green 2000).

The 2000 FIU poll, conducted six months after this controversy, also showed that 78.5 percent of Cuban Americans in Miami believed that Elián should have stayed in the United States, an opinion not widely shared by others in Miami (33.6 percent) or nationwide (28.3 percent). This lack of fit between Cuban exiles' perception and others is an example of what Andrew Shryock in his study of the Arab American community called "double remoteness" – a crisis of belonging. When a community "is properly linked to one dominant zone, this connection triggers feelings of impropriety in relation to another" (2004:291).

War by Another Name

In his analysis of the impossible triangle, Dufoix also noted that the attitudes of the home and host country toward the exiles were marked by a different logic. In the case of the host country (the United States), the predominant concern regarding the exiles who reside within it is surveillance: keeping an eye on them. At times of war, surveillance can turn into detention and internment. In the case of the home country (Cuba), the predominant concern regarding the exiles who reside elsewhere is to neutralize them. The Cuban government is aware that, while they successfully externalized their dissent, they also created a substantial opposition abroad.

The Trade Embargo

As Dufoix stressed, on a continuum of politics at one end and war at the other end, exile politics is closer to war (seeking the overthrow of the regime) than to what is usually called politics (the art of bargaining, compromise, and negotiation). Over nearly half a century, exile politics ranged from a warlike politics to open war. The preeminent example of a war by another name is the trade embargo. This policy has remained in place because the intransigent wing of the exiles insists on it, despite a very widespread lack of support for the embargo among the international community, as well as the moderate wing of the exile community. Examples of real war were described in earlier chapters: the Bay of Pigs invasion; other forays into Cuba organized by groups such as Alpha 66; and acts of violence aimed at particular exiles, killing or maiming those who openly supported the revolution or the reestablishment of relations. Even when exile politics most resembles normal politics (e.g., the creation of the Cuban American National Foundation, whose goal was to lobby the U.S. Congress), its intent was also to accomplish a warlike politics (the passage of the Helms-Burton Act, tightening the screws of the embargo).

Congressional Politics

A warlike politics also describes the role the Cuban American representatives in Congress, particularly Ileana Ros-Lehtinen and Lincoln Díaz-Balart, regularly play. For example, the U.S. Congress approved the softening of the trade embargo toward Cuba in October 2000, by the very wide margin of 86 to 8, allowing the sale of medicine and food to Cuba. Yet the Cuban American representatives curtailed the intent of the legislation by adding to the bill the provision that Castro could not buy from the United States on credit but only with cash. Díaz-Balart characterized this as the greatest victory since the passage of the Helms-Burton Act (Radelat 2000). Its intent was to make the softening of the embargo only symbolic.

Culture Wars

The experience of the revolution and the exodus politicizes and leaves no social sector untouched: artists, writers, religious groups, musicians all become split into pro- and antiregime factions. As a result, "culture wars" developed in Miami in the mid to late 1990s, when contemporary artists who lived in Cuba began to receive visas to come to the United States (Eckstein 2004). When they visited Miami, they often received a hostile welcome. Such was the case when the pianist Gonzalo Rubalcaba gave a concert. Those who entered the Gusman Center to hear him play were beaten or spat at. Worse was the case of Los Van Van. The band came to play in Miami in 1999, appearing on television, where the musicians apologetically told the Miami public they were bringing them their music with affection. Many Cubans defiantly attended the concert, but many others protested, throwing eggs and soda cans at the music fans who danced to the band's rhythms. The behavior was reminiscent of the *actos de repudio* typical of Cuban political culture – now on both sides of the Gulf.

As the Cuban immigrant community in Miami changes its social composition, and the recent immigrants become an increasingly larger part of it, it is natural they would want to hear the music they grew up with, fell in love by – the music of their generation. But to the old exiles – *los viejos Cubanos del exilio* – as Luis Martínez (1998) described himself in his angry letter to the newspaper, the musicians remained a symbol of a past they could not forget: family members assassinated, those executed before *el paredón*, those who suffered political imprisonment, "every imaginable abuse" committed by Fidel Castro for more than 40 years.

A musician par excellence, Omar Reyes-Canto (1997) also wrote to the newspaper. A former member of the Conjunto Folclórico de Cuba (Cuba's National Folklore Group), after arriving in Miami he went on to become director of the Miami Pop Orchestra. In his article, he played with the similarity in Spanish of the words *alma* (soul) and *arma* (weapon). He emphasized that in Cuba and Miami both, the *alma* of music had instead become an *arma*. In Cuba, he said, every artist who left the island was censored – his or her identity and work erased from the annals of Cuban culture, where they belonged. In Miami, musical groups who resided on the island were silenced. Reyes-Canto looked forward to the day when music would again be *alma*, the soul that unites us – not *arma*, the weapon that drives us apart. Such was the case in the concert Los Van Van gave in Toronto, Canada, at the end of 2006, to an audience full of Cubans from the various waves, myself among them.

Human Rights Denunciation

Yet another example of a warlike politics is the substantial effort in which Cuban Americans engage every year to take the Cuban case before the United Nations' Human Rights Commission in Geneva, Switzerland. To present their documentation on human rights violations by the Cuban government, Cuban Americans labor hard to prepare the substantial documentation that comes from informants in Cuba yet is compiled in Miami, mostly due to the work of the Comité Cubano Pro Derechos Humanos. In addition, they must find a country that will sponsor them by allowing them to present their case. In recent years, this was done by the United States and the European Union; Honduras, Uruguay, Peru, and Nicaragua; the Czech Republic and Poland; and Spain.

Since it began in 1988, with the sole exception of 1998, every year in April the commission approved the resolution presented and documented, condemning Cuba's human rights violations. At times, the margins were extremely narrow. But in 2005, the accusation was approved by a wider margin of 21 votes for, 17 against, with 15 abstentions – the result of Latin America's change in attitude (Alfonso 2005b). Only in 1998, the year that Pope John Paul II visited Cuba, did the commission not approve the resolution (cf. Rivero 1998).

Does it make a difference? Certainly, with respect to Cuba, these annual ratifications of its human rights violations have not contributed to their deterrence. However, they contributed to the healing of the victims and

293

survivors, to a sense of justice and closure for them and their families. Hopefully, they will also contribute to the development of a culture of human rights protection in the world (cf. Ratner 2005).

Neutralizing the Exiles

While the exiles were involved in these various forms of war by another name, the Cuban government sought to neutralize the exile opposition. One of its means was the use of language as a discourse of war. For example, Castro referred to the refugees who initially left Cuba as *gusanos* (worms). During the Bay of Pigs exile invasion of Cuba, Castro called the young men who risked their lives to restore a democratic government in Cuba, as well as the old society they knew, "mercenaries." They, however, called themselves "freedom fighters." Likewise, Castro referred to the *Marielitos* who left in 1980 as *escoria* (scum), though they were the very people in whose name the revolution was made.

Moreover, as we have seen, the Cuban government also learned to use the deep rifts within the Cuban community in the United States in its favor. Though united in its rejection of Castro's communism, the Cuban exile community is more heterogeneous than most imagine, embracing a wide range of political expression. Two major factions, or "wings," exist in the organized political community. They describe themselves as *los moderados* (the moderates) and *los intransigentes* (the intransigents). The two major groups share the goal of promoting the return to a democratic government in Cuba but radically disagree with respect to the means. More often than not, their attitude toward one another is acrimonious and contemptuous. *Los intransigentes* include exile organizations such as Unidad Cubana, la Junta Patriótica Cubana, el Presidio Político Histórico Cubano, and Alpha 66. *Los moderados* include exile organizations such as la Coordinadora Social Demócrata, el Partido Demócrata Cristiano de Cuba, la Unión Liberal Cubana, el Movimiento Democracia, and the Cuba Study Group. Outside these two major groups lie a small group of radical Cubans, who support the revolution, such as Francisco Aruca, Max Azicri, and the small remnant of the Brigada Antonio Maceo.

Los intransigentes see war and open confrontation with the Cuban government as the instrument to achieve that end, with violence an inevitable prelude. As the late Andrés Vargas-Gómez, then president of Unidad Cubana emphasized, "Castro will never sit at a negotiation table to negotiate his exit from power." Thus, they help the internal resistance in Cuba and the dissidents in Cuba, such as Marta Beatriz Roque, who condemn the present Constitution and propose a return to the 1940 Constitution. By contrast, *los moderados* see constructive engagement with the Cuban government, a dialogue, as the instrument to a negotiated, peaceful transition to democracy. As José Ignacio Rasco explained, "a dialogue is necessary to attain real reforms that will usher in a transition without concessions, violence, or fanaticism." Thus, they propose the development of nonviolent alternatives to develop in Cuba and support the dissidents, such as Oswaldo Payá, who work within the limits of the present Constitution yet propose real changes as a prologue to the achievement of democracy.

Recognizing this deep rift among the exiles, the Cuban government repeatedly reached out to *los moderados* and *los dialogueros* so as to neutralize the opposition of the exile community by placing those who were willing to engage in dialogue at the forefront. For example, in recent years three conferences took place in Havana (1994, 1995, 2003) called "La Nación y la Emigración" (The Nation and Its Emigration). The 1994 conference turned into a fiasco when, among the 200 or so Cuban Americans invited, lawyer Magda Montiel, apparently starstruck by Fidel Castro's charisma, shook his hand, kissed him, and called him *maestro* (a great teacher), all of which was captured on video. When she returned to Miami, she was treated as an outcast, harassed, and threatened. In 1992, Human Rights Watch issued a report documenting instances of harassment and intimidation against exiles who were sympathetic to Castro or held moderate views. Two years later, it issued a report on this conference, urging local government officials and civic leaders to take steps to correct the atmosphere of intimidation present in Miami: "The overall climate for free expression remains essentially unchanged in Miami" (1994). Moreover, the Cuban government's effort to neutralize the Cuban exile opposition by strengthening the moderate sectors within it backfired.

Dufoix's notion of the "impossible triangle" is an insightful way to make sense of the organization of exile politics by showing the inherent instability between the three sides of the triangle that poses distinct dilemmas for each.

Transitions in Cuba

After nearly a half century, several transitions are now taking place, both in Cuba and in the exile community. "What will happen after Fidel Castro dies?" is constantly asked. It is well, however, to keep two distinct transitions in mind: the succession in leadership that will take place when Fidel Castro dies or gives up his political role; and the transition to democracy, which may not take place at the same time as the succession (LeoGrande 2002).

Leadership Succession

Contrary to those who expected "that the transition will involve a trajectory moving from the totalitarian to the democratic in something akin to a straight line," as Irving Louis Horowitz (2004:32) put it, after Fidel came Raúl. On July 31, 2006, due to serious illness, Fidel ceded power to his younger brother. As expected, an orderly, dynastic succession took place with the support of the military. As defense minister, Raúl had the necessary authority, as designated by the Constitution and publicly by Fidel.

In Cuba, the armed forces is the one institution that consistently worked well, garnering the respect of the people, with its victories in the armed struggle against Batista, at the Bay of Pigs, and in conflicts in other Third World countries, notably Africa (Amuchastegui 1999). The military in Cuba was what Jorge Domínguez (1978a) called the "civic soldier" who fused civilian and military lives. As Brian Latell pointed out, in a country of about 11.2 million, "the number of Cubans who don uniforms totals well over 2 million" (2003:2), which constitutes roughly 18 percent. Only the Catholic Church rivals it in influence and competence. Thus, as Irving Louis Horowitz noted, we can expect a Cuba without Fidel Castro but with less than a democratic government for some indefinite period of time, especially given Cuba's small size, limited resources, widespread impoverishment, and, "indeed, its tradition of the anti-democratic now enshrined as tragic historical fact" (2004:33).

Although the military in Cuba has enjoyed enormous prestige, over the years its mission and policies have changed. After the 1980s, Cuba's ideology of proletarian internationalism, which led to overseas adventures in the 1960s and 1970s, waned, and the military came to play a central role in domestic economic production. As Latell put it, "the venerated civic-soldier now had a new companion: the 'technocrat soldier'" (2003:13). The latter applied Western management techniques, such as the System of Enterprise Perfection, to military enterprises.

In truth, the military has played quite different roles in the various transitions from communism. At one extreme, in Eastern Europe the various militaries did nothing to save the communist regimes; they refused to fire at or use force against the civilian protestors, as was particularly evident in the collapse of the Ceausescu regime, when the military and internal security force leaders first refused to support the government and then joined the opposition (Radu 2003). At the other extreme, in China, the army slaughtered large numbers of civilian, prodemocracy protesters. According to Domingo Amuchastegui (1999), formerly a Cuban intelligence and foreign affairs official, the military's new role in Cuba was the result of China's Tiananmen Square. He pointed out that in the debates among the political class, of which he was then part, all the events in 1989–91 – the collapse of the Soviet Union and Eastern Europe, the Tiananmen student revolt, and the failed expectations concerning the ability of the armed forces to save socialism – had a tremendous impact on the Cuban armed forces. But the dominant perception was that nothing like what happened in Eastern Europe would ever happen in Cuba. Tiananmen, however, was "entirely different. It became a haunting ghost for each and every debate within the Cuban political class."

Reportedly, Raúl Castro believed such crises could be averted by improved economic performance, providing food and welfare, not by rolling the tanks onto the streets. As a result, trusted military officers now manage the lion's share of the economy. For example, General Ulises Rosales del Toro is currently minister of the sugar industry, and General Luis Pérez-Rispide runs Gaviota (the tourism conglomerate of hotels, small airlines, tourist shops, and car rental agencies). As a result, yet a third type of military officer has emerged: the "entrepreneur-soldier" involved in for-profit activities that earn hard currency for the regime by doing business with foreign investors and dealing with the capitalist world. In effect, the transition to a society run by the military is already in place.

Democracy

The question then becomes whether, after Fidel's passing, such a militarized society guided by a military elite can effect a transition to democracy. While Raúl's legitimacy has always derived in large part from being Fidel's brother, he has been the world's longest-serving defense minister. He has always been known for being ardently pro-Soviet and for his iron will and discipline. Yet he is also known for his lack of charisma, inability to relate to the masses, and ruthlessness (LeoGrande 2002:18). Moreover, the memory of General Arnaldo Ochoa's execution in 1989, allegedly for his involvement in the lucrative drug trade and corruption, still haunts the Castro brothers (cf. Oppenheimer 1993; Montaner 2001). Roberto Ortega (2007), former colonel of the Cuban Armed Forces and former chief of medical services for the Cuban military who defected in 2003, was present at Ochoa's trial. In his view, Ochoa was eliminated due to his enormous popularity with the Cuban soldiers in Angola and Ethiopia and due to his sympathy for Gorbachev's reforms in the Soviet Union, for *glasnost* and *perestroika*. "Cuba was one before Ochoa's trial," Ortega said, "and another afterward."

Despite Fidel's efforts to ensure the future, the actual shape it will take may be quite different than expected. In my view, several conditions will help usher in the democracy transition: Raúl's lack of capacity to govern through either personal charisma or bargaining and compromise; the fissures that must exist within the military elite since Ochoa's execution; communism's loss of legitimacy as a system in the world arena; the economic stagnation of the country, now dependent on the influx of dollars and euros from tourism and the émigrés' remittances; the development of political alternatives within the island that, despite their discrepancies, stress the need for a contested political life and suffrage; and the dissatisfaction of a population exhausted from constant mass mobilizations and the continued lack of a viable future.

Though the transition may at first be a succession, Fidel's passing will release pent-up demands for further change (LeoGrande 2002). It will keep the transition from being "sequestered," as Rousseau and Cumerlato (2001) called it as the result of their experiences in the 1990s when they were working for the Agence France Press in Havana. In recent years, Fidel refused to engage in any substantial social and political reforms that may result, as they did in Eastern Europe, in the unraveling of communism, seemingly preferring China's strategy of combining limited economic reforms with tight political control. Limited as the reforms of recent years have been, they strengthened civil society at the expense of the state, to such an extent that Domínguez (1997) argued that Cuba is in the process of making a transition to a post-totalitarian, authoritarian regime. While Fidel, Raúl, and other hard-liners in government still wish they could draw the reins of the totalitarian society tightly, as they did in the past, they can no longer do so. Certain social groups have attained a measure of autonomy, in particular the church, intellectuals, and those in the informal economy and in the dissident movement. Moreover, the nationalism of the early years that entailed nationalization of foreign-owned industry was replaced by joint ventures with new foreign industries, which are provided incentives and privileges to operate in Cuba. Most important is the public's waning ideological commitment: "The revolutionary process in the 50's and 60's based itself, in part, on the absolute faith that the nation had taken in its hands the

298

reins of history," stressed Domínguez. "Today, that faith has disappeared, and has been replaced by fear, hope, doubt" (1997:9). The state itself has become weaker, as it has lost both the power it had and the fear it used to provoke.

Even more, Fidel and Raúl's stance makes it impossible for the voice of the reformists to be heard, much less for them to side with the regime opponents. It was such coalitions that made possible the "velvet revolutions" in Eastern Europe, the peaceful transitions from communism to democracy. In my view, the U.S. trade embargo and its policy of constant confrontation with Cuba make the development of such a coalition impossible, as they exacerbate the anti-U.S. nationalism on which the hard-liners in Cuba rely, making the voice of the soft-liners inaudible.

In any post-Castro Cuba, neither the dissidents nor the diaspora is likely to play a large political role. Without doubt, the émigrés will likely be a major problem, given the size and power of the Cuban diaspora, and the extent of the nationalizations in the early years of the revolution, which will raise substantial issues over property rights (Radu 2003:17). Still, as Sergio Díaz-Briquets and Jorge Pérez-López (2003) pointed out, the exile community has much to offer with its skills, knowledge, and capital to an emergent society, as well as by its capacity to influence U.S. policies.

Transitions in Exile

Time has not stood still. In an exodus that is now nearly half a century old, increasingly there are dramatic differences in attitudes across the various waves, as well as generations.

Political Attitudes

Chun and Grenier analyzed the data from the Florida International University polls of Miami Cubans conducted in 2000. As we have seen, the lived experiences of the early exiles and the recent exiles differed markedly. This is reflected in sharply contrasting attitudes toward Cuba, as Table 11.1 shows. Looking at several measures of an uncompromising political attitude toward Cuba, Chun and Grenier showed that the "hard," uncompromising attitudes toward Cuba are disproportionately held by the exiles from the early waves, whereas "soft" attitudes toward Cuba are quite common among the most recent exiles. In all of the measures, the *Marielitos'* attitudes fall in between. While more than 70 percent of the early exiles (1959–73)

Table 11.1. *Attitudes toward Cuba among Cuban Americans in the Miami Area, by Waves of Migration, in 2000*

	Percentage of Cuban Americans				
Year of Immigration	Favoring Continuing the U.S. Embargo of Cuba	Opposing Sale of Medicine to Cuba	Opposing Sale of Food to Cuba	Opposing Dialogue of Exiles and Cuban Government	Number
1959–64	71.3	41.9	55.7	57.1	172,000
1965–73	76.7	47.0	62.5	61.0	211,000
1974–79	62.1	41.9	51.7	62.5	31,000
1980	67.1	36.5	43.3	53.0	85,000
1981–89	63.3	37.3	44.1	45.4	59,000
1990–2000	40.7	14.9	22.9	33.3	127,000
U.S.-born	57.1	24.8	31.1	32.0	109,000

Source: Chun and Grenier 2004: table 3. Based on the Florida International University Cuban Poll of 2000 conducted by Guillermo Grenier and Hugh Gladwin.

favor continuing the U.S. embargo of Cuba, fewer than half (40 percent) of the recent exiles (1990–2000) share the same attitude. Those born in the United States are divided in their support (57 percent).

Likewise, whereas close to 60 percent of the early exiles oppose a dialogue between the Cuban exile community and the Cuban government, only a third of the most recent exiles do, as is also the case for the second generation. Attitudes toward the sale of food and medicine to Cuba are not as hard, but show similar patterns. While half to two-thirds of the early exiles oppose the sale of food to Cuba, only slightly more than 20 percent of the most recent exiles do. Whereas more than 40 percent of the early exiles oppose the sale of medicine to Cuba, only 15 percent of the most recent exiles do. Support for the Republican Party also varies markedly. A survey of Miami-Dade Cuban Americans conducted by Bendixen and Associates for the New Democrat Network showed that support for President George W. Bush is declining among Cuban Americans (in Lizza 2004). While he captured 82 percent of the Cuban American vote in 2000, the 2004 poll showed their support for Bush had declined to 66 percent. Bendixen noted that a new political bloc may well be forming that comprises those who came to the United States after 1980 and Cuban Americans born in the United States. The second generation supported Kerry over Bush by 58 to 32 percent. Moreover, the ranks of the early exiles are declining. According to Bendixen and Associates' polls, while they constituted 90 percent of the Cuban American electorate in 1990, now they are down to only 67 percent.

A number of factors seem to be at play with respect to these dramatic contrasts. First, clearly the era in which the exiles left the island matters most. The most recent exiles still have family in Cuba whom they want to be able to help and to visit. Few of the early exiles still do, because most brought all the family they wanted to the United States and severed their relationships with those left behind who supported the Cuban government. Second, the recent exiles also vividly remember the want and suffering they went through in Cuba due to the scarcity of food and other goods and the lack of transportation. By contrast, few of the early exiles went to bed hungry in Cuba or lived obsessed with the difficulties inherent in the task of feeding their families.

Even more, the differences in attitudes across waves also stem from the political culture the early exiles built in Miami. The core of that political culture – puzzling and contradictory to outsiders – is what Lisandro Pérez (1992) called "the exile ideology," which consists of various political traits: an unwavering anti-Castroism, militancy, conservatism, and an affiliation with the Republican Party. Successive waves of immigrants progressively joined the political culture established by the early exiles, but many of the recent immigrants have not.

Real differences in attitudes exist among the major "wings" of the exile community. The *intransigentes* view all forms of contact of the exiles with Cuba – through family visits, the sending of remittances – as treason to the exile community itself, a form of collaboration that makes those who engage in it suspect of being, at worst, potential spies; at best, *tontos útiles* – fools who lend themselves to being used politically. Trips to Cuba are seen as a form of support for the government and collaboration. This was true even in the case of the pope's visit to Cuba in January 1998.

Transnationalism

Despite this dominant political culture, transnational ties between the exiles and their families back in Cuba remain strong. Family reunification visits have never ceased, at the pace of around 100,000 a year. Cubans remit money to their families the same as other immigrant groups do. Family remittances are estimated at $813 million a year (Orozco 2000). Bendixen and Associates' (2001) survey of 1,000 remittance senders from the United States to different countries in Latin America showed that 67 percent of

Cubans had sent money to their family on the island – a larger percentage than Mexicans (65 percent), though less than Dominicans (78 percent) and Central Americans (82 percent). Despite the insistence of a very vocal part of the Cuban American exile community, whose political task is to insist that no dollars be sent back to Cuba because doing so props up Fidel Castro's regime, another sizable part of the Cuban American exile community insists on putting their families first – and quietly sends dollars to those left behind. This is a moral task in which women are centrally involved (cf. Pedraza 1991).

These forms of communication between the vast majority of the Cuban refugees and their relatives back in Cuba again fell victim to the exiles' warlike politics when President George W. Bush, seeking the electoral support of the Cuban American community, dramatically restricted both their travel and remittances in the summer of 2004. The new restrictions gave rise to sizable street protests in Miami, mostly from recently arrived Cubans who still have family in Cuba. Placards read "Liana, Lincoln, Mario, we will remember you in November." However, these congressional representatives were reelected in November 2004 by very wide margins. Though recent immigrants do not share these hard-line positions, they are also not yet citizens, able to exercise the power of the ballot box.

In my view, these restrictions will not be able to curtail the immigrants' transnationalism. In today's global economy, changes in the technologies of transportation and communication (jet air travel, faxes, electronic mail, the Internet, videos) have changed the qualitative experience of immigration. These modern communications enable immigrants to maintain more frequent and closer contact with their home countries and to participate regularly – both actually and vicariously – in the life they once left behind. As a result, immigrants now take actions, make decisions, and develop identities embedded in social networks across two or more nations (Basch et al. 1994). Thus, such government restrictions will only temporarily reduce the flow of people, goods, and money. Cuban immigrants, like all other immigrants, will find ways to get around the government's restrictions. Transnationalism is a fact of the modern world in which we live, the result of the new forms of communication (Pedraza 2006).

Party Identification

Given that Cubans in the United States are still very much an immigrant community, issues that pertain to the homeland, to Cuba, have primacy over "immigrant" issues regarding adjustment to life in the United States. Part of this popular culture is an uncompromising struggle to overthrow the Castro regime, help Cuba to exit from communism, and help reestablish a democratic government in Cuba. While virtually all of the Cuban exiles are united behind this goal, an important difference exists between *los intransigentes* and *los moderados* in the means to achieve this goal. Pérez pointed out the important role the Democratic Party had played toward Cuban Americans: "The measures that have greatly facilitated Cuban immigration and the adjustment of Cuban Americans in the United States have all been enacted by Democratic administrations: the Cuban Refugee Program and its resettlement efforts, the assistance given to the Cuban elderly and the dependent, the establishment of the airlift or freedom flights, and permission for the Mariel boatlift to take place, among others" (1992:96).

One might add that it was former president Jimmy Carter who visited Cuba in May 2002 and publicly acknowledged the importance of the dissidents' work on the island. While in Havana, Carter urged Washington in a forthright speech to repeal the embargo and permit unrestricted travel to the island. He also urged the Cuban government to permit civil and political freedoms and to respect human rights. However, the Republican White House reacted to Carter's speech by applauding his emphasis on human rights, while disagreeing with regard to the trade embargo (cf. Johnson 2002). Given the size, concentration, and political activism of the Cuban American community, Cuba is now not only a foreign policy issue but also a domestic politics issue. Hence, it is unlikely that the inconsistency in the public policies of the Democrats and the Republicans toward Cuba can be solved, tied as they are to electoral concerns.

Despite the frank efforts many Democratic administrations over the years have made toward Cuba, in my view the sense of betrayal at the hand of the Democratic Party is too strong to allow such party identification among many Cubans who otherwise do share many of the social democratic values espoused by the Democratic Party. In the only national political survey of its kind to date, Rodolfo de la Garza et al.'s *Latino Voices* (1992) sampled Mexicans, Puerto Ricans, Cubans, and non-Hispanic whites in 40 metropolitan areas about American politics. While overall their party identification contrasted sharply, most of them described themselves as moderate to conservative, only one-third as liberal. Despite this conservatism, the majority of all groups, particularly Puerto Ricans and Cubans, saw government as the solution to both national and local problems. Likewise, their positive attitudes toward increased government spending on a broad range of domestic issues were quite similar. Hence, Cubans' support for the role government should play in supporting social issues is that which is usually associated with the Democratic Party. Among the early exiles, this attitude is bound to issue from what was the predominant political attitude in Cuba prior to the revolution: the social democratic tradition expressed in the main political parties then, the Ortodoxos and the Auténticos. Among the recent exiles, this attitude is bound to issue from their experience of social life in a communist society. However, the exiles' anticommunism, their material success, and their feeling of betrayal at the hands of the Democratic Party have attracted them to the Republican Party.

Generations

Cuban American success along the standard indicators of education, income, occupation, and poverty is well known. The 2000 census data for Cubans as a whole (immigrant and U.S.-born) show that 21.2 percent have a college degree or higher education, 37.1 percent hold managerial and professional occupations, 14.6 percent live below the poverty level, and 7.1 percent are unemployed; the median household income is $36,671. These figures show that their structural assimilation into mainstream institutions has gone further than other Latinos'. Their level of education, in particular, approximates that of the white (non-Hispanic) population (26.1 percent of whom have a college education or higher) (U.S. Census Bureau 2002). Yet, at the same time, Cuban immigrants became structurally assimilated without becoming overwhelmingly culturally assimilated. Census data show that 86.3 percent speak Spanish at home. Moreover, they became fairly successful in Miami without speaking English well, or being bilingual and bicultural. In Miami, Cubans willfully retain a great deal of their culture. However, Cubans' material success does not translate to political success as exiles. As Max Castro (1999–2000) pointed out, ironically Cubans have failed as exiles (what they most wanted to be), while they have succeeded as immigrants (what they did not aspire to be).

Given the marked differences in political attitudes from the early exiles to the most recent exiles, it is clear that, as time passes, the defining political ideology of the Cuban community will change. Already the community is becoming more tolerant. This generational transition is symbolized by the figure of Jorge Mas-Santos, who inherited the leadership of the Cuban American National Foundation upon Jorge Mas-Canosa's death. Mas-Santos was not comfortable with the hard-line positions the CANF represented, while the hard-liners in the CANF felt his positions did not go far enough. Thus, it split into two groups: the Consejo Cubano por la Libertad (Cuban Liberty Council), where the old CANF warriors now reside, and the new CANF, which is now close to the positions represented by *los moderados*. The Cuban American National Foundation is now a member of the newly formed Consenso Cubano, an umbrella organization of *los moderados* that had earlier rallied around the Plataforma Democrática (Democratic Platform) in Spain (Montaner 2001). While many of the early exiles regret the changes that have taken place in *la Fundación*, as they call it, the new *Fundación* is, like the new generations born in the United States, like Mas-Santos himself, a more pragmatic organization, less of an ideological standard-bearer.

Even more, substantial change in attitudes has taken place. In the 1970s and 1980s, the idea of a dialogue between exiles and the Castro government was seen as treason. Even in the early 1990s, polls put the support for such a dialogue at less than a third of the exiles. But in 2003 two polls found the majority of Cubans in South Florida supported such a dialogue. One poll was conducted by the *Miami Herald*, the other was conducted by Bendixen and Associates for the Cuba Study Group, headed by Carlos Saladrigas. These polls also showed that the majority of Cubans in South Florida believe that dissidents on the island are more important than exiles to Cuba's political future. Indeed, for some years now, the political lead for change has been within Cuba, in the dissident movement – besieged and divided as this has been. Both "wings" of the Cuban exile community recognize this and have sought to help those inside the island to foster change. "We can't live in a time capsule," said Mas-Santos in an interview with the journalist Andrés Oppenheimer (2003). "The transition has to happen on the island, with the Cubans on the island, led by the opposition on the island, and by the members of the current government who want things to change. They are the ones that will initiate change."

Nonetheless, neither "wing" has succeeded in incorporating the most recent exiles. E. F. Kunz (1973) correctly noted that some refugee "vintages" are hostile toward one another. Cuba's early exiles blame the recent exiles for having collaborated with and propped up the regime, for having left Cuba too late; the recent exiles also blame the early exiles for not having given the more egalitarian society under construction a chance, for having left too early. Such distrust can hardly be overcome. Oscar Aguirre, the young man who came with his family from Russia, was enormously grateful to the Cuban American National Foundation for its Program Exodus. Yet,

305

he found himself insulted shortly after his arrival. Much to his surprise, at a meeting of *la Fundación* in Miami, he and his wife, Natalia Goderich, were deeply offended by a woman who stood up and called all who lived in Cuba cowards. She insisted they were unable to see the reality and the political abuse there because they did not want to see it, and she exhorted them to rise against the regime, rather than leave the island. Angry and hurt, Oscar replied: "*Señora*, it was you who created the problem, to begin with. If you left Cuba, there is no reason why I shouldn't." As the exile community ages, it is becoming more tolerant – but also less involved. The recent exiles are not being incorporated into the political organizations founded by the early exiles, not only because of the distrust that exists between different vintages but also because the recent exiles' need to create a private life away from politics, precisely the chance that life under communism denied them.

Refugees, Immigrants, Ethnics

Yet another transition is taking place. Over the time span of the exodus, nearly half a century, Cubans in the United States have been undergoing another profound attitudinal transition: from refugees to immigrants to ethnics. The first part of this transition in attitudes "from refugees to immigrants," under the impact of constant new immigration and the centrality of Cuba in the lives of the immigrants, has been slow to take place (cf. Rieff 1993). But to the degree that Cubans ceased to look backward (like Lot's wife) to Cuba as the only source for the meaning of their existence and identity, to the degree they started to look forward and to carve their future in this country as Cuban Americans, to that degree it has been achieved.

The second part of this transition in attitudes, "from immigrants to ethnics," is more inexorable because it corresponds to the demographic transition currently underway. Although quite young still, a second generation born in this country is now in our midst that was raised under American institutions and socialized in American schools, the great transmitters of tradition, culture, and values. These young Cubans' assimilation may have been delayed by their growing up in the Cuban enclave in Miami, as their parents succeeded in passing on to them a refugee identity. Tasoulla Hadjiyanni (2002) studied the children of Greek Cypriot refugees and argued that they had inherited a "refugee consciousness" grounded in the past and in their experience of force and loss. Despite this, these Cuban

Americans, like any people, are the soil in which they rooted and grew. Moreover, they lack the felt sense of a Cuba they do not know.

In "The Agony of Exile" (1991), Rubén Rumbaut pointed out that the meaning of exile is different across generations. To the parents' generation, who made the decision to leave, exile represents both a profound loss and a profound commitment. And it entails a worldview that will be defended. By contrast, to their children's' generation exile is an inherited circumstance. Typically, they are in solidarity with the family's predicament but do not need to protect their parents' worldview. Their focus is on the future in the new society.

In between these two lies the "1.5 generation" (my own): those who left at the dawn of their adolescence and are forever caught between two worlds, the land of their birth and the land that tended them. As one of them, it is my hope that those of the second generation that has now rooted in the United States will not be so American that they will lose touch with their history and culture, with their *Cubanía*. But as a sociologist, I have to recognize that such may well be the price to be paid for shedding the pain of exile.

Refugees as a Social Type

Refugees are as old as human history, but the 20th century – the age of genocide, two world wars, and most of the great social revolutions – created more refugees and displaced people than ever. The U.S. Committee for Refugees and Immigrants (2005) estimates that the number of refugees and asylum seekers who fled their countries in 2004 is 11.5 million people, with an additional 21.3 million people internally displaced. Such estimates use the narrow definition of refugees as *targets*, those who can demonstrate a well-founded fear of persecution. Using a broader definition of refugees not only as *targets* but also as *victims*, such as Zolberg et al. (1989) proposed and I emphasize, those numbers would be many times higher.

Yet sociology has paid scant attention to the refugee as a distinct social type. To date, the difference between refugees and other types of immigrants has been understood to be twofold. At the microlevel, it has been understood simply in terms of the nature of the "push" factors involved: persecution, lack of political or religious freedom, civil strife. At the macrolevel, it has been understood as the legal systems in two societies that direct or curtail the flows, also distinguishing those deserving of political asylum and refugee assistance. While both of these remain true, my research shows these formulations do not go far enough. At the microlevel, refugee migration results from distinct political experiences: dictatorship, civil war, revolution, genocide. Refugees are not only those who suffered outright persecution; they are also those whose lives became intolerable because their most closely held values were violated. At the macrolevel, refugee migration serves different functions. Refugees are not only those who "vote with their feet," symbolizing the rightness of a cause; they are also those who easily become pawns in a larger political chess game, such as the United States and the Soviet Union played for 40 years during the Cold War.

Not only are their motivations and experiences different. Once settled in a new society, refugees form distinctly different communities. Doing fieldwork in California, Steve Gold (1992) conducted a comparative study of Soviet Jews and Vietnamese refugees. Gold found these refugee communities marked by enormous diversity of background, interests, and experiences, as I also found in my own study. Such diversity was regional, religious, class, generational, ideological, and ethnic. Gold highlighted the relationship that exists between these refugee groups and entrepreneurship, as self-employment and ethnic enterprises proliferate among them. Such a relationship is also well known among Cubans in the Miami ethnic enclave (e.g., Portes and Bach 1985) and in Puerto Rico (Cobas and Duany 1997). Gold, however, stressed that the relationship had to do with the psychology of the refugee. "These refugees entered business," he concluded, "because it offered the independence needed to fulfill goals that would be unattainable through other conditions of employment" (1992:175). By becoming self-employed, refugees limited their contact with the larger, unfamiliar culture; they provided employment for relatives; and they enjoyed the autonomy of being their own boss. This autonomy allowed them to earn a living while at the same time accomplishing political or community service goals within the refugee community. In turn, this allowed them to become visible and to exert influence on the refugee community. Thus, they were able to achieve goals they felt were important given the community's history and its social needs. My own research corroborates this. In addition, my fieldwork also led me to believe their very drive to succeed was also spurred by the wounds they suffered as refugees, by their need to prove – to others and to themselves – that they were people of worth. Jews who came to America in the late 19th and early 20th centuries arrived at a time when they were neither legally nor sociologically recognized as refugees. Hence, their entrepreneurial success was never understood as part of their history as refugees. Contemporary studies of Soviet Jewish, Vietnamese, and Cuban refugees, such as Gold's and my own, indicate that it is.

The research reported in this book led me to conclude that a number of factors, not many of which were previously identified, make refugees a distinct social type: their psychology and motivations; their coerced homelessness; their deep attachment to the land (both as nation and as landscape) they came from; the histories of dictatorship, revolution, civil war, or genocide that propelled their flight and strengthened their very identities; the psychological trauma that left them with deep wounds that fail to heal with time; their sense of being victims of history; their attempt to pass on their refugee consciousness to their children; the international body of law that seeks to protect them and the international arenas where they hope to be heard; the distinct nature of the communities they form, marked by high levels of self-employment; their drive to achieve and to succeed; their constant political engagement with the homeland they left behind; and their intimate acquaintance with danger. Contrary to Alejandro Portes's (1999:27) assertion that in the study of immigration micro- and macrolevels of analysis cannot be integrated, "are not fungible," I argue that both micro- and macrolevels of analysis, in dialectical fashion, are needed to understand refugees as refugees. Social scientists, lawyers, and policy makers all need to heed these dramatic differences for a more enlightened understanding of the plight of refugees to develop and a more effective public policy to issue – all the more so when the total number of refugees and displaced people worldwide is as large as it is.

Even more, I stress, social scientists need to study refugees not only as individuals but as members of families, as these constitute the context in which their decisions are made, their trauma lived out. Beyond social class, race, gender, sexuality, and religiosity, social scientists should heed political generations as a fruitful concept to understand human behavior, for it is also a powerful structuring of human experience. In his study of the English working class, E. P. Thompson (1966) placed his fingers on the wounds left by experience, the experiences of groups of workers during the industrial revolution. People of all social classes, races, genders, sexual orientations, and religious convictions also became refugees due to the experiences that cumulated in their lives. As Thompson put it, they were casualties of history: their ideals may have been fantasies, and their insurrectionary conspiracies foolhardy, but "they lived through these times of acute social disturbance, and we did not" (1966:13).

W. R. Smyser (1985), an American diplomat who served as United Nations deputy high commissioner for refugees in Geneva, repeatedly saw and heard the experiences that turned people everywhere into refugees. As Smyser (1985:157) explained: "The common drive that compels refugees to leave their homes is fear: fear for their lives, for their families, for their future. Their stories have a depressing, even numbing, sameness. They may have seen their houses, shops or land burned, seized, pillaged or invaded, their countrymen – often friends or relatives – taken away without explanation. They may have been expelled from their jobs or from their homes. Their lives may have been threatened. They may have been injured, raped or robbed in their escape, and that escape may have taken them over hundreds of miles and many borders." When they finally reach safety, he continued, a distinct psychological attitude accompanies them: "They may reach their country of refuge exhausted, emaciated or dying. They often care little what happens to themselves but will do anything to ensure a safe future for their children. They worry continuously about those they left behind."

Like him, I also came to know their courage and their tenacity, as well as their plight. Writing in the mid-1950s, Maurice Merleau-Ponty expressed it succinctly: "Revolutions are true as movements but false as regimes" (1973 [1955]:207). It is good to remember, however, that a refugee community is a wounded community. It is a community of people who have experienced or witnessed violence, murder, torture – their own, their family's, or friends'. They are people whose lives were threatened, and who were forcibly separated from those they loved. Family separation, political division, left them with the deepest hurt. Andrés Vargas-Gómez was imprisoned due to the failure of the exile invasion at the Bay of Pigs. He spent 22 years in a Cuban prison, where he suffered enormously, sorrow he described to me unflinchingly. Yet his eyes misted over when he spoke about his brother, who chose to be on the other side. Fully integrated to the revolution, his brother deliberately repudiated him by their mother's deathbed.

Refugees are often imprisoned, subject to forced isolation and attempted brainwashing. Many are beaten, sometimes sexually abused, and denied health care when ill. The hurt and trauma they experienced often recurs in their memories, forming nightmares. The Harvard Program in Refugee Trauma studied the prevalence of such trauma among Thai, Cambodian, Laotian, and Vietnamese refugees (see, e.g., Mollica et al. 1987). My own interviews also elicited such experiences. Such deep wounds can also lead to collective behavior that others fail to make sense of, as with the Elián González case. Only on a few occasions was the church able to draw the reins in, to provide a moral leadership, to open a path for a wounded community to follow. Monsignor Agustín Román did so after Cuba's downing of the airplanes piloted by young men; so did Father Francisco Santana when the earthquake that devastated Cuba demanded the help of Miami's exiles.

False Hopes

The notion of hopes that proved false began this work. It is good to be precise about the many hopes involved. Those who fought against Batista's dictatorship placed their hopes on the return of a democratic, constitutional society. But, instead, the revolution was channeled toward the creation of a communist society. Those who fought against Castro's dictatorship, as part of an external invasion or the internal resistance, placed their hopes on the swift return to a democratic, constitutional society. But they were to see the longest-lasting dictatorship in Latin America. Those who believed democracy would soon be restored also hoped they would someday return to live out the rest of their lives in Cuba. But most of the early exiles were unable to return and will die in other lands, while most of the recent exiles do not harbor such hopes. Those who believed the Marxist-Leninist revolution would usher in a better world placed their hopes on the new society they enthusiastically helped to build. But they lived to see the collapse of communism in the Soviet Union and the Eastern European nations. And the long-standing scarcity and intolerance for dissent typical of those nations also thwarted their hopes. Those who vowed they would not leave Cuba remained, believing they could reform the society from within. But they found substantial economic and political reforms impossible to effect and eventually felt compelled to leave. Last, all who made the decision to leave Cuba placed their hopes on the better life they would thereafter find. Without doubt, Cubans who immigrated to the United States, Puerto Rico, Spain, Canada, and Costa Rica more often than not found a good life, economically speaking. But their hopes were frustrated by their felt lack of belonging, their loss of *la patria*, their homeland. Mariano Pérez, the *guajirito* from Matanzas who as an adolescent worked on an enormous farm, helping to milk cows, made this point. Due to his hard work in Michigan's auto factories, he prospered. He grew to own several properties and built a beautiful house near Key West, where he lived with his Czech wife. His children attended good schools and graduated from college at Michigan State. He was able to retire at 55, after traveling to 23 countries. "I should be grateful to Fidel because I would never have had any of this in Cuba," he stressed. "But I lost the opportunity to live the best years of my life in Cuba – only God knows how. Instead, I was sentenced to live them without my *patria*."

Among the exiles, the passage of time created different refugee "vintages" that at best can hardly understand one another and at worst may be hostile. Only in moments of sorrow – *en el dolor* – is the community able to come together, briefly. Such a moment is the Memorial to the Dead celebrated annually, a dramatic three-day memorial to the victims of Fidel Castro's regime. In 2005 fully 10,300 crosses made from white Styrofoam were planted in Tamiami Park in Miami. Each represented a known victim of Castro's regime, someone who died – either executed by his government, or fighting for the opposition, or in prison, or attempting to escape Cuba. In the center stood a large cross, nearly 20 feet high, for all those whose manner of death or time was unclear. Many had no other place to rest than this. In this memorial, the relatives expressed their sorrow for those they loved. In the wake held in the evening, they held candles (Steinback 2005; Cancio 2005). They were the relatives of those who were taken to the execution wall (*el paredón*) in the early 1960s, when the revolution veered toward communism; of those who were among the insurgents in the mountains of el Escambray in the mid-1960s; of those who drowned in the *13 de Marzo* tugboat incident in 1994; of the young pilots who became dust in the air, pulverized by the Cuban MiG airplanes in 1996. For that brief moment, at least, in their sorrow – *en su dolor* – they could understand one another.

Appendix

LIST OF INTERVIEWS

The list of interviewees is divided by the wave of immigration in which they participated. In the first wave, there are 38 interviews; in the second wave, 19; in the third wave, 24; and in the fourth wave, 39. The total number of interviews conducted in all four waves is 120. Interviews took place in the United States, Puerto Rico, Canada, and Spain – a majority of them, 71 (59 percent), in Miami, Florida. The interviews were conducted by Silvia Pedraza mostly between 1996 and 2000, with some as recent as 2006.

Wave 1

1. Jorge Duany	San Juan, Puerto Rico
2. Himilce Esteve	San Juan, Puerto Rico
3. Manolo Ray	San Juan, Puerto Rico
4. Ramón Alvarez (pseudonym)	Miami, Florida
5. Miguel González-Pando	Miami, Florida
6. Gastón Vázquez (pseudonym)	Miami, Florida
7. Fermín Mejía (pseudonym)	Boston, Massachusetts
8. Serafín García-Menocal	Miami, Florida
9. José Bober and Juanita Bober	Miami, Florida
10. Dolores Prida	Ann Arbor, Michigan
11. Rosario Rexach	New York, New York
12. Eulogio González	Miami, Florida
13. Raul Martínez	Miami, Florida
14. Pedro Reboredo	Miami, Florida
15. Fernando Roa	Miami, Florida
16. José Basulto	Miami, Florida
17. Alfredo Blanco and Liana Blanco	Miami, Florida

18. Ramón Espino — Miami, Florida
19. Eduardo Lorenzo — Flint, Michigan
20. Raúl Moncarz and Elisa Moncarz — Miami, Florida
21. Flavio Risech — Amherst, Massachusetts
22. Antonio Reyes and Cecilia Mestre (pseudonyms) — Miami, Florida
23. Ofelia García-Menocal — Madrid, Spain
24. Concha Besú — Miami, Florida
25. Eloísa Lezama-Lima — Miami, Florida
26. Prisciliano Falcón — Miami, Florida
27. José Ignacio Rasco — Miami, Florida
28. Eloísa García (pseudonym) — New Orleans, Louisiana
29. Marcelino Miyares — Miami, Florida
30. Juan Manuel Salvat — Miami, Florida
31. José Tenreiro — Elizabeth, New Jersey
32. Mariano Pérez — Miami, Florida
33. Anton Núñez (pseudonym) — Miami, Florida
34. Sergio Segarra — Miami, Florida
35. Carlos Méndez — Miami, Florida
36. José Antonio Costa — Miami, Florida
37. Bernardo Benes — Miami, Florida
38. Seferina Fernández-Yarzábal and Marcelino Heres — Miami, Florida

Wave 2

1. Angelina Rodríguez — Ann Arbor, Michigan
2. Carlos Franqui — San Juan, Puerto Rico
3. Luisa Calvo (pseudonym) — Miami, Florida
4. Adolfo Fernández and Cristina Fernández — Detroit, Michigan
5. Aimée Vázquez Simpson and Pedro Simpson — Chicago, Illinois
6. Silvio Olivio Lubián — Miami, Florida
7. Pablo González — Paterson, New Jersey
8. Yolanda Prieto — New York, New York
9. Olga Mallo — Miami, Florida

10. José Manuel Baracaldo and Alicia   Miami, Florida
    Baracaldo
11. Gladys Santana   Miami, Florida
12. Graciela Relloso   Miami, Florida
13. Cari Orozco Mount   Miami, Florida
14. Julio Rodríguez   Ypsilanti, Michigan
15. Nyurka Duarte   Chicago, Illinois
16. Alberto Duarte   Chicago, Illinois
17. José "Richard" Heredia   Miami, Florida
18. Jesús Cruz   Lansing, Michigan
19. Martha Oliva   Miami, Florida

Wave 3

1. Rogelio Santos (pseudonym)   St. Louis, Missouri
2. Rafael Peláez and Juanita Peláez   New York, New York
    (pseudonyms)
3. Andrés Vargas-Gómez   Miami, Florida
4. René Cifuentes   New York, New York
5. Oscar Suárez   Miami, Florida
6. Armando Alvarez-Bravo   Miami, Florida
7. Augusto Vidaurreta and Esther María   Miami, Florida
    Vidaurreta
8. Norberto Conde   Houston, Texas
9. Hilda Felipe   Miami, Florida
10. José Macías (pseudonym)   Los Angeles, California
11. Rafael Naranjo   Miami, Florida
12. Fidelia Suárez (pseudonym)   Madrid, Spain
13. Jesús Selgas   New York, New York
14. Roberto Lang and Maximina   Miami, Florida
    Domínguez-Poyo
15. Carlos Gómez   Miami, Florida
16. Lorenzo Dueñas-Fernández   Miami, Florida
17. Jorge Valls   Miami, Florida
18. Luis Zúñiga   Miami, Florida
19. Luis González-Infante   Miami, Florida
20. Víctor Mozo   Montreal, Canada
21. Juan Salces (pseudonym)   Miami, Florida
22. Nicolás Morejón   Miami, Florida

23. Juan Sánchez ("Novillo")   Miami, Florida
24. Ivanna Martín   Miami, Florida

Wave 4

1. Alberto Masa (pseudonym)   Lansing, Michigan
2. Salvador León (pseudonym)   Lansing, Michigan
3. Pedro García-Grau and Daisy   Lansing, Michigan
   Llorens
4. Eva Zaldívar (pseudonym)   New York, New York
5. Félix Fojo   Miami, Florida
6. Olga Gómez (pseudonym)   Lansing, Michigan
7. Pedro Cañas   Miami, Florida
8. Frank Fuentes   Lansing, Michigan
9. José Conrado Rodríguez   Miami, Florida
10. Juan López (pseudonym)   Miami, Florida
11. Pascual Cruz-Varela   San Juan, Puerto Rico
12. Oscar Alvarez   Miami, Florida
13. Rafael Saumell   Huntsville, Texas
14. Enrique Patterson   Miami, Florida
15. Lorenzo Dueñas   Miami, Florida
16. Moisés Asís and Teresa Hernández Asís   Miami, Florida
17. Oscar Aguirre and Natalia Goderich   Miami, Florida
18. Rafael Díeguez   Madrid, Spain
19. Radamés García de la Vega and Heriberto   Union City, New Jersey
    Leyva
20. Kenya González   Miami, Florida
21. Amelia Sosa and Arturo Llana   Miami, Florida
    (pseudonyms)
22. Tomás Medina (pseudonym)   Miami, Florida
23. Wilfredo Cancio   Miami, Florida
24. Luisa Suárez (pseudonym)   Lansing, Michigan
25. Juan Toledo (pseudonym)   Lansing, Michigan
26. Emma Tejera (pseudonym)   Lansing, Michigan
27. Lázaro Santamaría   New York, New York
28. Mariana Torres (pseudonym)   New York, New York
29. Georgina Mestre (pseudonym)   Miami, Florida
30. Alejandro Ríos   Miami, Florida

31. Wilfredo Beyra and Zaimar Campins	Phoenix, Arizona
32. Lazaro Argudín	Phoenix, Arizona
33. Enrique Naranjo and Ildelisa Rivera	Madrid, Spain
34. Teresita Sánchez	Miami, Florida
35. Arcadio Peguero	Miami, Florida
36. Joel Brito	Miami, Florida
37. Armando Añel	Madrid, Spain
38. Sergio Pérez (pseudonym)	Miami, Florida
39. Ricardo Blanco	Lansing, Michigan

References

Abreu, Juan. 1998. "Pequeño Elogio de la Escoria." *Encuentro: Revista de la Cultura Cubana* 8–9 (Spring–Summer): 135–38.

Ackerman, Holly, and Juan M. Clark. 1995. "The Cuban *Balseros*: Voyage of Uncertainty." Miami, FL: Cuban American National Council.

Agence France Press, la Habana. 2006. "Cuba Asegura que Crecieron las Compras a EEUU." *El Nuevo Herald*, January 18.

Agrupación Católica Universitaria. 1957. "Por Qué Reforma Agraria?" By Melchor W. Gastón, Oscar A. Echevarría, and René F. de la Huerta. Series B-Apologética Folleto No. 23. Havana: Buró de Información y Propaganda.

———. 1954. "Encuesta Nacional sobre el Sentimiento Religioso del Pueblo de Cuba." In *Religión y Revolución en Cuba*, by Manuel Fernández, 22. Miami: Saeta Ediciones, 1984.

Aguilar-León, Luis E. 1972. *Cuba: Conciencia y Revolución*. Miami, FL: Ediciones Universal.

Aguirre, Benigno E. 1976. "The Differential Migration of Cuban Social Races." *Latin American Research Review* 11: 103–24.

Aguirre, Benigno E., and Eduardo Bonilla-Silva. 2001. "Does Race Matter among Cuban Immigrants? An Analysis of the Racial Characteristics of Recent Cuban Immigrants." *Journal of Latin American Studies* 34: 311–24.

Aja-Díaz, Antonio. 2006. "Tendencia de la Emigración desde Cuba a Inicios del Siglo XXI." Centro de Estudios de Migraciones Internacionales (CEMI), Universidad de la Habana, Cuba.

Alarcón-Ramírez, Daniel ("Benigno"). 2003. *Memorias de un Soldado Cubano: Vida y Muerte de la Revolución*. Barcelona: Fabula Tusquets Editores.

Alfonso, Pablo. 2005a. "Camarioca: Cuatro Décadas de Exodo y Dolor." *El Nuevo Herald*, September 25.

———. 2005b. "Castro Aislado en la ONU." *El Nuevo Herald*, April 19.

———. 1999. "Comienza el Juicio al Grupo de los Cuatro." *Miami Herald*, February 27.

———. 1985. *Cuba, Castro, y los Católicos*. Miami, FL: Ediciones Hispamerican Books.

319

Amaro, Nelson, and Alejandro Portes. 1972. "Una Sociología del Exilio: Situación de los Grupos Cubanos en los Estados Unidos." *Aportes* 23: 6–24.

Amaro-Victoria, Nelson. 1981. "Mass and Class in the Origins of the Cuban Revolution." In *Cuban Communism*, ed. Irving Louis Horowitz, 221–51. New Brunswick, NJ: Transaction.

Aminzade, Ron, Jack A. Goldstone, and Elizabeth J. Perry. 2001. "Leadership Dynamics and Dynamics of Contention." In *Silence and Voice in the Study of Contentious* Politics, ed. Ronald R. Aminzade, Jack A. Goldstone, Doug McAdam, Elizabeth J. Perry, William H. Sewell Jr., Sidney Tarrow, and Charles Tilly, 126–54. Cambridge: Cambridge University Press.

Aminzade, Ron, and Doug McAdam. 2001. "Emotions and Contentious Politics." In *Silence and Voice in the Study of Contentious Politics*, ed. Ronald R. Aminzade, Jack A. Goldstone, Doug McAdam, Elizabeth J. Perry, William H. Sewell Jr., Sidney Tarrow, and Charles Tilly, 14–50. Cambridge: Cambridge University Press.

Amnesty International. 1992. "Cuba: Silencing the Voices of Dissent." New York: Amnesty International.

Amuchastegui, Domingo. 1999. "Cuba's Armed Forces: Power and Reforms." In *Cuba in Transition*, vol. 9, 109–19. Conference proceedings of the 9th annual meeting of the Association for the Study of the Cuban Economy, Miami, Florida. Washington, DC: Association for the Study of the Cuban Economy.

Anderson, Bonnie M. 1979. "The Execution of My Father." *Miami Herald, Tropic* magazine, April 25.

"Appeals Court Denies Asylum Hearing for Elián." 2000. *Japan Times*, June 3.

Aranguren, Emilio. 2003. "Memorias a mi Regreso." *Vitral* 9: 65–70.

Arenas, Reinaldo. 1992. *Antes que Anochezca*. Barcelona: Fabula Tusquets.

———. 1982. *Otra Vez el Mar*. Barcelona: Arcos Vergara.

———. 1981. *Termina el Desfile*. Barcelona: Seix Barral.

Arendt, Hannah. 1979 [1948]. *The Origins of Totalitarianism*. New York: Harvest/ Harcourt Brace Jovanovich.

Armony, Ariel. 2003. "Civil Society in Cuba: A Conceptual Approach." In *Religion, Culture, and Society: The Case of Cuba*, ed. Margaret E. Crahan, 17–35. Conference Report. Washington, DC: Woodrow Wilson International Center for Scholars.

Arteaga, Manuel, Cardenal de Cuba, y otros Obispos. 1960. "Circular Colectiva del Episcopado Cubano," August 7. In *La Voz de la Iglesia en Cuba: 100 Documentos Episcopales*, ed. Conferencia de Obispos Católicos de Cuba, 115–18. Mexico, DF: Obra Nacional de la Buena Prensa, 1995.

Asís, Moisés. 2003. "El Judaísmo en Cuba después de 1959." *Herencia* 9 (Spring): 84–96.

Bach, Robert, Jennifer B. Bach, and Timothy Triplett. 1981–82. "The Flotilla 'Entrants': Latest and Most Controversial." *Cuban Studies* 11–12: 29–48.

———. 1980. "The New Cuban Immigrants: Their Background and Prospects." *Monthly Labor Review* 103: 39–46.

Ballagas, Manuel F. 1983. "La Generación del Silencio II." *Término: Publicación Literaria Bilingue* 2 (Fall): 14–16.

320

References

————. 1953. "Poema Impaciente." In *Obra Poética de Emilio Ballagas*, ed. Cintio Vitier. Miami, FL: Mnemosyne.

Balmaseda, Liz. 1994a. "Balserita Violinista Toca pero También Escribe como los Angeles." *El Nuevo Herald*, October 19, 1B.

————. 1994b. "Cuba Bleeds, and the Drops Are Called Rafts." *Miami Herald*, August 17, 1B.

Baquero, Gastón. 2003. "El Negro en Cuba." *Herencia* 9 (Spring): 98–107.

Barbería, Lorena. 2004. "Remittances to Cuba: An Evaluation of Cuban and U.S. Government Policy Measures." In *The Cuban Economy at the Start of the Twenty-first Century*, ed. Jorge I. Domínguez, Omar Everleny Pérez Villanueva, and Lorena Barbería, 353–412. Cambridge, MA: David Rockefeller Center for Latin American Studies, Harvard University.

Barnet, Miguel. 2001. *Afro-Cuban Religions*. Princeton, NJ: Markus Wiener.

Barquet, Jesús. 1998. "La Generación del Mariel." *Encuentro: Revista de la Cultura Cubana* 8–9 (Spring–Summer):110–25.

Barquín, Ramón M. 1978. *El Día que Fidel Castro se Apoderó de Cuba*. San Juan, PR: Editorial Rumbar.

Basch, Linda, Nina Glick-Schiller, and Cristina Szanton Blanc. 1994. *Nations Unbound: Transnational Projects, Postcolonial Predicaments, and Deterritorialized Nation States*. Langhorne, PA: Gordon and Breach.

Bendix, Reinhard. 1977. *Max Weber: An Intellectual Portrait*. Berkeley: University of California Press.

Bendixen and Associates. 2001. "Survey of Remittance Senders: U.S. to Latin America." Washington, DC: Inter-American Development Bank.

Berezin, Mabel. 1997. *Making the Fascist Self: The Political Culture of Interwar Italy*. Ithaca, NY: Cornell University Press.

Betancourt, Ernesto, and Guillermo Grenier. 1999. "Measuring Public Opinion: Economic, Social, and Political Issues." In *Cuba in Transition*, vol. 9, 251–69. Conference proceedings of the 9th annual meeting of the Association for the Study of the Cuban Economy, Miami, Florida. Washington, DC: Association for the Study of the Cuban Economy.

Betto, Frei. 1985. *Fidel y la Religión*. Havana: Oficina de Publicaciones del Consejo de Estado. Translated as *Fidel and Religion* (New York: Simon & Schuster, 1987).

Bikel, Ofra, director. 2001. "Saving Elián." PBS *Frontline*. February 6. Boston: WGBH Educational Foundation.

Blue, Sarah A. 2004. "The Social Cost of Remittances: Race and Income Inequality in Contemporary Cuba." Paper presented at the meetings of the Latin American Studies Association, Las Vegas, Nevada, October 9.

Blumer, Herbert. 1969. *Symbolic Interactionism: Perspective and Method*. Englewood-Cliffs, NJ: Prentice-Hall.

Bodnar, John. 1985. *The Transplanted: A History of Immigrants in Urban America*. Bloomington: Indiana University Press.

Bofill, Ricardo. 2004. "El Respaldo de Reagan a Nuestro Movimiento de Derechos Humanos." *El Nuevo Herald*, June 14.

Bonachea, Rolando E., and Nelson P. Valdés, eds. 1972. *Cuba in Revolution*. Garden City, NY: Doubleday, Anchor Books.

Bonacich, Edna. 1973. "A Theory of Middleman Minorities." *American Sociological Review* 38 (October): 583–94.

Bonne-Carcasés, Felix, René Gómez-Manzano, Vladimiro Roca-Antuñez, and Marta Beatriz Roque-Cabello. 1997. "La Patria es de Todos." Havana: June 17.

Boza-Masvidal, Eduardo, Monsignor. 1997. *Voz en el Destierro*. Miami, FL: Revista Ideal.

———. 1960. "Es Cristiana la Revolución Social que se está Verificando en Cuba?" *La Quincena*, October 30. En *La Voz de la Iglesia en Cuba: 100 Documentos Episcopales*, ed. Conferencia de Obispos Católicos de Cuba, 131–34. Mexico, DF: Obra Nacional de la Buena Prensa, 1995.

Bremer, Fredrika. 1995 [1851]. *Cartas desde Cuba*. Havana: Editorial Arte y Literatura.

Brinton, Crane. 1965. *The Anatomy of Revolution*. New York: Vintage.

Brunet, Rolando C. 1959. "¡Así Torturaban los Esbirros de Batista!" *Bohemia*, January 11, 96–97.

Bustamante, Alberto S. 2003. "Notes and Statistics on Ethnic Groups in Cuba." *Herencia* 9 (Spring): 108–9.

Cabrera, Lydia. 1968. *El Monte*. Miami, FL: Ediciones Universal.

Cancio, Wilfredo. 2005. "Miles de Cruces en Memorial Cubano." *El Nuevo Herald*, February 20.

Cancio-Isla, Wilfredo. 2007. "Muere Mario Chanes de Armas, Símbolo del Presidio Político. *El Nuevo Herald*, February 25.

Cardona, Joe, and Mario de Varona, directors. 1999. *The Flight of Pedro Pan: An Untold American Story*. Miami, FL: Community Television Foundation of South Florida and Florida International University.

———, directors. 1998. *Havana: Portrait of Yesteryear*. Miami, FL: Community Television Foundation of South Florida and Florida International University.

Casa de las Américas. 1971. *Casa de las Américas*, XI, March–June.

Casal, Lourdes. 1987. "Images of Women in Pre- and Post-Revolutionary Cuban Novels." *Cuban Studies* 17: 25–50. (Edited by Virginia Domínguez).

———. 1979. "Cubans in the United States: Their Impact on U.S.-Cuban Relations." In *Revolutionary Cuba in the World Arena*, ed. Martin Weinstein, 109–36. Philadelphia: Ishi.

Castañeda, Carlos M. 1959. "Jamás en mi Vida Toleraré Conscientemente una Immoralidad." *Bohemia*, January 11, 68–70, 128.

Castro, Fidel. 1980. "Discurso Pronunciado en la Plaza de la Revolución José Martí." *Granma*, May 1.

———. 1973 [1953]. "La Historia me Absolverá." Havana: Instituto Cubano del Libro.

———. 1960. "*This* Is Democracy." In *Fidel Castro Speeches*, vol. 2: *Our Power Is That of the Working People Building Socialism in Cuba*, ed. Michael Taber, 25–37. New York: Pathfinder Press, 1981.

References

_____. 1959a. Television interview on *Meet the Press*, Washington, DC, April 19. Princeton University, Carlos Franqui Collection: Speeches, Press Conferences, and Declarations of Fidel Castro Ruz from March 1959–October 1970.

_____. 1959b. Television interview on CMQ station's *Before the Press*, Havana, Cuba, May 21. Interviewed by Jorge Mañach, Agustín Tamargo, Luis Gómez Wanguemert, Nicolás Bravo, and Carlos Castañeda.

Castro, Max J. 1999–2000. "De Agentes a Arquitectos." *Encuentro* 15: 187–94.

_____. 1999. *Free Markets, Open Societies, Closed Borders? Trends in International Migration and Immigration Policy in the Americas.* Coral Gables, FL: University of Miami North-South Center.

Central Intelligence Agency. 2003. *World Factbook.* http://www.theodora.com/wfb2003/cuba.

Chun, Sung-Chang, and Guillermo Grenier. 2004. "Anti-Castro Political Ideology among Cuban Americans in the Miami Area: Cohort and Generational Differences." *Latino Research* 2 (November):1–9. Institute for Latino Studies, University of Notre Dame, South Bend, IN. http://www.nd.edu/~Latino/ils_publications.htm.

Cifuentes, René. 1984. "Los Parametros del Paraíso." *Mariel: Revista de Literatura y Arte* 2 (Spring): 12.

Clark, Juan M. 1992. *Cuba: Mito y Realidad.* Miami, FL, and Caracas, Venezuela: Saeta Ediciones.

Clavijo, Uva. 1985. "El Legado de Elena Mederos." *Diario de las Américas*, January 3.

Clinton, William J., President. 1994. "Press Conference by the President." August 19. http://www.clintonlibrary.gov.

Cobas, José A., and Jorge Duany. 1997. *Cubans in Puerto Rico: Ethnic Economy and Cultural Identity.* Miami: University Press of Florida.

Collazo, José Enrique. 2001. "La Iglesia Católica Cubana durante el Siglo XX: Diez Acontecimientos Significativos." *Espacios* 4: 24–26.

Conde, Yvonne M. 1999. *Operation Pedro Pan.* New York: Routledge.

Conferencia de Obispos Católicos de Cuba. 1993. "El Amor Todo lo Espera," September 8. In *La Voz de la Iglesia en Cuba: 100 Documentos Episcopales*, 399–418. Mexico, DF.: Obra Nacional de la Buena Prensa, 1995.

Connor, Olga. 2005. "El Juego y el Antijuego de la Literatura Cubana del Exilio." *El Nuevo Herald*, part 1, December 18; part 2, December 25.

Córdoba, Efrén. 1995. *Clase Trabajadora y Movimiento Sindical en Cuba*, vol 1: *1819–1959*; vol. 2: *1959–1996*. Miami, FL: Ediciones Universal and Center for Labor Research and Studies of Florida International University.

Correa, Armando. 1996. "Sacerdote de Palma Soriano Dice fue Malinterpretado." *El Nuevo Herald*, November 1.

Corriente Socialista Democrática. 1992. "Así Pensamos . . . Declaración de Cuatro Puntos." Havana, June 31. Signed by Rolando Prats-Páez, Vladimiro Roca, Elizardo Sánchez, Nestor E. Baguer, Bernardo Marqués Ravelo, Néstor Castellanos, René del Pozo Pozo, Enrique Julio Patterson, Violeta Romero, Gladys Rodríguez, Guillermo Fernández Donate.

———. 1991–92. "Cuba: Proyecto de Programa Socialista Democrático." Havana, December–January. By Néstor E. Baguer, Manuel Díaz Martínez, Bernardo Márquez Ravelo, Enrique Julio Patterson, Omar Pérez, Rolando Prats, Vladimiro Roca, and Elizardo Sánchez-Santa Cruz.

Crahan, Margaret E., ed. 2003. *Religion, Culture, and Society: The Case of Cuba.* Conference Report. Washington, DC: Woodrow Wilson International Center for Scholars.

Cuba, Oficina Nacional del Censo. 2004. *Censo de Población y Viviendas, 2002.* República de Cuba. http://www.ccsr.ac.uk/Cuba/cepde2004/censomultimedia/c_iii.htm.

———. 1984. *Censo de Población y Viviendas, 1981.* República de Cuba, vol. 16. Havana: Comité Estatal de Estadísticas.

Cuesta, Tony. 1988. *Plomo y Fantasía.* Miami, FL: Editorial SIBI.

Cuesta-Morúa, Manuel. 1999. "Los No Blancos Irrumpen en las Filas de la Disidencia." *El Nuevo Herald*, October 2.

Cuza-Malé, Belkis. 1987. "La Patria de mi Madre" (My Mother's Homeland). In *Woman on the Front Lines.* Greensboro, NC: Unicorn Press.

de Céspedes, Carlos Manuel, Monsignor. 2002. "Influencia de la Iglesia Católica en la Cultura Cubana y en la Identidad Nacional." Paper presented at the conference on "Cuban Catholicism: Island and Diaspora" at the University of Notre Dame, Helen Kellogg Institute for International Studies and Institute for Latino Studies, South Bend, Indiana, June 20–21.

———. 1999. "Desafío del Sincretismo Religioso AfroCubano al Pensamiento Católico Integralmente Considerado." Paper presented at the symposium on "Mysteria, Initiation," Kraków, Poland, October 15.

———. 1995. "La Religiosidad del Pueblo Cubano" *Temas* 4 (October–November): 20–22.

de la Fuente, Alejandro. 2000. *A Nation for All: Race, Inequality, and Politics in Twentieth Century Cuba.* Chapel Hill: University of North Carolina Press.

de la Garza, Rodolfo O., Louis De Sipio, F. Chris García, John García, and Angelo Falcón. 1992. *Latino Voices: Mexican, Puerto Rican, and Cuban Perspectives on American Politics.* Boulder, CO: Westview Press.

de la Luz y Caballero, José. 1840. "Aforismos." In *Vida de Don José de la Luz y Caballero,* by José Ignacio Rodríguez. New York: N. Ponce de León, 1879. Facsimile edition, Miami, FL: Editorial Cubana, 2000.

de la Torre, Miguel A. 2003. *La Lucha for Cuba: Religion and Politics on the Streets of Miami.* Berkeley: University of California Press.

Degler, Carl N. 1971. *Neither Black Nor White: Slavery and Race Relations in Brazil and the United States.* Madison: University of Wisconsin Press.

del Castillo, Siro. 2005. "La Ley de Ajuste Cubano: Mitos y Realidades." Havana: Proyecto Demócrata Cubano. http://www.prodecu.org/documentos/leydeajuste.htm (accessed July 22, 2005).

del Cueto, Mario G. 1959. "El Aporte del Directorio Revolucionario en la Lucha contra la Tiranía." *Bohemia,* January 11, 56–59, 160–61.

del Pino, Rafael. 1991. *Proa a la Libertad.* Mexico, DF: Planeta.

References

Denzin, Norman K. 1978. *The Research Act: A Theoretical Introduction to Sociological Methods.* New York: McGraw-Hill.

Díaz, Ernesto. 1984. *La Campana del Alba.* Madrid: Editorial Playor.

Díaz, Jesús. 2000. "El Fin de Otra Ilusión." *Encuentro* 16–17: 106–21.

———. 1979. *De la Patria y el Exilio.* Havana: Unión de Escritores y Artistas de Cuba (UNEAC).

———, director. 1978. *55 Hermanos.* Documentary. Havana: El Instituto Cubano del Arte e Industrias Cinematográficos (ICAIC).

Díaz-Briquets, Sergio. 2006. "Cuban Global Emigration at the Turn of the 21st Century: Overall Estimate and Selected Characteristics of the Emigrant Population." In *Cuba in Transition,* vol. 16, 394–407. Conference proceedings of the 16th annual meeting of the Association for the Study of the Cuban Economy, Miami, Florida. Washington, DC: Association for the Study of the Cuban Economy and University of Miami, Cuban-American Studies.

———. 1983. "Demographic and Related Determinants of Recent Cuban Emigration." *International Migration Review* 17: 95–119.

Díaz-Briquets, Sergio, and Jorge Pérez-López. 2003. "The Role of the Cuban-American Community in the Cuban Transition." Miami, FL: Institute for Cuban and Cuban-American Studies, University of Miami, Cuba Transition Project.

Díaz de Villar, Delia. 1986. "Historia de la Devoción a la Virgen de la Caridad." Miami, FL: Ermita de la Caridad, 8 Septiembre.

Dixon, Rogelio. 1988. "Black Cubans in the United States: A Case of Conflicts between Race and Ethnicity." Paper presented at the annual meeting of the American Studies Association, Miami, Florida, October 27–30.

Domínguez, Jorge I. 2004a. "The Cuban Economy at the Start of the Twenty-first Century: An Introductory Analysis." In *The Cuban Economy at the Start of the Twenty-first Century,* ed. Jorge I. Domínguez, Omar Everleny Pérez Villanueva, and Lorena Barbería, 1–14. Cambridge, MA: David Rockefeller Center for Latin American Studies, Harvard University.

———. 2004b. "Cuba's Economic Transition: Successes, Deficiencies, and Challenges." In *The Cuban Economy at the Start of the Twenty-first Century,* ed. Jorge I. Domínguez, Omar Everleny Pérez Villanueva, and Lorena Barbería, 17–47. Cambridge, MA: David Rockefeller Center for Latin American Studies, Harvard University.

———. 1997. "Comienza una Transición hacia el Autoritarismo en Cuba." *Encuentro* 6–7 (Fall–Winter): 7–23.

———. 1992. "Cooperating with the Enemy? U.S. Immigration Policies toward Cuba." In *Western Hemisphere Immigration and U.S. Foreign Policy,* ed. Christopher Mitchell, 31–88. University Park: Pennsylvania State University Press.

———, series editor. 1985. "Crisis in Central America." PBS *Frontline,* aired April. A four-part report: "The Yankee Years," "Castro's Challenge," "Revolution in Nicaragua," and "Battle for El Salvador."

———. 1978a. *Cuba: Order and Revolution.* Cambridge, MA: Belknap Press, Harvard University Press.

———. 1978b. "Cuban Foreign Policy." *Foreign Affairs* 57 (Fall): 83–108.

References

Domínguez, Virginia R., and Yolanda Prieto. 1987. "Introduction to the Special Issue on Sex, Gender, and Revolution." *Cuban Studies* 17: 3–5.

Dufoix, Stéphane. 2000. "The Coriolanus Complex: War, Politics, and Aliens." Paper presented at the meetings of the Social Science History Association, Pittsburgh, October 26–29.

Dugowson, Maurice, and Pierre Kalfon, directors. 1997. *El Che*. Documentary. Paris: Cinétévé.

Eckstein, Susan. 2004. "On Deconstructing Immigrant Generations: Cohorts and the Cuban Emigré Experience." Working Paper no. 97, Center for Comparative International Studies, University of California at San Diego, May.

———. 1994. *Back from the Future: Cuba under Castro*. Princeton, NJ: Princeton University Press.

Eire, Carlos M. N. 2003. *Waiting for Snow in Havana: Confessions of a Cuban Boy*. New York: Free Press.

Elder, Glen H., Jr. 1979. "Historical Change in Life Patterns and Personality." In *Life- span Development and Behavior*, ed. P. B. Baltes and O. G. Grim, vol. 2, 117–59. New York: Academic Press.

Elder, Glen H., Jr., and Tamara K. Hareven. 1992. "Rising above Life's Disadvantage: From Great Depression to World War." In *Children in Time and Place: Developmental and Historical Insights*, ed. Glen H. Elder Jr., John Modell, and Ross D. Parke, 47–72. Cambridge: Cambridge University Press.

Encinosa, Enrique. 2004. *Unvanquished: Cuba's Resistance to Fidel Castro*. Los Angeles: Pureplay Press.

Encuentro Nacional Eclesial Cubano (ENEC). 1987. *Documento Final*. Rome: Tipografía Don Bosco.

Enzensberger, Hans Magnus. 1974. "Portrait of a Party: Prehistory, Structure, and Ideology of the PCC." In *Politics and Crime*, ed. Michael Roloff, 126–55. New York: Seabury.

Espina, Mayra. 2004. "Social Effects of Economic Adjustment: Equality, Inequality, and Trends toward Greater Complexity in Cuban Society." In *The Cuban Economy at the Start of the Twenty-first Century*, ed. Jorge I. Domínguez, Omar Everleny Pérez Villanueva, and Lorena Barbería, 209–43. Cambridge, MA: David Rockefeller Center for Latin American Studies, Harvard University.

Estévez, Abilio. 1998. "Autobiografía de un Desesperado." *Encuentro: Revista de la Cultural Cubana* 8–9 (Spring–Summer): 110–25.

Estrada, Joaquín. 2005. *Iglesia Católica y Nacionalidad Cubana: Encuentros Nacionales de Historia*. Miami, FL: Ediciones Universal.

Fagen, Richard R. 1969. *The Transformation of Political Culture in Cuba*. Stanford, CA: Stanford University Press.

Fagen, Richard R., Richard A. Brody, and Thomas J. O'Leary. 1968. *Cubans in Exile: Disaffection and the Revolution*. Stanford, CA: Stanford University Press.

Farber, Samuel. 2006. *The Origins of the Cuban Revolution Reconsidered*. Chapel Hill: University of North Carolina Press.

Fernández, Damián. 2000. *The Politics of Passion*. Miami: University Press of Florida.

References

Fernández, Gastón A. 1982. "The Freedom Flotilla: A Legitimacy Crisis of Cuban Socialism?" *Journal of Interamerican Studies and World Affairs* 24: 183–209.

Fernández, Manuel. 1984. *Religión y Revolución en Cuba: Veinticinco Años de Lucha Ateista*. Miami, FL: Saeta Ediciones.

Fernández-Robaina, Tomás. 1997. *Hablen Paleros y Santeros*. Havana: Instituto Cubano del Libro, Editorial de Ciencias Sociales.

———. 1994. *El Negro en Cuba 1902–1958*. Havana: Editorial de Ciencias Sociales.

Fernández-Yarzábal, Felo. 1976. "Discurso Pronunciado el 8 de Septiembre de 1976 en la Iglesia de la Inmaculada de Brownsville, Texas." *El Undoso* 62 (December): 6–7.

Ferreira, Rui. 2000. "Castro Amenaza con Otro Exodo." *El Nuevo Herald*, March 15, 1A.

Flexner, James Thomas. 1974. *Washington: The Indispensable Man*. Boston: Little, Brown.

Fox, Geoffrey E. 1971. "Cuban Workers in Exile." *Trans-Action* 8: 21–30.

Franco, José Luciano. 1978. *La Diáspora Africana en el Nuevo Mundo*. Havana: Osvaldo Sánchez.

Franqui, Carlos. 1983. *Family Portrait with Fidel*. London: Jonathan Cape. Translated by Alfred Macadam from *Retrato de Familia con Fidel* (Barcelona: Seix Barral, 1981).

———. 1980. *Diary of the Cuban Revolution*. New York: Viking. Translated from *Diario de la Revolución Cubana* (Paris: Editions du Seuil, 1976).

Free, Lloyd A. 1960. *Attitudes of the Cuban People toward the Castro Regime*. Princeton, NJ: Institute for International Social Research.

Fuentes, Carlos. 1981. "Farewell, Monroe Doctrine: Three Dates of Change in Latin America." *Harper's*, August, 29–35.

Fuentes, Norberto. 1999. *Dulces Guerreros Cubanos*. Barcelona: Editorial Seix Barral.

Galaor, Don. 1959. "Violeta Casal: La Voz Femenina de Radio Rebelde." *Bohemia*, January 18, 16–18, 142.

García, Maria Cristina. 1996. *Havana USA: Cuban Exiles and Cuban Americans in South Florida, 1959–1994*. Berkeley: University of California Press.

García-Pérez, Gladys Marel. 1998. *Insurrection and Revolution: Armed Struggle in Cuba, 1952–1959*. Boulder, CO: Lynne Rienner.

Gerth, Hans H., and C. Wright Mills. 1981. "Introduction: The Man and His Work." *From Max Weber: Essays in Sociology*. New York: Oxford University Press.

Godínez-Soler, Aleida. 2005. "Revelaciones sobre el 'sindicalismo independiente' en Cuba: Solidarias Invenciones." *Trabajadores*, August 2.

Goffman, Erving. 1963. *Stigma: Notes on the Management of Spoiled Identity*. Englewood Cliffs, NJ: Prentice-Hall.

Gold, Steven J. 1992. *Refugee Communities: A Comparative Field Study*. Newbury Park, CA: Sage.

Goldstone, Jack A. 2001. "Toward a Fourth Generation of Revolutionary Theory." *Annual Review of Political Science* 4: 139–87.

_____. 1982. "The Comparative and Historical Study of Revolutions." *Annual Review of Sociology* 8: 187–207.

Gómez, Andy S., and Eugenio M. Rothe. 2004. "Value Orientations and Opinions of Recently Arrived Cubans in Miami." Miami, FL: University of Miami, Institute for Cuban and Cuban-American Studies.

Gómez-Lubián Urioste, Agustín. 1978. *Versos*. Havana: Editorial Letras Cubanas.

González-Dalmau, Rafael. 1991. "Declaración de Profesores Universitarios." Havana. (Statement of Principles signed by 14 Faculty – 11 from the Instituto Superior Politécnico José Antonio Echeverría and 3 from the Instituto Superior Pedagógico Enrique José Varona. Statement signed by Rafael González-Dalmau; Pedro Rubio-Castillo; Miguel Morales Acosta; Georgina González-Corvo; Ramsés Pérez-Menéndez; María Martínez-Martínez; Carlos Delgado-Abad; Danilo Alonso-Santana; Nestor Castellanos-Martínez; Felix Bonne-Carcasés; Luis Brito-López; Rolando Martínez-García; José Ricardo Muñoz-Morgado; Rafael Sariol.)

González-Pando, Miguel, director. 1996. *Ni Patria Ni Amo: Voces del Exilio Cubano*. Documentary. Florida International University, the Cuban Living History Project, Miami.

_____. 1994. *"Calle Ocho": Cuban Exiles Look at Themselves*. Documentary. Florida International University, the Cuban Living History Project, Miami.

Granma. 1980a. Editorial: "La Posición de Cuba." April 7.

_____. 1980b. Editorial: "Nota de Granma." April 28.

Green, Eric. 2000. "Hispanics Vote 2–1 for Gore over Bush in U.S. Presidential Election." Washington Staff File Writer, November 14. http://www.usembassy.it/file 2000_11/alia/a011140h.htm (accessed October 10, 2005).

Grenier, Guillermo, and Hugh Gladwin. 2000, 1997. "The FIU/Cuba Polls." Florida International University. http://www.fiu.edu/orgs/ipor/cuba2000. Polls done in 1991, 1993, 1995, 1997, 2000, 2002, 2004.

Guerrero, Gustavo. 2002. "Ilusión y Desilusión." *Encuentro* 25: 10–18.

Guerrero, María Luisa. 1991. *Elena Mederos: Una Mujer con Perfil para la Historia*. Miami, FL: Ediciones Universal; Washington, DC: Of Human Rights.

Guevara, Ernesto Che. 1970. "El Hombre Nuevo." In *Los Dispositivos en la Flor – Cuba: Literatura desde la Revolución*, ed. Edmundo Desnoes, 525–32. Hanover, NH: Ediciones del Norte, 1981.

_____. 1968. *El Diario del Che en Bolivia: Noviembre 7, 1966–Octubre 7, 1967*. Havana: Instituto del Libro.

Guillén, Nicolás. 2002. *Poemas*. Ed. Efraín Huerta. Ciudad Universitaria: Universidad Nacional Autónoma de México.

_____. 1986. *Summa Poética*. Ed. Luis Iñigo Madrigal. Madrid: Ediciones Cátedra.

_____. 1929. "El Camino de Harlem." *Diario de la Marina*, April 21.

Gutiérrez-Aléa, Tomás, and Juan Carlos Tabío, directors. 1994. "Fresa y Chocolate." Cuba: Instituto Cubano del Arte e Industria Cinematográficos; México: Instituto Mejicano de Cinematografía (IMCINE); Spain: TeleMadrid. (1995 English version "Strawberry and Chocolate," distributed by Miramax Films.)

References

Hadjiyanni, Tasoulla. 2002. *The Making of a Refugee: Children Adopting Refugee Identity in Cyprus*. Westport, CT: Praeger.

Ham, Adolfo. 1977. "Evangelism in the Socialist Society of Cuba." *International Review of Mission* 66 (July): 279–84.

Handlin, Oscar. 1973 [1951]. *The Uprooted: The Epic Story of the Great Migration that Made the American People*. Boston: Little, Brown.

Hansing, Katrin, and Sarah J. Mahler. 2003. "God Knows No Borders: Transnational Religious Ties Linking Miami and Cuba." *Religion, Culture, and Society: The Case of Cuba*, ed. Margaret E. Crahan, 123–29. Conference Report. Washington, DC: Woodrow Wilson International Center for Scholars.

Havel, Vaclav. 1986. "Two Notes on Charter 77." In Vaclav Havel, *Open Letters: Selected Writings, 1965–1990*, 323–27. Ed. Paul Wilson. New York: Vintage.

——. 1978. "The Power of the Powerless." In Vaclav Havel, *Open Letters: Selected Writings, 1965–1990*, 125–214. Ed. Paul Wilson. New York: Vintage.

Heath, Jim F. 1975. *Decade of Disillusionment: The Kennedy-Johnson Years*. Bloomington: Indiana University Press.

Henken, Ted. 2005. "*Balseros, Boteros*, and *El Bombo*: Post-1994 Cuban Immigration to the United States and the Persistence of Special Treatment." *Latino Studies Journal* 3 (November): 393–416.

Hernández, Jose M. 1999. *The ACU at the Threshold of the Third Millennium*. Miami, FL: Agrupación Católica Universitaria.

——. 1981. *Agrupación Católica Universitaria: Los Primeros Cincuenta Años*. Miami, FL: Agrupación Católica Universitaria.

Higham, John. 1978. *Strangers in the Land: Patterns of American Nativism, 1860–1925*. New York: Atheneum.

Hirschman, Albert O. 1993. "Exit, Voice, and the Fate of the German Democratic Republic: An Essay in Conceptual History." *World Politics* 45: 173–202.

——. 1986. "Exit and Voice: An Expanding Sphere of Influence." In Albert O. Hirschman, *Rival Views of Market Society and Other Recent Essays*, 77–101. New York: Viking.

——. 1970. *Exit, Voice, and Loyalty: Responses to Decline in Firms, Organizations, and States*. Cambridge, MA: Harvard University Press.

Hollinger, David. 1995. *Postethnic America*. New York: Basic Books.

Horowitz, Irving Louis. 2004. "Transition Scenarios for a Post-Castro Cuba: Military Outcomes or Civil Prospects?" *Human Rights Review* (October–December): 27–34.

——. 2002. "One Hundred Years of Ambiguity: U.S.-Cuba Relations in the 20th Century." *National Interest* 67 (Spring): 58–64.

——, ed. 1995. *Cuban Communism*. New Brunswick, NJ: Transaction.

Human Rights Watch/Americas. 1994. "Dangerous Dialogue Revisited: Threats to Freedom of Expression Continue in Miami's Cuban Exile Community." *Human Rights Watch Free Expression Project* 6 (November): 1–9.

Inkeles, Alex, and Raymond Bauer. 1959. *The Soviet Citizen: Daily Life in a Totalitarian Society*. Cambridge, MA: Harvard University Press.

Instituto de la Memoria Histórica Cubana. 2000. "La Quema del Encanto." *Memoria* 1 (August): 1, 6–7.

Instituto Nacional de Investigaciones. 1952. "El 'Survey' Nacional de *Carteles* sobre los Candidatos Presidenciales." *Carteles* 33, no. 4 (January 27): 28–32; no. 5 (February 3): 28–32; no. 6 (February 10): 28–34.

Johnson, Haynes. 1964. *The Bay of Pigs*. New York: Norton.

Johnson, Jeffrey C. 1990. *Selecting Ethnographic Informants*. Beverly Hills, CA: Sage.

Johnson, Lyndon Baines. 1965. "Text of President's Speech on Immigration." *New York Times*, October 4.

Johnson, Tim. 2002. "U.S. Rejects Carter's Plea to End Embargo on Cuba." *Miami Herald*, May 2.

Jované de Zayas, Elvira. 1968. "Letter to the Reverend Agustin Román," August 29. Miami, FL. In *Ermita de la Caridad*, September 8, 1986.

Junta Revolucionaria Cubana. 1964. "Ideario de la Junta Revolucionaria Cubana." San Juan, PR. Programa Político.

Kaplan, Sender M., Raúl Moncarz, and Julio Steinberg. 1990. "Jewish Emigrants to Cuba: 1898–1960." *International Migration* 28: 295–310.

Kennedy, Edward M. 1981. "Refugee Act of 1980." *International Migration Review* 15: 141–56.

———. 1966. "The Immigration Act of 1954." *Annals of the American Academy of Political and Social Sciences* 367: 137–49.

Kennedy, John F. 1964. *A Nation of Immigrants*. New York: Harper & Row.

Kennedy, Paul P. 1961. "U.S. Helps Train an Anti-Castro Force at Secret Guatemalan Air-Ground Base." *New York Times*, January 10.

Kennedy, Robert F. 1971. *Thirteen Days: Memoir of the Cuban Missile Crisis*. New York: W. W. Norton.

Kirk, Jerome, and Marc L. Miller. 1987. *Reliability and Validity in Qualitative Research*. Beverly Hills, CA: Sage.

Kirk, John. 1989. *Between God and the Party: Religion and Politics in Revolutionary Cuba*. Tampa: University of South Florida Press.

Kornbluh, Peter, ed. 1998. *Bay of Pigs Declassified: The Secret CIA Report on the Invasion of Cuba*. New York: New Press.

Kunz, E. F. 1981. "Exile and Resettlement: Refugee Theory." *International Migration Review* 15: 42–51.

———. 1973. "The Refugee in Flight: Kinetic Models and Forms of Displacement." *International Migration Review* 7: 125–46.

Kunzle, David. 1997. *Che Guevara: Icon, Myth, and Message*. Los Angeles: UCLA Fowler Museum of Cultural History and Center for the Study of Political Graphics.

Laguerre, Michel S. 1998. *Diasporic Citizenship: Haitian Americans in Transnational America*. New York: St. Martin's Press.

Latell, Brian. 2003. "The Cuban Military and Transition Dynamics." Miami, FL: Institute for Cuban and Cuban-American Studies, University of Miami, Cuba Transition Project.

References

Laughlin, Meg. 1994. "A Letter from Samara." *Miami Herald, Tropic* magazine, November 6.

Lee, Everett S. 1966. "A Theory of Migration." *Demography* 3: 47–57.

LeoGrande, William M. 2002. "The Cuban Communist Party and Electoral Politics: Adaptation, Succession, and Transition." Miami, FL: Institute for Cuban and Cuban-American Studies, University of Miami, Cuba Transition Project.

———. 1998. "From Havana to Miami: U.S. Cuba Policy as a Two-Level Game." *Journal of Interamerican Studies and World Affairs* 40: 67–87.

———. 1980. "Cuba's Policy in Africa, 1959–1980." Berkeley: University of California, Institute of International Studies, Policy Papers in International Affairs.

Levine, Robert M. 1993. *Tropical Diaspora: The Jewish Experience in Cuba*. Gainesville: University of Florida Press.

"Leyes Cubanas contra el Homosexualismo." 1984. *Mariel: Revista de Literatura y Arte* 2 (Spring): 8.

Lezama-Lima, José. 1941. "Noche Insular: Jardines Invisibles." *Enemigo Rumor*. In *José Lezama Lima, Poesía*, ed. Emilio de Armas. Madrid: Ediciones Cátedra, 1992.

Lizza, Ryan. 2004. "Campaign Journal: Havana John (Bush's Support among Cuban-Americans)." *New Republic* 231 (July 26):1–2.

Lofland, John, David Snow, and Lyn H. Lofland. 2006. *Analyzing Social Settings: A Guide to Qualitative Observation and Analysis*. Belmont, CA: Wadsworth.

López-Blanch, Heriberto. 1999. "Religiosos Claman por Elián." *Juventud Rebelde*, December 25.

López-Levy, Arturo. 2003. "The Jewish Community in Cuba in the 1990s." In *Religion, Culture, and Society: The Case of Cuba*, ed. Margaret E. Crahan, 79–89. Conference Report. Washington, DC: Woodrow Wilson International Center for Scholars.

Loynaz, Dulce María. 1958. *Un Verano en Tenerife*. In *Dulce María Loynaz*, ed. Centro de las Letras Españolas, 109–18. Madrid: Ministerio de Cultura, Dirección General del Libro y Bibliotecas, 1993.

Lynch, Grayston L. 1998. *Decision for Disaster: Betrayal at the Bay of Pigs*. Washington, DC: Brassey's.

Mañach, Jorge. 1959. "El Drama de Cuba." *Bohemia*, January 11, 6–9, 163, 168, 172, 174.

Mannheim, Karl. 1952. *Essays in the Sociology of Knowledge*. New York: Oxford University Press.

Marill, Alicia C. 2000. "Coming Full Circle: Black Elk Speaks to a Cuban Refugee." In *The Healing Circle: Essays in Cross-Cultural Mission*, ed. Stephen Bevans, Eleanor Doidge, and Robert Schreiter, 37–47. Chicago: Chicago Center for Global Ministries.

Marrero, Leví. 1976. "Documentos: Juan Moreno Relata como Halló a la Virgen de la Caridad" and "La Virgen y el Esclavo" [1687]. In *Cuba: Economía y Sociedad*, El Siglo XVII, vol. 5. Madrid: Editorial Playor.

Martí, José. 1891. "Nuestra América." *Revista Ilustrada de Nueva York*, January 1.

Martínez, Luis R. 1998. "No Hay Música que Haga Olvidar al Exilio." *El Nuevo Herald*, September 2.

Martínez-Fernández, Luis. 2003a. "Population and Demographic Indicators." In *Encyclopedia of Cuba: People, History, Culture*, ed. Luis Martínez-Fernández, D. H. Figueredo, Louis A. Pérez Jr., and Luis González, vol. 1, 298–99. Westport, CT: Greenwood Press.

———. 2003b. "Racial Composition." In *Encyclopedia of Cuba: People, History, Culture*, ed. Luis Martínez-Fernández, D. H. Figueredo, Louis A. Pérez Jr., and Luis González, vol. 1, 300–1. Westport, CT: Greenwood Press.

Martín-Villaverde, Alberto. 1959. "Congreso en Defensa de la Caridad." In *La Voz de la Iglesia en Cuba: 100 Documentos Episcopales*, ed. Conferencia de Obispos Católicos de Cuba, 91–97. Mexico, DF: Obra Nacional de la Buena Prensa, 1995.

Marx, Gary. 2005. "U.S. Spending $23 Million This Year to Support Anti-Castro Movement inside Cuba." *Chicago Tribune*, March 30.

Massey, Douglas S. 1999. "Why Does Immigration Occur? A Theoretical Synthesis." In *The Handbook of International Migration: The American Experience*, ed. Charles Hirschman, Philip Kasinitz, and Josh DeWind, 34–52. New York: Russell Sage Foundation.

Massey, Douglas S., Rafael Alarcón, Jorge Durand, and Humberto González. 1987. *Return to Aztlán: The Social Process of International Migration from Western Mexico.* Berkeley: University of California Press.

Masud-Piloto, Felix. 1996. *From Welcome Exiles to Illegal Immigrants: Cuban Migrants to the U.S., 1959–1995.* Lanham, MD: Rowman & Littlefield.

Matos, Huber. 2002. *Como Llegó la Noche.* Barcelona: Tusquets Editores.

Matthews, Herbert L. 1961. *The Cuban Story.* New York: George Braziller.

McAdam, Doug. 1988. *Freedom Summer.* New York: Oxford University Press.

McAdam, Doug, Sydney Tarrow, and Charles Tilly. 2001. *Dynamics of Contention.* Cambridge: Cambridge University Press.

"Medio Millón de Campesinos Respaldan la Reforma Agraria." 1959. *Información*, July 28.

Menocal, Ondina. 2003. "La Iglesia Intramuros: Realidad y Retos." Paper presented at the meeting of the Unión de Cubanos en el Exilio (UCE), Miami, Florida, August 6.

Merleau-Ponty, Maurice. 1973 [1955]. *Adventures of the Dialectic.* Translated by Joseph Bien. Evanston, IL: Northwestern University Press.

Mesa-Lago, Carmelo. 2004. "Economic and Ideological Cycles in Cuba: Policy and Performance, 1959–2002." In *The Cuban Economy*, ed. Archibald R. M. Ritter, 25–41. Pittsburgh: University of Pittsburgh Press.

———. 2000. *Market, Socialist, and Mixed Economies: Comparative Policy and Performance in Chile, Cuba, and Costa Rica.* Baltimore: Johns Hopkins University Press.

———. 1981. *The Economy of Socialist Cuba: A Two-Decade Appraisal.* Albuquerque: University of New Mexico Press.

———. 1978. *Cuba in the 1970s: Pragmatism and Institutionalization.* Albuquerque: University of New Mexico Press.

"Microfaction Unmasked." 1968. *Granma*, February 4 and 11.

Mills, C. Wright. 1961. *The Sociological Imagination.* New York: Grove Press.

References

Mollica, Richard F., G. Wyshak, and J. Lavelle. 1987. "The Psychosocial Impact of War Trauma and Torture on Southeast Asian Refugees." *American Journal of Psychiatry* 144: 1567–72.

Monreal, Pedro. 2004. "Globalization and the Dilemmas of Cuba's Economic Trajectories." In *The Cuban Economy at the Start of the Twenty-first Century*, ed. Jorge I. Domínguez, Omar Everleny Pérez Villanueva, and Lorena Barbería, 91–118. Cambridge, MA: David Rockefeller Center for Latin American Studies, Harvard University.

Montaner, Carlos Alberto. 2002. "Cuba: A Century of Painful Apprenticeship." Paper presented at the University of Miami, Koubek Center, Institute for Cuban and Cuban-American Studies, May 9.

———. 2001. *Viaje al Corazón de Cuba*. Barcelona: Plaza & Janés Editores, S.A.

———. 1998. "Adíos, Miguel, Adíos." *El Nuevo Herald*, April 7.

Montgomery, Paul. 1981. "For Cuban Refugees, Promise of U.S. Fades." *New York Times*, April 19.

Moore, Carlos. 1988. *Castro, the Blacks, and Africa*. Los Angeles: Center for Afro-American Studies, University of California.

Morán-Arce, Lucas. 1980. *La Revolución Cubana (1953–1959): Una Versión Rebelde*. Ponce, PR: Imprenta Universitaria, Universidad Católica.

Morawska, Ewa. 2001. "Structuring Migration: The Case of Polish Income-Seeking Travelers to the West." *Theory and Society* 30: 47–80.

Morello, Carol. 1998. "A Family Divided: Reunion, Reconciliation as Pope Arrives Today." *USA Today*, January 21.

Moreno-Fraginals, Manolo R. 1978. *El Ingenio*. 3 vols. Havana: Editorial de Ciencias Sociales.

Muller, Thomas, and Thomas J. Espenshade. 1985. *The Fourth Wave: California's Newest Immigrants*. Washington, DC: Urban Institute.

Myrdal, Gunnar. 1975. "How Scientific Are the Social Sciences?" In *Against the Stream*, 133–57. New York: Vintage.

Nagel, Joane. 2003. *Race, Ethnicity, and Sexuality: Intimate Intersections, Forbidden Frontiers*. New York: Oxford University Press.

Novo, Mireya L. 1994. "Crónicas de la Historia en Vivo." *¡Exito!* November 9.

Oppenheimer, Andrés. 2003. "Best Anti-Castro Tool Is Exile Moderation." *Miami Herald*, February 16.

———. 1993. *Castro's Final Hour*. New York: Simon & Schuster.

Orozco, Manuel. 2000. "Remittances and Markets: New Players and Practices." Washington, DC: Inter-American Dialogue and the Tomás Rivera Policy Institute.

Orsi, Robert A. 1985. *The Madonna of 115th Street: Faith and Community in Italian Harlem, 1880–1950*. New Haven: Yale University Press.

Ortega, Roberto. 2007. Panelist in the discussion on "Transition and the Cuban Military," University of Miami, Institute for Cuban and Cuban-American Studies, February 27. Other panelists: Hal Klepak and Brian Latell. Moderator: Jaime Suchlicki.

Otazo, Julio. 1976. "Una Opinión." *Diario de las Américas*, December 1.

Padilla, Heberto. 1998 [1968]. *Fuera del Juego*. Miami, FL: Ediciones Universal.

_____. 1990. *Self-Portrait of the Other: A Memoir*. New York: Farrar, Straus, Giroux.

Pardo, Angel. 1992. *Cuba: Memorias de un Prisionero Político 1964–1988*. Miami, FL: Ahora Printing.

_____. 1988. "¿Derechos Humanos? Violaciones Jurídicas de los Derechos Humanos en Cuba Según la Declaración Universal de los Derechos Humanos." Reprint, Miami, FL: Casa del Preso, 1994.

Patterson, Enrique. 1999. "Reflexiones sobre Tres Cubanos." *El Nuevo Herald*, November 17.

Patton, Michael Quinn. 1990. *Qualitative Evaluation and Research Methods*. Newbury Park, CA: Sage.

Paull, Laura, ed. 1995. *"Havana Nagila": The Jews in Cuba*. Documentary. Schnitzki & Stone, San Francisco.

Payá-Sardiñas, Osvaldo. 2001. "Proyecto Varela." Havana: Movimiento Cristiano Liberación.

Pedraza, Silvia. 2006. "Assimilation or Transnationalism? Conceptual Models of the Immigrant Experience." In *The Cultural Psychology of Immigrants*, ed. Ram Mahalingam, 33–54. Mahwah, NJ: Lawrence Erlbaum.

_____. 2002. "A Sociology for Our Times: Alvin Gouldner's Message." *Sociological Quarterly* 43 (Winter): 73–80.

_____. 2000. "La Perspectiva desde la Isla." *El Nuevo Herald*, March 27.

_____. 1996a. "Cuba's Refugees: Manifold Migrations." *Origins and Destinies: Immigration, Race, and Ethnicity in America*, ed. Silvia Pedraza and Rubén G. Rumbaut, 263–84. Belmont, CA: Wadsworth.

_____. 1996b. "American Paradox." In *Origins and Destinies: Immigration, Race, and Ethnicity in America*, ed. Silvia Pedraza and Rubén G. Rumbaut, 479–91. Belmont, CA: Wadsworth.

_____. 1991. "Women and Migration: The Social Consequences of Gender." *Annual Review of Sociology* 17: 303–25.

Pedraza-Bailey, Silvia. 1990. "Immigration Research: A Conceptual Map." *Social Science History* 14: 44–67.

_____. 1985. *Political and Economic Migrants in America: Cubans and Mexicans*. Austin: University of Texas Press.

_____. 1982. "Reflections on a Revolution: Cuba Revisited." *Washington University Magazine* 52 (Fall):13–16.

Pérez, Lisandro. 1999. "The End of Exile: A New Era in U.S. Immigration Policy toward Cuba." In *Free Markets, Open Societies, Closed Borders? Trends in International Migration and Immigration Policy in the Americas*, ed. Max Castro, 197–211. Coral Gables: University of Miami North-South Center.

_____. 1992. "Cuban Miami." In, *Miami Now! Immigration, Ethnicity, and Social Change*, ed. Guillermo J. Grenier and Alex Stepich III, 83–108. Gainesville, FL: University Press of Florida.

Pérez, Louis A., Jr. 1995. *Cuba: Between Reform and Revolution*. New York: Oxford University Press.

Pérez-Díaz, Víctor M. 1993. *The Return of Civil Society: The Emergence of a Democratic Spain*. Cambridge, MA: Harvard University Press.

References

Pérez-Firmat, Gustavo. 1994. *Life on the Hyphen: The Cuban-American Way*. Austin: University of Texas Press.

Pérez-López, Daniel J. 2006. "Cubans in the Island and in the U.S. Diaspora: Selected Demographic and Social Comparisons." In *Cuba in Transition*, vol. 16, 371–80. Conference proceedings of the 16th annual meeting of the Association for the Study of the Cuban Economy, Miami, Florida. Washington, DC: Association for the Study of the Cuban Economy and University of Miami, Cuban-American Studies.

Pérez-López, Jorge F. 1991. *The Economics of Cuban Sugar*. Pittsburgh: University of Pittsburgh Press.

Pérez-Serantes, Enrique, Monsignor. 1960a. "Por Dios y por Cuba." May. In *La Voz de la Iglesia en Cuba: 100 Documentos Episcopales*, ed. Conferencia de Obispos Católicos de Cuba, 107–14. Mexico, DF: Obra Nacional de la Buena Prensa, 1995.

——. 1960b. "Roma o Moscú. Fiesta de Cristo Rey." In *La Voz de la Iglesia en Cuba: 100 Documentos Episcopales*, ed. Conferencia de Obispos Católicos de Cuba, 135–41. Mexico, DF: Obra Nacional de la Buena Prensa, 1995.

——. 1959. "El Congreso Católico Nacional." November. In *La Voz de la Iglesia en Cuba: 100 Documentos Episcopales*, ed. Conferencia de Obispos Católicos de Cuba, 88–90. Mexico, DF: Obra Nacional de la Buena Prensa.

Pérez-Stable, Marifeli. 1999. *The Cuban Revolution: Origins, Course, and Legacy*. New York: Oxford University Press.

Péristiany, John G. 1966. *Honour and Shame: The Values of Mediterranean Society*. Chicago: University of Chicago Press.

Pfaff, Steven. 2006. *Exit-Voice Dynamics and the Collapse of East Germany: The Crisis of Leninism and the Revolution of 1989*. Durham: Duke University Press.

Política Cultural de la Revolución Cubana: Documentos. 1977. Havana: Editorial de Ciencias Sociales.

Pollitt, Brian H. 2004. "Crisis and Reform in Cuba's Sugar Economy." In *The Cuban Economy*, ed. Archibald R. M. Ritter, 69–105. Pittsburgh: University of Pittsburgh Press.

Portell-Vilá, Herminio. 1986. *Nueva Historia de la República de Cuba*. Miami, FL: La Moderna Poesía.

——. 1975. "Carlos Prío Socarrás." In *La Enciclopedia de Cuba: Gobiernos Republicanos* 14: 348–443. Madrid: Editorial Playor.

Portes, Alejandro. 1999. "Immigration Theory for a New Century: Some Problems and Opportunities." In *The Handbook of International Migration: The American Experience*, ed. Charles Hirschman, Philip Kasinitz, and Josh DeWind, 21–33. New York: Russell Sage Foundation.

Portes, Alejandro, and Robert L. Bach. 1985. *Latin Journey: Cuban and Mexican Immigrants in the United States*. Berkeley: University of California Press.

Portes, Alejandro, Juan M. Clark, and Robert L. Bach. 1977. "The New Wave: A Statistical Profile of Recent Cuban Exiles to the United States." *Cuban Studies* 7: 1–32.

Portes, Alejandro, and Rubén G. Rumbaut. 1991. *Immigrant America*. Berkeley: University of California Press.

Power, Samantha. 2002. *"A Problem from Hell": America and the Age of Genocide*. New York: Basic.

Poyo, Gerald E. 2002. *"Vida Nueva*: Cuban Catholics, Reform, and Revolution, 1930s–1950s." St. Mary's University, Department of History. Unpublished manuscript.

Prats-Páez, Rolando. 1993a. "Lift the U.S. Embargo – and Force Castro's Bloody Hand." *Miami Herald*, January 29.

———. 1993b. "U.S. Embargo Helps Castro, Hurts Democracy." *New York Times*, May 10.

Prieto, Yolanda. 2001. "The Catholic Church and the Cuban Diaspora." Georgetown University Cuba Occasional Paper Series, December. Caribbean Project, Center for Latin American Studies.

Quigley, Thomas E. 2003. "The Catholic Church and Cuba's International Ties." In *Religion, Culture, and Society: The Case of Cuba*, ed. Margaret E. Crahan, 93–102. Conference Report. Washington, DC: Woodrow Wilson International Center for Scholars.

Radelat, Ana. 2000. "Deal Struck to Ease Embargo: House Leaders Approve Cuba Food Sales but Prohibit Financing by U.S." *Miami Herald*, June 28.

Radu, Michael. 2003. "The Cuban Transition: Lessons from the Romanian Experience." Miami, FL: Institute for Cuban and Cuban-American Studies, University of Miami, Cuba Transition Project.

Ramos, Marcos A. 1989. *Protestantism and Revolution in Cuba*. Coral Gables, FL: University of Miami North-South Center.

Rasco, José Ignacio. 1962. *Cuba 1959: Artículos de Combate*. Buenos Aires: Ediciones Diagrama.

———. 1961. *Movimiento Democrático Cristiano*. Programa Político.

Ratner, Steven. 2005. "The War Crimes Tribunals for Yugoslavia: Are Trials after Atrocities Effective?" Lecture presented at the Institute for the Humanities, University of Michigan, October 10.

Reno, Janet, Attorney General. 1994. "Press Briefing." August 19. http://www.clintonlibrary.gov.

Reyes-Canto, Omar. 1997. "La Música como Alma o Arma." *El Nuevo Herald*, March 31.

Rieff, David. 1993. *The Exile: Cuba in the Heart of Miami*. New York: Simon & Schuster.

Ripoll, Carlos. 1981. "The Cuban Scene: Censors and Dissenters." *Partisan Review* 48: 574–87.

Risech, Flavio. 1994. "Political and Cultural Cross-Dressing: Negotiating a Second Generation Cuban-American Identity." *Michigan Quarterly* 33: 526–40.

Ritter, Archibald R. M. 2004. *The Cuban Economy*. Pittsburgh: University of Pittsburgh Press.

Rivas-Porta, Guillermo. 1994. "El Pueblo Cubano: Protagonista, Víctima, y Espectador." *Desafíos* 1 (August–September): 4–5.

References

Rivero, Raúl. 1998. "1998. Cuba Libre y Ginebra Libre." *El Nuevo Herald*, April 26.

Rivero-Caro, Adolfo. 2007. "El Obispo del Pueblo." *El Nuevo Herald*, February 23.

Robaína, Frank. 2000. "Elián es de Aquí y de Allá." *Ideal* 294: 53.

Roberts, Churchill. 1999. "Measuring Public Opinion: Methodology." In *Cuba in Transition*, vol. 9, 245–48. Conference proceedings of the 9th annual meeting of the Association for the Study of the Cuban Economy, Miami, Florida. Washington, DC: Association for the Study of the Cuban Economy.

Roca, Sergio. 1981. "Cuban Economic Policy in the 1970s: The Trodden Paths." In *Cuban Communism*, ed. Irving Louis Horowitz, 83–118. New Brunswick, NJ: Transaction.

Rodríguez, Felix. 1989. *Shadow of a Warrior*. New York: Simon & Schuster.

Rodríguez, José Conrado. 1996. "Adíos Hermanos." *El Nuevo Herald*, October 4.

———. 1995. "Cuando la Patria Peligra." *El Nuevo Herald*, March 25.

Rodríguez-Chavez, Ernesto. 1996. *Emigración Cubana Actual*. Havana: Editorial de Ciencias Sociales.

———. 1993. "Tendencias Actuales del Flujo Migratorio Cubano." *Cuadernos de Nuestra América* 10: 114–37.

Rojas, Rafael. 2002. "Jesús Díaz: el Intelectual Redimido." *Revista de Historia Internacional* 2 (Fall): 166–76.

Ros, Enrique. 2005. *La Revolución de 1933*. Miami, FL: Ediciones Universal.

———. 2004. *La UMAP: El Gulag Castrista*. Miami, FL: Ediciones Universal.

———. 1995. *De Girón a la Crisis de los Cohetes: La Segunda Derrota*. Miami, FL: Ediciones Universal.

———. 1994. *Girón: La Verdadera Historia*. Miami, FL: Ediciones Universal.

Rose, Peter. 1993. "Tempest-Tost: Exile, Ethnicity, and the Politics of Rescue." *Sociological Forum* 8: 5–24.

———. 1981. "Some Thoughts about Refugees and the Descendants of Theseus." *International Migration Review* 15: 8–15.

Rousseau, Denis, and Corinne Cumerlato. 2001. *La Isla del Doctor Castro: la Transición Secuestrada*. Barcelona: Editorial Planeta, S.A. Translated by Catalina Ginard. Originally *L'Ile du Docteur Castro, ou La Transition Confisquée* (Paris: Stock, 2000).

Rumbaut, Rubén G. 1991. "The Agony of Exile: A Study of the Migration and Adaptation of Indochinese Refugee Adults and Children." In *Refugee Children: Theory, Research, and Practice*, ed. Frederick L. Ahearn Jr. and Jean L. Athey, 53–91. Baltimore: Johns Hopkins University Press.

Salazar, Manuel. 1959. "El Pueblo Juzgó a los Barbaros 'Tigres' de Masferrer y los Llevó ante el Paredón." *Bohemia*, February 1, 66–68.

Sandoval, Mercedes Cros. 1986. *Mariel and Cuban National Identity*. Miami, FL: Editorial SIBI.

———. 1975. *La Religión Afro-Cubana*. Madrid: Editorial Playor.

Schreiber, Anna P. 1973. "Economic Coercion as an Instrument of Foreign Policy: U.S. Economic Measures against Cuba and the Dominican Republic." *World Politics* 25: 387–413.

Scott, James C. 1990. *Domination and the Arts of Resistance: Hidden Transcripts*. New Haven: Yale University Press.

Semple, Robert B., Jr. 1965. "U.S. to Admit Cubans Castro Frees; Johnson Signs New Immigration Bill." *New York Times*, October 4, 1A.

Shayne, Julie D. 2004. *The Revolution Question: Feminisms in El Salvador, Chile, and Cuba*. New Brunswick, NJ: Rutgers University Press.

"The Shootdown of Brothers to the Rescue Aircraft: Truth and Justice for U.S. Citizens Murdered by Fidel Castro." 2006. http://www.hermanos.org.

Shryock, Andrew. 2004. "In the Double Remoteness of Arab Detroit: Reflections on Ethnography, Culture Work, and the Intimate Disciplines of Americanization." In *Off Stage/On Display: Intimacy and Ethnography in the Age of Public Culture*, 279–314. Stanford, CA: Stanford University Press.

Simmel, Georg. 1971 [1908]. "The Stranger." In *Georg Simmel: On Individuality and Social Forms*, ed. Donald N. Levine, 143–49. Chicago: University of Chicago Press.

Skocpol, Theda. 1979. *States and Social Revolutions*. Cambridge: Cambridge University Press.

Smith, Louis M., and Alfred Padula. 1996. *Sex and Revolution: Women in Socialist Cuba*. New York: Oxford University Press.

Smyser, W. R. 1985. "Refugees: A Never-Ending Story." *Foreign Affairs* 64: 154–68.

Sorensen, Theodore C. 1965. *Kennedy*. New York: Harper & Row.

Soto, Francisco. 1990. *Conversación con Reinaldo Arenas*. Madrid: Betania.

Stein, Barry N. 1981. "The Refugee Experience: Defining the Parameters of a Field of Study." *International Migration Review* 15: 320–30.

Steinback, Robert L. 2005. "Memorial Recalls Castro's Victims." *Miami Herald*, February 20.

Strauss, Anselm L. 1987. *Qualitative Analysis for Social Scientists*. Cambridge: Cambridge University Press.

Suárez-Cobián, Rolando. 2002. "El Desarrollo Institucional de la Iglesia Cubana en las Comunidades." Paper presented at the symposium on "Cuban Catholicism: Island and Diaspora," University of Notre Dame, Kellog Institute for International Studies and Institute for Latino Studies, South Bend, Indiana, June 20–21.

Szulc, Tad. 1961. "Anti-Castro Units Trained to Fight at Florida Bases." *New York Times*, April 7.

Tamargo, Agustín. 1997. "El Cardenal Prestado." *El Nuevo Herald*, June 22.

Tamayo, Juan O. 1999. "Four Cuban Dissidents Convicted." *Miami Herald*, March 16.

Tamayo-León, René. 2003. "Allí Estabamos Nosotros." *Juventud Rebelde*, April 13.

Telleda, Miguel L. 1995. *Alpha 66 y su Histórica Tarea*. Miami, FL: Ediciones Universal.

Thomas, Hugh. 1971. *Cuba or the Pursuit of Freedom*. London: Eyre & Spottiswoode.

Thomas, John F. 1967. "Cuban Refugees in the United States." *International Migration Review* 2: 46–57.

Thompson, E. P. 1966. *The Making of the English Working Class*. New York: Vintage.

Tilly, Charles. 1981. *As Sociology Meets History*. New York: Academic Press.

References

———. 1978. *From Mobilization to Revolution*. Reading, MA: Addison-Wesley.

Time. 1994. "Ready to Talk Now? Castro Hopes His Flood of Refugees Will Force the U.S. to Make a Deal." Magazine cover, September 5.

Tocqueville, Alexis de. 1955. *The Old Regime and the French Revolution*. Translated by Stuart Gilbert. New York: Doubleday.

Torreira, Ramón, and José Buajasán. 2000. *Operación Peter Pan: Un Caso de Guerra Psicológica contra Cuba*. Havana: Editora Política.

Torres, Agustín. 1980. "Files Remain Open in Slayings of Negrin and Judge Prizzia." *Jersey Journal*, December 12.

Torres, María de los Angeles. 2003. *The Lost Apple: Operation Pedro Pan, Cuban Children in the U.S., and the Promise of a Better Future*. Boston: Beacon Press.

Triay, Víctor Andrés. 1998. *Fleeing Castro: Operation Pedro Pan and the Cuban Children's Program*. Gainesville: University Press of Florida.

Tweed, Thomas A. 1997. *Our Lady of the Exile: Diasporic Religion at a Cuban Catholic Shrine in Miami*. New York: Oxford University Press.

United Nations. 1948. "Universal Declaration of Human Rights." Adopted and proclaimed on December 10. http://www.un.org/Overview/rights.html.

U.S. Bureau of the Census. 2003. 2000 Public Use Microdata Samples (5 percent). Washington, DC. Distributor: Public Data Queries, Inc., Ann Arbor, MI.

———. 2002. Census 2000 Summary File 4 (SF 4), American Factfinder. "Profile of Selected Social Characteristics" and "Profile of Selected Economic Characteristics."

———. 2000–5. American Community Survey (ACS) Public Use Microdata Sample. Washington, DC. Producer: Integrated Public Use Microdata Series: Version 3.0, by Steven Ruggles, Matthew Sobek, Trent Alexander, Catherine A. Fitch, Ronald Goeken, Patricia Kelly Hall, Miriam King, and Chad Ronnander. Minneapolis: Minnesota Population Center. Distributor: Public Data Queries, Inc., Ann Arbor, MI.

———. 1993. 1990 Public Use Microdata Samples (5 percent). Washington, DC. Distributor: Public Data Queries, Inc., Ann Arbor, MI.

U.S. Coast Guard, Seventh District. 1995. "Cuban Rescue Statistics: 1983–1995." Miami, FL: Public Affairs Office.

U.S. Committee for Refugees. 1986. "Despite a Generous Spirit: Denying Asylum in the United States." Washington, DC: American Council for Nationalities Service.

U.S. Committee for Refugees and Immigrants. 2005. *World Refugee Survey 2005*. Washington, DC, November 30. http://www.refugees.org.

"U.S. Opens Arms to Cuban Exodus." 1980. *Miami Herald*, May 6.

Valdés-Hernández, Dagoberto. 1997. *Reconstruir la Sociedad Civil: Un Proyecto de Educación Cívica, Pluralismo, y Participación para Cuba*. Caracas: Fundación Konrad Adenauer.

Valero, Roberto. 1983. "La Generación del Mariel." *Término: Publicación Literaria Bilingüe* 2 (Fall): 14–16.

Valladares, Armando. 1986. *Against All Hope: The Prison Memories of Armando Valladares*. Trans. Andrew Hurley. New York: Alfred A. Knopf. Translated from *Contra Toda Esperanza: Mis Memorias* (Barcelona: Plaza & Janes Editores, 1985).

Valls, Jorge. 1991. *Filo, Contrafilo, y Punta*. Caracas: Saeta.

———. 1986. *Twenty Years and Forty Days: Life in a Cuban Prison*. Washington, DC: Americas Watch Committee.

Varela, Presbítero Félix. 1996 [1835]. *Cartas a Elpidio: Sobre la Impiedad, la Superstición, y el Fanatismo en sus Relaciones con la Sociedad*. Miami, FL: Editorial Cubana.

Victoria, Carlos. 1998. "Fragmentos del Mariel." *Encuentro: Revista de la Cultura Cubana* 8–9 (Spring–Summer): 133–34.

———. 1992. "El Abrigo." In *Las Sombras en la Playa*. Miami, FL: Ediciones Universal.

Villegas, Agustín. 2003. "Francisco." *Ideal* 32, no. 320: 24–25.

———. 2002. "Rafael Díaz Hanscom." *Ideal* 31, no. 316: 52–55.

Wagley, Charles. 1968. "The Concept of Social Race in the Americas." In *The Latin American Tradition*, ed. Charles Wagley, 155–74. New York: Columbia University Press.

Wassem, Ruth Ellen. 1992. "U.S. Response to Asylum Seekers, 1946 to Present." Washington, DC: Library of Congress, Congressional Research Service.

Weber, Max. 1978. *Economy and Society: An Outline of Interpretive Sociology*. Ed. Guenther Roth and Claus Wittich. 2 vols. Berkeley: University of California Press.

Wright, James D. 1976. *The Dissent of the Governed: Alienation and Democracy in America*. New York: Academic Press.

Wyden, Peter. 1979. *Bay of Pigs: The Untold Story*. New York: Simon & Schuster.

Yero, Evelio. 1996. "Es Mejor Encender una Vela . . ." *El Nuevo Herald*, September 15.

Zeitlin, Maurice. 1966. "Political Generations in the Cuban Working Class." *American Journal of Sociology* 71: 493–508.

Zolberg, Aristide R., Astri Suhrke, and Sergio Aguayo. 1989. *Escape From Violence: Conflict and the Refugee Crisis in the Developing World*. New York: Oxford University Press.

Index

5th of August riots, 180, 183, 191, 222, 279

13 de Marzo tugboat drowning, 256, 261, 279

26th of July Movement, 10, 18, 37, 45, 48, 49, 50, 51, 52, 53, 54, 56, 63, 67, 75, 87, 109, 130, 131

30 de Noviembre Movement, 50, 102, 131

55 Hermanos (55 Brothers and Sisters), 139

Abdala, 106, 140
Abreu, Juan, 167
Acción Católica (Catholic Action), 57, 65, 140
Ackerman, Holly, 183, 198
Africa, 120, 140, 213, 242, 278, 296
Africa, influence on culture, 163, 195. *See also* Santería
Agence France-Presse, 290, 298
Agramonte, Roberto, 41
agrarian reform, 3, 47, 57, 58, 60, 64, 70, 79, 90, 108, 118
Agrupación Católica Universitaria (University Catholic Group), 25, 47, 57, 58, 64, 94, 96, 98
Aguilar-León, Luis E., 2
Aguirre, Benigno E., 6, 73, 123, 155, 157, 182, 198, 229

Aguirre, Oscar, 305
Alarcón-Ramírez, Daniel ("Benigno"), 119
Alejandre, Armando, Jr., 285
Alfonso, Pablo, 65, 87, 107, 108, 110, 120, 133, 280, 293
Allende, Salvador, 126
Almaguer, Xiomara, 244
Alpha 66, 6, 106, 291, 294
Alvarez-Bravo, Armando, 172
Alvarez-Guedes, Guillermo, 271
Amaro, Nelson, 3, 5, 16, 21, 36, 58, 78, 89, 110, 111, 122
América Libre prison, 135
American Community Survey, 181
Americas Watch, 128, 133, 280
Aminzade, Ron, 15, 37, 48
Amnesty International, 136, 278, 280, 281
Amuchastegui, Domingo, 296, 297
Anderson, Bonnie, 67, 78
Anderson, Howard, 78
Añel, Armando, 269
Angola, 120, 213, 217
Anido Gómez-Lubián, Marta, 30, 255
anti-Vietnam War movement, 139, 141, 144
Antonio Maceo Brigade, 31, 139–45, 294
Arango, Aureliano, 94

Arcos-Bergnes, Gustavo, 46, 118
Areíto, 139, 141
Arenas, Reinaldo, 151, 166, 167, 168, 172
Arendt, Hannah, 79
Ariza prison, 137
Armony, Ariel, 239
Arteaga, Manuel, 108
Artíme, Manuel, 94, 100
artisan markets, 206
artists, 8, 21, 61, 151, 153, 154, 166, 167, 168, 169, 171, 174, 175, 182, 224, 272, 292, 293
Aruca, Francisco, 294
Asís, Moisés, 241, 249, 273
assimilation, immigrant, 2, 259, 275, 304
Auténticos, 22, 41, 44, 93, 94, 304
authoritarianism, 160, 210, 229, 298. *See also* dictatorship; totalitarianism
Azicri, Max, 294

Bach, Robert L., 2, 6, 7, 123, 153, 154, 308
Bailey, Lee E., 143
Baker, James, 81
Ballagas, Emilio, 92
Ballagas, Manuel F., 167
Balmaseda, Liz, 184, 185
balsero crisis, 8–9, 180, 181, 191, 199, 200, 212, 250, 256, 259, 266, 267, 273, 279, 282, 312
Banco Nacional (National Bank), 118
bandidos (bandits), 125
Baquero, Gastón, 157
Barbería, Lorena, 207
Barnet, Miguel, 163
Barquet, Jesús, 167
Barquín, Ramón, 44
Basch, Linda, 302
Basulto, José, 98, 102, 107, 200, 285
Batista, Fulgencio, 36, 37, 40–44, 45, 46–54, 59, 70, 73, 90, 93, 98, 127, 129, 231, 240, 278, 311

Bauer, Raymond, 17, 175
Bay of Pigs invasion, 3, 21, 23, 25, 52, 68, 78, 79, 81, 84, 92–107, 109, 110, 115, 129, 146, 185, 200, 284, 286, 291, 294, 296, 310
Bay of Pigs Veterans Association, 119, 146
Beauvoir, Simone de, 172
Bendixen, Sergio, 290, 300, 301, 305
Benes, Bernardo, 145
Berezin, Mabel, 24, 80
Berlin Wall, 211, 230, 277
Betancourt, Ernesto, 182
Betancourt, Teresa and Bobby, 271
Betto, Frei, 242
Beyra, Wilfredo, 256
Biaín, Ignacio, 57
Bikel, Ofra, 289
biotechnology, 179, 228
Bissell, Richard M., Jr., 99
Bisset, Oscar Elías, 234
black market, 153, 154, 160, 161, 174, 175, 223
Blanco, Alfredo, 36, 38, 67
Blanco, Liana, 289
Blanco, Ricardo, 195, 197
Blue, Sarah A., 199, 207
Blumer, Herbert, 21
Bober, José, 59, 79
Bodnar, John, 205
Bofill, Ricardo, 118, 279
Bohemia, 44
Boitel, Pedro Luis, 130, 131
Bolívar, Natalia, 117
Bolivia, 119
Bonachea, Rolando, 49
Bonacich, Edna, 248
Boniato prison, 135
Bonilla-Silva, Eduardo, 182, 198
Bonne-Carcasés, Félix, 280
Borbonet, Enrique, 44
Bosch, Orlando, 126
Boza-Masvidal, Eduardo, 87, 88, 107, 108, 261, 262

Index

Brazil, 73, 157, 276
Bremer, Fredrika, 66, 73
Brigadas de Respuesta Rápida (Rapid
  Response Brigades), 222, 252,
  258
Brinton, Crane, 36, 51, 88
Brito, Joel, 225
Brotons, Elizabeth, 286
Brunet, Rolando C., 58
Buajasán, José, 82
Bulgaria, 276
Burns, Ken, 31
Bush, George H., 178
Bush, George W., 290, 300, 302

Cabrera, Lydia, 169
Cabrera-Infante, Guillermo, 271
Calvino, Italo, 172
Camarioca exodus, 4, 120, 121, 198,
  267
Cambodian refugees, 310
Campamento, Julio Antonio Mella, 142
Campins, Zaimar, 258
Campos, Miguel Angel, 60
Canada, 266, 274, 280
Canadian Jewish Congress, 244
Cancio, Wilfredo, 215, 312
Cardona, Joe, 82, 271
Caritas (International Catholic
  Charities), 244
Carrasco, Teok, 260
Carrillo, Justo, 94, 129, 130
Carter, Jimmy, 145, 152, 178, 279,
  303
Casa de las Américas, 77, 172
Casal, Lourdes, 76, 111, 126, 138, 139,
  140, 180
Castañeda, Carlos, 59
Castillo del Príncipe prison, 97, 104,
  105, 161
Castro, Fidel, 10, 12, 37, 46, 50, 51, 55,
  56, 68, 90, 91, 97, 102, 110, 116,
  118, 126, 129, 130, 131, 137, 144,
  146, 198, 207, 213, 226, 243, 245,
  246, 265, 287, 289, 294, 298

speeches, 49, 50, 55, 58, 59, 69, 74,
  78, 96, 116, 152, 166, 220, 277,
  279
Castro, Max J., 200, 304
Castro, Raúl, 51, 77, 89, 116, 130, 153,
  207, 212, 226, 296, 297, 298
Catholic Charities, 182, 195, 244
Catholic Church, 19, 24, 56–58, 65, 69,
  70, 123, 136, 249, 255, 258, 278,
  296, 298, 310
  clerical population, 241
  conflict with government, 89, 108
  expulsion of priests and nuns, 101,
    107, 240, 261
  and Santería, 213
  silenced, 3, 107–9, 240
census
  Cuban, 73, 155
  U.S., 4, 6, 73, 111, 121, 153, 155,
    158, 181, 182, 266, 304
Central American immigrants, 201, 302
Central de Trabajadores Cubanos
  (Cuban Workers' Confederation),
  39, 117, 127, 221, 225, 226, 228
Central Intelligence Agency (CIA), 71,
  78, 81, 84, 93, 94, 95, 98, 99, 100,
  102, 103, 109, 113, 117, 119, 125,
  126, 131, 157
Centro de Estudios sobre Alternativas
  Políticas (Center for the Study of
  Political Alternatives), 180
Centro de Estudios Sobre América
  (Center for American Studies),
  207
Centro Habana, 70, 180, 183, 221, 245,
  279
Césaire, Aimé, 232
Chanes de Armas, Mario, 137
Chavez, Cesar, 32, 233
Chevalier, Maurice, 70
Chibás, Eduardo, 41, 51, 90, 93
Chibás, Raúl, 51
Chicago, 85, 140, 159
Chicago Tribune, 59
Chile, 76, 266

China, 297, 298
Chinese, Cuban, 21, 59, 73, 156
Chovel, Elly, 67, 81
Chun, Sung-Chang, 299
Church of la Ermita de la Caridad, 260, 261
Church of Lucumí Babalú Ayé, 163
Church of San Antonio de los Baños, 268
Church of San Antonio de Miramar, 172
Church of San Rafael, 137
Church of Santa Teresita, 244
Church of the Immaculate Conception, 138
Church of the Sacred Heart, 245
Church World Service, 181, 195
Ciénaga de Zapata, 72, 96, 99
Cienfuegos, Camilo, 55, 63
Cienfuegos, Osmany, 97
Cifuentes, René, 166, 168
civil liberties, 31, 49, 58, 64, 183, 218, 235, 253, 303
civil rights movement, 18, 20, 139, 141
civil society, 3, 18, 51, 68–69, 80, 107, 113, 116, 171, 235, 239, 253, 264, 265, 267, 268, 269, 270, 271, 274, 275, 276, 282, 298
civil war, 308
Civil War, American, 31
Civil War, Spanish, 117, 270
Clark, Juan M., 6, 80, 122, 123, 158, 183, 198
Clavijo, Uva, 110
Clinton, William J., 179, 183, 187, 285, 286, 289, 290
Cobas, José, 308
Cohen, J. M., 172
Cold War, 97, 113, 123, 185, 203, 278, 308
Colegio de Belén, 84
Colegio de las Esclavas del Sagrado Corazón, 30
Colegio del Sagrado Corazón, 74
Collazo, José Enrique, 240, 244

Combinado del Este prison, 136, 138
Comisión Cubana de Derechos Humanos y Reconciliación Nacional (National Committee for Human Rights and National Reconciliation), 234
Comité Cubano Pro Derechos Humanos (Cuban Committee for Human Rights), 118, 279, 293
Comité de Ayuda al Preso Político (Committee to Help Political Prisoners), 117
Comité de Mujeres Oposicionistas Unidas (Committee of Women United in Opposition), 117
Comités para la Defensa de la Revolución (Committees for the Defense of the Revolution), 12, 13, 17, 89, 96, 123, 164, 213, 216, 219, 221, 224
Committee for Cuban Democracy, 18, 97
communism, 7, 8, 10, 14, 16, 19, 22, 24, 48, 51, 59, 62, 75, 79, 82, 89, 108, 109, 116, 118, 119, 145, 179, 180, 193, 205, 210, 211, 243, 249, 272, 286, 298, 303, 311
communists, old, 115, 231
Concilio Cubano (Cuban Council), 280
Conde, Yvonne M., 81
Confederación Nacional de Trabajadores Azucareros de Cuba (National Federation of Sugar Workers), 39
Confederación Obrera Nacional Independiente de Cuba (Cuban Confederation of Independent Labor Organizations), 227
Conferencia de Obispos Católicos de Cuba (Confederation of Cuban Catholic Bishops), 246
Congo, 119, 163
Congreso de Educación y Cultura (National Conference on Education and Culture), 166

Conjunto de Instituciones Cívicas
Cubanas (Association of Cuban
Civic Institutions), 71
Connor, Olga, 139
Conrado Benítez Brigade, 164
Consejo Cubano por la Libertad
(Cuban Liberty Council), 305
Consejo Revolucionario Cubano
(Cuban Revolutionary Council),
95
Consenso Cubano, 305
Constitution
of 1940, 38, 40, 41, 43, 45, 49, 52,
57, 80, 89, 130, 280, 295
of 1992, 280, 295, 296
Contramaestre, 247
Coordinadora Social Demócrata
(Social Democratic Party), 294
Córdoba, Efrén, 38, 40
Corrales, Maritza, 248
Correa, Armando, 248
Corriente Socialista Democrática
Cubana (Cuban Democratic
Socialists), 233, 234,
279
Cortázar, Julio, 172
Costa, Carlos, 285
Costa, José Antonio, 39, 53
Costa Rica, 76, 266, 274
Council for Mutual Economic
Assistance, 178
counterrevolution, 123–25, 172, 232,
233, 277
armed struggle, 10, 78, 79, 80, 81,
87, 94, 95, 102, 115, 127
Crahan, Margaret E., 262
Crespo, Jorge, 233
Cruz, Celia, 74
Cruz, Tomás, 105
Cuba Independiente y Democrática
(Cuba Independent and
Democratic), 65
Cuba Study Group, 294, 305
Cuban American Alliance Educational
Foundation, 275

Cuban American National Foundation,
18, 127, 179, 220, 230, 275, 286,
291, 304, 305
Cuban Coast Guard, 8, 183, 188
Cuban Hebrew Congregation, 248
Cuban Missile Crisis, 4, 21, 112–13,
127, 210, 286
Cuban Refugee Emergency Center, 82
Cuban Refugee Program, 4, 5, 111,
120, 127, 147, 303
Cubana airlines bombing, 126
Cubelas, Rolando, 71, 89, 130
Cuenca, Arturo, 225, 274
Cuesta, Tony, 127
Cuesta-Morúa, Manuel, 234
Cumerlato, Corinne, 298
Cuza-Malé, Belkis, 172, 283
Czechoslovakia, 12, 231, 262, 276, 280,
281

Dalrymple, Donato, 290
de Céspedes, Carlos Manuel, 243, 249,
250, 253
de la Cerra, Alberto, 140
de la Fuente, Alejandro, 199
de la Garza, Rodolfo, 303
de la Luz y Caballero, José, 205
de la Peña, Mario, 285
de la Torre, Miguel, 289
de Varona, Mario, 271
Declaración de Profesores
Universitarios (University Faculty
Statement), 193
Degler, Carl N., 157
del Castillo, Siro, 200
del Cueto, Mario G., 53, 129
del Pino, Rafael, 120
Delgado, Mario, 268
democracy, 32, 36, 37, 49, 53, 54, 55,
59, 63, 69, 90, 94, 114, 118, 128,
129, 131, 207, 255, 256, 257, 263,
269, 270, 271, 274, 275, 276, 282,
295, 296, 297, 303, 311
Democratic Party, 279, 285, 290, 303,
304

Denzin, Norman K., 20
Détente, 122
dialogue
United States and Cuba, 18, 22, 45, 84, 246, 295, 300, 305
Dialogue, the, 7, 72, 86, 139, 145–47, 151, 300
Díaz, Eloína, 86
Díaz, Ernesto, 115
Díaz, Jesús, 139, 144
Díaz, Manuel, 44
Díaz-Balart, Lincoln, 292, 302
Díaz-Balart, Mario, 302
Díaz-Briquets, Sergio, 153, 266, 299
Díaz de Villar, Delia, 250
Díaz-Hanscom, Rafael, 101
Díaz-Martínez, Manuel, 172
dictatorship, 45, 46, 54, 59, 60, 71, 91, 168, 278, 308, 311. *See also* authoritarianism; totalitarianism
Diéguez, Rafael, 250–51
Directorio Revolucionario Estudiantil (Revolutionary Students' Directorate), 25, 45, 49, 50, 52, 53, 71, 80, 94, 95, 98, 102, 103, 109, 128, 129, 140, 145, 234
dissent, externalized, 122, 128, 176, 268, 277
dissident movement, 14, 19, 21, 23, 128, 161, 164, 183, 190, 193, 220, 225, 227, 228, 246, 278, 279, 281, 298, 303, 305
human rights, 13, 18, 32, 207, 234, 279, 280, 293–94
nonviolent struggle, 233, 255, 280
Dixon, Rogelio, 159
doble moral (dual morality), 162, 163, 268
Dole, Robert, 290
dollarization, 207, 215
Domínguez, Jorge I., 2, 47, 54, 59, 67, 68, 105, 116, 117, 119, 120, 198, 206, 209, 296, 298, 299
Domínguez, Virginia, 76
Dominican immigrants, 302

Dominican Republic, 157, 266
Dorticós, Osvaldo, 65, 129
Duany, Jorge, 143, 308
Dubois, Jules, 59
Dueñas, Lorenzo, 137, 138
Dufoix, Stéphane, 283
Dugowson, Maurice, 119, 132
Dulles, Allen W., 99

Eastern European countries, 61, 119, 126, 177, 179, 203, 205, 206, 211, 219, 225, 229, 243, 249, 262, 271, 272, 276, 278, 296, 297, 298, 299, 311. *See also* Soviet Union; *countries by name*
Echeverría, José Antonio, 50, 53, 80, 90
Eckstein, Susan, 2, 179, 205, 206, 222, 292
Ediciones Universal, 174
education, 2, 6, 13, 23, 30, 31, 38, 40, 47, 49, 72, 74, 76, 89, 94, 107, 108, 120, 122, 153, 158, 159, 171, 182, 186, 188, 206, 213, 215, 216, 218, 221, 233, 240, 242, 255, 256, 289, 304
Eire, Carlos N., 84
Eisenhower, Dwight D., 68, 78, 99, 100
El Amor Todo lo Espera (Love Hopes All Things), 247
El Caimán Barbudo (The Bearded Cayman), 144
El Encanto Department Store, 44, 103
El Morro prison, 167
Elder, Glen H., 15
elections, 19, 32, 37, 41, 42, 45, 58, 59, 60, 62, 69, 80, 130, 191, 211, 215, 281, 290, 298, 300, 302, 303
Elizabeth, NJ, 127
embargo, trade, 6, 8, 18, 19, 22, 23, 68, 122, 140, 141, 143, 146, 153, 176, 178, 179, 207, 218, 234, 253, 255, 278, 285, 290, 291, 292, 299, 300, 303
Encinosa, Enrique, 125
Encuentro, 145

Encuentro Nacional Eclesiástico
Cubano, 240, 244, 255
Enzensberger, Hans Magnus, 117, 172
Escalante, Aníbal, 116
Escalona, Arnaldo, 117
Escambray, 10, 45, 53, 54, 71, 72, 87,
125, 132, 312
escoria (scum), 7, 14, 152, 167, 175, 217,
219, 277, 294
Escuela para Cuadros del Partido
(School for Party Leaders), 232
Espín, Vilma, 77
Espina, Mayra, 207
Espino, Ramón, 69, 101
Espiritismo (Spiritism), 222
Esteve, Himilce, 54, 60, 65
Estevez, Abilio, 167
Estrada, Joaquín, 249
Ethiopia, 120
European Parliament, 281
European Union, 208, 271, 280
executions, 78, 93, 101, 105, 132, 145,
292, 312
exiles
early vs. recent, 154, 271, 273, 299,
304, 305
intransigents vs. moderates, 22, 145,
285, 294, 301, 303
violence among, 116, 125–28, 145,
146
exit vs. *voice*, 267, 275, 276, 277, 279,
281, 282
Exodus, 204

Fagen, Richard R., 74, 79, 111, 158
family, 22, 24, 255, 294
divided, 22, 24, 26, 31, 109, 141,
143, 144, 162, 164, 173, 187, 209,
244, 247, 309, 310
reunification of, 6, 7, 27, 86, 121,
146, 151, 158, 198, 200, 207, 211,
213, 215, 235, 267, 301
reunion of, 24, 86, 143, 255
Farber, Samuel, 37, 40, 41
fascism, 24, 79, 204, 278

Federación de Mujeres Cubanas
(Cuban Women's Federation), 77,
89, 131, 216, 221, 224
Federación Estudiantil Universitaria
(University Students' Federation),
50, 53, 80, 87, 89, 130, 131, 132,
145
Federación Sindical de Plantas
Eléctricas, Gas y Agua de Cuba en
el Exilio (the labor union for
electrical, gas, and water workers
in exile), 227
Felipe, Hilda, 117
Fermoselle, Joaquín, 85
Fernández, Damián, 15
Fernández, Gastón A., 153, 154
Fernández, Manuel, 241
Fernández-Robaina, Tomás, 75, 163
Fernández-Yarzábal, Felo, 130, 135,
137, 138
Fernández-Yarzábal, Seferina ("Fefé"),
130, 137
Ferreira, Rui, 198
Finlay, Pancho and Berta, 84
Flexner, James Thomas, 204
Fojo, Felix, 210
food rationing, 153, 174, 179, 206, 221,
222
Ford, Gerald, 178
foreign investments, 206, 280, 297, 298
Fort Chaffee, 166
Fox, Geoffrey, 158
Foyaca, Manuel, 57
Franco, Francisco, 270
Franco, José Luciano, 163
Frankfurt School, 233
Franqui, Carlos, 47, 50, 51, 52, 54, 56,
109, 172
Frayde, Marta, 117
Free, Lloyd A., 67, 77
Frente Revolucionario Democrático
(Democratic Revolutionary
Front), 94, 101, 129
Fuentes, Carlos, 77, 172
Fuentes, Frank, 187, 195

Fuentes, Osilía, 190
Fuentes, Rita, 75
Fuentes, Teresita, 190
Fundación Lawton (Lawton
    Foundation), 234

Galaor, Don, 90
Gandhi, Mahatma, 32, 233, 234, 257,
    280
García, Eloísa, 74, 140
García-Bárcenas, Rafael, 44, 54
García-Márquez, Gabriel, 172
García-Menocal, Serafin, 11
García-Pérez, Gladys Marel, 76
generations, 299
    demographic, 139, 206, 209, 218,
        244, 272, 306, 307
    political, 2, 7, 9, 15, 16, 31, 139, 151,
        154, 168, 180, 272, 309
genocide, 242, 308
German Democratic Republic, 225,
    230, 262, 276, 278, 282
Germany, 266
Gladwin, Hugh, 290
glasnost and *perestroika*, 16, 178, 192,
    218, 226, 230, 297
Goderich, Natalia, 229, 306
Godínez-Soler, Aleida ("Vilma"), 227
Goffman, Erving, 154
Gold, Steven J., 308
Goldstone, Jack, 36, 48
Gómez, Andy, 181
Gómez, Carlos, 10, 11
Gómez, Máximo, 32, 128, 129
Gómez, Olguita, 10, 13
Gómez-Lubián, Agustín, 30, 104
Gómez-Lubián, Clara Estrella, 68
Gómez-Manzano, René, 280
González, Elián, 276, 286–91, 310
González, Juan Miguel, 286
González, Kenia, 221
González, Lázaro, 286
González-Alvarez, Gerardo, 135
González-Corso, Rogelio
    ("Francisco"), 100

González-Dalmau, Rafael, 193
González-Infante, Luis, 131, 134, 138
González-Pando, Miguel, 146
Gorbachev, Michael, 178, 297
Gramsci, Antonio, 233
Granada, 217
Grau, Pola and Ramón, 84
Grau-San Martín, Ramón, 41, 43
Green, Eric, 290
Grenier, Guillermo, 182, 290, 299
Guantanamo Bay, U.S. Naval Base, 8,
    69, 99, 181, 183, 184, 185, 187,
    190, 194–95, 199, 203, 259
Guarch, George, 82–83
Guerrero, Gustavo, 144
Guerrero, María Luisa, 61, 63, 110
Guevara, Che, 51, 53, 63, 67, 71, 94,
    101, 115, 118–20, 132, 169,
    178–79
Guillén, Nicolás, 74, 75, 191
Guiteras, Antonio, 90
gusanos (worms), 14, 78, 104, 144, 146,
    152, 186, 187, 217, 219, 222, 230,
    294
gusanos rojos (red worms), 229
Gutiérrez-Alea, Tomás, 225

Habana Elegante (Elegant Havana), 233
Hadjiyanni, Tasoulla, 306
Haitian immigrants, 199, 202, 274
Ham, Adolfo, 242
Handlin, Oscar, 155, 201
Hansing, Katrin, 244
Hareven, Tamara K., 15
Hart, Armando, 77
Harvard Program in Refugee Trauma,
    310
Havana, 26, 47, 55, 163, 271, 282
Havana Country Club, 73
Havel, Vaclav, 107, 265, 279, 280
health care, 6, 13, 31, 38, 40, 47, 49,
    108, 122, 140, 171, 208, 211, 256,
    310
Heath, Jim F., 112
Hemingway, Ernest, 272

Henken, Ted, 200
Heredia, José ("Richard"), 130, 136
Heres, Marcelino, 130
Hermanos al Rescate (Brothers to the Rescue), 93, 98, 180, 200, 261, 285, 286, 311, 312
Hernández, José M., 25, 49, 54, 57, 64, 65, 88
Hernández, Melba, 46
Hernández, Teresa, 241
Hevia, Carlos, 41, 42
Higham, John, 202
Hirschman, Albert O., 15, 264, 275, 276, 278, 282
history, American, 201
history, immigrant, 201
Hollinger, David, 275
homosexuality, 7, 8, 76, 123, 144, 153, 154, 164, 165, 166, 168, 169, 171, 173, 175, 216
Horowitz, Irving Louis, 2, 77, 296
Hoy (Today), 117
human rights, 109, 118, 128, 136, 146, 204, 235, 252, 253, 257, 269, 281, 303
Human Rights Watch, 295
Humboldt #7, attack on students, 53, 129
Hungary, 276

Immigration and Naturalization Service (INS), 153, 286, 290
incentives, moral vs. material, 119, 126, 178, 179, 206
independence movement, 31, 32, 77, 117, 128, 129, 132, 140, 242, 253, 258, 260, 281
Inkeles, Alex, 17, 175
Instituto Cubano del Libro, 224
Instituto de la Memoria Histórica, 103
Instituto de la Víbora, 30

Instituto Nacional de Investigaciones, 41, 44
Instituto Nacional de Reforma Agraria (National Institute of Agrarian Reform), 118. See also agrarian reform
intellectuals, 7, 8, 29, 57, 61, 75, 145, 153, 154, 167, 174, 183, 207, 225, 232, 280, 298
intelligence, 193, 284. See also spies
Inter-American Development Bank, 207
International Labour Organization, 227
internationalism, proletarian, 118
Iriondo, Silvia, 289
Irish immigrants, 281
Isle of Pines prison, 97, 133, 135
Israel, 242
Italian immigrants, 260, 281
Italy, 266

Jackson, Jesse, 129
Jehovah's Witnesses, 123, 242
Jewish Solidarity, 244
Jews, American, 308
Jews, Cuban, 21, 59, 145, 241, 248, 273
John Paul II, 26, 244, 250, 258, 261, 280, 293, 301
Johnson, Haynes, 103
Johnson, Lyndon B., 120, 185
Johnson, Tim, 303
Jované de Zayas, Elvira, 260
Joven Cuba (Young Cuba), 141
Jóvenes Rebeldes (Rebel Youth), 164, 218
Junta Central de Planificación Económica (Central Economic Planning Board), 178, 212
Junta Patriótica Cubana (Cuban Patriotic Board), 129, 294
Junta Revolucionaria Cubana (Cuban Revolutionary Board), 110

Juventud Católica Cubana (Young
    Cuban Catholics), 57
Juventud Obrera Católica (Young
    Catholic Workers), 57

Kaflon, Pierre, 119, 132
Kaplan, Sender M., 248
Kennedy, Edward M., 199, 202
Kennedy, Jackie, 105
Kennedy, John F., 95, 97, 99, 100, 105,
    112, 201
Kennedy, Paul P., 100
Kennedy, Robert, 112
Kerry, John, 300
Key West, FL, 155
Khrushchev, Nikita, 112
King, Martin Luther, Jr., 32, 233, 280,
    285
Kirk, Jerome, 22
Kirk, John, 242
Kornbluh, Peter, 99, 100
Kunz, E. F., 2, 3, 5, 27, 111, 120, 155,
    199, 305
Kunzle, David, 120

La Cabaña prison, 101, 125, 132, 133,
    136
La Casa del Preso, 25, 139
La Gaceta de Cuba, 172, 216, 225
La Patria es de Todos (Our Nation
    Belongs to All), 234, 253, 280
labor unions, 38, 39, 47, 51, 53, 57, 68,
    78, 117, 127, 131, 213, 225, 231
Laguerre, Michel S., 272, 274
Lansing, MI, 187, 195
Laotian refugees, 310
Las Damas de Blanco (Ladies in
    White), 282
Lasaga, José Ignacio, 57, 65
Latell, Brian, 296
Latin America, 11, 38, 40, 49, 57, 76,
    90, 95, 119, 120, 169, 211, 215,
    225, 242, 262, 271, 278, 293, 301,
    311
Laughlin, Meg, 145

Lazarus, Emma, 201
League against Cancer, 138
Lee, Everett S., 2, 27
legitimacy, governmental, 49, 50, 60,
    67, 68, 91, 122, 130, 180, 205, 297
LeoGrande, William M., 120, 198,
    296, 297, 298
Letelier, Orlando, 126
Levine, Robert M., 248
Levy, Eddie, 244
Ley de Ajuste Cubano (Cuban
    Adjustment Act), 123, 198, 200
Ley de la Peligrosidad (Potentially
    Dangerous Persons Act), 153
Ley de Patrimonio Nacional (National
    Patrimony Law), 168
Leyes Cubanas contra el
    Homosexualismo (Cuban Laws
    against Homosexuality), 166
Lezama-Lima, José, 35, 167, 168, 172
liberation theology, 242
Linden Lane, 168
Literacy Campaign, 64, 81, 89, 122,
    123, 164, 210
Lizza, Ryan, 300
Llorente, Amando, 25, 57
Lofland, John, 20
Lofland, Lyn H., 20
López, Juan, 191
López-Blanch, Heriberto, 288
López-Castillo, Eddie, 118
López-Fresquet, Rufo, 130
López-Levy, Arturo, 243
López-Santiago, Pury, 82
Lorenzo, Eduardo, 108
Los Van Van, 292, 293
Loynaz, Dulce María, 264
Lyceum, 61
Lynch, Grayston L., 95

Maceo, Antonio, 90, 140, 234, 250
Machado, Gerardo, 9, 37, 39, 41, 43,
    61, 117, 128
machismo, 76, 144, 169, 186
Macías, José, 164

Index

Mahler, Sarah, 244
Malcolm X, 232
Mallo, Olga, 43
Mañach, Jorge, 40, 41, 44, 52, 53, 54
Mannheim, Karl, 8, 154
Mariel, 168
Mariel exodus, 7, 12, 13, 21, 77, 118,
    140, 141, 151–55, 158, 163, 167,
    168, 173, 177, 180, 183, 185, 192,
    198, 199, 214, 216, 217, 219, 232,
    248, 277, 294, 303
    and crime, 154, 168, 173
Marill, Alicia, 260
Marrero, Leví, 250
Marshall Plan, 273
Martí, José, 1, 32, 52, 80, 90, 109, 258
Martín, Ivanna, 242
Martínez, Lizbet, 184
Martínez, Luis, 292
Martínez, Mel, 84
Martínez, Raúl, 93, 104, 200
Martínez, Urbano, 93
Martínez-Fernández, Luis, 157
Martín-Villaverde, Alberto, 65
Marx, Gary, 227
Marxism, 3, 11, 36, 65, 75, 77, 91, 92,
    110, 114, 117, 118, 141, 166, 232,
    240, 311
Masa, Alberto, 185, 194, 195
Mas-Canosa, Jorge, 179, 230, 286, 304
Mas-Santos, Jorge, 304, 305
Massey, Douglas S., 26, 27
Masud-Piloto, Felix, 199
Matos, Huber, 55, 62, 65, 66, 68, 90,
    161
Matthews, Herbert L., 45
McAdam, Doug, 15, 20, 36, 37
Mederos, Elena, 62, 110
Medina, Tomás, 211
Meissner, Doris, 289
Mejía, Fermín, 84
Memorial to the Dead, 312
Méndez, Carlos, 36, 65
Menocal, Ondina, 108, 240
mercenarios (mercenaries), 97, 294

Merleau-Ponty, Maurice, 310
Mesa-Lago, Carmelo, 7, 38, 40, 43, 76,
    123, 126, 177, 178, 179, 206, 207
Mestre, Cecilia, 36, 46, 51
Mestre, Georgina, 218
methodology, 2, 15, 19–26, 181
Meurice, Pedro, 252
Mexican immigrants, 201, 262, 302,
    303
Mexico, 266, 268, 280
Miami, 19, 25, 96, 118, 126, 139, 143,
    144, 145, 146, 152, 173, 223, 247,
    260, 261, 272, 275, 285, 286, 287,
    292, 295, 302, 304, 312
Miami-Dade College, 138, 225
Miami Herald, 305
Michigan State University, 195
micro and macro analysis, 28, 197, 307,
    309
microfaction, 116, 118
migration policy
    Cuban, 123, 138, 154, 168, 191, 242
    joint U.S. and Cuban, 5, 6, 9, 23, 73,
        81, 120, 122, 158, 180, 184, 198,
        200, 266, 267, 279
    U.S., 8, 120, 185, 199, 202, 203, 204
Mikoyan, Anastas, 68, 80
Milián, Emilio, 126
milicianos (militia), 12, 72, 82, 89, 94,
    96, 105, 107, 137, 172, 210, 231
military, 44, 55, 131
    Batista's, 44, 45, 94, 131, 162, 231
    Haiti's, 275
    revolution's, 72, 116, 120, 130, 132,
        162, 217, 242, 296, 297
    United States', 107
military service, 122, 153, 154, 159,
    172, 185, 216, 224, 242
Miller, José, 248
Miller, Marc L., 22
Mills, C. Wright, 28
Ministerio de Hacienda (the Treasury),
    130, 145
Ministerio de Salud (Health Ministry),
    131

Ministerio del Interior (Ministry of the Interior), 104, 118, 190
Ministry of Culture, 12, 215
Miranda, Fausto, 271
Miró-Cardona, José, 63, 94
Miyares, Marcelino, 96
mobilizations, mass, 24, 114, 178, 224, 252, 287, 298
Mollica, Richard F., 310
Moncada barracks, attack on, 10, 37, 46, 48, 110, 137
Monreal, Pedro, 208
Montaner, Carlos Alberto, 69, 146, 297, 305
Montecristi Movement, 94, 129
Montgomery, Paul, 7, 153, 154
Montiel, Magda, 295
Moore, Carlos, 120
Mora, César, 233
Mora, Menelao, 53
Morales, Pablo, 285
Morán, Francisco, 233
Morán-Arce, Lucas, 54
Morawska, Ewa, 271
Morejón, Nicolás, 72
Morello, Carol, 30, 250
Moreno-Fraginals, Manolo R., 38
Mosquere, Marilyn, 227
Mother Teresa, 257
Mothers against Repression, 289
Movimiento Cristiano Liberación (Christian Movement for Liberation), 255, 281
Movimiento Democracia (Democracy Movement), 18, 294
Movimiento Demócrata Cristiano (Christian Democratic Movement), 25, 45, 57, 94
Movimiento Nacional Revolucionario (National Revolutionary Movement), 44
Movimiento Nacionalista (Nationalist Movement), 127

Movimiento Pro Derechos Humanos, Carlos Manuel de Céspedes, 257
Movimiento de Recuperación Revolucionaria (Revolutionary Movement for Recuperation), 25, 80, 94, 98, 101, 102
Movimiento Revolucionario del Pueblo (Revolutionary Movement of the People), 10, 18, 72, 87, 102, 110, 132
Mozo, Víctor, 123
Mujal, Eusebio, 53, 127
Müller, Alberto, 80, 98, 103
Muller, Thomas, 201
musicians, 12, 74, 169, 214, 292–93
Myrdal, Gunnar, 29

Nagel, Joane, 169
Naranjo, Enrique, 244
National Assembly of Popular Power, 280
National Catholic Congress, 65
National Endowment for Democracy, 227
nationalism, 16, 36, 49, 53, 66, 67, 68, 77, 91, 98, 129, 169, 207, 250, 259, 260, 262, 289, 298, 299
nationalizations, 3, 6, 16, 49, 66, 67, 68, 71, 77, 78, 79, 92, 110, 118, 206, 240, 248, 259, 298, 299
Negrín, Eulalio José, 127
Netherlands Antilles, 266
New Democrat Network, 300
New Jersey, 127, 140
New York, 74, 167, 168, 281
New York Times, 45, 100
Novo, Guillermo and Ignacio, 127
Novo, Mireya L., 146
Nuevo Herald, 173, 184, 234
Nuñez, Antón, 43

Oak Grove School, 85
Ochoa, Arnaldo, 230, 297, 298
Of Human Rights, 110
old communists, 116–18

Index

Oliva, Erneido, 95, 100, 107
Oliva, Martha, 131, 134, 135, 136, 138
Omega 2, 126, 127
Operation Pedro Pan, 21, 81–86, 289
Oppenheimer, Andrés, 297, 305
Ordoqui, Joaquín, 116
Organización de Instituciones
  Revolucionarias Integradas
  (Integrated Revolutionary
  Organizations), 109, 116
Organization of American States, 122,
  178
Orozco, Manuel, 207, 301
Orsi, Robert A., 260
Ortega, Jaime, 245, 248
Ortega, Roberto, 297
Ortodoxos, 22, 41, 304
Orwell, George, 193
Otazo, Julio, 130, 135
Ovando-Bravo, Miguel, 245

Padilla, Heberto, 154, 171
Padula, Alfred, 77
País, Frank, 50, 51, 54, 210
Palacio de los Deportes (Sports
  Palace), 96, 105
Palestinians, 242
Palma Soriano, 246, 247, 256, 257, 258
Palo Monte, 137, 163
parásitos (parasites), 123
Pardo, Angel, 134–35, 137
Paris, 169
Partido Comunista de Cuba (Cuban
  Communist Party), 13, 14, 16, 17,
  30, 86, 116, 126, 145, 161, 162,
  163, 165, 190, 191, 205, 207, 212,
  213, 216, 219, 225, 226, 228, 233,
  243, 246, 256, 257, 280
Partido de Acción Unitaria (United
  Action Party), 41
Partido Demócrata Cristiano
  (Christian Democratic Party), 45,
  97, 294
Partido Social Revolucionario
  Democrático de Cuba (Cuban

Revolutionary Social Democratic
  Party), 138
Partido Socialista Popular (People's
  Socialist Party), 21, 48, 53, 74,
  109, 116, 279
Partido Unido de la Revolución
  Socialista (United Party of the
  Socialist Revolution), 111
Patronato Synagogue, 248
Patterson, Enrique, 231
Patton, Michael Quinn, 20
Paull, Laura, 249
Payá, Oswaldo, 255, 281, 295
Paz, Octavio, 151, 172
Paz, Senel, 225
Pazos, Felipe, 49
peasant markets, 178, 179, 206, 226
peasants, 39, 44, 47, 58, 70, 75, 89, 90,
  105, 119, 122, 123, 134, 137, 171,
  311
Pedraza, Fidelia, 85
Pedraza, Rafael, 30, 86, 143, 191
Pedraza, Silvia, 2, 7, 30, 73, 153, 180,
  201, 259, 272, 288, 302
Pedraza, Victoria, 32
Pedraza-Bailey, Silvia, 17, 31, 37, 111,
  123, 162, 185, 203, 268
Peláez, Amelia, 175
Peláez, Rafael, 10, 18, 48, 50, 62, 63,
  87, 103
PEN Club, 136
Peña, Lázaro, 116
Pensamiento Crítico (Critical Thinking),
  144, 232
Pérez, Claudia, 184
Pérez, Faustino, 51
Pérez, Humberto, 178
Pérez, Lisandro, 200, 301, 303
Pérez, Louis A., Jr., 90
Pérez, Mariano, 93, 104, 311
Pérez, Omar, 233
Pérez-Díaz, Víctor, 265, 269
Pérez-Firmat, Gustavo, 273
Pérez-López, Daniel, 156–57, 181
Pérez-López, Jorge F., 38, 299

Pérez-Rispide, Luis, 297
Pérez–San Román, José, 95, 100
Pérez-Serantes, Enrique, 48, 56, 65, 87
Pérez-Stable, Marifeli, 97, 109, 140,
    141
período especial (special period), 8, 14,
    104, 177, 179, 180, 185, 186, 199,
    205, 206, 209, 211, 214, 222, 223,
    227, 239, 255, 264, 265, 279, 280,
    289
Péristiany, John G., 76
Perry, Elizabeth, 48
Peruvian Embassy, 152, 167
Pfaff, Steven, 262
Phoenix, AZ, 258
Piñera, Virgilio, 168
Pino, Julio, 104
Pioneros (Pioneer Students), 89, 192
Plataforma Democrática (Democratic
    Platform), 305
Poder Popular (Organs of People's
    Power), 126, 190
Poland, 253, 262, 276, 278
Polish Solidarity Movement, 262
Política Cultural, 171
political parties
    in Cuba, 22, 41, 233
    in U.S., 45, 84
political prisoners, 7, 10, 13, 19, 22, 23,
    25–26, 36, 45, 48, 50, 65, 72, 78,
    97, 101, 103, 107, 110, 115,
    128–39, 146, 151, 152, 153, 162,
    168, 180, 183, 191, 192, 211, 242,
    277, 280, 281, 310
    population, 133, 146
    progressive plan for, 133, 136
    reeducation plan for, 133, 134, 136
politics
    attitudes, 3, 14–16, 22, 23, 26, 28, 71,
        119, 144, 169, 171, 192, 215, 220,
        263, 285, 299, 303, 304
    corruption, 40, 49, 67, 212, 226
    disaffection, 1, 2, 3, 8, 10, 15, 16, 17,
        18, 23, 27, 28, 36, 71, 72, 144, 152,
        160, 167, 180, 185, 187, 192, 203,

210, 215, 217, 218, 220, 225, 226,
        227, 228, 231, 235, 241, 243, 245,
        256
    identity, 24, 79, 97, 126, 139, 141,
        144, 248, 260, 262, 270, 307, 309
    participation, 12, 16–18, 21, 23, 28,
        79, 164, 175, 183, 185, 191, 224,
        228, 229, 268, 269, 301, 306
Pollack, Detlef, 277
Pollitt, Brian H., 207
population
    of Cuba, 1, 22, 296
    who emigrated, 1, 2, 4, 5, 7, 8
Portes, Alejandro, 2, 3, 5, 6, 26, 78,
    110, 122, 123, 308, 309
Posada-Carriles, Luis, 126
poverty, 8, 14, 27, 31, 39, 45, 47, 51,
    57, 61, 64, 72, 91, 93, 94, 106, 109,
    117, 144, 167, 171, 179, 204, 213,
    219, 220, 224, 240, 253, 260, 272,
    273, 290, 304
Power, Samantha, 26
Poyo, Gerald E., 56, 57
Prats-Páez, Rolando, 233, 234
Presidential Palace, 55
Presidential Palace attack, 50, 53
Presidio Político Histórico Cubano
    (Historical Political Prisoners
    Association), 294
Prieto, Plinio, 87
Prieto, Yolanda, 76, 140,
    243
Prío-Socarrás, Carlos, 41
Program Exodus, 128, 230,
    305
prostitution, 173, 208
Protestant Churches, 123, 135, 193,
    242, 258
Proust, Marcel, 143
Provisional Government, 51, 62, 63,
    68, 110, 130
Proyecto Varela, 255, 280, 281
Puerto Rican immigrants, 303
Puerto Rico, 127, 143
Pujol, Juan and Aidée, 84

Index

¿Qué Pasa? (What's Going On?), 194,
 197
Quigley, Thomas E., 244

race of Cubans
 in Cuba, 26, 31, 44, 47, 73, 74, 75,
  90, 91, 105, 120, 131, 134, 137,
  140, 158, 162, 164, 165, 169, 185,
  208, 212, 232, 234, 252, 280, 282
 who emigrated, 7, 23, 73, 95, 107,
  139, 153, 155, 182, 198, 208, 269
Radelat, Ana, 292
Radio Esperanza (Radio Hope), 194
Radio Martí, 189, 234, 259
Radu, Michael, 297, 299
Ramírez, Porfirio, 87, 93, 132
Ramos, Marcos A., 242
Rasco, Estela, 81, 112
Rasco, José Ignacio, 36, 45, 57, 60, 63,
 94, 97, 295
Ratner, Steven, 294
Ray, Manolo, 51, 94, 110
Reagan, Ronald, 178, 279,
 285
Rectification of Errors Campaign, 178,
 190, 230
Red Cross, 175
Refugee Act of 1980, 199, 203
refugees
 defined, 2, 3, 5, 6, 7, 8, 27–29, 32,
  111, 120, 155, 185, 199, 202, 260,
  305, 306, 307–11, 312
 population worldwide, 307
Regalado, Tomás, 118
religion, 123, 289
 participation in, 58, 168, 172, 183,
  193, 239, 241, 265
 revival of, 240, 243
Relloso, Graciela, 240
remittances, immigrant, 199, 207, 214,
 220, 298, 301, 302
Reno, Janet, 8, 183, 185,
 289
Republican Party, 279, 285, 300, 301,
 303, 304

Rescate Revolucionario (Revolutionary
 Rescue), 84, 94
Restano, Aurelina, 117
return
 repatriation, 223
 settlement, 23, 27, 29, 175, 200, 270,
  271, 272, 273, 274, 299, 311
 visits, 7, 14, 26, 140, 142, 146, 151,
  165, 218, 250, 273, 301, 302, 303
revolution
 armed struggle, 10, 45, 48, 49, 52,
  57, 76
 causes of, 26, 36, 46, 47, 54, 89–91
 ideals of, 5, 7, 10, 11, 58, 110, 117,
  118, 119, 126, 298
 stages of, 2, 35, 36, 58, 66, 92, 110,
  177, 210
 triumph of, 1, 3, 10, 162, 174, 210
revolutions, defined, 22, 32, 37, 48,
 299, 308, 310
Rexach, Rosario, 61
Reyes, Antonio, 36, 46, 51
Reyes-Canto, Omar, 293
Rieff, David, 306
Rincón, 259
Ríos, Alejandro, 223
Ripoll, Carlos, 172
Risech, Flavio, 143, 144
Ritter, Archibald R. M., 208
Rivas-Porta, Guillermo, 134, 183
Rivera, Ildelisa, 244
Rivero, Raúl, 281, 293
Roa, Fernando, 36, 41, 246
Robaína, Frank, 289
Roberts, Churchill, 181
Roca, Blas, 234, 280
Roca, Sergio, 7, 126, 153
Roca, Vladimiro, 234, 280
Rodríguez, Carlos Rafael, 51
Rodríguez, Coiré, 132
Rodríguez, Felix, 119
Rodríguez, Israel, 125
Rodríguez, José Conrado, 246, 247,
 257, 279, 282
Rodríguez, José Ignacio, 205

Rodríguez, Julio, 45, 125
Rodríguez, Marcos, 129
Rodríguez, Myriam, 125
Rodríguez-Chavez, Ernesto, 8, 180, 185
Rodríguez-Santana, Carlos, 93
Rojas, Rafael, 145
Román, Agustín, 108, 261, 311
Romania, 276
Romero, Oscar Arnulfo, 257
Roque, Marta Beatriz, 280, 295
Ros, Enrique, 97, 99, 113, 123, 128
Rosales del Toro, Ulíses, 297
Rose, Peter I., 2, 27, 203
Ros-Lehtinen, Ileana, 97, 292, 302
Rothe, Eugenio, 181
Rousseau, Denis, 298
Rubalcaba, Gonzalo, 292
Ruíz, Albor, 140
Rulfo, Juan, 172
Rumania, 262, 276
Rumbaut, Rubén G., 26, 272, 307
Rusk, Dean, 112
Rutgers University, 140

Sakharov, Andrei, 281
Sakharov prize, 281, 282
Saladrigas, Carlos, 305
Salvador, David, 51
Salvat, Juan Manuel, 80, 94, 102, 103
Sánchez, Celia, 56, 77
Sánchez, Juan, 46
Sánchez, Teresita, 152
Sánchez–Santa Cruz, Elizardo, 118, 233
Sandoval, Mercedes Cros, 154, 163, 214
Santa Clara, 71, 252
Santamaría, Haydée, 46, 77
Santamaría, Lázaro, 213
Santamaría, Ramón, 214
Santana, Francisco, 311
Santana, Raísa, 184
Santería, 58, 74, 75, 137, 163, 169, 182, 213, 214–15, 228, 253, 289

Santos, Guillermo, 162
Santos, Juan, 162
Santos, Lázaro, 162
Santos, Raúl, 162
Santos, Rogelio, 159
Sartre, Jean-Paul, 172
Saumell, Rafael, 10, 13, 18
Schreiber, Anna P., 122
Scott, James C., 231
Scull, Haydée, 272
Seguridad del Estado (State Security), 113, 165, 188, 190, 234, 245, 247, 257, 258
self-employment, 123, 178, 179, 206, 208, 226, 298, 308
Selgas, Jesús, 166, 168, 170
Semple, Robert B., Jr., 120
Senghor, Leopold, 232
Shayne, Julie D., 76
Shryock, Andrew, 291
Sí, Juan, 225
Sierra Maestra, 45, 46, 48, 50, 60, 162
Simmel, Georg, 202
Skocpol, Theda, 37
Smith, Lois M., 77
Smyser, W. R., 310
Snow, David, 20
social and economic conditions
    in Cuba, 90, 153, 178, 179, 186, 198, 208, 226, 229, 244, 298, 301
social class of Cubans
    in Cuba, 9, 12, 13, 18, 19, 26, 31, 40, 45, 46, 69, 70, 72, 89, 90, 91, 93, 118, 122, 127, 130, 137, 159, 164, 173, 182, 185, 192, 212, 213, 216, 226, 231, 242, 252, 256
    who emigrated, 3, 5, 6, 7, 11, 23, 78, 95, 96, 110, 122, 123, 140, 141, 152, 153, 155, 159, 183, 268
social movements, 32, 45, 126, 290, 302
socialism, 16, 53, 68, 107, 144, 171, 256
sociology, as discipline, 2, 29, 32, 307
Sorensen, Theodore, 99
Sorí-Marín, Humberto, 101

Sosa, Amelia, 183, 192, 195, 243, 273
Soto, Francisco, 167
Soto, Valero, 167
South Florida, 260
Southern and Eastern European
    immigrants, 201, 202
Soviet Jewish refugees, 308, 309
Soviet Union, 8, 12, 17, 19, 51, 67, 68,
    77, 80, 89, 93, 97, 109, 112, 116,
    118, 119, 123, 145, 175, 177, 178,
    179, 185, 192, 205, 206, 216, 229,
    231, 233, 242, 243, 246, 262, 273,
    278, 297, 311
Spain, 6, 70, 123, 173, 175, 240, 242,
    247, 250, 265, 266, 268, 269, 270,
    273, 274, 276, 280
    migration to Cuba from, 39, 44, 70,
    93, 117, 155, 212, 258
    migration to Europe from, 270
spies, 131, 227, 284, 301. *See also*
    intelligence
Statue of Liberty, 120, 201
Stein, Barry N., 27
Steinback, Robert L., 312
Stevenson, Adlai, 100
Strauss, Anselm L, 21
Suárez, Fidelia, 174
Suárez, Rosa, 85
Suárez-Cobián, Rolando, 240, 244
sugar harvest, mobilization for, 12, 117,
    126, 137, 144
sugar industry, 6, 39–40, 67, 119, 178,
    206, 210, 297
Szulc, Tad, 100

Tabío, Juan Carlos, 225
Tamayo-León, René, 227
Tejera, Emma, 258
Telleda, Miguel L., 106
Tenreiro, José, 127
Tercera Opción, 233
Término, 168
Thai refugees, 310
Thomas, Hugh, 95, 122
Thompson, E. P., 309

Tiananmen student revolt, 297
Tilly, Charles, 29, 36
Time, 198
Tocqueville, Alexis de, 40
Torreira, Ramón, 82
Torres, Agustín, 127
Torres, Guillermina, 86
Torres, María de los Angeles, 81
Torres, Mariana, 245
totalitarianism, 145, 279, 298. *See also*
    authoritarianism; dictatorship
tourism, 179, 191, 206, 208, 214, 220,
    228, 297, 298
transition
    from capitalism to communism, 16,
    152, 154, 180
    from communism to democracy, 18,
    19, 32, 205, 216, 228, 234, 255,
    262, 273, 295–99
    from fascism to democracy, 270
    from feudalism to capitalism, 205,
    273
    from refugees to Americans, 299–307
transnationalism
    church's, 244
    immigrant, 274, 275, 302
Triay, Victor Andrés, 81
Trinidad, 11, 99
Triple A, 94
Trueba, Domingo, 101
Turkey, 268
Tweed, Thomas, 259

U Thant, 112
U.S. Agency for International
    Development, 227
U.S. Census Bureau, 304
U.S. Coast Guard, 8, 180, 183, 184,
    188, 194, 199, 200, 201, 203
U.S. Committee for Refugees and
    Immigrants, 199, 307
U.S. Congress, 61, 65, 97, 123, 128,
    286, 287, 290, 291, 292, 302
U.S. Interests Section, 227, 234, 287
UNESCO, 281

Unidad Cubana (Cubans United), 18, 129, 138, 294
Unidades Militares de Ayuda a la Producción – UMAP, (Military Units to Aid Production), 123
Unión Cubana (Cuban Union), 230
Unión de Estudiantes Secundarios (High School Students League), 231
Unión de Jóvenes Comunistas (Communist Youth League), 11, 13, 16, 18, 89, 159, 160, 164, 191, 192, 213, 219, 225, 228, 231, 256
Unión Liberal Cubana (Liberal Party), 294
Unión Nacional de Escritores y Artistas de Cuba (Cuban Writers and Artists Union), 13, 18, 74, 145, 172
Unión Nacional Obrera (National Labor Union), 127
United Nations, 100, 112, 199, 228, 310
United Nations Human Rights Commission, 136, 293
United Nations' Universal Declaration of Human Rights, 136, 138, 233, 257, 280, 285
United States policy toward Cuba, 3, 23, 38, 41, 52, 60, 67, 68, 77, 79, 90, 246, 299
Universidad Pontificia de Salamanca, 247
University of Chicago, 31, 141
University of Havana, 26, 44, 52, 117, 130, 131, 138, 145, 157, 180, 215, 219, 224, 232, 241, 249
University of Michigan, 31, 141
University of Villanueva, 84, 87, 240
University of Wisconsin, 140
university students, 44, 45, 46, 49, 50, 52, 123, 128, 130, 141, 182, 208
Unveiling Cuba, 168
Urban Reform Law, 68, 71, 213
Urioste, Josefina, 104

Urrutia, Manuel, 59, 63
Valdés, Dagoberto, 255, 265, 266, 267
Valdés, Nelson, 49
Valero, Roberto, 167
Valladares, Armando, 136
Valls, Jorge, 36, 52, 56, 69, 79, 128, 130, 133, 137, 138, 147
Varela, Félix, 239, 281, 282
Vargas Llosa, Mario, 172
Vargas-Gómez, Andrés, 128, 132, 136, 138, 294, 310
Varona, Antonio ("Tony"), 84, 94, 129
Vázquez, Gastón, 67, 70, 73, 92, 101
Vedado, 55, 173
Vega, Juan, 225
Venceremos Brigade, 141
Venezuela, 266, 274
Victoria, Carlos, 166, 173, 177
Vidaurreta, Augusto, 71, 113, 136, 138
Vidaurreta, Esther María, 113
Vietnam War, 122
Vietnamese refugees, 309, 310
Villa Marista, 192, 234
Villegas, Agustín, 101
Virgen de Guadalupe, 108, 249
Virgen de la Caridad del Cobre (Our Lady of Charity), 59, 65, 82, 107, 108, 138, 169, 245, 246, 249, 250, 253, 259, 260, 262, 279
Virgen de Regla (Our Lady in Regla), 170, 259
Vitral, 255, 268
Vuelos de la Libertad (Freedom Flights), 4, 6, 120, 125, 303

Wagley, Charles, 157
Walhs, Sinesio, 87
Walsh, Bryan, 81, 84
Washington, George, 204
Wassem, Ruth Ellen, 199
waves of migration, 1–9, 14, 16, 18, 21, 22, 36, 78, 81, 95, 110, 120–23, 139, 151–52, 157, 175, 177, 180, 201, 208, 264, 266, 277, 299

Weber, Max, 24, 31, 50, 159
West Palm Beach, FL, 11, 195
Western Europe, 269, 270,
    271
women, 2, 6, 23, 26, 90, 91
    in Cuba, 31, 43, 46, 60, 61, 76–77,
    117, 135, 159, 175, 280, 281, 282
    who emigrated, 122, 174, 260, 302
World Bank, 207
Wright, James D., 16, 17, 269
writers, 7, 13, 74, 167, 168, 169, 174,
    216, 224, 225, 292

Wyden, Peter, 95, 97, 98, 99

Yero, Evelio, 247, 257
Yoruba, 163
Yugoslavia, 262

Zacchi, César, 136
Zaldívar, Eva, 228
Zeitlin, Maurice, 9
Zolberg, Aristide R., 154, 203,
    307
Zúñiga, Luis, 127